Appalachian Mountain Religion

Appalachian
Mountain Religion

A History

Deborah Vansau McCauley

University of Illinois Press
Urbana and Chicago

Publication of this book was supported by the 1990 Bancroft Award and by a grant from the National Endowment for the Humanities, an independent federal agency.

This book is printed on acid-free paper.

Library of Congress Cataloging-in-Publication Data

McCauley, Deborah Vansau, 1954–
    Appalachian mountain religion : a history / Deborah Vansau
McCauley.
        p.   cm.
    Includes bibliographical references (p. xxx-xxx) and index.
    ISBN 0-252-02129-0 (alk. paper). — ISBN 0-252-06414-3 (pbk. :
alk. paper)
    1. Christian sects—Appalachian Region—History. 2. Appalachian
Region—Religious life and customs. I. Title.
BR535.M38   1995
277.4'08—dc20   94-18247
                                                                          CIP

For

Hannah Vansau McCauley

and dedicated to the memory of

Deborah Jordan Vansau   Moye Demascus Vansau
1904–91   *1899–1972*

Coy Miser
1918–92

As big as the world is, as many people as there are,
that's the only place that God has got to live in this world
is in the hearts of people, men and women.
He's big enough to fill the universe,
but yet he is small enough to live in our hearts.
The only place right now he has got to live
is in the hearts of the people,
and that's just the ones that will let him come in.

—Brother Coy Miser

Contents

Illustrations follow page 338

Acknowledgments

The literature on religious life and history distinctive to the mountain regions of Appalachia is skimpy, to say the least. Supported by an Appalachian Studies Fellowship, I began my research in the Weatherford-Hammond Mountain Collection, the grandmother of all resource collections on Appalachia, housed in Special Collections at Hutchins Library of Berea College in Kentucky. Dr. Gerald Roberts, Director of Special Collections and board member of the Fellowship Committee, expressed his grave concern to me that I would have to dig very deeply and for a very long time in order to come up with the material I needed to begin to paint a comprehensive portrait of the development of Appalachian mountain religion and its differentiation from what became the dominant religious culture of the United States in the nineteenth and twentieth centuries. What I needed most for my research was participant-observation in the variety of church traditions making up mountain religion today, coupled with a broad familiarity with American religious history in order to be able to discern and understand the historical echoes reverberating in what I observed.

I slowly compiled a large bibliography of both primary and secondary sources through research that took me from Berea to other major Appalachian resource collections (see the "Essay on Sources"), incorporating every scrap of information I found as far back as I could reach and no matter how small, a necessary first step that had yet to be taken by other scholars who had written on mountain religion. Indeed, until the late 1980s, nearly all of the published material on mountain religion had been generated by social scientists and home missionaries. Studies by humanities scholars—and especially those guided by a religious studies perspective—were virtually nonexistent until that time. We shall explore throughout this book the evolution of the study of mountain religion, addressing it most directly in the "Essay on Sources."

Publication of this book was made possible in part by subventions from Columbia University's Bancroft Award and the National Endowment for the Humanities. My thanks to the committees for their affirmation of this work and, by extension, mountain people's religious culture and history. I also have many individuals to thank. First and foremost recognition must go to Robert T. Handy, Henry Sloane Coffin Professor Emeritus of Church History at Union Theological Seminary (New York City), who had faith in this project from its beginnings and pointed me to major clues that eventually led to how I came to understand mountain religion's significant role in American religious history. If it weren't for Bob Handy, there would be no book.

Loyal Jones was the founding director of the Appalachian Center at Berea College, the first center of its kind which set the standard for all the Appalachian centers attached to academic institutions that followed. The Appalachian Center and Hutchins Library administer the Appalachian Studies Fellowships, made possible by a grant from the Andrew W. Mellon Foundation. Loyal Jones is considered by many to be the leading interpreter of religious life and history in the mountains of the Appalachian region. He read drafts of the book manuscript, offering incisive comments and encouragement. He also read my original research proposal many years before, making observations that directly and profoundly affected the book's final outcome. While he is always generous, kindly, and accessible, the modesty of the man belies his preeminent stature in Appalachian studies (often referred to as its unofficial dean) and the deep affection with which he is regarded by his colleagues in the field.

Warren Brunner is widely and fondly known as the "Appalachian Photographer." Warren has had a studio in Berea, Kentucky, for over thirty-five years. His Mountain Collection and War on Poverty Collection, consisting of tens of thousands of photographs, are slated for Special Collections at Hutchins Library of Berea College. For more than seven years now, Warren and I have been working on a photography project featuring mountain churches and religious life and culture in the central Appalachian region with the goal of publishing a photographic essay. Many of my observations included in this book have come from our numerous field trips. Warren has absorbed most of the costs of these endeavors, and is, therefore, as much responsible for funding my work as any fellowship or grant or award or appointment or employment geared directly to my research needs I have been fortunate to receive.

Randall H. Balmer, Associate Professor of Religion at Barnard College of Columbia University, also guided my research. James M. Washington, Professor of Church History at Union Theological Seminary (New York City), gave encouragement and support over many years. Howard Dorgan, Professor of Communication Arts at Appalachian State University in Boone, North Carolina, generously shared more than two hundred pages of field notes and some early chapters on Old Regular Baptists before their publication in book form as *The Old Regular Baptists of Central Appalachia: Brothers and Sisters in Hope* (1989).

Special thanks are due Professor John Faulkner of the English Department at Ohio University–Lancaster who, several years ago, when I expressed my perplexity about finding early primary sources on mountain religion, told me about the journals of Jesuit missionaries which were the earliest principal primary sources on Native Americans with the beginning of European exploration of the North American continent. His point led directly and quickly to my recognizing the importance of home mission literature for investigating the history of mountain religion.

For 1992–93, I was a scholar in residence at the Center for American Culture Studies at Columbia University, an appointment that made possible the final extensive revisions of the book manuscript, as well as research for the manuscript of the photographic essay I am creating with the photographer Warren Brunner. My thanks to Professor Jack Salzman, Director of the Center, who first invited me to apply for the appointment.

For eighteen months, beginning in January 1987, I was research consultant in curriculum and bibliographic development for the study of Appalachian mountain religion for the Appalachian Ministries Educational Resource Center (AMERC), based at Berea College. Established in 1985, AMERC quickly achieved the distinction of being by far the largest consortium of graduate schools in the nation—made up of seminaries and theological and divinity schools, many of which are attached to universities. AMERC's founder and executive director, Mary Lee Daugherty, made sure that I had every opportunity to accomplish the research I needed for my own work as well as fulfill my duties to AMERC. Mary Lee was also the first to bring to my attention, back in the late 1970s, that the study of mountain religion was a wide-open field and virtually untouched, its history unexplored and, hence, all but unwritten. This was the mustard seed that germinated quickly into a focus that brought together all my interests, academic training, and personal history.

The staff of Special Collections at Hutchins Library of Berea College assisted my months of research in innumerable ways. Thanks go to director Gerald Roberts, archivist Shannon Wilson, the poet-author Sidney Saylor Farr who serves as collections staff member as well as editor of *Appalachian Heritage* (in which my first article on mountain religion was published), and *AH*'s editorial assistant and collections staff member Donna Lakes. Eric J. Olson, Director of the Appalachian Collection at Appalachian State University, and Dr. Clyde R. Root, then Special Collections Librarian of the Pentecostal Research Center at Lee College in Cleveland, Tennessee, both made my many weeks of research in their collections very profitable.

Specialized bookdealers are often the unsung heroes of research. George Brosi of Berea, Kentucky, is very much a "regional treasure," as he was characterized in a recent issue of *Appalachian Heritage*. Through his book concern, Appalachian Mountain Books, George has placed in my hands several extremely important—and little known—works. His unsurpassed knowledge of regional literature was invaluable to my bibliographic efforts, especially when I was first starting out.

The students enrolled in the course I taught at Columbia University during spring semester 1992, "Appalachian Women and American Religion," expanded my thinking on how the *land* itself has had such a compelling role in making Appalachian mountain religion a regional religious tradition without parallel on the American landscape. Their insight in the midst of the concrete canyons of Manhattan was astonishing. My gratitude goes to Natan Meir, Alissa Nourse, Natanya Pearlman, Carol Rosenthal, Shana Sippy, Cory Sparks, and Anita Wadhwani.

My investigations into the mountain origins of the Church of God (Cleveland, Tennessee) were assisted by several people. Foremost is the gift of extensive original research into the mountain roots of the Church of God through the Spurling family that the Pentecostal scholar Rev. Wade H. Phillips, D.D., then Bishop of the Churches in Canada of the Church of God of Prophecy, gave to me carte blanche, making this book the first venue for Phillips's meticulously documented information that completely restructures the earliest formative history of the Church of God through its first founders. Brother Phillips said that he was "anxious to get the correct focus of this history in print in the proper context," a context that he identified with the broader framework of mountain religious history. I am honored that he considered this book to be "the proper context."

Brother James Marshall and Sister June Glover Marshall of Cleveland, Tennessee, have spent a lifetime devoted to the discovery and preservation of the artifacts and obscure documents of the Church of God's earliest mountain roots. Brother and Sister Marshall spent many hours with me sharing the fruits of their decades of labor. I am indebted to them both. Dr. Donald M. Bowdle of the Church of God School of Theology faculty provided several helpful insights in the interview he granted me. Dr. Charles W. Conn, official church historian of the Church of God and former General Overseer, was extremely generous with his time and intimate knowledge of his denomination, entertaining with precision and directness my numerous questions.

Dr. Harold Hunter, now scholar in residence at the Pentecostal Research Center at Lee College (founded by the Church of God) and past president of the Society for Pentecostal Studies, was at the time of my interview with him an administrator in the World Headquarters of the Church of God of Prophecy, also in Cleveland, Tennessee, and of which he was then a member (Dr. Hunter has since placed membership with the Church of God). Dr. Hunter arranged for me to have an interview with Brother M. A. Tomlinson, then General Overseer of the Church of God of Prophecy and a son of A. J. Tomlinson, first General Overseer of the Church of God until the early 1920s when he founded the Church of God of Prophecy. Brother Tomlinson's fervent prayer for my work at the end of our interview shook me to my core and was an unexpected gift of affirmation I still treasure.

There are several very special people to thank. Without them there would have been no field research. Warren Brunner and I have often stayed at

Cranks Creek Survival Center in Harlan County, Kentucky. My deep appreciation goes to Becky and Bobby Simpson, who founded and operate the Survival Center, a local self-help effort for and by the mostly rural residents of this corner of southeastern Kentucky and southwest Virginia. Becky and Bobby have generously allowed us to stay at no cost, often including us at their table. This enabled us to make many trips to that area we could not otherwise afford. Sister Mae June Hensley, founding mother of Cranks Holiness Church, opened the door to many church communities in southeastern Kentucky and southwest Virginia. Without Sister Mae June, we would never have been as widely accepted and welcomed as family. Brother Coy Miser and Sister Hassie Miser opened up their hearts and their home to us. Brother Coy was an independent Holiness preacher who started many small churches throughout central Appalachia. His steadfast support of my work and his gift of time and frank, in-depth responses to my persistent questions over several years provided a significant part of the backbone of this study. Thank you, Brother Coy, for teaching me far more than you ever knew while you were still living among us. To your memory, along with that of my grandparents, I dedicate this book.

Other preachers and pastors in the central Appalachian region, especially Brother Kenneth Banks and Sister Marilyn Banks, Sister Lydia Surgener and her nephew Junior, Brother Lee Crider (d. 1990), Brother Loyd Haskell Underwood, and Brother James Fee, have all made inestimable contributions to this study. The open-heartedness of the congregations of Cranks Holiness Church and Red Hill Holiness Church made this work possible, as well as Rex Holiness Church and other congregations that permitted photography of church interiors and the tape recording and photography of worship services. Sister Edna Alexander and Brother L. L. Bradley have lent significant insight to this study. Special thanks go to Brother Terry Galloway of Wolf Creek Baptist Church, on Wolf Mountain in Jackson County, North Carolina, for providing his history of the church and for talking with me at length.

Pat Parker Brunner of Berea, Kentucky, has opened up her home to me many times while I have worked on this book. Pat's own family roots in the mountains run to the earliest years of settlement, along with her family members' active participation in the religious life of the region. Her wisdom has been an important sounding board for me and her intimate knowledge of both sides of the river—mountain religion and the denominations of American Protestantism, especially the Southern Baptist Convention—has been invaluable. Carroll and Kae Parker of Brevard, North Carolina, provided housing, warm hospitality, and guided access to many churches in the area. So did Francis and Margie Hammond of Lewisburg, West Virginia, who were very generous with their time and resources. Through the Parkers and the Hammonds, we found many treasures tucked far out in the mountains that were accessible to us only because of their lifetime of familiarity with the lay of the land.

Laura Porter, friend and colleague, has accompanied me on many of these trips and has spent long hours discussing mountain religion with me. Laura's sophisticated knowledge of word processing and her tent ministry as a computer consultant calmly solved all of my computer quandaries—which were numerous. I also can never repay my debt to Laura for reading and thoughtfully commenting on every phase of the book manuscript over many years as it developed and matured. In addition to content, Laura was unceasingly frank in her critique of my writing style when it confounded what I was trying to convey, but she also mercifully helped to diagnose whatever problems my sentences posed.

Kathryn Hammond Bell, lifelong friend, generously provided expertly rendered transcripts of the oral history interviews excerpted in this book and essential to this study. She did so as a gift of support, for which I am very grateful.

Dr. Patricia Hollahan, Associate Editor of the University of Illinois Press, brought extraordinary skill to the copyediting of this book. Her own highly developed religious sensibilities endowed her efforts with great sensitivity and respect for the subject matter the manuscript addressed. I am grateful for the care and well-honed gifts Pat gave to her labors.

Dr. Judith McCulloh, Executive Editor of the University of Illinois Press, has carefully guided the journey of this work from manuscript to book. Her integrity as a scholar and her professionalism as an editor combine to set the highest standards for the creation of a "good book." Judy believes that a large part of her work is to educate authors in the publication process. I am fortunate to have been one of her students.

My deepest thanks go to my mother, Hannah Vansau McCauley, whose steadfast, loyal love has opened more doors of opportunity for me than I can ever acknowledge. I have written this history for her. This book is dedicated to the memory of my grandparents, Deborah Jordan Vansau and Moye Demascus Vansau, "plain folk" whose religious heritage was my first teacher about Appalachian mountain religion.

Appalachian Mountain Religion

Introduction

In 1986, Martin E. Marty issued the second edition of his *Righteous Empire: Protestantism in the United States,*[1] a bold historical synthesis and interpretation of American Protestantism that did not at all neglect or diminish its diversity. Indeed, within that diversity he heard the historical echoes that were primary clues. They pointed to the repetitions—the commonalities and variations on commonalities—that made it possible for him to posit a historical framework from which conclusions could be drawn. Religious historians write macroscopic studies as well as microscopic. They involve different emphases in historical research, but use the same skills. Just as we can outline the history of American Protestantism and identify its characterizing features and trends, we can also draw out and interpret its implications in order to see what made it significant and unique in different historical periods. We can make such generalizations about American Protestantism even though it is made up of a plethora of church traditions and religious movements. (Throughout this book, "American Protestantism" refers to denominational Protestantism, usually mainstream.) I propose that we can do the same for Appalachian mountain religion as a regional religious tradition. Appalachian mountain religion is also made up of a veritable garden of church traditions and religious movements, nearly all of which share highly pronounced characteristics as well as common historical roots. The diversity of individual features lets us hear the repetitions, the primary historical echoes that are the clues to mountain religion's history within the Appalachian region as well as within the much larger setting of American Christianity.

This book is not about "religion in Appalachia" or even "Appalachian religion," which I understand to be any kind of religion that goes on in the region. It is about Appalachian *mountain* religion, "mountain religion" being the distinguishing term accepted by Appalachian studies scholars such as Loyal Jones and American religious historians such as Catherine Albanese.[2] Mountain people also accept the term without pause when they hear it but do not use it themselves, though they often talk about "mountain churches" when speaking in general. I distinguish between those church traditions that are in the Appalachian region but not largely of it, mostly the denominations of American Protestantism, and those church traditions that exist predominantly—or almost exclusively—in the region and are very special to it. The historical echoes of what is unique to religious life in Appalachia are much weaker in the Appalachian churches of American Protestantism in general, but they are there. For several denominations in Appalachia, particularly the United Methodists and Southern Baptists, their presence is great and their history is long in the region. Unlike most of their urban/county-seat/larger-town churches, many of their small mountain churches have been profoundly affected by the distinctive religious culture of the region. It is precisely the defining configuration of land, people, history, and traditions that constitutes Appalachian mountain religion as a regional religious tradition. I focus on those church traditions in the mountains that most densely concentrate within themselves the characterizing features of mountain religious life. Here the historical echoes reverberate most consistently and at their loudest, spelling out patterns, thus making it possible to identify much weaker echoes elsewhere.

Appalachian mountain religion is one of the very few uniquely American regional religious traditions to which Protestantism in the United States can lay claim. It is made up of church traditions found almost entirely in the region's mountains and small valleys. Generally, they do not exist beyond Appalachia, except through out-migration. These church traditions, nearly invisible to the outside world and to much of the Protestant mainstream even within Appalachia,[3] make up what is exclusive to religious life in Appalachia. Moreover, they have had profound impact on the overall religious character of Appalachia, extending their influences even into large, urban, and broad-valley mainline Protestant churches in subtle, indirect ways. However, mountain church traditions are scarcely influenced by the presence of American Protestantism in Appalachia today. Mountain religion embodies the distinctive religious ethos of Appalachia. The Appalachian churches of American Protestantism are affected by that ethos—although many mainstream Protestant clergy in Appalachia, native and "foreign," would disclaim this—for it permeates Appalachian culture well beyond the doors of the mountain "church house."

The history of Appalachian mountain religion involves more than just what is special and unique to religious life in Appalachia. It also concerns nearly two hundred years of interaction with the dominant religious culture of American Protestantism. Throughout that history, mountain religion's values have clashed with—and challenged—the values of its more powerful Protestant counterparts in American Christianity. Was mountain religion, existing almost entirely in an insular environment, solely acted upon? Did this road of religious influences lead only up the valleys and into the mountains? How Appalachian mountain religion came to be, how it has interacted with the nation's dominant religious culture, and what contributions it has made to American Christianity form the triple focus of this book.

I do not find it necessary to be drawn into a debate about "what is Appalachia." The definition has changed many times over many years, and involves more than just geography. In 1965, the federal government created the Appalachian Regional Commission (ARC), which for purposes of funding eligibility established political boundaries by counties, from Coharie County in New York State to Kemper County in Mississippi. These areas are only very loosely bound to the geography of the mountain chains of the Appalachians, which reach deep into Canada and down to the panhandle of Florida. For my purposes, John C. Campbell's map of the region in *The Southern Highlander & His Homeland* (1921) best represents the geographic range, especially the central areas, in which we find mountain religious culture at its most pronounced. If we follow the prolific Kentucky writer Jesse Stuart's rubric, "Appalachia is anywhere there's coal under the ground,"[4] then we, like the ARC, should include significant parts of southeastern Ohio and southwestern Pennsylvania, where many mountain people have migrated.

My own definition of the boundaries of Appalachia has to do as much with culture as with geography, a culture that has shrunk in upon itself over the decades and thus has shifted geographically depending upon the era. Karl B. Raitz and Richard Ulack wrote in "Regional Definitions," "To our knowledge, no cultural geographers or other cultural regionalists have explicitly delimited an Appalachian cultural region. Most cultural regionalists, however, do recognize a distinctive 'upland' culture subregion, at least in the southeastern portion of the United States," a geographic area dominated by the foothills and mountains of Appalachia. "The two characteristics that differentiate this type of region from others are the great variety of ways in which it manifests itself on the landscape (e.g., house type, religion, dialect, dietary preferences) and the self-consciousness on the part of the participants."[5] Cultural "landscape" and individuals' cultural "self-consciousness" combine with geography to create the identity and character of Appalachian mountain religion as a regional religious tradition.

Not by any means do the entire populace within the cultural-geographic borders of Appalachia consider themselves to be "mountain people." Campbell made the extremely pertinent, yet commonplace, observation about the basic division: "Obviously, if the term Southern Highland be allowed for the land, native-born residents of the region are Southern Highlanders. Yet within the Highland area are many native-born inhabitants of urban or valley residence who do not regard themselves as mountain people. The writer has two friends, one living in the Greater Appalachian Valley and one in a prosperous mountain city, and both devoted to the interests of their own people, who refer in conversation to 'those mountain folks,' although at other times jocosely alluding to themselves as 'mountain whites.'"[6] As we shall see, home missionaries to Appalachia before and since Campbell had made this same distinction in their literature, focusing their efforts not on the urbanite and large-valley dwellers but on "mountain people."

This division between valley and mountain populations is a worldwide

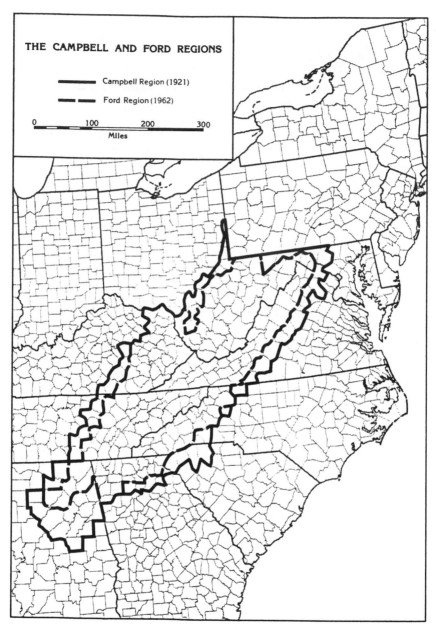

Map 1. The boundaries for Appalachia as determined by John C. Campbell (1921), with the boundaries determined by the Ford *Survey* (1962) superimposed on it. Reprinted from Karl B. Raitz and Richard Ulack, with Thomas R. Leinbach, *Appalachia, a Regional Geography: Land, People, and Development* (Boulder, Colo.: Westview Press, 1984), p. 20. Used by permission.

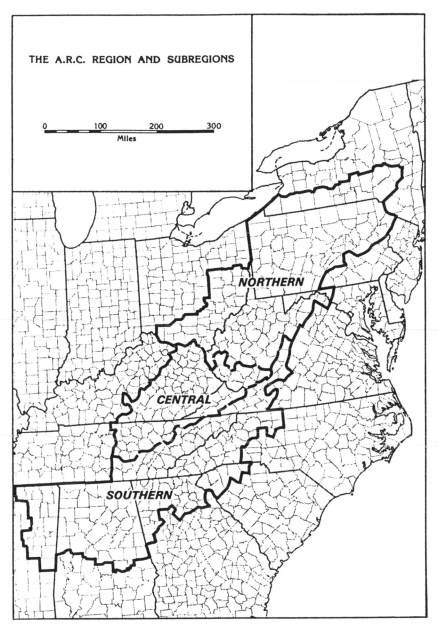

phenomenon, not at all unique to Appalachia. John F. Schermerhorn first noted it during his 1812–13 tour of the Old Southwest (a large part of which later became known as Appalachia), concerning its "religion and morals."[7] In the more than seventy years since Campbell wrote, the division between valley dwellers and mountain people has remained quite pronounced (although many would say less), even with the steady advance of urbanization. Transportation networks nonexistent in Campbell's day have greatly increased mutual accessibility, yet the vitality of mountain religious culture persists. Mountain people have carried their religious traditions into the larger towns and cities and broad valleys of Appalachia as they have moved to where they could find jobs more readily, just as they have carried them to Detroit and Cincinnati and Chicago and Columbus. But by far the strongest concentration of the components unique to religious life in Appalachia remains in the mountains, where they came together to create Appalachian mountain religion.

This study explores the historical development of Appalachian mountain religion and its differentiation from what became the dominant religious culture of the United States in the nineteenth and twentieth centuries. I look at the variety as well as the continuity and historical integrity of the worship practices, belief systems, religious experiences, and church traditions making up Appalachian mountain religion as a regional religious tradition. Mountain religion is essentially an oral religious tradition because it is known primarily through its oral literature and material culture, which accounts for its virtual invisibility in the study of American religious history. Nonetheless, Appalachian mountain religion has played an extremely significant role in American religious history, from the continuing traditions of Calvinist theological heritage to the Holiness-Pentecostal movements, providing the setting for the most dramatic events of the Great Revival period that continued to inform the development of mountain religious life long after the last camp meeting of the era had passed. Moreover, mountain religion has consciously continued doctrinal traditions of *grace* and the *Holy Spirit,* especially by maintaining the centrality of *religious experience* (from the ordinary to the extraordinary) in the worship life of mountain church communities. The expression of these doctrinal legacies in mountain church traditions remains closer to the conversion and revival traditions of Jonathan Edwards in the 1730s than of Charles Grandison Finney, the "father" of modern revivalism, in the 1830s. These traditions mark what is perhaps most theologically distinctive about Appalachian mountain religion when compared with the broader theological and institutional developments of Protestantism in the United States.

This theological distinctiveness goes beyond mere traditionalism, the myth that mountain Christians are simply a subgroup of American Protestantism left behind by a changing world that more modern, more progressive (and more powerful) Protestant denominations have met head on. Mountain religion has its own historical integrity that informs its uniqueness. First of all there is geography itself, the reality of the *land:* the mountainous terrain that is the Appalachian region has had enormous impact on its character, its texture, and its religious values. This makes it absolutely necessary to underscore at the outset that mountain religious life and history should not be subsumed under "Southern religion" or "religion in the South," treated simply as one more variant of this broadly encompassing label. Although there are certainly many significant similarities, the distinctions are far more pronounced, lodged primarily in geography. Nor do the variety of church traditions identified with Appalachian mountain religion have direct kinship today with denominational entities such as the Southern Baptist Convention and the United Methodist Church; indeed, mountain religion strongly eschews national, denominational, organizational church structures. Nor is it to be identified or equated with the religious ethos of well-known evangelical fundamentalists, ranging from the North Carolina Piedmont native Billy Graham to the Virginia Tidewater independent Baptist Jerry Falwell, as well as other popular televangelists today characterized by more charismatic-pentecostal flavors.

And finally, mountain religion is most certainly not "the religion of the poor." This pernicious, insidious, and condescending interpretation of the church traditions unique to Appalachia is favored by many representatives of mainline Protestantism and Catholicism. The presence of American Protestantism in Appalachia has been historically conditioned by a home missions posture centered on evangelization, education, and especially social needs relating to the region and its people's general welfare at the immediate level, but also in terms of the region's needs at the national level as a constituent of American society (which, as we shall see, was not always as benevolent as this sounds). As a consequence, the work of Protestant reformers in Appalachia today is, for the most part, simply a continuation of old-style Social Gospel home missionary efforts which framed their home missions ideology into the first few decades of the twentieth century. Their approach to "the work in Appalachia" was reconfigured under the War on Poverty of the 1960s and, most recently, they have been recasting their home missions ideology in the more modern guise of a liberation theology adapted to (in fact, superimposed on) mountain people, the antithesis of a theology ostensibly coming from the grass roots or, in its own argot, "base communities."

American Protestantism in particular has historically and consistently interpreted the worship practices, belief systems, and church traditions of mountain people as the religion of a subculture of poverty and the product of powerlessness and alienation. The current romance of delimiting mountain people as "the oppressed" is wedded to the traditional Protestant romance, beginning in the late nineteenth century, with Appalachia as a region in extremis, waiting for the salvific actions of the home missionaries to "help" mountain people and their region partake of "Christian civilization." As the key term and defining impetus of Protestant churches of the nineteenth and early twentieth centuries, Christian civilization meant specifically the nation's dominant religious culture of American Protestantism and the broader world of "progress" and "modernization" it represented to the designated deprived, like the mountain people of Appalachia. Today Appalachia is hyped as the "Third World" in America (as the latest wave of Protestant and Catholic reformers in Appalachia so often refer to it—with obvious implications). It is seen to be waiting for champions willing to put themselves on the line to help "empower" Appalachia's "oppressed" to name and address "for themselves" what these champions have identified as the region's "social justice issues" (what were originally "home mission concerns"). As the next step, social justice champions "help" mountain people do battle with more powerful "oppressors" otherwise out of the reach of their means and skills, but within the reach of the national institutional resources of these Christian reformers.

As we shall see, however, America's dominant religious culture—which has been especially characterized by the "helping" heritage of liberal values and their theological traditions—has found itself caught up for nearly two centuries now in a fundamental clash of religious values when confronted with the reality of Appalachian mountain religion. If anything, mountain religion has been a radical sign of contradiction within the broader religious culture. Even today, with widespread talk of "helping" to build up "base communities" in the mountains of Appalachia à la liberation theology, there is next to no interest in—apart from startlingly strong resistance to—exploring and appreciating mountain people's own worship communities and their distinguished and long-lived religious heritage. Gathered under the heading of Appalachian mountain religion, these worship communities and the ongoing and very strong influences of mountain religious culture beyond the doors of the mountain church house are arguably the most important and most prominent stabilizing force in the sociocultural life of the region. Instead, mountain religion is ignored by most Protestant reformers in the region when it is not dismissed with distaste. This is an extraordinary and seemingly very puzzling response to the worship life and religious traditions distinctive to mountain people on the part of a much larger and still widely dominant Protestant national culture that claims to thrive on appreciating what is "different," "unique," and "other" than itself—especially if accorded the ideologically loaded title "Third World" and its people designated among "the oppressed"—all in the name of laboring fearlessly to help bring God's reign on earth to fruition.

Labeling mountain religion as "the religion of the poor" in a region proclaimed to be America's "Third World" is much more than a ploy in large funding appeals to powerful foundations for projects such as education programs specializing in training mostly mainstream denominational clergy for a ministry tooled to Appalachia and its pressing social needs. This condescension toward mountain religion as "the religion of the poor" actually continues to serve a larger purpose with deep roots going back nearly two centuries. Throughout the history of its interaction with Appalachia—both within and beyond Appalachia's borders—American Protestantism has consistently sought to exorcise the power of mountain religion as a major threat to its own self-image by trivializing mountain religion as being primarily compensatory for deprivation, and suited for little else. Rejected as stagnant and regressive, mountain religion has always been portrayed by the nation's dominant religious culture as simply marking time in the lives of mountain people until they are finally lifted out of their isolation and poverty. How this scenario plays itself out today is but one more variation on the same theme: as mountain people seek to "liberate" themselves, they will transcend the oppressive fetters of their religion (a red flag in this clash of religious values), thus transforming it into an expression more true to who they are as a people on the way to liberation.

The actual meanings behind this scenario were put in more straightforward form by home missionaries of another age: with the coming of Christian civilization to the mountains, mountain people would surely discard not only their religion but many other sociocultural features that held them back. As one home missionary described the inevitable outcome of this plan of redemption, "What was merely temporary backwardness in their peculiar life is left behind" (1909). Only then could mountain people be assimilated into the national culture of accumulation and consumption, "merging"—as this same home missionary described mountain people's salvific absorption—"with the common life of the nation." Protestant reformers today express horror over any suggestion of diminishing the sociocultural features that have come to make Appalachia dear to the national consciousness about what is special to America. Their goal is to "lift up" what is unique and precious and true to Appalachia, while joining Appalachia in "the struggle" with national and international power blocs that destroy its environment and keep its people in poverty and in a position of "powerlessness." But mountain religion is not included in this list of treasures to be "lifted up." Protestant reformers exercise a deliberate selectivity in what they choose to affirm about Appalachia, a selectivity that has to do more with the Protestant reformers and their larger history than with Appalachia per se, effectively excluding what a significant majority of mountain people would likely include at the head of their own list of treasures.

If mountain religion can be characterized as "the religion of the poor," it can only be understood as such in the terms of the biblical injunction found in Jesus' Sermon on the Mount: "Blessed are the poor in spirit: for theirs is the kingdom of heaven. . . . Blessed are the pure in heart: for they shall see God" (Matt. 5:3, 8).[8] At the outset, this may appear to be a reverse form of romanticization. But this claim is based on a very particular type of theological temperament undergirding nearly all mountain church traditions and how it translates into social identity. It is also based, as we shall see throughout this book, on the characterizing features of mountain worship life and the efforts to transform the values they embody into concrete social action once the concluding hymn, such as "Brethren We Have Met Again," is sung and the worshipers depart to go about their daily lives. Being "poor in spirit" has to do with the condition of one's heart. It also has to do with what the Apostle Paul called not being proud and "puffed up." It values humility, a quality tied directly to "charity" or a loving heart where individuals do not vaunt themselves over others. Wrote Paul, "Charity vaunteth not itself, is not puffed up" (1 Cor. 13:4), an admonition mountain people take to heart in their religious culture which establishes and reinforces the value of humility through the central role of doctrines of grace: "humbleness" is the only appropriate response in a grace-centered religious culture that emphasizes a worldview recognizing all the many things or "blessings" that come as an unmerited gift from God, starting with salvation itself, a recognition to which all human efforts that may have had a part in bringing them about are subordinated. Such "humbleness" eschews hierarchies of merit; it is an equalizer.

In mountain religion, "charity" also takes ascendancy over "knowledge," keeping firmly in check the rationalistic conceit of placing primary value on the personal merit of one's own intellect, to which the heart is made subordinate, that invariably leads to spiritual pride about matters of religion through a self-righteous sense of certainty and superiority. Paul goes right to the point: "Knowledge puffeth up, but charity edifieth" (1 Cor. 8:1), confirming mountain religion's normative values of grace and humility that emphasize listening with the openness that discernment requires as the principal avenue of religious knowledge, trusting the Holy Spirit speaking within one's own heart to separate the wheat from the chaff, and rejecting a dogmatism open to no other view but its own that tears at the fabric of church life by dividing individuals and promoting hardness of heart.

Paul also addresses the essentially spiritual character of mountain religious life, declaring, "Let no man beguile you of your reward in a voluntary humility and worshipping of angels, intruding into those things which he hath not seen, vainly puffed up by his fleshly mind" (Col. 2:18). Observers of mountain religious life, from Schermerhorn to one home missionary pastor who in 1931 dismissed mountain people's religious experiences as "intense and strange spiritual vagaries," would be exasperated and dismayed by mountain religion's overwhelming emphasis on the spiritual realm—"those things which [are] not seen." Mountain people would reject outsiders' efforts to "intrude into" the spiritual core of their religious culture with the rationalistic, evidential criteria of the "fleshly mind" which emphasizes the material values enshrined by the "works righteousness" mentality characteristic of so much of American Protestantism. Not being "puffed up" points to the one theological focus that most comprehensively expresses the religious values embodied by Appalachian mountain religion. The spiritual condition of the human heart and how that condition translates into everyday living is the only evidential criteria mountain people require of each other; carefully tending the condition of their hearts, in order to love one another rightly, is the primary demand they believe God makes of them (John 13:34–35).

"These are humble people," says Brother Coy Miser, and their humility resides most of all in their tenderheartedness. Brother Coy should know. He is a "mountain preacher" (in his own words) in the independent Holiness tradition, mountain religion's most "invisible" and least documented church tradition. "Mountain preacher" is a universal designation for native ministers in the mountains, preachers and pastors alike, be they independent Holiness or Old Regular Baptist. The most significant and recurring theme in mountain preaching is that of the broken heart, tenderness of heart, a heart not hardened to the Spirit and the Word of God. Mountain people teach through their churches that the image of God in each person lives in the heart, that the Holy Spirit takes up residence in the heart, that the Word of God lodges itself in the heart, and the heart is meant to guide the head, not the other way around. "God speaks to the heart. The Devil speaks to the head," says Brother Coy. His admonition is not peculiar to him but highly representative of the basic orientation of mountain people in terms of how they conduct their lives and understand the world about them—an understanding which places one of the highest premiums on the value of intuition or "listening to the heart"—as expressed in their religious culture. So many mountain people identify that intuition with the phrase, "God laid on my heart." Coupled with its placing grace at the forefront, mountain religion pursues a distinctly nonrationalist mode of religious experience and a radical emotional and psychic vulnerability that flies in the face of the rationalist, nonemotive traditions of mainstream American Protestantism once characterized as "muscular Christianity." Mountain religion's emphasis on the heart guiding the head, rather than the other way around, epitomizes this fundamental divide in basic orientation not only to religion but to the world itself.

It is no surprise that one of the most frequent charges leveled against mountain religion is that it is "anti-intellectual," lacking, in the words of one recent writer, "common sense" (1981). This criticism has been an ongoing theme throughout mountain religion's history of interaction with American Protestantism, as we shall see when we explore the first home missions evaluation of religious life in the Appalachian region. In 1814, Schermerhorn, the first to make extensive observations about the central place of the Holy Spirit in what later became distinctively mountain church traditions, wrote, "It is the mistaken notion of this Spirit that has caused so much ignorance, error, and enthusiasm." He also used words like "fanaticism," stating that the worship practices soon to become normative in mountain religion were based on what he called "desires," "impressions," "feelings," and "delusion." His was a distinctly rationalist response that knew little what to do with the nonrational in religious experience. Schermerhorn was also on the cutting edge of his times, helping to translate new theological developments into the new institutional features characterizing the American Benevolence movement of his era, a movement whose larger purpose was to promote the also newly defined political goals and social agendas of American Protestantism.

At the end of the nineteenth century and at the height of the Christian America movement—a continuation and further refinement of the earlier American Benevolence movement—one sympathetic speaker, a Congregationalist and home missions church official, nonetheless criticized mountain religion for having excessive "religiosity" and "too little of intelligence" (1891). This attitude remains strong today; indeed it underlies the historical, ongoing divide between mountain religion and the Protestant mainstream, especially that part known best for its liberal values and traditions.

In an essay for *Mountain Review,* "Stripping Appalachian Soul: The New Left's Ace in the Hole" (1979), Bill Best recounted that "a very well known" theologian first visited Appalachia in the early 1930s. At that time a college president gave him this charge: "You are here to build a golden bridge from an impossible mountain theology to the modern world." This charge had echoed throughout the history of mountain religion's interaction with American Protestantism. Forty years later Best's "very well known" theologian returned to Appalachia, only to make essentially the same statement in Best's presence: "We must rid these mountaineers of their impossible theology just as we must rid them of the worms in their stomachs."[9] His statement expressed an attitude made up of the bricks of superiority and paternalism; but these bricks were mortared with fear.

As we shall see, the nation's dominant religious culture had always been deeply frightened of mountain people's distinctive religious culture: in part because American Protestantism could not control it; in part because it was so "other," even though mountain people shared the same racial, ethnic, and national origins, as well as the same religious heritages, as their counterparts in mainstream American Protestantism; in part because mountain religion's communal worship traditions—centered on the emotional, nonrational religious experiences of the individual—made American Protestants feel too vulnerable, too exposed, and too threatened; in part because mountain religion's primary theological values of grace and humility "convicted" American Protestantism's overweening pride expressed through its values promoting individual and institutional merit and achievement; in part because mountain religion challenged American Protestantism's will to power pursued through its colonial-type dominance of the less powerful embodied in its political goals and social agendas which have persisted for nearly two centuries; in part because mountain religion's own institutional structures were very small, very local, and very autonomous, in complete opposition to the national hierarchical institutionalism of denominationalism, the linchpin in American Protestantism. Fear translated into loathing, and even into outright hatred. In reaction to that fear, American Protestants accused mountain religion of deviance, bringing to its practitioners "moral and religious degradation," and of being unresponsive to the pressing social needs of the broader community—a clear sign of its irresponsibility and decadence. Other than the reasons briefly stated, what else was behind these accusations?

At the core of these fundamental theological differences between mountain religion and what had been historically America's dominant religious culture was the centrality of doctrines of grace and the Holy Spirit on an experiential level in the worship life of mountain church communities. The comparable tradition in American Protestantism was almost entirely supplanted during the first three to four decades of the nineteenth century by the theology of free will, with its subsequent foregrounding of rational decision in the experience of salvation or conversion. For nineteenth-century religious leaders, especially Charles Grandison Finney, the "father" of modern revivalism, salvation was no longer a "miracle" (in Finney's words), dependent on the uncontrollable and unpredictable quickening of the Holy Spirit in a movement of grace (as it was for Jonathan Edwards and continued to be in mountain church traditions). Instead, according to Finney, revivalism—which is all about salvation or the conversion experience—was now approximating a science; it was a rational and logical process dependent almost exclusively on "the right use of constituted means" which could, and should, be skillfully manipulated by the trained expert to achieve the desired effect, the actual experience of conversion precipitated by the expert but culminating in the individual's own act of will, of decision (*Lectures on Revivals of Religion*, 1835).

From this seismic shift along the theological fault line of the experience of salvation arose a whole new category of religious professionals: revival specialists who were expert in the "science" of winning souls for Christ, souls "won" or "saved" through persuasion by compelling them to reach the point of decision. Finney's work thus paved the way in an unbroken line from Dwight L. Moody to Billy Graham for a revival tradition that created a carefully managed, controlled environment where people were encouraged to make "a decision for Christ," "to dedicate your life to Jesus," "to accept Christ." With the displacement of grace by rational decision in the foreground of the experience of conversion, human initiative and God's cooperation supplanted God's initiative and human cooperation. The much broader implications of these two very different theological traditions—one centered on grace and the Holy Spirit, one centered on free will and rational decision—translated into two very different sets of religious values and worldviews. Indeed, these differences can be understood and appreciated only within the encompassing context of the history of American Protestantism and the history of Appalachian mountain religion.

Finney's synthesis of classic revival techniques with the major theological developments defining his era transformed revivalism itself. For the first time, revivalism was deliberately incorporated into the institutional framework of American Protestantism and used as a tool ("the right use of constituted means") for its own purposes. One of the most important uses of revivalism was as an aggressive and highly effective means for building church membership. Another was the redirection of people's postconversion energies to American Protestantism's own social and political ends through sanctioned activities centered on moral reform and social benevolence. What became the revival traditions of a now evangelically based Protestantism—and which were tools rather than components integral to its identity—were no longer the revival traditions that had created the foundations of Appalachian mountain religion and continued to sustain it.

By the turn into the twentieth century, the Old Regular Baptists—among the most doctrinally sophisticated of all mountain church traditions—had developed what has become normative as their doctrine of atonement or salvation. It strikes a mediating position between Calvinism and Arminianism that very much represents the general position on grace found in nearly all mountain church traditions. The Old Regular Baptist atonement doctrine is summarized as "election by grace" through the "sanctification of the Holy Spirit." It falls between the more Calvinist "particular election" traditions of the Primitive Baptists and the more Arminian "general" or "universal" atonement traditions attributed to the Free Will and Missionary Baptists. However, for all of these groups, emphasis is upon religious experience—from the experience of conversion or salvation itself to emotional expressions in a worship service. The centrality of religious experience was a result of the revival movements infusing mountain religious history that became regionally specific to mountain religion, from pietism and Scots-Irish sacramental revivalism, to early American Baptist revival culture and plain-folk camp-meeting religion. Religious experiences are found especially in expressive and ecstatic worship practices, with the breadth of their traditional possibilities represented (some more, some less) in nearly all mountain church traditions. These vibrant, immediate religious experiences, which not only occur in the communal setting of mountain people's worship services but permeate their more private, everyday lives, are what mountain people call "a blessing," mediated by grace through the galvanizing presence of the Holy Spirit.[10]

Throughout mountain religious life, there is a dominant emphasis on the purity of God-generated or God-instituted emotion or religious experience, unmediated by direct human manipulation. Expressive and ecstatic worship traditions have a very long heritage in mountain religious life, reaching back to the earliest years of the first settlements on the Appalachian frontier near the beginning of the eighteenth century. These traditions involve intensely physical and emotional behavior in the worship environment where spontaneity is highly valued because it marks the immediate presence of the Holy Spirit. Such emotional expressions, to a greater or lesser degree, cut across almost all mountain church traditions, from the most doctrinally conservative to the more free-flowing. A preacher is supposed to experience emotion while preaching, not generate it or "whip it up." Most television evangelists are seen by a significant number of mountain people as generators of emotion or religious experience, not leaning on the unmanipulated movement of the Holy Spirit. The same applies to the call to conversion or salvation: for most mountain church traditions, from independent Holiness to Old Regular Baptist, one cannot make "a decision for Christ," as evangelical Protestants have come to express it. One can only be open to the experience of saving grace in one's life. The preeminence of grace over rational decision in the conversion experience goes hand in hand with the centrality of the Holy Spirit in mountain worship life.

Since the division between mountain religion and American Protestantism in their attitudes toward grace and nonrational religious experience was well established by the time of Finney, it is clear that mountain religion's complementary emphasis on the movement of the Holy Spirit in the community of believers has its roots not in the late nineteenth and early twentieth centuries' Holiness-Pentecostal movements but in classic Calvinist theological tradition reaching back to the Synod of Dort in 1618–19 and ultimately to Calvin himself. In terms of the traditions of the doctrines of grace and the Holy Spirit, Calvinism is alive and well in mountain religious life. It binds together church traditions such as Old Regular Baptists and Primitive Baptists, who share a strong Calvinist doctrinal heritage, as well as Free Will Baptists and independent Holiness who, though "general" or "universal" in their atonement doctrines, make a wide berth for Calvinist traditions of grace and the Holy Spirit that firmly tamp down the free-will/ human-initiative aspect of fully developed Arminianism. Thus, uniting these four church traditions with many others found mostly in the mountains of Appalachia are predominant emphases in their worship practices and belief systems on grace and profoundly expressive religious experiences through the mediation of the Holy Spirit. Included in their numbers are many small mountain churches belonging to mainstream Protestant denominations, primarily the Methodists and Southern Baptists, which usually have more in common with the traditions distinctive to Appalachia than with the large, nationally based denominations with whom they are formally affiliated.

Other features complimenting the experiential traditions of doctrines of grace and the Holy Spirit also distinguish the variety of church traditions making up Appalachian mountain religion as part of a regional religious tradition: preachers assume more of a prophetic stance than a charismatic one; free church polity (a universal throughout mountain church traditions), expressed primarily through a firm belief in democratic equality and the priesthood of all believers, makes church life very much a corporate, collegial reality. This latter fact has to do especially with how corporate decisions are reached in rural Appalachian communities about matters affecting the group. An emphasis on humility—also a product of the doctrines of grace— makes leadership in church life a highly subtle and extremely deferential affair on the part of those who are recognized religious leaders, both women and men. Indeed, church leaders—ordained or not, for many are the fluid and variegated leadership roles in mountain churches—function primarily to call forth the gifts and full participation of others. In mountain churches, preachers and pastors in particular are rarely the center of church life, in contrast to the more typical leadership models for clergy characterizing most of American Protestantism.

Grace and religious experience, mediated by the Holy Spirit, are at the core of this regional religious tradition. The individual is affirmed in the worshiping community through an autonomy of spontaneous self-expression, the integrity of which is valued by the group. The worshiping community itself achieves an often spectacular "transformative power" where the community as a whole experiences an ontological shift creating, however briefly, a unity of being expressing what heaven must be like.[11] Indeed, this collective experience gives tangible substance to what so many mountain people call their "hope of heaven." These experiential realities confound two of the most popular labels that have been glued onto all of the traditions making up Appalachian mountain religion: that it is a "pie-in-the-sky" religion for a socially and economically "disadvantaged" people who see little reason to hope for a better life or that it is a "fatalistic" religion that drains its adherents of power over their own destinies. As we attempt to understand mountain religion more on its own terms and less on the terms of those who have to date provided the most readily available interpretations—from home missionaries to social scientists—the veracity of such labels and the purposes behind them form a significant part of our investigation. We begin that investigation in the next section.

Mountain Preachers, Mountain Religion

Mountain religion and mountain preachers suffer the fate of being portrayed either as drab, oppressive, narrow purveyors of doctrinal darkness (read "Calvinism") or as emotional exotics left over from the worst excesses of the Great Revival. In the popular mind, in fiction, and in scholarship, these apparent extremes have been located as contradictions commingling in the archetypical figure of the mountain preacher, a pattern of representation that has persisted up to the present. When applied to Appalachian mountain religion, this either/or palette of portrayal obliterates mountain religion's broad spectrum of worship practices, belief systems, church traditions, and religious culture, focusing instead on what appear to be two widely divergent—indeed, completely opposite—groups. One group emphasizes what is perceived to be the doctrinally "drab and oppressive" and the other the "emotionally exotic" poles of mountain religion, like opposite sides of the same coin. These seemingly "opposite poles," however, do not define the spectrum's limits because they do not set its ends: they are not opposites at all, nor are they contradictions.

Nonetheless, since the mid-twentieth century, serpent handlers and Primitive/Old Regular Baptists have dominated as the "two" church traditions most closely identified with mountain religion, embodying the "opposite poles" model. The literature has rarely differentiated between Primitive and Old Regular Baptists, usually blending them together and ignoring altogether the many other Calvinist-based groups in the mountains closely related to them through shared history and doctrinal traditions. Serpent handlers are, of course, what an overwhelming majority of "outsiders" consider to be mountain religion's most fascinating tradition and its primary claim to fame.[12] They too are painted with a broad, monochrome brush, wiping out what are otherwise clear and significant distinctions among subregionally and doctrinally diverse traditions of serpent handlers such as Oneness or Jesus Only groups (located primarily in central Appalachian areas, especially southern West Virginia, eastern Kentucky, and southwest Virginia) in contrast to Trinitarian groups (usually found in the southern areas of Appalachia, such as northern Georgia and southeast Tennessee).

Although their origins go back to around 1910, serpent handlers have been a focus of attention only since the 1940s. From popular culture to social science research, they were elevated to the position of being the primary representative of what is special and unique about "religion in Appalachia" only in the late 1950s to early 1960s. Indeed, serpent handlers are today what most people usually mention first when asked, "What comes to mind when you think about religion in Appalachia?" Historically, however, Primitive and Old Regular Baptists have tended to be seen as the quintessential expression of Appalachian mountain religion because of their pronounced traditionalism in worship practices and belief systems. The reasons for this are straightforward. Just as the Appalachian region, and the social behaviors usually identified with the region, are invariably labeled "traditional" or unchanging, reflecting a world once common to "long ago," so the Primitive and Old Regular Baptists seem to embody this myth of traditionalism within the religious life of the region. Implicit in this portrayal is extreme passivity, commonly characterized as "fatalism," which drags with it the weight of stagnation and a regressive traditionalism, rather than active self-determination.

Such a portrait has served well the interests of industrial colonizers and home missionaries and has been exposed in a few publications in Appalachian studies.[13] This stereotypical portrayal of Old Regular and Primitive Baptists as passive traditionalists has then been overlaid onto all mountain church traditions in nearly all of the available—and spotty—literature. Not only a stereotype, passive traditionalism is also one of the most prominent and frequently repeated prejudices (expressing bigotry and intolerance) infusing the cumulative layers of myth and distortion enveloping Appalachian mountain religion. Passive traditionalism does not stand alone but is joined by an assortment of stereotypes that also have crossed over the line to become the prejudices that have vaguely defined the religion of mountain people in the national consciousness. All of them are propagated by an inability to hear historical echoes in what one observes and reads about, factual errors, and unmitigated prejudice. These three basic sources of distortion have predetermined the tone and the conclusions of most descriptive and interpretive writings about mountain religious life and history.

Primitive and Old Regular Baptists are, in fact, a large window into mountain religion, but they have been elevated by outsiders to the status of a totem, telling the story of the "family" of mountain religion, for all the wrong reasons. In many respects the Primitive and Old Regular Baptists are indeed totemic, one of the region's deepest canyons producing many of the loudest reverberations of historical echoes that spell out patterns of repetitions found throughout mountain religious culture. Those repetitions or commonalities are significant clues to the uniqueness of the region's religious history, despite ideological differences ranging from the strict or modified Calvinism of some (such as the Primitive and Old Regular Baptists) to the free-will Arminianism of others (including independent Missionary Baptists, Free Will Baptists, and independent Holiness, all of whom, as I have noted previously, do modify their Arminianism by incorporating the influences of Calvinist traditions of grace and the Holy Spirit). Throughout this book, repeatedly we will return to the Primitive and Old Regular Baptists who concentrate within themselves certain traditions that are major clues to mountain religion's history. The development of these clues will illuminate the strong ties between seemingly disparate church traditions such as Old Regular Baptist and independent Holiness. In turn, this will lead to discerning the patterns of commonalities and thence to what can be said more generally about the characterizing features of mountain religion.

Within the field of American religious history, a tunnel of silence prevails about religious life that became normative to the mountains of Appalachia from soon after the Great Revival on the Appalachian frontier (which crested in 1801 and ebbed away a few years later, leaving in its wake plain-folk camp-meeting religion) until John C. Campbell's *The Southern Highlander & His Homeland* was published in 1921. Prior to Campbell, the only sources on Appalachia's mountain church traditions and distinctive religious culture were local-color novelists and the home missionaries of American Protestantism, introduced into the region to evangelize and educate "mountain whites" in the last decades of the nineteenth century. The home missionaries habitually dismissed the religious culture unique to mountain people by acting as if it were virtually nonexistent or proclaiming it deviant: mountain people were "unchurched," indeed, they were "religiously destitute," or their religious culture reduced them to a state of "moral and religious degradation." This willful blindness to the pervasive presence of mountain religious culture and its vital importance in the lives of mountain people, coupled with a posture of offended sensibilities in reaction to its defining features such as strong emotional piety, have persisted until today and permeate much of the very limited literature on mountain religion.

The viewpoints of social scientists, responsible for producing a preponderance of the secondary literature, have tended to pick up where the home missionaries left off. They too habitually describe and analyze various aspects of mountain religious life as both products and causes of deprivation—psychological, social, and economic. Like the home missionaries, they very often conclude that mountain religion is a significant retardant standing in the way of "needed" social change. They usually base this conclusion on the "hard science" of statistical studies (so favored by a disproportionate number of social scientists who have written on mountain people and their religion) by which they generate their profiles of "the role of religion (and whatever else) in such-and-such mountain community." More often than not, these profiles are predetermined by a functionalistic orientation that, predictably, casts mountain religion as the creation of a subculture of poverty.

The starting point, then, for too many scholars' "firsthand" information about religious life and traditions distinctive to Appalachia's mountain regions has been the observations and interpretations of home missionaries and social uplift workers, past and present, that by now form the foundations for most of the standard descriptive information available in secondary sources.[14] Primary sources from within mountain religion have yet to be identified and collected in any systematic manner for one basic reason: mountain religion is principally an oral religious tradition. As such, most of its primary sources lie in the underexplored realms of oral history, oral tradition, and material culture. Worship—the preaching, singing, and praying—is the "text," the primary source "document" of mountain religious life. So are the carefully sculpted conversion narratives and the oft-repeated testimonies that so frequently are minor masterpieces of oral literature, along with the oral compositions embodying the visions, dreams, and trances of religious experience. Material culture, from church houses to religious art, also offers a wealth of primary sources. Oral history is equally indispensable to the investigation of mountain religion, for mountain people bear in themselves the clearest, living chronicles of their distinctive religious culture.

Written primary documents providing historical narratives about the region's religious life from the early eighteenth century up to the present are exceedingly sparse, or at the least have yet to be identified and examined. Largely absent or unknown are the memoirs, diaries, letters, and journals of mountain people. Church records, formal and informal, are scattered and at this time their extent is undetermined. Moreover, many mountain churches are not known for creating and preserving documentation about themselves. However, some groups, notably Primitive Baptists, have collected documentation about themselves. Everything from spiritual diaries to associational minutes can be found at the Primitive Baptist Library in Elon College, North Carolina. But this material, for the most part, has yet to find its way into writings about mountain religious life and about Primitive Baptists in particular. Given the overwhelming absence of traditional research material, most scholars and commentators on mountain religion have been unduly influenced by the accounts of "outsiders" over the past two centuries.

Scholars and commentators also get caught up in the underlying ideological and political agendas of published denominational histories. As a result, Old School or anti-missionary Baptists, such as the Primitive Baptists in particular, are not portrayed as the significant social movement they developed into during the first half of the nineteenth century. The leaders of American Protestantism at that time were caught up in the consequences of important changes in theological direction, manifested both individually and institutionally in the drive for merit and achievement and denominational hierarchy and power.[15] Such developments stood in complete contrast to the theological traditions and institutions of mountain Baptists, whose emphasis was on grace and humility. Old School Baptists actively challenged the leadership of the evangelical Protestant denominations, especially Baptist denominational leaders, who were moving forward with their plans to translate into concrete expression major theological shifts precipitated by the New Haven Theology, which stemmed from the New Divinity that in turn had its own foundations in the theology of Jonathan Edwards. The New Haven Theology had been most fully developed during the first years of the nineteenth century by Nathaniel W. Taylor and Lyman Beecher, New Englanders drawn to the center of theological activity under Timothy Dwight at Yale. One of their primary theological tasks was to liberate free will and rational decision in the experience of conversion or salvation from the fetters of Calvinism without losing the moorings of their heritage. As such, their overriding task was to facilitate the "Arminianization" of Calvinism.

Denominational leadership in the eastern United States created the perfect vehicle for the institutionalization of what Sydney Ahlstrom called the New Haven "rationalistic 'revival theology' " which was translated into "moral reform and social benevolence."[16] What had been the expressive and ecstatic energies of the conversion experience of an earlier revival tradition, centered on religious experience understood to be mediated by grace through the Holy Spirit, were now channeled directly into national, church-based institutions and their suborganizations, where these energies were transformed into social action with very specific goals and agendas, from temperance to abolitionism. Old School Baptists were alarmed. What they challenged in particular was the convergence of these developments into a movement that came to be called American Benevolence. Promoted in the form of missionary, educational, and benevolent societies, its purpose was to achieve American Protestantism's social and political ends. Making a rational "decision for Christ"—a recent conversion tradition reflecting these new theological shifts and very different from the conversion tradition of the Old School Baptists— was now validated by aggressively doing a very specific type of "good works" identified with promoting American Protestantism's moral vision for the world at large by addressing the pressing social issues American Protestantism identified.

The tenor that would define what became known over the next two centuries as "liberal Protestantism," centered on social justice theology and social action—apart from a more specific focus on aggressive evangelization equally influenced by the "decision for Christ" theological orientation that would soon characterize many conservative Protestant movements—was now fully formed. The Old School Baptists raised the debate over the inherent implications of these developments, coming down squarely on issues of power and major theological significance. They did so by creating their own counterresponse through the short-lived Anti-Mission movement. The theology undergirding the overwhelming movement toward missions, especially as it altered the basic character of the Baptist tradition in the United States and ushered in its denominational structuring on a national level, summed up all the issues raised by the larger and more encompassing American Benevolence movement that the Old School Baptists felt compelled to address.

The social and political objectives of American Benevolence were shared by all of the denominations making up the Protestant mainstream at that time. As the Old School Baptists saw it, more than just theology was at stake. With the ascendancy of a "works righteousness" mentality, a pernicious form of judgmentalism and even a virulent form of nativism manifested themselves among many who were now feverishly working their way into God's kingdom by changing the world according to their perception of God's plan of salvation. What the Old School Baptists saw as a serious, and even destructive, trespass of their religious culture—and their style of life and the system of values it embodied—soon came to pass. Within a few short years many denominations targeted Appalachia through home missions for "assimilation" into their collective vision of a homogeneous "Christian America"—a later development following on the heels and under the sway of American Benevolence. Home missionaries aggressively promoted this vision by working to superimpose on "unassimilated" populations such as mountain people the values of the nation's dominant religious culture.

The "losers" of such power struggles rarely win much prominence in the historical record. As a result, Old School Baptists have been portrayed in denominational histories as a small group of disruptive, embarrassing malcontents who stood in the way of progress and the national good at the behest of a few narrow, zealous, ignorant leaders. Although a nationwide movement, Old School or anti-missionary Baptists were most heavily concentrated in the Appalachian region and its immediate border areas. A significant number of prominent Old School Baptist leaders outside of Appalachia had strong roots in the region. Through the Old School Baptists, during the early years of the nineteenth century (especially ca. 1827–40), mountain Christians made their only concerted effort to openly defend the integrity of their religious lives and values against the national denominational institutions. Old School Baptists also laid down the challenge of their opposition for the good of their much more influential Protestant brothers and sisters. Instead of confronting the issues raised by the anti-missionary Baptists—issues of power and of enormous theological import—mainstream Protestantism all but wrote them out of American religious history.

By the time J. H. Spencer wrote *A History of Kentucky Baptists from 1769 to 1885,* he labeled not only Old School Baptists but other Baptist groups characteristic of the mountain regions of Appalachia as having "seceded from the Baptists, and still retain the Baptist name" (confusing who historically had "seceded" from whom). Even though these other groups embraced a theology of free will and general atonement, by 1885 not even basic theological similarities were enough to win parity. Spencer's highly representative prejudice was that all mountain Baptist traditions not associated with national Baptist denominational structures were only peculiar, perplexing aberrations, not "real" Baptists but mere "sects" and doomed to extinction. Spencer wrote,

> As we have seen, there are in the State, four sects, which have seceded from the Baptists, and still retain the Baptist name: viz. *Hypercalvinistic Baptists,* derisively called "Hard-Shells," or "Iron-Jackets," and calling themselves by a variety of names as "Particular Baptists," "Regular Baptists," "Predestinarian Baptists," "Old School Baptists," and "Primitive Baptists," *General Baptists, Free-Will Baptists,* and *United Baptists.* The first named have continued to diminish in numbers from soon after their secession, and, without some unforseen [*sic*] change, must, in a few years more, come to nought. The General Baptists, also, appear to be diminishing, while their numbers are already small. The Free-Will Baptists have scarcely more than a nominal existence in the State, and their [*sic*] seems to be no probability of their increasing to any considerable extent.

Only the United Baptists received some approval, despite "their opposition to missionary and other benevolent societies." In Spencer's estimation, "This sect has made some progress in numbers and influence, and is manifestly approximating nearer the denomination from which it seceded."[17]

Apparently "numbers and influence" were Spencer's principal measure for "progress" that "approximated" denominational status, well within the norm of the cult of accumulation that had overtaken the churches of American Protestantism by this time (large memberships, fine church buildings, a high premium on a clergy certified by first-rate theological education, institutional networking on a national level, influence identified with elevated rank in a hierarchy of prestige). Contrary to Spencer's predictions of demise (except for the United Baptists), all but one of the groups he named form a significant part of Appalachian mountain religion today, suggesting an entirely different standard of "progress." Free Will Baptist churches in particular are settled well within popular culture. They were even characterized in the mid-twentieth century as "the miner's church" by one serious student of how to bring denominationalism—and especially Presbyterianism—into the mountains.[18]

Given the selectivity of the historical record, most people today know little about Appalachian mountain religion and even less about Primitive and Old Regular Baptists apart from the stereotypes. Among the principal carriers of mountain religious culture are mountain preachers, whom John C. Campbell identified as "one of the strong links with the past which here in the Highlands have not yet been broken" (1921). Brother Ray Collins, while moderator of the Thornton Union Association of Old Regular Baptists, published a piece in the inaugural issue of *Mountain Review* (September 1974) in which he takes strong exception to the ways mountain preachers have been portrayed, understanding full well that to many a commentator the archetypical figure of the "mountain preacher" has always pointed directly to Primitive and Old Regular Baptist elders whose traditions combine the doctrinal conservatism (Calvinism) and expressive worship practices (emotionalism) requisite to that archetype.

Brother Ray addresses how that archetype is construed, which, for him, comes down to all the flesh-and-blood brethren he has known and loved. Brother Ray writes,

> The point I am wanting to make is this: that "education" won't preach the Gospel and neither will ignorance, but that in order for a man to preach the Gospel he must be called and qualified by God, and then he will do the job. That is the reason that it hurts me greatly for someone to make fun of the preachers that have gone without money, suffered many hardships, rode through the rain, the snow, in the nighttime, in the heat of day just for the cause of Jesus Christ. Then for someone without much learning, but a lot of education (maybe a degree), to write these derogatory remarks about the mountain preachers. There are a lot of articles in the little magazines that are put out by Alice Lloyd College that tend to degrade the mountain preacher and, also, it degrades the mountain people. People that write those articles should not be allowed to teach or write in the mountains.[23]

One hopes very much that Brother Ray never saw Robert H. Hartman's article in *Appalachian Heritage* back in 1981 titled "Origins of the Mountain Preacher," though *Appalachian Heritage* may have been the "little magazine" then published by Alice Lloyd College in eastern Kentucky that Brother Ray was referring to.[24] It is curious that Hartman's article was published at all in a periodical devoted to Appalachian life and culture. The fact that it was published in *Appalachian Heritage* indicates the grip of the tyranny over mountain people of what have become the prevailing stereotypes and prejudices about their religion and its worth, not only to them but in the broader scheme of American Christianity.

As a scholar claiming to look at mountain religion and mountain preachers from the perspective of American religious history, Hartman nonetheless adopted the stereotypes about them found in fiction not only as his starting point but as true-to-life. Hartman invoked Cratis Williams's landmark study, "The Southern Mountaineer in Fact and Fiction" (1961),[25] as his justification for accepting as realities Williams's summaries of how mountain preachers were portrayed in literature about Appalachia: "In his own words, Williams sums up the character of the mountain preacher as 'a Calvinist fundamentalist . . . , an emotional, irrational man of ranting zeal who always clung literally to the Bible.'"[26] Hartman failed to note that this seemingly damning quotation came, however, from a section Williams labeled "Sociological Opinion." Hartman also failed to note that Williams wrote of one of John Fox, Jr.'s characters who appeared in several of his early twentieth-century novels about Appalachia, "Sherd Raines is one of the better fictional portraits of the Calvinistic mountain preacher whose ministry is motivated by a genuine passion for service. Self-sacrificing, shrewd, intelligent, and [with] a genuine zeal for his ministry, he is a well-presented figure of what is frequently merely a stock character."[27] Hartman, as we shall soon see, was far more interested in the "stock character" than he was in the "well-presented figure," which may account for his failure to include this particular quotation along with all the other material he mined from Williams on the mountain preacher; for indeed, this single quotation would have foiled Hartman's basic premise and exposed the extent to which he misconstrued Williams's material.

Hartman focused his attention almost exclusively on Calvinist mountain preachers, accepting without any question the ideological agenda reflected in most of the denominational histories and secondary scholarship on religion distinctive to Appalachia. He especially voiced prejudice against expressive and ecstatic worship traditions, which he identified as manifestations of "ignorance," a term he used repeatedly and equated with a lack of formal education in the pulpit. Finally, Hartman concluded that mountain religion was both compensatory for low socioeconomic standing and a primary explanation of Appalachia's disengagement from the rest of the nation. He believed that the doctrines preached were degenerate, and that this degeneracy was due to illiteracy and an accompanying susceptibility "to embrace almost all of the popular conceptions they [mountain people and mountain preachers especially] encountered."[28]

Hartman even went so far as to claim that throughout history the mountain preacher "emerges out of that segment of society. . . regarded as disreputable." With this statement, Hartman showed that understanding of the mountain preacher had simply marked time since the first decade of the nineteenth century, when William Fristoe wrote, "The cant word was that they are an ignorant, illiterate set and are of the poor and contemptible class of people,"[29] referring to the people and preachers making up the Baptist revival in colonial Virginia, a tradition from which came many of the most important components of Appalachian mountain religion. If the mountain preacher's background was "disreputable," mountain religion itself fared no better. As a religion, it did not "do" what religion was supposed to do, but just the opposite. Hartman declared, "The excesses of this type of religion we have dwelt upon at some length. It was a religion which, rather than bringing much in the way of comfort, strength and hope to its adherents, brought estrangement, isolation, and a sense of helplessness."[30] Once again, and into the 1980s, mountain religion was blamed for keeping mountain people in an arrested state of alienation and powerlessness.

Hartman advanced his thesis by interpreting the Great Awakening in the South and the Great Revival as roiling, disruptive, and even dangerous excesses of human emotion. With such a religious heritage untempered by the restraint of rationalism and education, mountain people had pursued a misguided search for true religious experience and some sense of control over their otherwise dismal, if not defeated, lives. Melanie Sovine wrote of this type of scholarship about mountain religion (although not about this specific article), especially when directed toward its most doctrinally traditional groups, "Even the more recent histories of the Primitive Baptist Church continue to interpret their formation within a theological-denominational context, perpetuating a popular image of the Primitive Baptists as unenlightened, uneducated men and women who would not, indeed because of their lower social status could not, progress with other Baptists to a position among the powerful and competitive American denominations."[31] This stereotype of ignorance and lower-class status, focused on the Primitive and Old Regular Baptists as totemic of mountain religion, had long been universally applied to all of mountain religious culture. Hartman's article was no exception. As Sovine has indicated repeatedly in her essays about Primitive Baptists, the national power base and values of the denominations making up American Protestantism were used as the measure of the worth and viability of mountain religion by those who were not part of it. Again, Hartman's article broke no new ground.

Tracing further the portraits drawn of mountain preachers in literature about Appalachia as guided by Cratis Williams's descriptive analyses, Hartman concluded the following about the literary "figure" of the mountain preacher: "He is a figure conspicuously devoid of human compassion. He lacks common sense and common grace. His preaching is emotional to the point of being ludicrous. His religion is one of dissent and negation, one of continually harping on the people's sins which cover everything that brought simple pleasure to the people, such as playing the fiddle and dancing. At times he seems to be little higher in status than the village fool."[32] With this cache of ammunition, Hartman went two startling—yet, by now, not unanticipated—steps beyond his filtered summary of the mountain preacher as literary "figure," culminating, according to his reading of Williams, as the religious variant of the communal role accorded "the village fool": Hartman concluded that not only was this portrait solidly based in reality, it was also representative; indeed, it was the norm to be found among the mountain preachers of Appalachia. Throughout his article, Hartman enhanced the illusion of the legitimacy of his scathing attack by making reference to reputable secondary literature in American religious history, using it to buttress his claims by highlighting to the point of distortion whatever confirmed his composite (and secondhand) rendition of the mountain preacher's fictional portrait as emblematic of mountain preachers in general.

Hartman's article is astonishing. It parades under the guise of solid scholarship while giving vent to the worst of the major stereotypes and prejudices about mountain preachers and mountain religion. Most disturbing of all, it was written, not at the end of the nineteenth century, but near the end of the twentieth. Hartman's vitriol, even at this late date, tells us much more about the values and worldview out of which he wrote than about mountain preachers and mountain religion. His article stands as simply one more entry into the "canon" of material that predominates on mountain religious life in the Appalachian region. At most, it is a useful—though troubling—compendium of prevailing opinion in the available literature about Appalachian mountain religion. It also poses a larger question: What accounts for the force propelling such expressions of hostility and condescension toward mountain religion found in varying degrees throughout most of the literature? We shall approach this question from different directions throughout this book.

When considering the "Origins of the Mountain Preacher," surely the first question should be "Who is the mountain preacher?" In 1947 *Mountain Life & Work*, the publication of the Council of the Southern Mountains, held what it called "A Reflective Symposium by Seven Rural Ministers of the Mountains."[33] The "rural ministers of the mountains" selected for the symposium were Episcopal, Evangelical, Lutheran, and Dutch Reform, including one minister who spoke on behalf of the Methodists, Disciples, and Presbyterians, and two representatives called "undenominational." Except perhaps for "undenominational," it is difficult to recognize a representative example of the mountain preacher in this group. Numerous organizations with strong ties to American Protestantism over the decades have been committed to work exclusively in Appalachia, including the recently defunct Council of the Southern Mountains (disbanded in 1989 after more than seventy-five years), which was the first. Today many channel strong religious motivations into focusing on social justice issues in Appalachia. The most influential of this type is the interdenominational Commission on Religion in Appalachia (CORA), founded during the earliest years of the War on Poverty and affiliated with the National Council of Churches. As we shall see, these helping bodies, no matter how sympathetic, have always had a very difficult time recognizing and acknowledging the mountain preachers who make up the overwhelming majority of "rural ministers of the mountains."

Is the mountain preacher Brother John Sherfey, whose Fellowship Independent Baptist Church in Page County, Virginia, has its immediate roots in the Free Will Baptist tradition with many pietistic elements and plain-folk camp-meeting traditions (now identified especially with independent Holiness churches) intermixed in its services?[34] Is it Elder Millard Pruitt of the Laurel Glenn Regular Baptist Church in Allegheny County, North Carolina?[35] Is it Preacher Dan Gibson from near Hindman, Kentucky, who stands in a long tradition of angry, passionate, and very smart men and women who are committed to protecting and preserving the land for their children's children?[36] Is it Brother Joe Turner from near Camp Creek, West Virginia, a former miner whose Baptist and Methodist background led him eventually to serpent handling and a church built on his own property?[37] Or is it Sister Edna Alexander, who lives in the foothills of the Cumberlands in Kentucky, an independent Holiness woman now into her early sixties whose active prayer ministry for more than thirty years touches the lives of all of her family and neighbors? She has no small building for gatherings, but calls together her kith and kin for prayer and exhortation or goes alone to a small cabin atop the mountain on her property line set aside solely as a place to be with God.

Whoever he or she is, the mountain preacher deserves much, much better than most of what has been published so far. A very small handful of regional scholars and humanities scholars influenced by a religious studies perspective (whose first monographs have appeared only since the late 1980s) are beginning to contribute to the variegated portrait of the mountain preacher and mountain religion, and to wrestle with the inaccuracies and caricatures that have long since become the staple of discussions about mountain religious life. More important than documenting the case against Appalachian mountain religion in the available literature is the need to begin to identify and explore with care and an open heart the "primary source material" of this oral religious culture—the preaching, singing, and praying; the visions, dreams, and trances; the conversion narratives and testimonies; the material culture of church houses and religious art; the private letters, diaries, and memoirs; the interviews recounting religious life in the mountains of Appalachia. These resources are the primary clues that will make it possible to illuminate the tradition histories and symbol systems of mountain people's worship practices and beliefs.

Only through the historical echoes reverberating in these resources may we begin to identify the primary components—the large streams of foundational historical influences—without which mountain religion would not exist today. Once they are identified, we may begin to see how these streams of influence coursed together, allowing us to suggest a historical framework that will help to guide our understanding of the history of Appalachian mountain religion as a regional religious tradition. Only through the resources of this oral religious culture—resources that are primarily flesh and blood, people who graciously allow us to enter the intimate realm of their religious lives that they so carefully nurture and fiercely guard as perhaps the clearest and most cherished expression of who they are—will we begin to hear and understand mountain religion in a way that will allow a more authentic portrait to emerge in secondary literature. We shall know we are getting closer to such a portrait only when those who give life to the religious culture unique to the mountains of Appalachia are able to begin to recognize and affirm that portrait as akin to their own self-understanding.

An Itinerary for Our Journey

The first two sections of this introduction have sketched out the larger, overarching historical drama of Appalachian mountain religion and American Protestantism in relation to each other, suggesting the significance of their interaction within the framework of American religious history. The rest of the book attempts to fill out many of the particulars, especially with regard to mountain religion itself, that have generated this ongoing conflict between a major regional religious tradition and the nation's historically dominant religious culture. Nearly twenty chapters in four parts make up the rest of this work. In order to clarify the design of the book and how the chapters interact with each other, I provide here a brief summary. The first few pages of each numbered part will introduce that part's focus and some of the interpretive highlights of each of the chapters within it.

Part 1 presents distinguishing characteristics of mountain religious life from different periods of the twentieth century and from different places in central Appalachia. We begin by looking at an early 1930s account of W. H. Callaway, an independent Holiness preacher in northwestern North Carolina who represents the independent nondenominational church tradition critical to any understanding of mountain religion. Next, we recount Emma Bell Miles's portrait of a generic worship service near her home on Walden's Ridge in southeast Tennessee at the turn into the twentieth century. Miles was the first to name the pronounced sense of "persecution" mountain people had about their worship lives by the time she published in 1905. Then we look at Ron Short's description of Old Regular Baptist worship life in southwest Virginia in the late twentieth century and the role of grace-centered religious experience.

Part 1 also puts forth my thesis that, by the years 1825–27, Appalachian mountain religion had clearly and decisively separated itself from what was rapidly becoming the burgeoning Protestant mainstream. I identify as signposts the establishment of the New Salem Association of Old Regular Baptists in 1825; the unambiguous movement of the Methodist denomination at the national level away from camp-meeting revivalism by 1825; the Kehukee Declaration of Old School Baptists in 1827, which established the division between anti-missionary and missionary Baptists; and the years when Old Father Nash and Charles Grandison Finney worked together in the revival campaigns of western New York State in 1825–27. The role Finney played in the history of revivalism and Protestant religious culture in fact marked the very juncture when Appalachian mountain religion had distinctly differentiated itself from the prevailing national religious culture. I propose that Nash and Finney embodied in their personal relationship the larger, more far-reaching relationship between Appalachian mountain religion and what became mainstream American Protestantism.

Part 2 is about the roots of mountain religiosity—religious life, religious feeling, religious sentiment. Four major streams of historical influences—pietism, Scots-Irish sacramental revivalism, Baptist revival culture during the Great Awakening in the mid-South, and plain-folk camp-meeting religion—became primary currents in the creation of mountain religious life and its distinctive regional character, ranging from the worship practices and belief systems embodied by independent Holiness to those of the Old Regular Baptists. I examine each of these four streams of historical influences against the backdrop of the contrast between mountain religion and denominationalism—the phenomenon of national church institutions based on voluntaryism and organized around a national purpose and identity. Denominationalism was the established hallmark of American Protestantism well before the end of the first half of the nineteenth century.

The fundamental divide between denominationalism and mountain religion, though it was set in concrete by the late nineteenth century, was not given a clear statement until the publication of John C. Campbell's *The Southern Highlander & His Homeland* (1921), the first—and what many still consider to be the best—survey of the Appalachian region. Campbell, a Congregationalist and home missionary to Appalachia, was the first to identify mountain religion as a fully developed tradition with its own internal and historical integrity, worthy of respect. We explore Campbell's insights along with those of Elizabeth R. Hooker (1933) and Catherine L. Albanese (1981), the only two "outsider" scholars of mountain religion to appreciate the importance of the distinctions Campbell first named.

Pietism was perhaps the earliest influence on the religious life of the Appalachian region and a major source of mountain religion's distinguishing features and formative traditions. I begin this chapter with a brief history of pietism and some of the most prominent pietist groups to settle in Appalachia, especially the Moravians, Mennonites, and German Baptist Brethren (Dunkards). We then look at how pietist sensibilities express themselves today in the lives of two people. Brother L. L. Bradley is an independent Holiness preacher whose family members were Old Order Dunkards in southern West Virginia. Sister Edna Alexander is an independent Holiness woman in eastern Kentucky who in recent years has spent several months each year living in a traditional Mennonite community in south-central Tennessee.

Sacramental revivalism, the next component of our investigation, was characterized by the conversionist preaching and communion practices of Scots-Irish evangelical Presbyterians from Ulster and especially from western Scotland. These staunch Calvinists came into the Appalachian region in great numbers during the earliest decades of settlement. I propose that the historical memory of Scots-Irish sacramental revivalism is long in the Appalachian region. This longevity is manifested in part by the preeminence of Leonardo da Vinci's *Last Supper* as the single most important piece of religious art in mountain churches and homes today. The vital importance of conversion as the heart of mountain religious experience is traced in large part to its roots in Scots-Irish religiosity. For the Scots-Irish, revivalism *was* the religious ideology of the laity, centered on a communal conversion experience that was renewed and strengthened time and again throughout the people's earthly pilgrimage.

The sacramental revivalism of the Scots-Irish merged with the revival traditions of the Baptists. We explore next the tradition histories and symbol systems of worship practices and beliefs, along with the organization and transmission of church life, in the Baptist revival culture of colonial Virginia and North Carolina, where Scots-Irish people became Baptists in large numbers, joining with the contingent of English and Welsh Baptists already in the area. The sacramental revivalism that became the distinctive ethos of mountain religious culture was born at this time. Centered on conversionist preaching and a collection of ritual practices such as footwashing, it culminated in the public rite of baptism by immersion that broke through social distance and confirmed community; it also confirmed the autonomy of the individual within the communal worship setting and in church life as part of a group made up of equals. The worship practices expressing mountain religion's sacramental revivalism today continue these original purposes.

Plain-folk camp-meeting religion as one of the major streams of mountain religiosity does not have its own chapter in this section but is discussed throughout the book, including in "Methodism in Appalachia—A Clash of Religious Values." The history of the Methodists in Appalachia is a particularly useful case study of the clash between denominationalism and mountain religious life, as we examine in the concluding chapter of part 2, which started out exploring this foundational divide. More so than most other denominations, the Methodists, along with the Southern Baptists, are distinguished by their long frontier history in the Appalachian region. The Methodists were the largest Protestant denomination in the United States by 1850 and are the next largest today in Appalachia, second only to the Southern Baptists. Since it is one of the "old denominations" Elizabeth Hooker identified as long associated with the Appalachian region, to see how the Methodist church moved, during the first half of the nineteenth century, from identification with to objectification of mountain religious culture is both telling and cautionary in terms of the fundamental clash of religious values dividing mountain religion from American Protestantism. Comparison of the connectional, bureaucratic, hierarchical structure of the Methodist church as a denomination with the autonomous, nonhierarchical, nondenominational character of mountain church life clarifies the basic features that distinguish mountain religion from American Christianity's most distinctive institutional construct—denominationalism.

Throughout this study I claim that the independent nondenominational church stands at the center of the spectrum of church traditions making up mountain religious life. The introduction to part 3 details the spectrum model I refer to throughout this book to describe the variety of church traditions identified with mountain religion. The nondenominational church tradition is primarily independent Holiness and independent Baptist, generic terms meant to characterize those individual church communities that do not belong to national, denominational, organizational structures, or even to subregional structures (such as associations) like Free Will Baptists and Old Regular and Primitive Baptists. The centrality of autonomy and free church polity in Appalachian mountain religion influences to a greater or somewhat lesser extent its core church traditions. It is seen especially in the independent nondenominational church tradition. As the American religious historian Catherine Albanese stated, "[T]he growth of nondenominational churches . . . carried the tendencies within mountain religion to their logical conclusion," a conclusion born out of the powerful, defining influences of land, people, history, and traditions.

One of my principal claims is that independent, nondenominational Holiness churches and Baptist traditions such as independent Missionary (which is, for the most part, a distinctly Appalachian phenomenon) distill to their essence many of the features and qualities creating mountain religion. Part 3 focuses on the independent Holiness church, mountain religion's most "invisible" and least documented church tradition, notwithstanding its understated prominence throughout significant portions of the region for more than a century. In the first chapter of this section I propose a tradition history for the independent Holiness church, placing its primary roots in plain-folk camp-meeting religion and identifying it as a product first and foremost of Baptist-dominated mountain religious culture, and of the national Holiness-Pentecostal movements only secondarily. This tradition history directly challenges the assumption, found in much of Holiness-Pentecostal scholarship today, that Wesleyan-Holiness tradition is the overwhelming source of Holiness-Pentecostal theology and religious culture. I offer support for my claims from George W. Henry's book, *Shouting* (1859), which sees the expressive and ecstatic worship practices associated with Holiness-Pentecostal worship life as reaching their zenith and definitive forms on the Appalachian frontier of the Great Revival era, attributing them as much to Calvinist and Arminian (including Baptist) traditions as to a specifically Wesleyan-Holiness provenance.

We then look at the mountain roots of the Church of God (Cleveland, Tennessee), the second largest Pentecostal denomination in the South today.[38] A commanding percentage of its membership is now outside of the continental United States. This denomination was formed out of a single independent mountain church at the turn of the century, the Holiness Church at Camp Creek (est. 1902) on the southernmost tip of western North Carolina. This chapter incorporates much new information about the family and religious heritage of Richard Spurling and his son, Richard G. Spurling, to whom the Church of God attributes its initial origins in the Spurlings' Christian Union (est. 1886) in southeast Tennessee near the border of North Carolina. Mountain religious culture defined the formative years of this denomination. I explore the factors behind the early shift in the Church of God from the amorphous organizational independence and autonomy of its first churches—highly characteristic of mountain churches in general—to its becoming a denominational entity. I claim that this shift was precipitated by A. J. Tomlinson, who was not native to the region and who had long-standing ambitions to create a "world-wide" religious "movement," ambitions reaching back to his earlier days as a home missionary in the mountain regions of the tristate area of western North Carolina, east Tennessee, and north Georgia.

Part 3 concludes with extensive excerpts from an oral history interview I recorded in 1989 with Brother Coy Miser, whose voice is heard throughout this book. The interview with Brother Coy gives a platform to a mountain preacher who represents the widespread independent Holiness church, basically overlooked or disregarded in studies of mountain religion (except for serpent handlers). Brother Coy's reminiscences give an immediacy to many of the generalizations I make throughout this work about the features characterizing mountain religious life.

Part 4 looks closely at the emergence of the images of mountain religious culture through the home missions movement to Appalachia and mountain people. In 1814 John F. Schermerhorn published the first home mission report focused specifically on the "religion and morals" of the Appalachian frontier, which scholars later called the Old Southwest. His investigative journey concentrated on western Pennsylvania, "New Virginia" (West Virginia), Kentucky, and Tennessee. Schermerhorn is especially important for his insights into the central role of the Holy Spirit in Old-Time Baptist traditions of the region that became normative for most of mountain religious life up to the present day. With Schermerhorn we also see the unambiguous beginnings of the objectification of the variety of church traditions specific to the mountains of the "Southwest" by the nation's major Protestant denominations, which, with the emergence of their own national identity and purposes, came to see Appalachia and mountain people—and their religious culture— as the "Other." In a few short decades after Schermerhorn's report, mountain religion was seen as standing totally apart from—and in conflict with— the norms and goals of American Protestantism. These perceptions would provoke the largest home missions movement to white American Protestants by other white American Protestants, beginning in the last two decades of the nineteenth century.

Appalachia began to be identified for the first time as a distinctive region around 1850, when national roads bypassed the region and new settlement in Appalachia dropped off precipitously. This development had the effect of introducing the "isolation" factor that would come to predominate in tales and accounts and critiques of life in Appalachia. During this time Hamilton W. Pierson, a Presbyterian and graduate of Union Theological Seminary in New York City, was a colporteur or Bible distributor in the 1840s for the American Tract Society in Virginia and then in the 1850s for the American Bible Society in Kentucky. Pierson provided the earliest positive, sympathetic, and richly detailed descriptions of religious life in what he called "the 'wilderness' or 'forests' or 'hills' or 'mountains' of the Southwest," especially in Kentucky. Most of the values and traditions Pierson recounted as distinctive to mountain religion continue to thrive today.

During the latter half of the nineteenth century, American Protestantism was caught up in the Christian America movement, represented by the English-speaking evangelical denominations that thought of themselves as making up the religious mainstream of the nation. They also believed themselves to be charged with the task of making America a Christian nation, a

Christian civilization, by which they meant Protestant. The Christian America movement defined all home mission work to Appalachia throughout this period and determined how mountain religion was portrayed in home mission literature. Home missionaries' characteristic descriptions of Appalachian mountain religion, beginning especially in the 1880s, near the height of the Christian America movement, developed parallel to widely circulated local-color writing about Appalachia, which first identified the region as "a strange land and peculiar people" (1873). At about the same time, industrialists discovered the region's exploitable resources, especially timber and coal. Appalachia's industrialization over the next fifty years would determine most of the home missionaries' goals for the region's people. H. Paul Douglass (1909), a Congregationalist, stated with approval that "the millionaire and the missionary" presided "over the future of the mountains," sharing between them the task of transforming the "mountaineer" into the "normally equipped American" through the region's "nationalization."

Pierson's profoundly respectful and affectionate accounts of mountain religious life in the 1850s and Campbell's clarion call in 1921 were the only efforts to take seriously the "native churches" of mountain people on their own terms until the early 1930s. Elizabeth R. Hooker's 1933 social science study, *Religion in the Highlands: Native Churches and Missionary Enterprises in the Southern Appalachian Area*, contrasted religious life and traditions "native" to the Appalachian region with the home mission efforts of major Protestant denominations in the area. Hooker's study was commissioned by a national coalition of home mission organizations and the Federal Council of Churches, which wanted to know how to have effective home missions in Appalachia. Hooker's research strategy was to determine the actual nature of religious life already existing in the mountains of Appalachia. Her strategy was based on the quite logical premise that home missionaries could no longer afford to ignore or dismiss mountain people's deeply rooted "native churches" and highly developed religious values. I present a summary of Hooker's conclusions about the "common characteristics" shared by mountain religion's "native churches," as well as mountain people's ongoing conflict with home missionaries and their denominations. Hooker identified that conflict "in differences regarding basic conceptions as to the nature of religion," which she evaluated as "[a]n almost insurmountable barrier."

Brother Terry Galloway's brief historical portrait of Wolf Creek Baptist Church from 1886 to 1987 serves to highlight and illustrate many of the features and practices Hooker identified as being both characteristic of and distinctive to religious life in the mountain regions of Appalachia at the time of her research. The history of Wolf Creek Baptist Church demonstrates not only the longevity but the continuity and commonness of those characteristics today. Brother Galloway, who has been a member of this independent Missionary Baptist Church in the Blue Ridge Mountains near Brevard, North Carolina, since the mid-1930s, is an extremely reliable witness.

The concluding chapter of "The Home Mission to 'Mountain Whites'" is about home missions in Appalachia today. The overriding emphasis of the major Protestant denominations and American Catholicism on liberation theology as their interpretive matrix has shifted home missions to Appalachia and mountain people to the priorities of "social justice." With this shift has come the characterization of mountain people as "victims," "the poor," and "the oppressed," an "exploited" people "powerless" to help themselves without the help of American Protestantism and American Catholicism, who see themselves commissioned by God to "stand at the side of" in order to "be involved" in the "struggle for justice" (all of the words and phrases set apart by quotation marks appear in various documents discussed in this chapter). I argue that this new ideological framework, which serves as the latest justification for home missions to Appalachia and mountain people— one that continues to ignore or dismiss mountain religion as irrelevant or, worse, as a barrier to efforts that will "help the people"—is no different in substance than the motivations and rationale of previous home missions, to save mountain people from themselves and their religion. That mountain religion tenaciously persists is a testimony to its viability as a regional religious tradition and its ongoing value in the lives of so many people in Appalachia. The divide between American Protestantism and mountain religion, and the grounds of their mutual antipathy, I argue throughout this book, is a difference in religious values.

Finally, I discuss how the study of Appalachian mountain religion as a regional religious tradition poses major issues and offers significant contributions to the study of American religious history. The afterword addresses the questions "Why is this journey important? What can we see now that we did not see before?" Here is a clue to guide you on your way: certain ways of looking at who God is and who people are in relation to God and to each other mark what are most characteristic about Appalachian mountain religion in terms of values and worldview. These values and worldview distinguish mountain religion from the surrounding national religious culture from which it continues to differentiate itself. They have also placed mountain religion in fundamental conflict with that surrounding national religious culture throughout a shared history. Despite that shared history, Appalachian mountain religion is among the most poorly understood and least explored of the very few uniquely American regional religious traditions to which Protestantism in the United States can lay claim. Mountain religion's values and worldview—and how they express themselves through a specific configuration of worship practices, belief systems, and church traditions centered around land, people, and history—can be understood only within the context of their interaction with what was America's dominant religious culture during the eighteenth, nineteenth, and much of the twentieth centuries.

Although it is a far larger story than what unfolds in the following pages, I attempt nonetheless to begin to sketch out mountain religion's basic historical framework, identifying specific trends and coming up with certain generalizations about what characterizes mountain religious life and the church traditions in which it thrives. This task is difficult. I hope not to have done too much violence to the individual integrity of mountain people and the numerous church traditions—from Old Regular Baptist to independent Holiness—that give life and sustenance to Appalachian mountain religion.

PART 1

Mountain Religious Life, Mountain Religious History: Redolence and Beginnings

It is fruitless to try to talk about the history of Appalachian mountain religion unless a serious attempt is made to create a feel for the sights and sounds of mountain worship life. At the same time, to begin to create such a feel is to talk about worship practices, belief systems, and the redolence—the powerful, evocative scent of historical memory—they exude. As Catherine Albanese observed, American religious history has been written mostly about main events, institutional developments, and prominent individuals, all leaving an avalanche of written documentation. Albanese attests that religious history should also be about the quieter, more subtle, and largely undocumented story of a people's inner religious life and how that life finds outward expression, personal and communal, because the record of that story is revealing and valuable. Here we will begin to lay the groundwork for understanding some of the basic features of mountain religion's inner religious life and how it finds outward expression. At the same time, we will attempt to start placing this largely undocumented story within a broader framework of historical narrative.

In this section, two purposes meet. The first is to help the reader unfamiliar with Appalachian mountain religion to have some sense of its sights and sounds. We begin by looking at a brief account of an independent Holiness preacher in the very early 1930s, Brother W. H. Callaway of Avery County in western North Carolina. Brother Callaway represents the independent nondenominational church tradition that stands at the epicenter of mountain religious life. I introduce along with Brother Callaway other religious leaders representing this church tradition living today in central Appalachia, particularly Brother Coy Miser[1] of Pennington Gap, located in Lee County on the farthest southwest tip of Virginia, close to the Cumberland Gap that has always marked the symbolic heart of Appalachia.

We then scrutinize the spirited and moving portrait Emma Bell Miles created of a mountain worship service in southeast Tennessee at the turn into the twentieth century. The generic character of this service and the bridge it creates between the nineteenth and twentieth centuries is especially revealing. Miles was also the first "insider" to name the protectiveness mountain people had developed by this time about their worship lives when confronted with the attitudes expressed by "summer people" or "visitors" (meaning non-Appalachian people, but also including large-town, urban, and broad-valley Appalachian residents).

Finally, we explore Old Regular Baptist life and worship in the late twentieth century by looking at Ron Short's brief account of his growing-up years in an Old Regular Baptist community in southwest Virginia. The Old Regular Baptists are of particular importance to the story of Appalachian mountain religion. Unlike many other mountain church traditions, they maintain a doctrinal heritage of modified Calvinism that has been the primary source of their continuity and longevity in the Appalachian region. They are also a window into free church polity that has had profound influence on all of mountain religious life. In addition, consideration of the founding of the New Salem Association in eastern Kentucky in 1825, the parent association for all Old Regular Baptist churches today, leads into this section's second purpose—a discussion of the earliest period I can identify by which Appalachian mountain religion had clearly and decisively emerged as a distinctive regional tradition in American religious history.

The mid-1820s, especially the years 1825–27, were a very important time for the unmistakable differentiation of Appalachian mountain religion from evangelical Protestantism and its burgeoning national institutions. This time was marked by signposts both inside and outside the Appalachian region, the first one noted being the organization of the New Salem Association. The year 1825 was also when the Methodist church, on a national denominational level, unambiguously completed its move to detach itself totally from its initial embrace of the expressive and ecstatic worship practices characterizing plain-folk camp-meeting religion that had drawn so many people into the Methodist church during the early years of the Great Revival on the Appalachian frontier. Plain-folk camp-meeting religion, and the egalitarian values it expressed, was one of the major streams of historical influences that have continued to shape much of mountain worship life.

Along with the Methodists, I discuss the Kehukee Declaration of 1827, the line of demarcation establishing the "Great Split" between Old School Baptists, perpetuating a Calvinist-based doctrinal heritage, and New School Baptists, fully Arminianized in their theology (embracing free will and rational decision in the experience of conversion). This "Great Split" was institutionally expressed through New School Baptists' commitment to national and especially international missionary work that was highly organized from the "top down," and their simultaneous emergence into national denominational structures that made such work possible. Both of these developments ran totally contrary to the highly localized institutional features of Old

School Baptists and the values they expressed. By the mid-nineteenth century, New School Baptists made up the vast majority of Baptists on the American scene, with the Old School Baptists mostly concentrated in Appalachia and its immediate border areas. The anti-mission controversy of ca. 1800–1840, especially between 1827 and 1840, was the keystone—like the American Revolution in U.S. history—in the history of Appalachian mountain religion after it had fully emerged as a regional religious tradition.

Finally we look at Old Father Nash and Charles Grandison Finney. Their relationship symbolically embodied the historical relationship of Appalachian mountain religion with what became the dominant religious culture of the United States. Nash and Finney parted company at the very moment and for the same reasons that mountain religion and American Protestantism did. The period when Nash and Finney worked together in the revival campaigns of western New York State, 1825–27, saw the conclusion of the process by which Appalachian mountain religion decisively differentiated itself from the rapidly evolving Protestant mainstream and the national religious culture Finney came to represent. Like mountain religion in relation to American Protestantism, Father Nash remained in Finney's life the unobtrusive but firm, loving voice that was always his radical sign of contradiction.

churches, schools and community centers" in Appalachia. But Hooker also sought to address one other group of readers: "Finally, the general American public may well be interested in the church life of a people long isolated from the rest of the world, because it reproduces to a considerable extent the churches and religious attitudes of their ancestors of colonial days."[2] Hooker's research had led her to a critical insight into mountain religious life. Worship practices, belief systems, religious experiences, and church traditions characterizing Appalachian mountain religion had not followed the same lines of development that now defined the mainstream Protestant denominations which for some years had been engaging in benevolent work in the region. Instead, Hooker found that "native" mountain church traditions (encompassing a large majority of churches) maintained at their core shared features and modes of expression once well known in the earliest years of the now predominant Protestant bodies. Hooker found that the same applied to many churches which were part of Southern Baptist associations and Methodist districts, the denominations with the largest presence in the mountains. Unlike many of their long-established mountain churches, the Methodists and Southern Baptists, in step with the other denominations of American Protestantism, had moved far beyond such features and expressions on a national level by the mid-nineteenth century.

But Hooker had assumed wrongly, like those before her and even today, that "isolation" had created a passive religious traditionalism that simply "reproduced" itself with each generation, basically unmodified since the church life "of their ancestors of colonial days." This assumption corresponded to what was by then a mythical image of "Appalachia" cemented into American consciousness as a type of frontier traditionalism producing a subcultural regionalism that was anachronistic and somehow frozen in time. Instead, the active character of mountain churches' choices and the decisions they made within specific social historical contexts had much more to do with the development and definition of Appalachian mountain religion.[3] An awareness of the historical self-determination of mountain religion's church traditions with regard to their worship practices and the beliefs they embodied would have negated the romantic image of these various traditions as living religious history. This alternative interpretive model for understanding mountain church traditions, and subsequently mountain religious history, would not be on the horizon for another fifty years, and even then limited to only a few voices.

Hooker and so many others before and since dipped the religious traditions they found in Appalachia in a vat of wax, preserving them as dusty museum pieces. Indeed, Hooker's remarks echoed a long-popular perception of mountain people as keepers of the flame of America's colonial era. However, to reiterate, any attempt at a long view of Appalachian mountain religion, especially its differentiation from the nation's dominant religious culture, needed to take into account the active character of mountain people's choices and the decisions that they made. This meant that Hooker's attempt at a long view needed to reach beyond the perception of mountain religion as a sort of hothouse, preserving—through its religious flora and fauna kept alive in a regionally unique and protective "isolation"—living specimens of American religious history, especially as it had been on the early frontier of the Old Southwest in the eighteenth to mid-nineteenth centuries. This task was difficult because Hooker, like so many other observers of mountain religious life, was not altogether wrong. The historical echoes she perceived were strongly present. Many traditions represented in worship practices and belief systems long abandoned or radically transformed by other American churches continue today in pronounced fashion in a preponderance of mountain churches. But how we interpret those historical echoes and the contexts we give them are the primary issues in any attempt to study Appalachia's mountain religious culture within the larger historical framework of American Christianity.

At the time Hooker wrote, mountain people were widely characterized, in the words of William Goodell Frost, as "our contemporary ancestors" and by others as "yesterday's people," preservers of the past resisting change.[4] Their religious life was cast in the same terms. Only the emergence of Appalachian studies and studies of regionalism and colonialism in the 1960s and 1970s would challenge these designations and the assumptions behind them. Not until the 1980s would mountain religious life begin to be viewed as a subject for serious investigation by a very small but growing number of humanities scholars using terms other than those established by home missionaries and social scientists. More often than not, social scientists mirrored home missionaries' assumptions about the developmental movement of churches from small sectlike groups "up to" the financially and institutionally powerful, culturally dominant denominations seen as the epicenter of America's religious life. At the bottom of the evolutionary heap were the very small and very local independent nondenominational churches so characteristic of Appalachia's mountain regions. This social Darwinism had exacted a high price on the self-identity of mountain people. Their religious traditions were often singled out by commentators concerned with the region's economic and social development, especially in the War on Poverty years of the 1960s. Many who were committed to social justice issues saw mountain religion as the clearest manifestation—and even one of the primary sources—of Appalachia's "problems." Mountain religion was seen as a window into mountain character. Indeed it is, but for the most part it has been seen "through a glass darkly."

Loyal Jones, in his best-known and most reprinted essay "Appalachian

Values," puts "Religion" at the top of his list, writing, "Mountain people are religious. This does not necessarily mean that we all go to church regularly, but we are religious in the sense that most of our values and the meaning we see in life spring from religious sources. *One must understand the religion of mountaineers before [one] can begin to understand mountaineers."*[5] Following Jones's lead, it is important for us to see that religion is not simply a facet of an umbrella-like entity called mountain culture but is the very core of it. Mountain people derive "most of our *values* and the *meaning* we see in life from *religious* sources," not from a vaguely defined mountain culture from which mountain people supposedly gain and partake of their identity. Instead, each generation of "mountaineers" not only transmits and reformulates but creates that culture, since it exists only at the level of cultural landscape (among examples of which cultural geographers Raitz and Ulack list "house type, religion, dialect, dietary preferences") and individuals' cultural self-consciousness.

Again, "One must understand the religion of mountaineers *before* [one] can begin to understand mountaineers," or more generally, the broader culture that "mountaineers" are always creating anew, like the variegated rings of a large tree trunk that tell its story with each passing year. Mountain religion is the key that unlocks mountain culture in terms of values and worldview. It is, in many ways, the core of the tree trunk. Mountain religion does not, therefore, stem like a shoot from the main vine of a mountain culture that determines what makes mountain religion distinctively "Appalachian," or even unique on America's religious landscape. Nor is it merely one among many other by-products or subunits of an overarching mountain culture, existing like some Platonic ideal, which make up what is supposedly *really* special about Appalachia—apart from its grinding poverty—in the national consciousness. Religion itself—not mountain culture, or economics, or psychology, or colonialism, or ethnography, or a host of other possibilities—provides the only appropriate predominant matrix of interpretation for understanding Appalachian mountain religion as a regional religious tradition.[6]

Loyal Jones offers a corrective to my emphasis on religion itself in our understandings and interpretations of mountain religion. He writes in the next paragraph of his "Appalachian Values" essay, "Religion shaped our lives, but at the same time we shaped our religion, since religion and culture are always intertwined."[7] Indeed, cultural landscape (of which religion is a part) and individuals' cultural self-consciousness combine to create the only level at which exists what we call "culture." What is distinctive about mountain religion are the various streams of religious movements that became regionally specific to Appalachia. Mountain religion called upon these streams to create itself—or more accurately, mountain people called upon them to create mountain religion, especially pietism, Scots-Irish sacramental revivalism, Baptist revival culture in the mid-South during the Great Awakening, and early nineteenth-century plain-folk camp-meeting religion. All can be characterized as revival movements, influencing all mountain church traditions in some form or another, from the most doctrinally conservative to the most free-flowing. These revival movements as social movements invested mountain people with the power to define themselves as a people of faith by creating their own distinct style of life as expressed in a distinct set of values. In this way, the groundwaters of religious movements that fed what became Appalachian mountain religion were most certainly shaped by the land, its people, and their shared history and traditions.

The world beyond Appalachia's ridges and small valleys has long understood what Loyal Jones dares to attest in his essay: that mountain religion is the truest mirror reflecting who *are* mountain people, apart from which they cannot be understood. American Protestantism especially has recognized this since the very beginnings of its interaction with the Appalachian region, clearly seeing that its own power to control how mountain people in particular were defined in the national consciousness was based largely, if not primarily, on its control over how mountain religion was construed. Whoever controls religion (or how religion is perceived) controls social identity and social action (or how they are perceived) at their foundations and in their most potently symbolic forms. Since mountain religion could not be controlled, it had to be overcome, if not by ignoring or dismissing its broad authority, then by generating destructive stereotypes, prejudices, myths, and all but unrecognizable caricatures. Such treatment not only trivialized mountain religion's significance and demeaned its values in the lives of so many people but reduced it—and hence, the basic identity of mountain people themselves—to something that was either dangerous, out of control, and a threat to the common weal, or laughable and pathetic, not to be taken seriously (both attitudes—fear and condescension—have been equally damaging). "Through a glass darkly," mountain religion's portrayal by the "outside" world determined to a large extent how this brightest of windows into the lives of mountain people was manipulated and abused as justification to construe the worst, the darkest, about them.

As we have seen in the introduction, Appalachian mountain religion has been portrayed monolithically in stereotypical terms that focus on an archetype called the "mountain preacher" who oscillates between two extremes: as either a strict, suffocating Calvinist or an emotionally unstable religious fanatic with a penchant for serpent handling. In fact, mountain religion, like mountain preachers, exists only as a range or spectrum of worship life and traditions sharing "regional" characteristics. This claim, at the outset, is as much a thorny nutshell as "mountain culture." But Catherine Albanese incisively helps us out of this apparent methodological dilemma. Regional religion may be looked at primarily through the interplay of what Albanese calls *creeds* (what people believe), *codes* (how people live), *cultuses* (how people worship), and *communities* (the people who are bound together by shared traditions, history, and place).[8] Regional religion, writes Albanese, is "religion born of natural geography, of past and present human history, and of the interaction of the two."[9] By the second half of the nineteenth century, Appalachia's regional character had clearly sharpened and defined itself. Well before that time, the variety of church traditions making up Appalachian mountain religion were already firmly established in having more in common with each other—notwithstanding theological differences—than with the large denominations and religious movements, both within and outside of Appalachia, with whom they shared their earliest roots.

If we depict Appalachian mountain religion as a spectrum (a linear, two-dimensional model useful only for purposes of discussion), the independent nondenominational church—Brother Callaway's church—stands at the center of that spectrum. Very often Baptist, even more often Holiness-Pentecostal, these churches carry on today the worship practices and belief systems of pre-1850 plain-folk camp-meeting religion more fully than any other mountain church tradition. Indeed, plain-folk camp-meeting religion was localized almost exclusively in the Appalachian region of the upland South. Dickson D. Bruce defines "plain-folk" as a term descriptive of the vast majority of Southerners, most of whom were farmers, who were not of the planter class that came to dominate the economic, political, and social fabric of the South. Instead, Bruce writes, "The small farms and domestic economy of these plain-folk therefore came to dominate certain upland areas of the South—the uplands and highlands of middle and western North Carolina, poorer lands in the Valley of Virginia, the northern parts of Georgia and Alabama, the foothills and mountains of Tennessee and Kentucky, and the mountainous regions of west Virginia."[10] In other words, the plain-folk of the upland South whose camp-meeting religion Bruce writes about were overwhelmingly the people of Appalachia.

The independent nondenominational church—part of a long heritage beginning with the first years of settlement in the eighteenth century and crystallized especially through plain-folk camp-meeting religion—is perhaps the most common form of religious organization in many areas of rural Appalachia, especially central Appalachia. It is also the most invisible and least considered in writings on mountain religious life—with a few notable exceptions. Some social scientists have zeroed in on how well they believe such churches epitomize a subculture of poverty model and models of powerlessness and alienation.[11] Commentators have also pointed to such churches as the premier example of mountain religion as sectarianism-run-amok.

It follows that such commentators believe a church-sect typology is the most appropriate for looking at mountain religious life.[12] Despite their bad reviews in the available literature, the foundational, shared characteristics of independent nondenominational churches nonetheless serve as a benchmark for looking at other mountain church traditions and seeing what they have in common, how they influence each other, and how they may be influenced by traditions nearer the ends of the spectrum, or—far less likely—by church traditions and religious movements clearly beyond the spectrum's range.

On the surface, this may seem to be an extraordinary claim: that not only does mountain religion have a church tradition consisting of churches that are nearly invisible yet exceedingly numerous, widely scattered, totally autonomous from each other, as local and grassroots as possible, and almost always extremely small (often limited to a single room, either as a free-standing structure or in a private home), but that this church tradition is exceptionally significant; indeed, it is indispensable to our understanding of mountain religion and its history. Autonomy and free church polity expressed in varying degrees are two of the most basic threads found throughout mountain church traditions. Embodying a radical autonomy and a highly spontaneous free church polity, independent nondenominational churches distill to their essence many of the normative institutional features and qualities of popular piety defining mountain religion throughout its history. This interpretation negates the church-sect typology model. It means that each of these churches does not constitute a random, discrete "sect," unconnected and peculiar unto itself, but that each is part of a large, intelligible church tradition.

Like the smallest of molecular units capable of retaining its identity with the substance in mass, each of these churches emerges and organizes itself (retains its identity) within the defining structure (the substance in mass) of Appalachia's mountain religious culture. These churches also, in apparent contradiction, constitute a major mountain church tradition created solely by a myriad of totally "disconnected" churches (which are actually "disconnected" only organizationally, as the long-standing and highly valued tradition of "fellowshiping," or constantly traveling around to worship at each other's churches, firmly attests). It is a church tradition that lacks any kind of subregional institutional framework, like the associational systems of traditions such as the Old Regular Baptists. Its churches are also unremittingly characterized as highly "individualistic" (and therefore "sectarian"), because of each of its churches' personal, freely self-determined variations on the firm foundation of shared worship traditions. These variations make the independent nondenominational tradition all the more obscure as a clearly differentiated mountain church tradition. However, its churches' shared worship traditions have long been faithfully transmitted with an uninterrupted integrity through the oral tradition of a regionally specific culture of popular piety that historically has infused all of mountain religion.

This pronounced ad hoc character defining independent nondenominational churches deceptively demonstrates a randomness and "chaos" in organization, features that physicists in their realm of investigation have so recently begun to see (and are barely beginning to understand) as having an extraordinarily subtle and creative "logic" that is redefining what is logic. Indeed, complexity theory, rather than chaos theory, is a more intelligible approach to understanding mountain religion's independent nondenominational church tradition. Today no greater challenge exists to the mechanistic rationalism dominating the conceptual framework of the western world, including its religious traditions (and the representatives of American Protestantism who have felt compelled to try to overcome mountain religion), causing those who prize "good order" and logical progression and the rationalism of institutionalism above all else to be confounded and outraged—and threatened—by such absurdities. Inevitably, despite our overwhelming need to be in control of the world around us, the logic of randomness and chaos—which we will eventually come to recognize never were what we have perceived them to be—will lead to our understanding the elemental forces indispensable to shaping the universe itself, as well as our everyday lives.

On a much more humble level, the highly creative, surprising, unpredictable, and seemingly fragmented and illogical progression of mountain religion's independent nondenominational church tradition has been indispensable to shaping mountain religion itself—even though it is made up of churches that seem to have as much logic to their emergence, organization, and demise on the mountain landscape as the ceaselessly changing contours of flowing waters in a small creek (a perception contradicted by the long historical presence of so many of these churches). Their influence on the religious life of Appalachia's mountain regions stands as silent witness challenging the parochialism (and injustice) of attitudes that habitually dismiss them not only as utterly insubstantial on the playing field of American religious history but as merely one of mountain religion's stranger peculiarities, treating them as an odd little sideshow tucked into the very outskirts of the midway in the carnival of American religions. Above all else, they are perceived as random and chaotic, which means that they are irrational and a cause for concern (when any attention is paid to them at all).

We cannot understand mountain religion without beginning to understand and appreciate its independent nondenominational churches. Like the history of the elemental forces creating the universe, the tradition history for independent nondenominational churches—converging into a church tradition indispensable to the creation of Appalachian mountain religion, crystallizing many of its normative features—is not entirely lost in the mists of time, despite the apparently elusive randomness and chaos of these tiniest of forces on the religious landscape of Appalachia's mountain regions. An earlier, though most immediate, heritage is the essentially oral tradition of plain-folk camp-meeting religion which laid much of their foundations. Throughout this study, in various chapters, I develop a tradition history for mountain religion's independent nondenominational church tradition. Conceptually, this should make more accessible and concrete—especially to those who understand church life almost exclusively in terms of highly structured institutionalism—how these churches can be understood as part of a long-lived, organic religious movement in the mountains, while simultaneously making up a definable church tradition constituting one of the largest—if not the largest—in Appalachian mountain religion.

Throughout the rest of this chapter, as well as throughout most of this book, when speaking of the independent nondenominational church tradition in the mountains I shall address almost exclusively independent Holiness churches, churches like Brother Callaway's. I shall make much more limited reference to the independent Baptist church tradition, represented predominantly by independent Missionary Baptist churches, nonaligned with any Baptist denominational structures. The formulation of the Holiness and Pentecostal movements through mountain religion's independent nondenominational church tradition skews well-established distinctions for these movements in Holiness-Pentecostal history in the United States, pointing to a unique formulation of these traditions in the Appalachian mountains influenced primarily, as we shall see in later sections of this book, by the history of mountain religion itself and only secondarily by the Holiness-Pentecostal movements.

"Holiness" is the universal generic term for the presence of the Holiness-Pentecostal movements in the mountains through independent nondenominational churches. The Holiness-Pentecostal movements in the mountains are represented only secondarily, but with a significant presence, by denominations whose national identity and national institutionalism define them, rather than being defined primarily by their spiritual character or religious ethos like mountain religion's independent nondenominational churches. The Holiness and Pentecostal movements both have numerous denominations and church traditions and submovements, as well as thousands of loosely affiliated or unaffiliated churches throughout the United States, churches that are also nondenominational. Unlike mountain people who make up Appalachia's nondenominational church tradition of independent Holiness, Holiness and Pentecostal denominations use the terms "Holiness" and "Pentecostal" in the manner of organized religion, as terms that clearly differentiate themselves from each other, referring to a denominational institutionalism defined by codified creeds and doctrines and polity, whose institutional life is bureaucratic and quantifiable by statistics, the quantifier of things tangible as the primary, controllable reality.

By "religion," when they use it to make their all-important distinction between "religion" and "faith," mountain people invariably mean organized religion as represented primarily by the mainstream denominations of American Protestantism, from the Southern Baptists to the Presbyterians to the Methodists, as well as by Holiness and Pentecostal denominations, from the Church of God (Cleveland, Tennessee), the second largest Pentecostal denomination in the South today and known especially for its episcopal authority structure, to the Church of the Nazarene, the largest Holiness denomination in the United States. Outsiders invariably designate as "Pentecostal" mountain people who align themselves with mountain religion's independent Holiness tradition, primarily because speaking in tongues, which served in the first years of the twentieth century to differentiate between the Holiness and Pentecostal movements, is widely practiced in these churches. When asked if they are Pentecostal, people who attend independent Holiness churches in the mountains will usually say yes, but they refer to themselves almost universally as Holiness. Their use of the term Holiness eschews the organizational categories distinguishing Holiness and Pentecostal denominations, and points to a very different formulation of the Holiness-Pentecostal movements in the mountains. In a later chapter, "Mountain Religion and the Holiness-Pentecostal Movements," we will explore in greater depth this different tradition history.

Albanese confirms the central place of the independent nondenominational church in mountain religion, which she describes more poetically as "the fruit of the mountain spirit and the mountain religious tradition" that "carried the tendencies within mountain religion to their *logical* conclusion" (emphasis added):

> [N]ondenominational churches . . . carried the tendencies within mountain religion to their logical conclusion, as one individual or another (usually male) among the people became convinced that God was calling him to preach and exhort. So he would set about establishing a church of his own, often on his property, either in his house or a separate building he might construct. Like a patron to his neighbors in a lonely mountain hollow, he invited them to join with him in seeking the Word and will of God. Here all the characteristics of mountain religion came together at their fullest expression: the uneducated preacher, the independent church, the primacy of the Bible, and the strong emotionalism of religious worship. The nondenominational church was the fruit of the mountain spirit and the mountain religious tradition.[13]

How accurate is Albanese's portrait? The field notes or schedules completed during 1931 for Hooker's survey of mountain religious life provide some important clues. The field notes supply limited but precise information on native ministers, sermons, and worship services not included in the published studies. Some of the ministers were born in the 1850s and 1860s, and so the data provide a glimmer of religious life in the Appalachian region during the second half of the nineteenth century and into the early twentieth. However, the field notes are fraught with the biases of the field-workers (repeatedly, education and cleanliness were of paramount concern).

One handwritten summary about a mountain preacher stands out in particular, because it is a good example of much of what the survey uncovered. W. H. Callaway of Avery County, North Carolina, was born in 1858. A farmer with no schooling, he had been pastor of the "Independent Church of God," the name he gave to the church house he built on his own property, for nearly twenty-five years at the time of his interview:

> Mr. Callaway is an elderly farmer who has spent his whole life in this place. He has no education and could not read until after he was grown. He has spent a great deal of time reading the Bible, which he regards as inspired in every detail, and as a result knows it remarkably well. Feeling called upon to preach the Gospel, he set up a building on his own land, at his own expense and with his own hands, and established a church independent of other denominations. At present the church has only 12 resident members, mostly relatives or life-long friends of his. For 24 years he has served as the pastor to the best of his ability, and received almost nothing in return. He is a kindly, lovable old man, always ready to help any who need it, and sometimes is imposed upon. Although his own beliefs are very definite, he very often allows men who differ with him to preach in his building.[14]

The parallels between Albanese's 1981 composite portrait and this quick sketch from fifty years before are striking. Other mountain preachers and religious leaders we shall meet along the way embody this portrait in their lives today—Brother Coy Miser of Pennington Gap, Lee County, Virginia; Sister Lydia Surgener and Sister Mae June Hensley of Cranks Creek, Harlan County, Kentucky; Sister Edna Alexander of Red Lick, Jackson County, Kentucky; and Brother L. L. Bradley of Peterstown, Monroe County, West Virginia.[15]

Let's take a closer look at the features outlined in the 1931 interview with Brother Callaway. He was seventy-three years old at the time, and had started his church when he was forty-nine, around 1907. It is not uncommon for the call to preach and pastor to come late in life. Mountain preachers tend to be older people to whom young people will often apprentice themselves in order to become preachers, frequently for several years, before striking out on their own. Sister Lydia Surgener of Cranks Creek, who began her ministry as an independent Holiness preacher in her thirties, several years ago opened her home to her nephew Junior, now in his late twenties, who "apprenticed" himself to her. As of this writing, they share a symbiotic ministry, Junior supporting and helping the ministry of his now aged aunt through the skills and talents he has developed by working with her, and Sister Lydia continuing to provide Junior mentorship, access, and opportunity to exercise his call.

The name Brother Callaway gave to his church, the Church of God, is one of the most popular names given to independent Holiness churches. The usage has no connection with the Church of God (Cleveland, Tennessee), whose own roots go back most immediately to an independent Holiness church in the mountains of western North Carolina at the turn of the century. They go back still further to an independent "meeting house" in east Tennessee in the mid-1880s, which was built for a nondenominational group called the "Christian Union" where participants were invited "to set together as the Church of God." This mid-1880s occurrence of "Church of God" indicates that the name was already in use at that time by independent nondenominational churches, whether belonging to the Holiness or Baptist movements (the founder of the Christian Union was a Baptist elder). "Church of God" was not adopted as the official name for the Cleveland, Tennessee, denomination until its second annual assembly, in January 1907.

Brother Callaway was a "farmer," self-supporting. In mountain ministry the tradition is that of Pauline tent-making: in Acts 18:3 the Apostle Paul is described as a tent-maker by trade; in 1 Cor. 9 Paul outlines what are the apostolic rights and then waives his own in favor of supporting himself by his own labors. Like Paul, mountain preachers look to God to supply their needs, not to those who hear them preach. Like Paul, they support themselves in labors other than ministry, which is a gift they give freely, without price. Brother Coy Miser of Pennington Gap, an independent Holiness preacher who has founded many small churches in Virginia, Kentucky, Tennessee, and Ohio, was a coal miner and a laborer who built what he called "dwelling houses" (a common expression, serving to distinguish them from "church houses"). Sister Lydia Surgener, who has two little Holiness churches she owns and preaches in, runs a used clothing store that caters to miners. The term "bi-vocational" does not exist in their vocabulary. There is no "professionalization" of the ministry, which has always been a bone of contention between mountain people and the institutionalized ministries of mainline denominations. American Protestantism crossed the mark in the eighteenth and early nineteenth centuries, when ministry clearly became a profession, a "career opportunity," by which clergy earned their living, entirely or at least in part.

Mountain people historically have a strong antipathy toward providing for the financial support of their preachers. This produces a leveling influence that keeps mountain preachers on a par with those to whom they minister. As we shall see in later parts of this book, this "leveling influence" did not spring up *de novo* in mountain religion, demonstrating, as Schermerhorn believed in 1814, "an unwillingness to support the gospel," a judgment repeated endlessly in the generations of criticisms about mountain religion. Rather, it is firmly planted in the heritage of colonial Baptist revival culture and the still earlier revival culture of Scots-Irish Presbyterian laity. As the report on Brother Callaway attests, "For 24 years he has served as the pastor to the best of his ability, and received almost nothing in return." Mountain preachers have always labored like everyone else to support themselves, offering as preachers and pastors their time and resources without charge or any expectation of recompense. The best-known exception to this norm is the early frontier tradition of "a pounding," where periodically people would get together and bring for the preacher and his family a pound of coffee or butter or flour or sugar or whatever else was at hand. Today, in independent nondenominational churches, many of whose people tend to be cash poor but rich in other resources, I have witnessed the continued practice of this tradition, still called "a pounding," with no apparent elaboration of its original purpose, indicating that such churches are part of a larger, deeply rooted tradition.

Brother Callaway had "spent his whole life in this place." There is a strong attachment to "place," to the land where you are planted. Mountain people most certainly do move about, often covering extensive areas of the Appalachian region, and at times in their lives may well have lived outside the region. But "place," home, is marked by ridges and valleys, not by property lines. Throughout his life, Brother Coy Miser has traveled fairly widely in the Appalachian region and lived for many years in southern Ohio. Today he lives in Pennington Gap, where he grew up and where his people are clustered. Like Brother Coy, Sister Edna Alexander lived for several years in southern Ohio, only to return with her husband and five children to live in a cabin on the same property as her childhood home, a two-story log house her father built at the base of a small ridge in Red Lick, Kentucky. Sister Lydia Surgener has always lived in the Cranks Creek area, where her people are found, even though she too has traveled widely, preaching in small churches and at revivals, commuting daily the nearly ten miles to Pennington Gap where her used clothing store and one of her two churches are located.

Brother Callaway had "no education" and learned to read as an adult, probably from reading the Bible. Brother Coy Miser's public education went only to the second grade and he is totally illiterate at the age of seventy-four, but he has a strong, comprehensive oral memory of the Bible. So does Sister Lydia Surgener, whose reading skills at age sixty-seven are minimal except for the Bible. Sister Edna Alexander, now in her early sixties, also reads little except for the Bible, a copy of which she wears out every few years. As did Brother Callaway, they too know the Bible "remarkably well."

Brother Callaway felt "called upon to preach the Gospel." In mountain traditions, a preacher and pastor is "called upon" by God, and equipped by God, not made through a seminary education or even necessarily by being ordained. It is a duty and a responsibility to answer that call, knowing that God will provide the means and the opportunities. For the mountain preachers of independent nondenominational churches, answering that call is very much an act of faith, because there is no loop or professional route, as in the denominations of American Protestantism, that opens the doors to fulfilling that call. Instead, always listening on tiptoe, seeing where God will lead, makes for a life of variety and uncertainty, except for the certainty of the "call" itself.

Like the Baptist revival preachers of colonial Virginia and North Carolina during the Great Awakening, mountain preachers rise up within their own neighborhoods, not as charismatic leaders but as individuals recognized for their capacity to inspire others. They are deemed by those who know them best to be especially adept at exercising the qualities that entitle them to be preachers or pastors within their particular church traditions. For church traditions such as independent Holiness, the process is very informal: personal qualities and the apprenticeship of practical experience—leading to recognition and affirmation within their own very local communities of family, friends, neighbors, associates, and acquaintances—is the traditional path that invests individuals with the authority to be preachers. For independent Holiness churches, the path made up of personal qualities, the apprenticeship of experience, and communal recognition is usually understood to be all that is necessary for the "ordination" of Holiness preachers such as Sister Lydia, whose religious authority and communal standing no one disputes. Upon occasion, preachers may gather, formally or informally, to lay hands on a brother or sister in recognition of their ministry, although this step is in no way a requirement.

The same fundamental path for the creation of mountain preachers is taken in church traditions such as the Old Regular Baptists, with basic differences stemming from their well-developed institutionalism. The candidate's apprenticeship—inaugurated by his being officially given "liberty to preach"—is carefully observed within the local church community. It is more structured (the candidate's preaching is limited to those churches with whom the local church, through the associational system, is "in fellowship"), and it is often very long, culminating in ordination only when it is deemed timely by the elders in his own church. Ordination is strictly a local matter; the association to which the church belongs does not determine in any way who may or may not be ordained by a local church. This totally ground-level control over ordination, unmonitored by any "higher authorities," Schermerhorn found especially troubling and judged it as a clear example of the degeneracy of the ministry throughout the region, epitomized by its traditional Baptist churches.

This particular mountain tradition for forming "native clergy" stands in stark contrast to the denominations of American Protestantism, which consider ministry to be as much a profession as a calling. As such, most denominations of American Protestantism compel an arduous, highly controlled, and institutionally complicated "ordination process"—usually requiring a postundergraduate, three-year professional degree as its foundation—making all the meticulous, incremental steps leading to ordination as much of a hoop-jumping marathon as it is supposed to be a biblically based rite of passage for responsibly forming their clergy.

The field notes on Brother Callaway reveal still other major features indispensable to our understanding Appalachian mountain religion. They report that Brother Callaway "set up a building on his own land, at his own expense and with his own hands, and established a church independent of other denominations." This autonomy and direct responsibility of action for meeting immediate local worship needs is the institutional keystone of mountain religious life. Establishing an independent church or place of worship is extremely widespread in the Appalachian region. Individuals hold public worship either in their home, in a building on their own property which they most likely pastor or at least serve as the caretaker for, or in a small, usually one-room structure somewhere nearby. It is a tradition that reaches back to the earliest days of settlement on the Appalachian frontier. Mountain people today continue to affirm without wavering the appropriateness and legitimacy of such totally autonomous, independent, and nondenominational churches, even if their own churches are not of that tradition. For example, the Church of Christ in Sand Gap, Kentucky, attends the Christmas play each year at the Sand Gap Holiness Church (est. 1913), and the Holiness Church returns the favor. Indeed, in their earliest years these two churches shared the same building. A local Church of Christ in Peterstown, West Virginia, provides Bible studies every Sunday afternoon in Brother L. L. Bradley's House of Prayer, an independent Holiness church which he built twenty-five years ago on his own property and which he pastors.

That many Churches of Christ in the mountain regions of Appalachia acknowledge the legitimacy of independent Holiness churches is an especially striking example of their wide acceptance. The Church of Christ is also an independent nondenominational tradition, neither Baptist nor Holiness, although it has historically interconnected with its autonomous churches through periodicals, a large body of theological literature reaching back to the early nineteenth century, and numerous cooperative events like debates

the term even applies) in very low profile locations with usually meager resources, if any. Their primary, if not sole, purpose is to ordain their own preachers, which—for legally incorporated groups—gives these individuals the legal right to issue marriage certificates, as well as baptismal certificates that are legally recognized in several states, often providing the only proof of birth date for mountain people who lack birth certificates. It also gives them legal access as ministers to hospitals and accident scenes, and additional sites and activities from which they might otherwise be restricted (however, mountain hospitals in particular rarely stand in the way of "uncredentialed" mountain preachers).

In addition, these loose networks sometimes establish their own churches (made possible more often by gift than by purchase, or by a property owner who allows a location to be used without financial encumberment to the organization, apart from the most basic of maintenance), which may, in turn, also have legal standing. Otherwise, these loosely centralized and completely grassroots networks have little real authority or institutional and financial control over their local preachers and churches, which in turn generally act with as much autonomy as independent nondenominational preachers and churches—and are, therefore, all but indistinguishable from them, except for their possible legal status. These loose networks are not an attempt to become part of "the system," but to get around the system by meeting the minimum of its requirements in order to overcome the restrictions imposed on the ministry essential to those churches and preachers that are a product first and always of mountain religious culture. This variation on the independent nondenominational church tradition presents an intriguing case in church-state relations. It also demonstrates flexibility and adaptability, without losing the essence of who and what they are, qualities well-pronounced in the nondenominational tradition of independent churches and preachers.

Indeed, there is no more rudimentary example of this variation than the initiative taken by Brother Coy Miser, which, in fact, is not really a variation on the independent nondenominational church tradition, so much as it is a refinement. Brother Coy Miser, ordained in 1948 at Harber's Chapel, an independent Holiness church in which he grew up in Pennington Gap, felt hindered by the legal restrictions imposed on his ministry, as well as on the ministry of other independent preachers, to the point that, in 1961, he incorporated his church work—consisting solely of himself—as the Pentecostal Church of God. Brother Coy's purpose was not to establish a "sect" or "subdenomination," but to free himself and others from legal restrictions. None of the nearly one dozen churches personally established by Brother Coy in four different states goes by the name Pentecostal Church of God. All of them are unincorporated and independent, in no way connected to each other, or even to Brother Coy once he moved on. (Brother Coy has expressed to me a wistful desire to revisit some of the churches he founded long ago to see whatever became of them.) There is no loosely organized group or network whatsoever, like the models illustrated in the preceding paragraphs, only Brother Coy.

Since 1961, Brother Coy has carried with him his seal of incorporation and licensing papers wherever he goes, so that, if he has a chance meeting with a preacher, or knows someone who he discerns is growing in the ministry, he can legalize their standing as ministers on the spot. After that, the preacher is totally autonomous from Brother Coy, only needing periodically to renew his or her license. Brother Coy's only goal is to enable others, in the most unencumbered way possible, to do that which God has called them to do. This is a remarkable achievement by an individual who is not merely functionally but totally illiterate, unable to tell the difference between pinto and kidney bean cans on a grocery store shelf except by the picture on the label.

Almost universally, the leveling influence of egalitarian norms in mountain church life—despite whatever forms of institutionalization distinguish mountain church traditions from each other—is personified by an oft-repeated motto, found over and over again throughout the mountains on churchhouse signs (if a church house even has a sign) that can be characterized as mountain religion's signature piece: "Where everybody is somebody and nobody is anybody" (or more important than others). The fear of losing autonomy and direct responsibility—two characteristics indispensable to mountain religion—for meeting the worship needs of the people in one's immediate area (especially family and neighbors) translates into a basic fear of any form of hierarchical institutionalism and, hence, hierarchies among individuals, as well as a deeply ingrained fear of losing local control in its most elemental forms.

For example, Sister Edna Alexander of Red Lick, Kentucky, holds "meetings" or worship services in her small mountain cabin located far off of the county road. Sister Edna makes a distinction between "Pentecostal" and "Holiness" in her vocabulary that encapsulates the anti-organizational or anti-institutional outlook of mountain religious life. She says that "Pentecostal" means denominationalism, organized control of religion that gets in the way of the will of God, whereas "Holiness" means "going where the Spirit tells you." Other mountain people do not necessarily make the same distinction in the two terms, but share the same attitudes. They talk about the difference between "religion" and "faith." Denominationalism or organized "religion" simply makes no sense to them, and is seen as a major hindrance to worshiping God as the Holy Spirit directs and responding unencumbered to the work God would have you do. This attitude has been maddening to the denominational workers who have entered Appalachia as home mission territory. Not only maddening, it has been seen as an indication of antisocial, "individualistic" religion that needs to be eradicated if "effective" ministry (embodying the social agendas and ideals of American Protestantism) is ever to succeed in the mountains.

A memoir entitled *Dorie, Woman of the Mountains* confirms this attitude toward denominationalism. In 1988, Florence Cope Bush published locally a wonderful account of her mother's oral memoirs about life in the Great Smokies from the turn of the century to the 1940s. Dora Woodruff Cope recalled one of the numerous locations where she lived during those years and where, typically, the local schoolhouse was shared by various church communities in the area. "The church was nondenominational. . . . Appalachian people were not 'joiners.' They felt no allegiance to any particular denomination so long as they felt they were preaching the Word of God. . . . The denomination idea made no sense to them. . . . We had folk who were Methodist, Holiness, Missionary Baptist, Primitive Baptist, footwashing Baptist, a sprinkling of Presbyterians and a few Campbellites [what Church of Christ people were often called]. . . . With so many preachers using the same church, it was difficult for us to know which denomination was visiting us when one came to call."[18] I drafted the phrase in the preceding paragraph, "Denominationalism simply makes no sense to them," two years before reading this passage in *Dorie*. Dora Cope's nearly exact verbatim repetition, "The denomination idea made no sense to them," which we may accept as coincidence, is also unimpeachable confirmation of this general attitude, which Cope's longer statement summarizes so well, complementing numerous statements very much like Cope's I have heard in personal interviews or as a result of participant-observation.

In our line-by-line examination of the 1931 field notes about Brother Callaway, we have reached the place where the field-worker recorded that Brother Callaway's church was attended mostly by family and neighbors. The number who attended was comparatively small, "only 12 resident members." Most mountain congregations are by necessity small in number. The worship practices are extremely intimate and personal, and heartfelt; larger numbers are a hindrance to such intimacy. Again, denominational church workers in the mountains of Appalachia have looked balefully upon the proliferation of so many small churches with their small numbers of attendees, calling instead for consolidation.[19] In their system of values, large churches are "successful"; small churches are not. But mountain people who are churchgoers usually do not attend just one church; they travel around to each other's churches, many attending several services a week at different churches where they are not merely "visitors" but are often well known to the core congregations.

Among church traditions nearest the center of the spectrum making up Appalachian mountain religion, church meeting schedules are almost always arranged in an area so as not to conflict with each other. For church traditions such as the Old Regular Baptists, churches making up an association carefully avoid cross-scheduling their local memorial meetings, homecomings, and sacramental meetings (combining communion with footwashing)—all annual events—because of the high value they place on "fellowshiping" or members traveling from their home church to worship at other churches. This is especially true for these particular annual occasions, which are held during the summer months (mountain religion's "high days" of the year), as demonstrated by the meeting schedules for the coming year published for each church in the annual minutes of the association. More locally among Old Regular Baptist churches, which meet only once a month, care is taken here also to avoid scheduling conflicts. One church will meet on the first Saturday and Sunday of the month, another will meet on the second, and so on, setting aside the periodic fifth Sunday for what are called "union meetings" when local, as well as farther away, Old Regular Baptist churches will all worship together. Old Regular Baptists are famous for traveling great distances to worship in each other's churches on Sunday and enjoying a wide variety. They rarely limit themselves to the once-a-month service at their home church, unless infirmity has restricted their mobility.

For Holiness churches and many independent Baptist churches, which meet weekly rather than monthly (and typically hold more than one full worship service a week), avoiding scheduling conflicts locally in order to encourage fellowshiping introduces an entirely different factor: the main service is at night, and as likely to be on any weeknight as it is on a Sunday. This also means that Sunday morning—if they even meet at that time—is usually not the main service of the week (which skews completely the mentality that puts communal worship in a once-a-week box labeled "Sunday morning," after which we all go have brunch). Warren Brunner and I have photographed hundreds of posted meeting schedules covering every night of the week. The tradition of night services held during the week is very long in the mountains—going back to plain-folk camp-meeting religion that emerged out of the Great Revival on the Appalachian frontier and matured into a regionally specific tradition during the first half of the nineteenth century; and back further to the Baptist revival particularly in colonial Virginia; and further yet to the seventeenth-century revivalistic sacramental meetings of Scots-Irish Presbyterians in Ulster and especially western Scotland. Each of these streams of tradition is a linchpin in the history of Appalachian mountain religion. Together they create a highly intelligible tradition history for night meetings not as ancillary worship services like mid-week Bible studies and prayer meetings but as the very heart of the worship life of innumerable mountain church communities. Careful consideration of the pivotal role of night meetings in the mountain churches which continue this centuries' old tradition should erase any perception that night meetings, especially when held during the week, are in no way comparable to the bedrock tradition of Sunday morning worship, the norm around which revolve the churches of American Protestantism within and outside of Appalachia.

This cooperative character among so many small clusters of local churches throughout the mountains is not prompted, then, just by extraordinary occasions, like revivals, but to facilitate people's access to each other's churches for the ordinary occasions of worship—the very reason for the existence of these churches. Their careful efforts at avoiding conflict with each other in the scheduling of their worship services enfleshes an enviable expansiveness and generosity that flies in the face of the typical insularity, only infrequently breached, of much more institutionalized churches, especially among the denominations of American Protestantism. It also exposes the lie of the long-standing stereotype created and promoted by American Protestantism throughout its history in the region that mountain churches are "uncooperative" with each other, willfully existing only as isolated entities in an isolated region that reinforces such self-centeredness.

We see a clear illustration of this cooperative character in the fluid meeting schedules of the microscopic locus of churches represented by Brother Coy Miser, Sister Mae June Hensley, and Sister Lydia Surgener, schedules that are adjusted over time as personal circumstances change. What had been Brother Coy's church in Pennington Gap, Red Hill Holiness Church, met Saturday and Sunday nights, with Saturday the main service. At that time, Sister Lydia's House of Prayer in Pennington Gap met Sunday and Wednesday evenings, with Sunday the main service. Her New Church at Mill Creek, at Cranks Creek less than ten miles away, met on Tuesday and Saturday evenings (it was never clear to me or anyone else which, if either, was the main service). Sister Mae June Hensley's church, Cranks Holiness Church, met Monday and Friday evenings, with Friday the main service.

The goal of these three religious leaders—not peculiar to them, as we have seen, but well represented in the history of mountain religious life—is to create opportunity for people to gather for worship, an important goal in the church life of more sparsely populated areas. It personifies a values system that flatly rejects the competition—so well known in the annals of American religious history—among local churches for as many bodies in the pews as possible as *their* church members, even to the point of depriving other churches of worshipers by deliberately and unnecessarily scheduling regular services or periodic events (like homecomings and revivals) at the same time. If people are planning to travel a greater distance to a service on a given night, as many do, competitive scheduling is not at issue. Even within a microscopic locus of church communities, scheduling conflicts are, at times, inevitable. There are only so many days (or rather, nights) in the week.

Sister Mae June and Sister Lydia grew up together and are cousins. They have spent a significant part of their lifetimes traveling with each other to worship services in all kinds of settings (homes, church houses, brush arbors or outdoor meetings, usually in a wooded clearing), as well as revivals and an assortment of other religious gatherings. They are also fiercely independent of each other in how they live their everyday lives, reflecting the seeming paradox of interdependent autonomy. Although not a preacher like Sister Lydia or a pastor like Brother Coy, Sister Mae June is very much a recognized religious leader within the limited geographic compass of her immediate area, as well as within the somewhat larger compass of the informal network of independent Holiness churches in that small corner of central Appalachia. She is also known in her local area to many religious leaders of other mountain church traditions, such as Free Will Baptist.

Sister Mae June illustrates a well-established leadership model in mountain religion that carries as much influence, although of a different sort, as preachers and pastors. She is the founder and caretaker of Cranks Holiness Church, its "church matriarch" (a term not used by mountain people), using her meager financial resources to pay its expenses, which are minimal, consisting mostly of utilities and property tax, levied because it has no legal, nonprofit—and, therefore, tax exempt—status. Sister Mae June assumes these costs because an "offertory" (or "passing the plate" or "taking up a collection") rarely occurs in many mountain church traditions such as independent Holiness and Old Regular Baptist. The usual exceptions are extraordinary needs, such as unexpected church maintenance requirements like a new coal-burning stove. More often the exceptions are drastic needs, such as a local family being burned out of their home or someone's funeral expenses, financial help that is in no way dependent on church membership or, for that matter, any history of involvement with the church, but determined simply by their being part of the immediate community to which the church belongs. No one dismisses Sister Mae June's religious authority, her standing being a result of her age, experience, wisdom, and uncommon spiritual maturity. Indeed, Cranks Holiness Church is known generally as "Sister Mae's Church" (a type of intimate, personalized designation for churches, apart from their proper names, that is common throughout the mountains), even though it too was pastored by Brother Coy until recently.

Brother Coy has had to step aside from Cranks and Red Hill for health reasons—the insidious advance of black lung disease from his years as a coal miner and his constant, suffocating battle with the ravages of emphysema. As of this writing, Cranks Holiness Church is pastored by Brother James Fee, a position he assumed not by any ordination—for Brother James is not "ordained" in a formal, institutional sense—but by the communal recognition and affirmation of his maturing gifts, as well as his steadfastness and constancy to the worship life of this very tiny church. When I first met Brother James, while Brother Coy was still active as the pastor of Cranks Holiness Church and Red Hill, Brother James was referred to as a "lay preacher," indicating not a place in a hierarchy of prestige within the informal network of Holiness churches but simply a developmental stage. All of these religious leaders—Brother Coy, Sister Lydia, Sister Mae June, and Brother James—attend each other's churches on a regular basis, as well as a large selection of other churches in the area (usually Holiness, but, frequently enough, churches of other mountain traditions), as do their core congregations.

Among mountain churches of all traditions, size is of no relevance whatsoever to a church's viability or worth, as innumerable churches like Cranks Holiness Church attest by their very presence, just so long as "two or three are gathered" (Matt. 18:20). Old Time Baptist traditions such as the Old Regular Baptists have always required a minimum number of founding members, duly baptized by immersion and covenanting together, in order to constitute a new church. However, their churches are not closed if membership dwindles to the point of being negligible, so long as a qualified male can still serve as moderator and preach some, supported by the preaching itinerancy of other elders within the association.

Cranks Holiness Church came to be only because of Sister Mae June's belief ("God laid on my heart," as she reported it) that the dormant church house was meant to be a living church again. It had been entrusted to her care (which Sister Mae June gave freely, without remuneration) years before by an independent Baptist preacher, Brother James L. Turner, who owned the property and had built the one-room structure for worship. An African-American, Brother Turner and his family and some of his neighbors making up the small church community left the Cranks Creek area when their economic circumstances had improved. Asking an individual in the immediate neighborhood, like Sister Mae June, who was otherwise unaffiliated with the worship life of a church house, to assume the care or oversight of a now dormant church house is a common and widespread tradition in the mountains. Church houses no longer in use are rarely simply abandoned and left to decay. They tend to be cared for with a loving attentiveness that is an ongoing legacy of the worship life they once sheltered. I have come across this pattern of behavior toward dormant church houses of all mountain church traditions repeatedly in my sojourns, especially in the central Appalachian region.

Brother Coy had a chance meeting with Sister Mae June when, traveling one Friday evening for the first time down the one-lane road (part pavement, part dirt) running beside Cranks Creek, he saw her praying on the front step of the church house ("holding services by myself," as she said), after she had checked on the building and swept it out. Brother Coy recognized the hand of God on her conviction of the church house's viability and came to preach to her for weeks on end, every Friday night, in the otherwise empty church house. Brother Coy and Sister Mae June did not launch a campaign to drum up people to come worship with them. Indeed, "membership drives," a long-established technique in many of the denominations of American Protestantism, are nonexistent among church traditions nearer the center of the spectrum making up Appalachian mountain religion.

Aggressive evangelization that works to get as many people as possible to "join" a specific church, as though a large membership makes a church "successful" and is indisputable evidence that God has specially favored a church (which translates into a lust for temporal power in the larger community, especially at the level of influence and prestige), sticks in the craw of most mountain people and runs completely contrary to religious values that eschew equating conspicuous accumulation with God's blessings. Indeed, a very large number of mountain churches, like Cranks Holiness, keep no membership rolls, in fact, no records whatsoever to track and validate their progress in the world. This absence of any kind of records or written documentation of church life stands in radical contrast to the denominations of American Protestantism, such as the Methodists, who are legendary for their extremely meticulous record keeping, through which they generate reams of statistics, charts, and mathematical quantifications, using them as the principal measure from which they draw their conclusions about their progress and success during a calendar year.

The nationally based, bureaucratic church world of the denominations of American Protestantism that governs how to go about establishing a new church—with regulations and guidelines and standards and legal requirements far beyond the simple, biblically based prescriptions of mountain church traditions—could not be any further removed from the very local, extemporaneous world of independent nondenominational churches in the mountains. Brother Coy and Sister Mae June simply worshiped together in the little church house, week after week until the weeks became months, praying that God would allow the church house to fulfill its purpose. And eventually, in ones and twos and threes, a small but steady stream of people started to come to the church house on Friday night to worship with them.

Just days before the very first people came, Brother Coy had what he describes as "a vision" of two angels standing on either side of the church house's entryway, and he saw people passing between them, walking into the church house to worship. Brother Coy told Sister Mae June about that vision. In obedient response, they anointed each bench in the church house with oil and prayed over it on what was the last Friday night before a few people started to come. Apparently the first who came to worship with Brother Coy and Sister Mae June were motivated by no more than word of mouth that culminated in their availing themselves of a new worship opportunity, although Brother Coy and Sister Mae June attributed it to the movement of the Holy Spirit. They do not accept as mere coincidence the timing of their taking prayerful, symbolic action on Brother Coy's vision and people starting to come for worship the very next week after so many months (indeed, years in Sister Mae June's case)—and each week thereafter without interruption in this church's constantly fluid worship population.

Since 1982, the dormant church house has been a living entity, reborn as Cranks Holiness Church, nourishing the lives of people in the immediate area of Cranks Creek, including those who never set foot inside it (the values of mountain worship life are made concrete beyond the doors of the church house by the plainest and most direct, everyday social action). It also provides yet another locale for people whose religious culture instills in them the desire to travel any distance accessible in order to worship. Over the years, the Turner family has charged Cranks Holiness Church (that is, Sister Mae June) no rent for use of the property. Within the broad and deeply rooted tradition of giving freely in support of local worship life, especially in the independent nondenominational church tradition, it would have been surprising and disturbing if they had. Indeed, this church house, originally built by Brother James Turner as an independent Baptist church, was always a part of that tradition. In 1989, Brother Turner's son, his father now deceased, sold the small patch of land, with the building, for a nominal sum to Sister Mae June. Even though nominal, the price was not within Sister Mae June's apparent resources; yet, somehow, she managed to meet the terms of purchase. No one ever asked her how, and Sister Mae June never said:

We know Brother Callaway—who has inspired so many pages of discussion—only from the chance meeting of a field-worker, gathering data for a sociological study of mountain religion, who thoughtfully crafted a few notes about him that remained hidden and unknown for decades in a large archival collection. Brother Callaway was characterized in the notes of that field-worker as "a kindly, lovable old man, always ready to help any who need it, and sometimes is imposed upon." Somehow, in a short span of time, Brother Callaway obviously touched the heart of this anonymous field-worker who felt justified in making such a personal and revealing assessment. This characterization of Brother Callaway fits Brother Coy in particular, a mountain preacher of a later era continuing in Brother Callaway's tradition of the independent Holiness church. Brother Coy lives in poverty today, but his days are filled with service and availability to others as his health permits, from simply helping out to prayer and visitation, and he too "sometimes is imposed upon."

The concluding sentence about Brother Callaway in the field notes is extremely telling about mountain religious life in general: "Although his own beliefs are very definite, he very often allows men who differ with him to preach in his building." There is a wide streak of tolerance for dissenting viewpoints on doctrinal issues, a fundamental humility that no one person has a corner on God's truth. Pastors like Brother Coy do have real concern for basic doctrinal agreement with those who preach in their pulpits, but they tend not to get caught up in the particulars, so long as harm is not brought to the auditors. In this attitude there is genuine respect for the intelligence and discernment of those who hear the preacher preach. As my own grandmother said to me more than once, "If you know your Bible, you know if they're preaching right or not." The people whom preachers address more often than not do know their Bible, many times finishing verses and supplying out loud additional verses or verse fragments to support or even redirect what they hear coming from the pulpit. But the basic attitude is one of humility and openness. Who knows how God will speak to them when they gather?

"[T]ake no thought beforehand what ye shall speak, neither do ye premeditate: but whatsoever shall be given you in that hour, that speak ye: for it is not ye that speak, but the Holy Ghost" (Mark 13:11). This particular text introduces one of the biblical bases for a highly challenging preaching tradition in the mountains that is vibrantly alive today and reaches back to the earliest years of settlement on the Appalachian frontier. It is a preaching tradition that relies exclusively on what is experienced and perceived to be the direct inspiration of the Holy Ghost. By far, this is one of the most troubling of all aspects of mountain religion to the nation's historically dominant religious culture of American Protestantism, which places its highest premium on a learned clergy and their self-control, their self-consciousness and deliberative intentionality, in the pulpit. The basic difference between these two preaching traditions is that, in mountain churches, God speaks *through* the preacher who does everything in his (or her) power to step aside, simply to be "a willing instrument" and not get too much in the way. In the churches of American Protestantism, and this is especially characteristic of movements such as evangelical fundamentalism, the preacher speaks *for* God, like an official spokesman. Although the differences between these two approaches may seem subtle, more apparent than real, they represent two profoundly different—indeed, contradictory—sets of religious values and worldviews. One self-consciously values "humbleness," where the preacher seeks to fade as a personality into the background of the words spoken through him; one self-consciously values assertiveness, which is the indispensable component in the charismatic leadership model.

Not surprisingly, the King James Version is the preferred English translation of the Bible in mountain churches and among mountain people in general. Even though they are "people of the Book," it is a Book that many mountain people—literate or not—know primarily as oral literature. Their knowledge of the Bible as oral literature results in a mode of text interpretation not grounded in the abstraction of ideas from their linguistic environment, so favored by their more "literate" and generally better educated counterparts in American Protestantism who tend to prize rationalism and, thus, what makes sense to the head, more than they value what makes sense to the heart and the intuitive discernment that involves. Instead, mountain people's way of interpreting the Bible is normatively more concrete, more midrashic, allowing texts to "interpret" each other, following the lead of a text by listening deep within to its own embedded literary structures (which is possible only through a comprehensive oral memory of the Bible).

This mode of text interpretation—not at all unique to mountain people in the history of world religions—is demonstrated not just by mountain preachers while preaching but by mountain people in general when they gather for "Sunday school," which is exceeded in importance, as Elizabeth Hooker observed, only by the worship service itself and revivals. Calvinist-based traditions are the exception to this norm in mountain religion, having no "educational" institutions whatsoever. However, Sunday school functions in church traditions such as independent Holiness and Free Will Baptist, as well as in many independent Baptist churches, not as an educational institution where people are taught a preformulated body of knowledge about the Bible through study guides but as an opportunity for people to gather, read a Bible text, and then have each person present discuss it among themselves, from the youngest to the oldest who are able. Sunday schools in churches such as these are not age- or sex-segregated with assigned "Sunday school teachers." Sunday school teacher is a role that generally does not apply, except in some churches such as Brother John Sherfey's Fellowship Independent Baptist Church in Page County, Virginia (studied by Jeff Titon in *Powerhouse for God*), where, preceding the Sunday morning worship service, Brother Jesse Comer leads the communal Sunday school (here too people rely exclusively on the Bible and interpret it to each other verse by verse). Brother Jesse assumes the "teaching" role in that setting which, biblically, he identifies as one of the gifts of the Holy Spirit, and which Brother John and Brother Jesse both make clear that they understand (quite biblically) is distinct from the "preaching" gift—Brother John's gift—of the Spirit.

Although Red Hill Holiness Church under Brother Coy's tenure as pastor, as so many other churches like it, held no Sunday morning worship service, a small handful of people would gather at the church house around ten o'clock on Sunday morning to read and interpret the Bible to each other.

The Bible is passed to each person who can read (the people gathered almost never bring their own Bible). This serves only to get the various texts—sometimes a whole story, sometimes only a verse or two—out on the table for discussion. Those who cannot read, like Brother Coy, do not feel in any way hindered from full participation, given the essentially oral base of knowledge of the Bible shared by all, literate or not, as the norm. Pastors like Brother Coy also do not "lead" or "take charge of" or "guide" the discussion, but are simply one among the rest. Indeed, there is no place or clearly defined role for Sunday school teachers like Brother Jesse in churches such as these, only a general recognition that some individuals seem to have greater insight into the Bible than others, but they assume no greater standing than others. Hooker noted, at the time of her survey, that the Bible itself was the sole text informing Sunday school in "native" mountain churches. No Sunday school literature found its way into these churches. This is still very true today. We find a growing number of exceptions among churches like Wolf Creek Baptist Church, an independent Missionary Baptist church in the Blue Ridge near Brevard, North Carolina, where the Bible was the only text in Sunday school until recent years. Now this church uses Sunday school literature.

By far mountain people's preferred texts are the historical narratives and the stories, where their mode of text interpretation is the most effective. Mountain people, especially those who are influenced by church traditions nearer the center of the spectrum defining mountain religion, generally shy away from much of the legal or prescriptive material in both the Hebrew Scriptures and the New Testament. Their preferences in biblical literature differ profoundly from a preponderance of evangelical fundamentalists in particular, whose clergy tend to focus in their preaching extensively on the New Testament Epistles or "Letters to Young Churches," substantially made up of instructions. Frequently (indeed, for some, almost always) in their preaching, evangelical fundamentalists will attempt to unpack in excruciating detail, by picking at this word and that, what they see as the divinely inspired blueprints for how the everyday world of a Christian should be structured. Preachers of this genre will often paint that world with a palette of black and white, tolerating only the lightest and most superficial shades of ambiguity. Proponents of this perspective are found scattered throughout the mountains. However, my observation is that, more often than not, mountain people and their preachers accept ambiguity—running deep and broad—as an indisputable fact of life. They do not feel driven to resolve it in their preaching with semantically fancy footwork that artificially overcomes ambiguity by forcing all the pieces to fit together in neatly packaged "biblical solutions" or "answers" to the pressing problems of daily living, from personal finances to moral dilemmas dividing the nation.

Instead, mountain people of nearly all mountain church traditions, from Old Regular Baptist to independent Holiness—and, indeed, mountain people in general—believe it is the Holy Spirit who should speak when preachers preach, and that the Holy Spirit should speak through them freely, unpredictably, and without our second-guessing or presuming to gainsay (embodying the theological model of God's initiative, human cooperation). For the overwhelming majority of mountain people, preaching is not about preselected topics addressed by carefully crafted exegeses of biblical texts making up "sermons" that are "delivered" (embodying the theological model of human initiative, God's cooperation). Indeed, when several preachers are called upon in a service (a common and ancient tradition in the mountains), as Schermerhorn observed in his 1814 report on religious life and morals in the region, they will often "contradict each other," which Schermerhorn concluded debunked their claims to be preaching under the direction of the Holy Ghost. Schermerhorn's proof of these preachers' theological erraticism and instability in the pulpit assumed that the Holy Spirit, if it spoke through them at all, should speak with one voice (that is, all the preachers speaking under the power of the Holy Ghost in any given meeting should say basically the same things about the same subjects), a premise mountain people do not accept. Instead, mountain preachers like Brother Coy attest that the Holy Spirit needs to say the same things hundreds of different ways, many of which may seem blatantly contradictory (which is also how they understand apparently contradictory texts in the Bible), in order to accommodate the kaleidoscopic varieties of needs and personal histories of the legions of people the Holy Spirit addresses through such preachers.

This attitude about the meaning or function of "contradiction" embraces ambiguity rather than fleeing from it, manifested in a profound acceptance of differences and variety that puts a firm lid on judgmentalism and self-righteousness (which nonetheless persist as unavoidable temptations in mountain people's lives, as in all people's), and expressed in a profound humility which mountain religion's normative theological heritage has carefully nurtured as one of its most important values. Indeed, humility, or not putting oneself forward (so often dismissed by outside observers as passivity), is a value generalized throughout everyday life in the mountains, demonstrating the power of mountain religious values in shaping the overall sociocultural life of the region. This attitude toward ambiguity, manifested as an acceptance of differences and variety—or tolerance—and also expressed in the normative value of "humbleness," founds itself on a deeper bedrock for understanding God's world and God's will than the fissures and cracks of a rationalism that demands definitive answers in order to negotiate its way in God's world and meet its overwhelming need for certainty about God's will—

attaining what certainty is achieved, more often than not, as a clearer artic-
ulation of human will than of divine will.

In the brief portrait of Brother Callaway and our exploration of the several major clues embedded in it, we have witnessed up close three of the four
components Catherine Albanese identified in which "all the characteristics
of mountain religion came together at their fullest expression: the uneducated preacher, the independent church, [and] the primacy of the Bible." Her
fourth component, "the strong emotionalism of religious worship," we shall
explore next with the help of Emma Bell Miles.

2

Emma Bell Miles and
"The Old-time Religion"

Emma Bell Miles (1879–1919) was born in Evansville, Indiana. About a year later her schoolteacher parents moved to Rabbit Hash, Kentucky, near Cincinnati. Around the age of nine Emma moved with her family to Red Bank, in southeast Tennessee, at the foot of Walden's Ridge very near Chattanooga. Emma Bell spent the rest of her life on Walden's Ridge, except for two years in St. Louis where she studied art, marrying Frank Miles, a "mountain man" (as she called him) whose people had lived on the ridge since before the Civil War. Emma Bell Miles lived a bicultural existence, dividing her time between Chattanooga where her artwork made her popular among the moneyed classes, and the small cabin on Walden's Ridge she shared with Frank and their four surviving children.[1]

In 1905 Miles published a book-length work called *The Spirit of the Mountains,* a work that was little noticed when it was published, and in fact was known mostly to historians and literary scholars until the mid-1960s. It was rediscovered at that time by regional activists who saw it as a welcome counterbalance by an "insider" to all of the condescending "outsider" publications that were then flooding the popular press about Appalachia and mountain people, as well as to the same type of materials that had been written by home missionaries and local-color essayists and novelists at the time of its original publication. In a chapter entitled "The Old-time Religion," Miles provides a portrait of mountain religious life, of worship practices and belief systems, that is very close to generic in the sense that there are shared features and emotional textures found in mountain churches then and now, be they Old Regular Baptist, Missionary Baptist, Holiness, Free Will Baptist, Primitive Baptist, Church of Christ, or a host of other traditions. I provide a composite summary of her account and commentary on it in the following paragraphs.

Brother Absalom Darney maintained a preaching circuit of four churches. "There is preaching every third Sunday in the month at the King's Creek log church. . . . On the first Sunday it is the same at Filmore's Cove; on the second, at a settlement in Sequatchie; and the fourth is claimed by a forsaken little 'shack' church away back in the Cumberland range."[2] This four-point preaching charge was the norm for many mountain Baptist and Methodist preachers well into the twentieth century, as Brother Terry Galloway makes clear in his account of the history of Wolf Creek Baptist Church, beginning in 1886. Miles makes no mention of whether these four churches and "Brother Ab" are Baptist or Methodist. Historically, this factor was of little import to mountain people; what mattered was if and when "preaching" was going to take place.

As we heard from the oral memoirs of Dora Woodruff Cope, who lived in this same general vicinity and at about the same time, "Appalachian people were not 'joiners.' They felt no allegiance to any particular denomination so long as they felt they were preaching the Word of God." And as we noted in the previous chapter, today numerous churches still meet only once a month, although people will attend services at various churches every Saturday or Sunday (or, for many independent Baptist and Holiness people, any weeknight), traveling some distance to get there. Invariably, people will have a "home church" they attend regularly. Log churches from Miles's period, like Brother Ab's "King's Creek log church," still stand and are in use today. Warren Brunner and I have photographed several, including the Band of Hope Missionary Baptist Church (est. 1893) near Lewisburg, West Virginia, and Mt. Olivet Methodist Church (est. 1877) next to Beartown, West Virginia.

Miles does not know what Brother Ab is paid by his four charges, only that he gives freely of his preaching and that neither he nor any other mountain preacher would consider taking up a collection as payment for their service to the Lord: "[W]hat comes to him is also given freely—slipped into his hand at the close of the service, a handful of dimes and pennies, by whomsoever feels inclined." Like Brother Callaway and Brother Coy Miser, preachers of a later era, Brother Ab "does not think of depending on his ministry for his daily bread." He has a large family and a farm whereby he maintains his keep, like the members of his congregations (p. 120). Collections are rarely taken up in churches nearest the center of the spectrum making up Appalachian mountain religion, except in times of need. The same applies to other church traditions less close to the spectrum's center, although not as uniformly. The norm in mountain churches is either to put money on the "stand" or in the preacher's hand. Miles underscores about Brother Absalom what is normative for traditional mountain preachers in each generation: God may call you to be a preacher, but responding to that call is a gift you give to God; it does not then become the financial obligation of those to whom you preach. You support yourself just like everyone else.

Miles remarks at length about the absence of class distinctions or of ministry as a profession set apart. No special titles are used that suggest "patronage": "You hear no cant in the mountains about respect due to the cloth; our preacher is never called a clergyman or a divine; even the term 'pastor of the flock' savors of patronage which would indicate a false relation; Brother So-and-So, preacher of the gospel, is title enough. He is not of a class set apart from life, from the labors, sins and sorrows of his world, nor does he pander to any class distinctions." He is, first of all, "sincere, a man among men" (p. 121). Miles characterizes Brother Ab's preaching style as "impressively simple." He provides "strong Scriptural meat" and avoids divisive doctrinal subjects such as close communion, free will, and original sin—issues stemming from the early nineteenth-century anti-mission controversy that took particular hold in the Appalachian region—while at the same time presenting "no false doctrine" (p. 122). Clarity of belief and a desire not to incite divisiveness over doctrinal issues are characteristics we have seen before and have commented on in the account of Brother Callaway. It may manifest itself as openness to allowing others with whom you are not in total agreement to share your pulpit. In the case of Brother Ab, it is a desire not to open the door to acrimony about "questions over which the mountain people are so fond of splitting hairs."

"Taking up church" or beginning the church service depends on when enough people are gathered. The time is not rigidly punctual but flexible, even up to half an hour or more beyond the customary gathering time. The people are called into the building not by the ringing of a bell but when the preacher and "some of the amen-corner members raise a hymn . . . . They sing without books, for these hymns have never been printed: 'They'll pray for me,' 'We have mothers up in heaven,' 'Father's gone to glory,' and a hundred like them" (p. 122). Mountain hymns typically emphasize communal bonding in the here and now, based on the model of the family, as well as family ties stretching beyond the bounds of death itself. Services today for many churches are still regularly convened by those gathered inside "raising up a hymn," especially in traditions such as the Old Regular Baptists. Singing without instrumental accompaniment, without pianos or organs, is common still today among the "primitive" church traditions ("primitive" here is a technical term, not a pejorative) indigenous to the Appalachian region—Old Regular Baptists, who are known especially for the ancient practice of hymn lining, Primitive Baptists, Church of Christ people. Unlined hymnals or hymnals without musical notation are found often even in Holiness churches, where the hymn tunes are part of oral tradition. Holiness churches use a wide array of instruments today—guitars especially, pianos, even banjos, mandolins, and harmonicas.

Brother Ab rises after the singing and reads a chapter from the Bible. "Then he asks the congregation to kneel with him in prayer," and the people go to their knees on the hardwood floor, with no kneelers attached to the benches to soften the posture (pp. 123–24). As Miles notes, it is an act of "simplicity and humility," perhaps the two premier values of mountain religious life. Kneeling on the floor at times of prayer is yet another practice cutting across distinctions among mountain church traditions still today. Missionary Baptist churches, Free Will Baptists, Holiness, Old Regular Baptists, all kneel on the floor at this opening prayer, many gathering up front near the preaching "stand" or at the "altar."

More hymns are sung and then Brother Ab announces his text. For a topic such as "Prayer," he will draw together all the Bible texts he knows that deal with the subject from both the Old and New Testaments, "abridged from the very words of the Book." His comprehensive oral memory is impressive. At different points he will address specifically someone in the congregation: "That, Brother Jim, is the kind of prayer God Almighty loves to hear" (p. 124). This specificity of address, speaking to someone present by name, is a universal preaching device in the mountains. It lends immediacy and an intimate, personal touch; it is also an equalizer. The preacher is addressing people who are as capable as he is of appreciating the depths and meaning of the message the Holy Spirit gives him that day.

"Like other mountain preachers, he speaks readily on his feet without preparation, scarcely once opening a book of which he can repeat whole pages by heart" (p. 126). It is extremely rare for a mountain preacher to preach with Bible in hand, flipping through it to find the texts that form part of the sermon, a practice so pronounced in evangelical fundamentalist traditions. Instead, preaching is spontaneous, "unprepared," with no index cards or notebooks or sermon guides. Oral memory is the norm, and behind it is the assumption of oral memory on the part of the hearers. This oral memory allows the greatest leeway for the tradition of seeking the Holy Spirit to guide the words of the preacher and the audible, interactive responses of "the church" (that is, the congregation).

"This informality, this direct simplicity, is the strength of Brother Absalom's sermons." Babies fret with the heat, people come and go, the dipper is passed from the water bucket. None of this disturbs the preacher. He preaches in the "slightly nasal pitch of a mountain preacher's voice, and its cadence, rather like an energetic chant, is well calculated to put any one to sleep; there is more than a little mesmerism about it" (p. 125). The chanting preaching style Miles mentions is a hallmark of mountain religious life, one that has long been noted in writings on mountain religion and continues still today among many traditional mountain preachers, although until recently it has received very little formal academic attention.[3]

Informality is integral to mountain services, from the eighteenth century to the present. There is much movement in mountain worship services. Children are permitted to move about at will, and they tend to be discreet. People will take a break from the service—which typically lasts three hours or more—to stand outside to talk or smoke a cigarette. People will often move to another bench or pew to visit quietly a few minutes with someone they haven't seen for a while. At the same time, there is another level of awareness operating, an attention to what is being said and what is happening from the pulpit and in the service generally. Mountain preachers are not disturbed by such behavior; it is normal and acceptable, although outsiders from denominational traditions where very rigid church behavior is the norm are often aghast at the informality and assume—wrongly—that there is inattention and an obliviousness to what is taking place in the service. Indeed, this informality would become a stock example of denominational church workers of what was "wrong" with mountain religion. Ellen Myers in her 1884 article on "Mountain Whites in Kentucky" in *American Missionary Magazine* would complain about mountain people's "habits of worship," setting a pattern in future commentary by other observers of remarking that mountain worship services were more of a social gathering than anything else.

Later in her chapter on religion, long after concluding her account of Brother Absalom's meeting, Miles mentions another feature of meetings, that of testifying: "'I desire an interest in all your pra'ars, and hope I may hold out faithful to the end,' and 'I want to get a home in heaven,' are favorite formulas for the closing of these intensely earnest, mystical 'experiences' recounted at meeting" (pp. 143–44). Testimonies usually occur after the sermon, although this is not necessarily a set pattern. Mountain people frequently recount their visions and dreams during the period of testimony, and these are often the most moving accounts of what God has done in their lives. Each person who wishes to is given an opportunity to speak. Some testimonies are quite brief, perfunctory, and highly formulaic, and some are minor masterpieces of oral literary composition. It is a mistake to think that this particular worship practice is confined only to Pentecostal churches or is of recent vintage. It goes back at least to the Puritan era, when people were required to give testimony of their conversion experience, and what saving grace meant in their lives, in order to gain access to church membership. This practice was also observed as the "love feast" by several pietist traditions such as the Moravians and appropriated by the early Methodists, as well as being a strong tradition of the early revival Baptists who had an extraordinary impact on mountain religious culture. Testifying, through this multiple heritage, was soon integrated in mountain worship life as a practice that was generalized as part of the worship service itself.

Brother Absalom ends his sermon "with an appeal to the sinners to come forward and be prayed for. Six or eight responded, . . . they gave the preacher their hands, while the congregation sang" (p. 126). Those who came forward were most likely not only *sinners* or non-church members (a nonpejorative but descriptive term stemming from plain-folk camp-meeting religion for people who are in the preconversion state) but also people who were already church members yet who were *backsliders* (another nonpejorative term stemming from plain-folk camp-meeting religion, which describes people who are in need of a renewal of their experience of conversion, the episodic conversion experience being a mainstay of mountain religious life). Finally, they were also quite probably people who simply had a burden on their hearts and were in need of prayer.

Inviting people in need—be they sinners, backsliders, or burdened in their hearts—to come up to be prayed over is nearly universal in mountain worship services, and the type of prayer style Miles notes is just as widespread today: the prayer is one "in which all the leading men of the church joined—all praying at once at the top of their voices, or at least ejaculating 'Lord grant it' from time to time" (p. 127). Mountain people—not only men but women equally—simultaneously pray out loud together their personal prayers of praise and thanksgiving, as well as their prayers of needs and concerns. In fact, different points of mountain worship services are meant for either praise or expression of need. This form of prayer has a wonderful melodic quality, and no self-consciousness about it on the part of the participants. In Holiness churches, women and men together pray over individuals along with the preacher and pastor (who may or may not be one and the same person). Simultaneous group prayer (called in print "concert prayer" by some observers) is practiced not just over individuals at the end of a service but whenever prayer is called for in the service, whether standing or on one's knees. For some it may simply be a matter of calling out "Yes, Lord," or "Bless him, Jesus" as one person starts and closes the prayer, while the rest pray out loud with him. This too is a practice of ancient vintage in the mountains, going back at least to the Baptist revival in colonial Virginia and North Carolina. A close but inexact parallel is the Jewish practice of davening, praying out loud together yet individually at one's own pace from the prayer book.

"After prayer, . . . the 'right hand of Christian fellowship' was called for. The ceremony is frankly a general hand-shaking and a hearty song; it promotes good feeling, and signifies little else. 'Let all who hope to meet me in the Promised Land give me their hands'" (p. 127). If mountain religion is known for anything it is "the right hand of fellowship." Hugging and embracing accompany the ubiquitous handshake. It may come at the beginning of the service, or at the end, and often both; it always precedes a communion and footwashing service, which in mountain churches usually happens only once a year after a regular "meeting," though sometimes more often. Old Regular Baptists are known in particular for their handshaking, although it is a tradition crisscrossing nearly all mountain church traditions. Latecomers to a worship service will take their time, going from person to person shaking hands, even as the service progresses. Such actions enhance rather than disrupt the service. In part 4 of this book, Hamilton W. Pierson expounds at length about the prevalence and importance of handshaking and embracing during worship services in the Appalachian wilderness of the 1850s. The right hand of fellowship goes back to Puritan times as a sign of welcoming a new member into the church covenant. Mountain people have generalized the practice as a form of greeting and affection for all their brothers and sisters in Christ and for the strangers in their midst who have come to worship with them.

Singing accompanies the right hand of fellowship. At the conclusion of Brother Absalom's service, Miles notes the number of songs built on simple repetition about family and meeting one another again in heaven.

> The preacher's voice strikes through the words of the song with encouraging shouts of goodwill; the singers throng and press about him on the floor, grasping hands right and left. . . . Tears are running down seamed and withered faces now, as the repression and loneliness of many months find relief; the tune changes again, and yet again—they do not tire of this. . . .
>
> Broken ties restored, old pain of lonely nights to be no more—that is the dearest promise of this religion; the aching of old griefs is suddenly caught up and whirled away in the aroused hope of glory. . . .
>
> "Glory to God, my soul's happy!" It is a woman's scream that rings high over all. Several break into sobbing; the woman throws herself down with her head and arms across a bench. One touches her in a friendly fashion; the rest sing on. (pp. 128–29)

Encouraging shouts of goodwill, tears and sobs, screams of joy. These are the emotional features so common in mountain worship services, the very features that set on edge the teeth of the outside observers who castigate mountain religion for its "emotional excesses." Such expressions of emotional release and rapture go back several eras before the Great Revival, which simply built on traditions of such emotional expressions in worship, reaching back at least to the Scots-Irish in early seventeenth-century Ulster and western Scotland. Mountain religion is very much a religion of the heart, and of heartfelt expressions. It stirs the emotions and counts as good the expression of vibrant, direct feeling about one's salvation and hope, and about the love you feel for the people around you.

"At last the wave of emotion spends itself; the handshaking is over. A few more songs and they are ready to go home, after Brother Absalom's benediction" (p. 130). Sunday dinner is an important time after meeting. Brother Absalom receives many invitations, but he goes home with a "poor widow."

Miles spends the next few pages talking about other religious gatherings: a revival or "a big meetin'," held night after night as long as there is interest; "brush meetings" or brush arbors held in the woods; and "baptizings," which always take place in a pool of water, or the deepest part of a creek, or in a small river, no matter what the season of the year. Even today it is not uncommon for ice to be cut through. Indeed, Miles writes of a form of baptism that still remains normative for mountain church traditions: "Baptism could hardly have been simpler as taught by the early Apostles themselves. . . . Most of the converts [the newly baptized] are shouting by the time they gain the bank, and nearly run amuck in the crowd before they can be persuaded to retire to a hastily erected brush shelter and change to dry clothing. No attempt is ever made to check the excitement" (pp. 132–33).

Mountain people today, almost universally, continue to place great importance on baptism by immersion "in living waters," an extremely common expression meaning out-of-doors in a natural setting; indeed, most cannot imagine any other form of baptism as acceptable. Baptism "in living [running] waters" is a tradition established in the Appalachian region during its first years of settlement by Anabaptist groups, especially pietists such as the German Baptist Brethren (Dunkards). As we shall see in chapter 10, "The Baptist Revival and the Power of Self-Definition," the public rite of baptism by immersion became the point of entry into mountain people's earthly pilgrimage of salvation, while at the same time serving to break through social distance and confirm community. It was also the rite that established the autonomy of the individual within that community, a community made up of equals.

Miles also speaks of the simple beauty of "foot-washing":

> I hesitate to say much of this, for there is a tendency among certain classes of city people to make jest of these peculiarities, to which we of the mountains are becoming more sensitive year by year. It ought not to be so—God knows what the old ceremonies mean to those who take part in them; but such is the persecution in some places where the curiosity of the town is pressing close in on us that even after a congregation has met together to hold a foot-washing, if any city people are present who are not well known and trusted, the occasion will be quietly turned into an ordinary preaching. It requires considerable courage in men, and especially in women, to go through with the primitive ceremony in the face of unsympathetic onlookers. (pp. 133–34)

God does indeed know what the old ceremonies mean to those who take part in them. The conjoining of communion with footwashing—which forms the annual "sacramental meeting" of Old Time Baptist traditions such as the Primitive and Old Regular Baptists, and is sometimes held with greater frequency in traditions such as independent Holiness—complemented baptism by immersion to create the sacramental high points of mountain religious life. Their importance for mountain people, their sacredness and the rever-

3

The New Salem Association
of Old Regular Baptists, org. 1825

"Regional religion" is a precarious description for religious life and church traditions unique to Appalachia, just as the term "Appalachian mountain religion" is problematic when not carefully delineated. Albanese's interpretive matrix for regional religion as the interplay of creeds, codes, cultuses, and communities is especially helpful. It places emphasis first on belief systems and the worship practices embodying them, factoring in the historical, social, geographic, and other data that qualify the internal integrity of worship practices and belief systems, rather than the other way around. This is a significant shift in emphasis in the study of mountain religious life that only a small handful of scholars, notably Loyal Jones, Melanie Sovine, and John Wallhausser, have pursued in recent years in short articles and essays. It may be characterized as a "religious studies" perspective heretofore lacking in descriptions of mountain religion.

Some of the most significant work by early Appalachian studies scholars of the late 1960s and 1970s redefined Appalachia as an economic colony of the United States. The lack of social and economic development in the region was understood in terms of industrial exploitation. Appalachian "traditionalism" was also reinterpreted as a mode of resistance to "cultural imperialism." Mountain religion was interpreted in the same terms as one of the key features of Appalachian "traditionalism" functioning as an internal technique of resistance to exploitation.[1] The problem with such an analysis when applied to religious life distinctive to the mountain regions of Appalachia was that it misdirected attention away from the intrinsically religious character of worship practices and belief systems and made mountain religion a type of "nativistic resistance to cultural change," a perspective that was very little improvement over the earlier portrayals of mountain religion as "the result of having been locked into the past."[2] In addition, the analysis of Appalachia as an economic colony emphasized the regional character of Appalachia, which in turn isolated certain religious groups in the region who were known especially for their faithful adherence to traditional ways in their worship life and theology. These groups were identified as being particularly characteristic of what was special about religion in Appalachia, which was not necessarily a problem in itself, except that these groups' identities came to be defined in exclusively regional terms. They existed because they were "Appalachian," not because of how their worship practices and belief systems interacted with their immediate as well as broader social historical context over an extended period of time. Again, this picked up on the tendency in earlier writings to isolate Old Time Baptist groups such as Old Regular and Primitive Baptists as the quintessential expression of Appalachian mountain religion.

As with most stereotypes, there is a kernel of truth that gets skewed and is usually lost altogether in the broader, ill-informed generalizations. Old Regular and Primitive Baptists are strongly traditional, and a preponderance of their churches, especially for Old Regular Baptists, are found still today in the mountains of the Appalachian region. Baptist history in general is extremely complex, and the history of Primitive and Old Regular Baptists has been, until quite recently, confined mostly to primary sources.[3]

In 1824 George Tucker published *The Valley of Shenandoah*, "perhaps the first book to propose that mountaineers constituted a distinct group."[4] The following year, 1825, the New Salem Association was formed in Kentucky, "armed off" of the Burning Spring Association of United Baptists.[5] The New Salem Association is the parent, the mother association of all Old Regular Baptist churches and associations today, the earliest associations arming off from New Salem Association by the mid-nineteenth century. As for New Salem itself, J. H. Spencer wrote in his *History of Kentucky Baptists* (1885), "This small fraternity [New Salem Association] is located in the counties of Letcher, Floyd, Perry, Breathitt and Pike, in the extreme eastern border of the State. . . . The country in which they are located, is rough and mountainous, and is thinly populated, even at the present time."[6] Today Old Regular Baptists are represented by "at least" fifteen associations concentrated in eastern Kentucky and southwest Virginia, some reaching into southern West Virginia and southern Ohio. A smattering of "isolated fellowships" (individual churches) are found as far afield as Florida, Arizona, Michigan, and Washington State, products of out-migration after World War II and retirement locations.[7]

From 1825 to 1853 the New Salem Association maintained the name United Baptists, and then changed its name in 1854 to Regular United Baptists. The evolution of New Salem's name epitomizes the history of many mountain Baptists in central Appalachia. The Union of 1801 between Regular Baptists and Separate Baptists in Kentucky had produced the United Baptist bodies in that state and a modified Calvinist creedal statement that allowed for a softening of the Philadelphia Confession's strict promulgation of the Calvinist doctrines of limited atonement and double predestination. While maintaining the doctrinal points of total depravity and perseverance of the saints "through grace to glory" (Articles 3 and 5), the new statement opened the door to a historic compromise between Arminian and Calvinist positions. The pattern thus set would become normative to nearly all mountain church traditions, theologically distinguishing them throughout their history from the nationally dominant religious culture of American Protestantism. The key was in Article 9 of the 1801 joint creedal statement, which read, "And that the preaching [that] Christ tasted death for every man shall be no bar to communion." Sydney Ahlstrom observed that the 1801 confession was not a product of "frontier faith" or the "religion of democracy" but a Calvinist theology with concessions made only to a more Arminian interpretation of atonement.[8] Unlike the Separates, who did not want "manmade" creeds to get in the way of God's work in revival, Regular Baptists had made an early decision to affirm creedal statements. For the Old Regular Baptists, "This creedal faith is the historical backbone that has given these communities their tenacity, resilience, and theological toughness."[9]

The Great Revival, also born in Kentucky and reaching its zenith with the 1801 Cane Ridge camp meeting in Bourbon County, had a profound effect on the churches and associations which were to be identified at the latter part of the century as Old Regular Baptist. An "emotional rawness" was added to doctrinal faith; "subjective experiences of grace given to the reborn joined the objective standards of orthodoxy."[10] Old Regular Baptist churches are known for their expressive worship practices and tactility, traditions that originated prior to the Great Revival—most immediately through colonial Baptist revival culture in the mid-South (where there was little distinction between Regulars and Separates)—but were intensified by it. Emphasis on grace is coupled with an emphasis on the presence of the Holy Spirit in worship services where people's immediate experience of the Holy Spirit occurs through singing, preaching, and praying; such religious experience is identified with physical-emotional behaviors that have long been institutionalized as traditional, ritualized worship practices. Shouts of encouragement, tears and sobs, screams of joy are today as much a part of many Old Regular Baptist worship services as they were of Brother Absalom's meeting and are still in mountain Holiness churches, as well as many other Calvinist and non-Calvinist mountain church traditions.

As indicated earlier, this emphasis on the Holy Spirit—intertwined with grace and the centrality of religious experience characterizing nearly all mountain church traditions—is not at all a product of the Holiness-Pentecostal movements making inroads into a basically Calvinist tradition. Emphasis on the "grace covenant," which Old Regular Baptists still speak of today, and its mediation by the Holy Spirit is classic Calvinist theological tradition reaching back to the Synod of Dort in 1618–19 and ultimately to Calvin himself.[11] Emphasis on the worshiping community as the People of God in possession of the Holy Spirit is a product of Anabaptist or free church polity, one of the most important features defining Old Regular Baptists and complementing the continuity of their Calvinist doctrinal heritage and the influence of the Great Revival's emphasis on subjective religious experience ("subjective experiences of *grace*") that is centered on the individual especially within a communal worship setting. In free church polity, the focus is not on ecclesiology or doctrine but on submitting the mind and especially the heart to obedience to God's will.[12] Authority resides not in ecclesiastical or political structures but in "the inner leading of God within the community of faith. The congregations claimed to be governed by the Holy Spirit."[13] The Holy Spirit leads one to know the mind of Christ, and subsequently the will of God.

The principle of consensus is thus essential in the government of church life for Old Regular Baptists and mountain church traditions generally, where all are in like mind in knowing the will of God for self-government of their common life. Such an attitude leads not toward the anarchy of self-willed individualism but to the goal of a disciplined church, bound together in a covenantal relationship and governed from within. Old Regular and Primitive Baptists in their constitutions still hold to the position that all disputes among church members, especially serious disputes involving civil legal questions, should be mediated and settled within the church community and not in a court of law. Freedom is understood principally as the freedom to participate in decisions that are arrived at democratically, a product of the free church emphasis on the priesthood of all believers. More than that, the individual needs to be assured the freedom to obey God. Implicit in this assurance is trust in the regenerated individual's ability to discern the will of God in his or her life. The proclamation of the gospel is given not to a priestly class but to the whole community of faith. The church is a gathered church, a regenerated membership maintained through believers' baptism (adult baptism by immersion) and believers' discipline (codes of conduct).

Early Baptists recognized the need for a wider fellowship with other congregations to express the church universal through congregational membership in what came to be called "associations." Their confessional statements made clear this concern, while at the same time seeking to maintain the free church tradition of local autonomy. Although we might anticipate just the opposite development, in fact, among the early General Baptists—or Baptists who held to a general or universal atonement doctrine rather than a doctrine of particular atonement or election like Calvinist Baptists—the trend in polity was toward centralization or a strong central government developing "an organizational life along denominational lines."[14] A desire for stricter control over the churches produced among General Baptists a church order that was more presbyterian than congregational. The association or connectional system for General Baptists became one in which authority was mediated upward, in contrast to the associational system of the early Particular Baptists, and later the Regular Baptists, which emphasized noncentralized fellowship with other churches in like agreement. This trend toward centralization in the United States played itself out in emerging Baptist state organizations of the early nineteenth century. The General Association of Virginia, organized in 1823 as a statewide body uniting Virginia's Baptist associations under its umbrella and a leader in the creation of the Southern Baptist Convention in 1845, exemplified the centralized polity of the General Baptists, which in turn gave strong impetus to shaping the ecclesiology of the Southern Baptist Convention into a hierarchical, denominational model.[15]

For the Regular Baptists—out of which developed most of the Old Time Baptist church traditions characteristic of Appalachia's mountain regions—the association could "disfellowship" or break relations with an individual church or with another association with whom it was "in correspondence" (that is, in receipt of letters during an association's annual meeting), but the association itself technically had no direct control over any of the local churches belonging to it, and certainly not over any other association. Today Old Regular Baptist associations invoke a standard and historic clause during their annual meetings when debating and deciding on doctrine, polity, and lifestyle issues raised by local churches: "We believe . . . that each Church . . . holds the key to its own door," a phrase that has been generalized throughout mountain church life. Moreover, delegates to the annual association meetings "shall have no power to lord it over God's heritage, nor shall they have any clerical power over the churches of union." However, at the same time, the association itself "shall have the power to provide for the general union of the churches, and to preserve an inviolate chain of communion among them," in partial opposition to the principle that "each Church holds the key to its own door."[16]

At the annual meetings of associations such as Old Regular Baptist, debate about lifestyle, polity, and doctrine is extremely democratic. Decisions are reached by painstaking consensus, not by rulings that are handed down. The annual agenda is based on the individual problems and concerns raised by local churches, rather than being set by any layered structure of committees (an institutional form nonexistent among mountain church traditions) or any focus on national or international issues and plans of action, like the denominations of American Protestantism. It is, however, the association itself, not a local church which belongs to it, that stands as the final arbiter of such issues for those churches choosing to remain in correspondence with it and, hence, in fellowship with each of the churches that make up the association. Like the free church polity infusing the life of the local church itself, it is not self-willed individualism but a disciplined church in covenantal relationship and governed from within which directs the life of the associa-tion. The local church is an integral and highly respected part of that larger body.

An individual association is limited in size to a small, subregional orga-nization of churches in a given area. No national, or even regional, organi-zation beyond each individual association exists today for Old Regular Bap-tist churches and for many other Calvinist and non-Calvinist mountain church traditions such as Regular, United, Primitive, Free Will, and Sepa-rate Baptist, other than associations being in correspondence and, therefore, in fellowship with each other—and not even necessarily with all associations representing their own church tradition within Appalachia. The same ap-plies for non-Baptist church traditions not having organizational structures such as the association, but nonetheless fellowshiping with each other in the same manner, represented by church traditions such as the Church of Christ, as well as by many Holiness churches belonging to some sort of very loose or informal subregional network.

Underscoring the preeminence of local autonomy, many disputes be-tween or within Primitive Baptist churches especially in Appalachia would lead to conflict over the propriety of deferring a dispute to the association.[17] But for many Arminian-based Baptist churches which later formalized in the South as the Southern Baptist Convention, much stricter associational and eventually national control was maintained. This created a wedge between mountain church traditions such as the Old Regular Baptists, with their emphatic rejection of hierarchical institutionalism, and denominational Bap-tists such as the Southern Baptist Convention. That rejection is grounded in fundamental differences in doctrine and polity.

Free church polity is a widely characterizing feature not just of Old Regular Baptists but of mountain church traditions in general. The princi-ple of consensus in mountain religious life is critical to any understanding not just of ministry in the mountains but of how Appalachian people espe-cially in rural areas come to corporate decisions about any and all matters of communal concern. Within the church, a pastor makes an irreversible error in not quietly going to key leaders, women and men, whether or not they hold formal positions of authority such as elder or deacon, before the church gathers to decide about how to proceed on an issue. Outsiders who have come to do ministry in the mountains and who have maintained in their thinking and practice hierarchical structures of authority are doomed to fail-ure. It is key to make sure that old Sister So-and-So, church matriarch, agrees with your intentions. Or that you not start the business meeting until Brother You-Know-Who is able to get there, even if he is late and holds no appoint-ed, elected, or ordained position.[18]

Free church polity has a strong heritage in mountain religious life in

Dorgan suggests the possibility that the 1892 name change to Old Regular Baptist may well have been a formalization of a self-designation that had been in use for some time. Other churches and associations calling themselves Regular Baptist, which held identical doctrinal positions (even matching New Salem's exact wording), nonetheless also employed revivals and Sabbath schools. They were also less traditional in their worship practices, having relegated hymn lining, for which Old Regular Baptists had taken a very strong stand even to the point of disfellowshiping churches that used notated hymnals, to special occasions such as the yearly communion-foot-washing service. In addition, the 1892 resolution rejecting both absolute predestination and "the work of the creature to be essential to eternal salvation" made clear Old Regular Baptists' mediating position between Calvinism and Arminianism on the issue of atonement. Dorgan writes, "Neither redemption nor damnation, therefore, were predestined ends; nevertheless, this didn't leave man in total control of his own salvation, able on his own and at any time to work his way into redemption or will his way there. According to this emerging Old Regular doctrine, man could not . . . simply exercise autonomous power to choose redemption by opting to believe."[21] This mediating position between Calvinism and Arminianism maintained the centrality of grace itself as it was understood in earlier centuries in American religious history, an understanding shared by nearly all mountain church traditions.

For Old Regular Baptists, all people are in a state of original sin from which they cannot escape simply by a "decision for Christ," as evangelical Protestants have come to express it. Instead, all people are personally called to "repentance and belief," and this call constitutes their "election by grace." It is by grace—not by a rational act of will—that one responds to that call, "sealed with the Holy Spirit of promise." Christ's atonement is for those who, by a movement of the Holy Spirit, respond to that call. No one is excluded by preordained election. As Howard Dorgan has determined, in 1905 New Salem's associational minutes formalized this doctrine of atonement. Their formalization represented in writing what had long been the normative position of a majority of mountain church traditions, be they Calvinist or Arminian, striking a mediating position between the two:

> 3. We believe in the doctrine of election by grace, for by grace ye are saved through faith.
> 4. We believe in the doctrine of original sin, and of man's inability to recover himself from the fallen state he is in by nature; therefore the Savior is needed for our redemption.
> 5. We believe that sinners are called to repentance and belief in the gospel and regeneration of the same, and sealed with the Holy Spirit of promise, and none shall fall away and be lost. . . .

13. None of the above Articles shall be so considered as to hold with particular election and reprobation so as to make God partial, directly or indirectly.[22]

Mountain church traditions that were "general" or "universal" in their atonement doctrines would be strongly in tune with the substance that the faith statements of the Old Regular Baptists helped to crystallize. As a consequence, the free-will/human-initiative aspect of fully developed Arminianism did not advance to the forefront of non-Calvinist traditions. They shared instead a common emphasis on the preeminence of grace and the Holy Spirit that governed their everyday faith and was magnified in their worship lives where ardent traditions of religious experience in a communal setting were a very large part of these doctrinal legacies.

In their 1905 articles of faith, the New Salem Association of Old Regular Baptists thus captured in writing the essence of what had long been the normative theological position of Appalachia's mountain church traditions, which had been flourishing since the earliest years of the nineteenth century. Grace and the Holy Spirit, mediating the centrality of religious experience in their worship lives, from the nature of the conversion experience itself to expressive and ecstatic worship practices, have continued to be the shared bedrock of belief and practice for nearly all mountain church traditions, regardless of other ideological and theological distinctions.

This Old Regular Baptist understanding of the nature of grace—of God's initiative and human cooperation—and the role the Holy Spirit plays in the administration of God's grace is, therefore, a hallmark not just of Old Regular Baptists but of almost all of mountain religious life. A telling example is that mountain Free Will Baptist churches still express this view of grace in matters such as revivals, precluding any prearrangement or planning to make them happen, despite their early historical position on general atonement. Such an understanding of grace places them much closer to Jonathan Edwards than to Charles Grandison Finney. The same is true for most independent Holiness churches and independent Missionary Baptist churches, as well as other church traditions characteristic of Appalachian mountain religion. Today the doctrinal centrality of grace, and its mediation by the Holy Spirit as manifested by religious experience, is the premier feature distinguishing mountain religious life from what became in the early nineteenth century the most significant theological features of American Protestantism. In the twentieth century, American Protestantism's defining theological emphases have culminated on the one hand in a liberal tradition focused on social justice theology and social action, and on the other in the widely held and highly aggressive evangelical interpretations of the role of free will and rational decision for acquiring souls "won" or "saved" for Christ. In order to

Churches always have available some form of water, either "a communal water bucket and dipper," more often a portable water cooler with styrofoam or plastic cups shared by the congregation. The water cooler will be either up by the pulpit or in the back, and people will get a drink at any point of the worship service. Often a small container of rock candy or peppermints is placed on the stand, and children as well as others will help themselves in the midst of the preaching. As Short observes, "anyone may come and go at will during the service," and this is "in no way considered a breach of etiquette." As we have seen with Brother Absalom's composite service, worship is not about rigid, programmatic church behavior. Participants are meant to be physically at ease. Indeed, there is a practicality and common sense about this at-easement in mountain worship services, which last an average of three hours. In many, many church houses of all mountain church traditions closest to the center of the spectrum, pews will have a scattering of pillows, often handmade.

Again, like all mountain preachers, Old Regular Baptist elders are "called" by God, not equipped by a seminary education. They are accorded great respect, and rely not on any extensive sermon preparation but solely on a comprehensive oral memory of the Bible and "a double portion of the Sweet Spirit," both of which are indispensable to a successful "preaching." They receive no pay, but assume whatever costs their ministry incurs. A full day's travel may be required to get to a preaching appointment, and the time and expense are given up as a gift to God.

The practice of hymn lining—where a precentor (an elder or deacon) chants unaccompanied two lines of a hymn at a quick pace and then the congregation sings the same lines at a much slower, more drawn-out pace (also unaccompanied by any musical instruments)—was predominant among the Welsh American churches of seventeenth- and eighteenth-century America as well as in Puritan churches and goes back to sixteenth-century Scotland and England.[14] Earlier observers of mountain religious life, demonstrating how quickly conscious historical memory evaporated in the larger religious culture, characterized such a singing style as "ignorant." Wrote one home missionary in western North Carolina in 1891, "Some of them are very ignorant, very few can read, and so the hymn is 'deaconed' off, two lines at a time, and they sing it in a dragging minor tone; there is a sad undertone in all of their singing, which seems to me like a wail of their past oppressions."[15] Hymn lining or some version of it was a widespread practice in mountain churches of nearly all traditions in the nineteenth century, in part because of the absence of songbooks. Today it is a practice that persists in the United States among white Christians only in Appalachia and only among the Old Regular Baptists in particular, in some Primitive Baptist and Regular Baptist churches, as well as in many African-American Baptist churches throughout Appalachia and the rural South.[16]

Short observes that the practice of hymn lining in Old Regular Baptist churches today has nothing to do with the absence of hymnals; rather, it has to do with melodies following no standard notation, having "depended on the oral tradition for their continuation. The melodies are closely 'modal' and are hard to follow using the standard scale of music. Without drastic changes they cannot be translated for musical accompaniment. Although there are now abundant songbooks, they contain only words, no music. The songs maintain the 'long meter' tradition with great emphasis on feeling rather than rhythm. To some, the sound is melancholy and mournful; for others, it is a glimpse into the very soul of man."[17] Although the analogy may seem contrived and superficial to those who have never heard Old Regular Baptist hymn lining, in fact the sound is very much like the droning of bagpipes in a human voice.

Frequently a preacher will be "sung down" by the congregation. Short attributes this to long-windedness or a disjointed sermon that fails to catch the flowing power expected. Dorgan has observed that this may have been true in the past, and is sometimes still the case, but today the congregational-preaching dynamic is much more complex. Indeed, evidence strongly indicates that this has been the norm reaching well back into the early nineteenth century as a tradition shared with plain-folk camp-meeting religion, if not earlier through Baptist revival culture. Today in Old Regular Baptist services, when the first preacher especially reaches a point of exuberance and some in the congregation have started shouting, an elder will begin lining a hymn which others in the congregation will follow. The preaching, shouting, and hymn lining continue together apace, with the exhorter increasing his volume "and the shouters, further stimulated by the volume and intensity of everything else, will reach for a more forceful level of expression."[18]

"Singing down" a preacher is a competition of sound dynamics, with each expression—the preaching, shouting, and hymn lining—providing a counterforce. It involves an intricate sense of timing that younger, less-skilled preachers learn over a period of years. By the second or third couplet of the lined hymn, the congregation is standing, shaking hands, and embracing each another. The preacher, who does not merely place himself behind the pulpit but walks continually about the large stand area, keeps up his chanted sermon, now moving from the stand into the congregation, an integral part of this tradition. After all three sound dynamics have subsided, the rest of the service is ideally positioned for maximum effect centered on the communal experience of conversion, like the early Scots-Irish in their sacramental meetings, not as an act of individuals "getting saved" in a church service but as a collective experience of what heaven must be like. For all, church members and congregation alike, it is a profoundly satisfying, indeed, a thrilling renewal of their "sweet hope." Singing down a preacher thus creates a powerful arena of worship experience.

The Old Regular Baptist preacher's movement from the stand into the congregation at the height of being "sung down" occurs when God's power in the worship service is at its most operative, manifested in the congregation's expressive and ecstatic behavior through this competition of sound dynamics. The preacher's movement from the stand into the congregation at the peak of group emotional impact is also an act of equality, a type of role reversal. It is a practice serving the same purpose of egalitarian norms in a similar competition of sound dynamics that so often prevailed in early nineteenth-century plain-folk camp-meeting religion. While the camp meeting was organized in every aspect to achieve the goal of conversion, it was more than mere method. It expressed for the believers and the seekers what they themselves understood to be the very essence of conversion, expressed in group terms (like the early Scots-Irish) rather than in individual ones.

This vision of what conversion or salvation really is, and what the world is supposed to be like—and a taste in the here and now of what heaven surely must be like—was found in the structure of the camp-meeting night service when the power of God would fall, resulting in "an equality of action" within the service itself. Dickson D. Bruce writes,

> First, the pattern of clergy-initiation—audience-response was broken. *Congregational singing became a constant accompaniment to ministerial exhortations and invitations, leading to an equality of action,* with each performance-group taking the initiative for its own activities. Second, in physical terms *there was also an equality of position as the ministers stepped down from the raised stand to enter the pen where they continued their activities.* The good singers and praying persons also entered the pen, thus canceling out their separation from the mourners while avoiding any further distinction between themselves and the clergy. Third, all accounts indicate that within the pen sexual segregations were either not pronounced or ceased to exist. Hence, no structural distinctions . . . were in force in either physical setting or performance patterns.[19]

At this point the power of God in the camp-meeting service was an immediate reality and at its greatest effect. All people worked together toward completing the experience of conversion for those in the altar, milling about preaching, praying, singing, shouting, crying, comforting, encouraging—all at the same time. For Old Regular Baptists today, who incorporate many of the same expressive and ecstatic behaviors when singing down a preacher, this happy combustion of sight and sound rips through the church house like an electrical current. Its impact is physically tangible, even to observers who, experiencing it for the first time, wonder what just happened.

As Bruce's statement indicates, the role structures and social distinctions of everyday life are purposefully negated through role reversals at this moment of greatest emotional impact. Now clergy are equal to laity and women to men and children to adults, and in this way the experience enacts a vision of what heaven must be like. In most mountain churches today, from Old Regular Baptist to independent Holiness, the role of the mountain preacher is to do what he or she can to help further this vision of heaven as a place of equality—for the mountain preacher works much as a good manager, encouraging all to participate as fully as possible according to their gifts. Such a tradition of egalitarian values embodied in the worship life of mountain church communities, especially among independent Holiness where the heritage of plain-folk camp-meeting religion is most pronounced, could not be further removed from the hierarchical institutionalism that completely overtook the denominations of American Protestantism by the mid-nineteenth century, the effects of which fully infiltrated their worship life.

Short refers to one other practice of particular import to Old Regular Baptists, what both Old Regular and Primitive Baptists refer to as "declaring the church at peace." This is a tradition likely having its origin in the early worship life of Scots-Irish Presbyterians as part of their sacramental meetings, which continued for several days, before the communion elements could be served. It was a process incorporated into these sacramental meetings for worshipers coming to terms with their own sinfulness and fulfilling their need for reconciliation with each other. The Scots-Irish were initially Appalachia's largest immigrant group of settlers and one of its earliest, having profound cultural and religious impact on the region. A large portion of them became mountain Baptists of all stripes.

For Old Regular and Primitive Baptists today, on the Saturday before the annual footwashing the church members meet to see if the church can be declared at peace, or the communion-footwashing service cannot take place the next day. In the Old Regular Baptist community in which Short grew up, as in all Old Regular Baptist church communities, the practice of declaring the church at peace has been generalized, taking place not only on the Saturday before footwashing but on the Saturday before all monthly worship services.[20] Today the question of whether the church is in "love and fellowship" is called at the monthly church conference. Short's statement makes clear the intention of the practice, the same as it was for the Scots-Irish: "The Old Regulars also believe that the church must exist with total harmony among members. Each person must carefully search his heart and mind and there must be full harmony before the services begin. Any dissent must be voiced with the full recognition that the unity of the church is broken, the most grievous state which can exist; but to stifle a question one feels should be asked is just as harmful."[21] This tradition parallels individuals' "falling under conviction of sin" in classic revivalism, but it is tightly focused on a very specific communal context.

"[T]he unity of the church" is equated with a powerful, shared, communal identity and cohesiveness, while at the same time affirming the primary value of the autonomy and integrity of the individual within the community of faith. The priorities accorded the communal and the individual are delicately yet effectively balanced, with neither assuming ascendancy over the other. Given this extraordinary dynamic in mountain worship life, declaring the church at peace by determining if its members are in "love and fellowship"—a tradition stemming at least from early Baptist revival culture which is given its own time the day before the monthly worship service—is much more than the perfunctory confession of sin incorporated into the church service itself as in liturgical traditions.

Melanie Sovine records verbatim the account of a Primitive Baptist woman about one church conference the Saturday before the annual communion-footwashing meeting. Many people, including people from the neighborhood who were not Primitive Baptists, had come to see if the church would be declared at peace, because two church members had been caught up in a well-known, yearlong dispute over a property line. They had even threatened to go to court. Mrs. Carolyn P. Alston recounts,

> They knew these two men had to be peaceful else there couldn't be any foot-washing. So, up gets this Bro. Johnson and up gets this Bro. Jones and they just come "Zip!" right to the middle of the Church. And he says, "Bro. Jones, I'll cut down the tree." And, Bro. [Jones] says, "No, I'll move the fence on the other side of the tree." And, they embraced each other. And, they had been fussing almost a solid year over the boundary line. And, they had fussed . . . and they had threatened to go to court to make them move. They embraced and were in tears. Everybody in the church was in tears. And everybody rejoiced to see how strict the Primitive Baptist Church was.[22]

The emotional content in the practice of declaring the church at peace can be explosive, resulting in powerful expressions of forgiveness, reconciliation, and accommodation.

Sovine's record of this Primitive Baptist account demonstrates the persistence of the original intent of this ritual practice before the Scots-Irish could hold their own annual "sacramental meetings." Short calls the practice of declaring the church at peace the reflection of "a cooperative spirit among people in the communities of Appalachia that has its roots deep in the historical development of the region and, I believe, in the development of the Church."[23] This "cooperative spirit" was lodged especially in the tradition of free church polity's emphasis on consensus in the common governance of church life, with the goal of achieving that consensus in "love and fellowship." We have already seen in a previous chapter an illustration of this cooperative character in the scheduling of local worship services. This "cooperative spirit" Short writes of, rooted in the region's religious history, is a key value normative to Appalachian mountain religion.

As for how Old Regular Baptists are perceived beyond their cultural-geographic bounds, Short recognizes that "in an age of massive cultural and technological advancement, it [the Old Regular Baptist church] is often viewed as a unique sect of backwoods Christians with neither the mentality nor the spirit to survive. But to me, this church, which embodies the spirit of unity, cooperation, harmony and fellowship, is the very essence of Christianity."[24] As we saw in the introduction concerning Spencer's *History of Kentucky Baptists* (1885), Old Time Baptists such as the Old Regular Baptists have often been declared on the verge of demise, their vitality and persistence a baffling mystery to the representatives and historians of powerful denominational traditions with a nationwide identity. But the success of mountain church traditions such as Old Regular Baptist is rooted not in institutional influence and the prestige of national standing but in their system of values, which Short identifies with "the spirit of unity, cooperation, harmony and fellowship . . . the very essence of Christianity." Such success is not quantifiable; it is manifested in mountain church traditions' vitality and larger sociocultural impact on the positive values so often identified by "outsiders" as characteristic of mountain people especially and the Appalachian region more generally.

Indeed, Short concludes his article with this statement: "A part of me refuses to be totally swept up by a culture that has long forgotten the *values* that I have taken for granted most of my life."[25] The conflict between Appalachian mountain religion and the nationally dominant religious culture of American Protestantism, a story indispensable to understanding mountain religion and American Protestantism, is about a fundamental clash of religious values nearly two centuries old. The next chapter, "Baptists, Methodists, and the Radical Decline of Religious Experience, 1825–27," outlines when that clash, growing and intensifying for some years, had clearly and unmistakably crystallized in American religious history.

Short is quite right that mountain church traditions in Appalachia such as Old Regular Baptist are invariably viewed as "dying sects," whether it be in the 1880s or the 1990s, even by those familiar with the Appalachian region and supposedly sympathetic to a regional perspective.[26] Short is also quite right that the "cooperative spirit among people in the communities of

Old Father Nash and Charles Grandison Finney: A Parting of the Ways, 1825–27

Both the American Benevolence movement and its counterresponse, the Anti-Mission movement, were direct products of the Second Great Awakening or Great Revival, for which William G. McLoughlin delineates three phases: 1795–1810 ("Southern camp meetings and Methodist contributions to the Awakening"); 1810–25 ("the conservative New England phase of the Awakening"); and 1825–35 ("the Midwestern, perfectionist contribution to the Awakening").[1] The first phase of the Great Revival took place on the Appalachian frontier of the Old Southwest. The personal experience of "vital religion" in the crisis event of the conversion experience was taken to new heights, and ecstatic worship practices were the most vivid memory of this period, giving birth to the plain-folk camp-meeting religion of the upland South dominated by the Appalachian region. The second phase marked the development of the New Haven Theology at Yale, formulated principally by Nathaniel W. Taylor[2] and advanced by Lyman Beecher, which laid the theological groundwork needed to incorporate the newly raised issues about freedom of the will in the salvation process into the evangelical Calvinism of Jonathan Edwards and Samuel Hopkins. The efforts of the New Haven Theology scholars were instrumental in realizing the full Arminianization of Calvinism, producing a new evangelical consensus that would be strongly in tune with the Jacksonian democracy of the 1830s.

The third phase of the Great Revival spanned the active revival career of Charles Grandison Finney, the "father" of modern revivalism. It centered on efforts to achieve the ecclesiastical reform necessary for the new evangelical consensus to take place in the practical framework of church order and worship. In the words of McLoughlin, it was the period that marked "the process by which revivalism was tamed and harnessed to the institutional structure of the churches."[3] Revivalism, for the first time, was deliberately incorporated into the organizational framework of the denominations of American Protestantism to promote their moral visions and social agendas for the nation—and almost simultaneously for the world beyond the

United States—as well as to ensure their ongoing institutional development through ever-increasing church membership.

The primary tools for such ecclesiastical reform and consensus building were the techniques of revivalism now formulated as a "science." One hundred years after Jonathan Edwards published *A Faithful Narrative of the Surprising Work of God in the Conversion of Many Hundred Souls in Northampton* (1737), about a revival occurring in his church during 1734–35, Finney published his first work, *Lectures on Revivals of Religion* (1835), in which he stated as a matter of fact that, contra Edwards, a revival "is not a miracle, or dependent on a miracle in any sense. It is a purely philosophical [scientific] result of the right use of constituted means—as much so as any other effect produced by the application of means."[4] No longer was a revival understood to be the result of a quickening of the Holy Spirit in a movement of grace, as it had been for James McGready and his Presbyterian congregations in Logan County, Kentucky, who beginning in 1796 had prayed and waited on God for nearly a year before the revival came that gave birth to the Great Revival on the Appalachian frontier. Now revivals were promoted as a product of human initiative and God's cooperation, of organizational advance planning that set the time and place for God's work in revival—a view that would clear the path for Finney's successors in Dwight L. Moody, Billy Sunday, and Billy Graham.

Finney's understanding of revivalism was a product of the New Haven Theology's blending of sectarian piety with eighteenth-century rationalism that caused a complete break with the doctrinal viewpoints undergirding the evangelical Calvinism of Jonathan Edwards. Revivalism was now adapted to the needs of denominational development, a process managed to some extent by Finney's own growing conservatism over the years, but much more so by revivalism's conservative opponents, who recognized its advantages when applied to their own designs. Revivalism was seen by its strongest proponents as being basically incompatible with denominationalism, a product of pietistic radicalism which continued unabated in mountain church traditions of the Appalachian region. Nonetheless, denominations in the East harnessed the engines of revivalism and used its forces to organize churches and increase church membership dramatically over the decades of the nineteenth century. Indeed, the powerful utility of revivalism for organizing immigrant churches in larger eastern cities during this period did not escape the notice of the foreign-born and budding native clergy of the Roman Catholic church.[5]

The active evangelistic career of Charles Grandison Finney from 1825 to 1835 was the consolidation, summation, and transmutation of the trends and practices endemic in the Great Revival, especially as they came to fruition in the East. Finney would provide the "theologization" of the revival in his writings after 1835, especially in his *Lectures to Professing Christians* (1837) and *Lectures on Systematic Theology* (1851). More than any other person or movement, Finney institutionalized revivalism by making it part of the church system of the "western frontier" (that is, western New York State) and eastern cities. He adapted "western revivalism" (that is, the revivalism characteristic of western New York State) to the needs and climate of a large urban apostolate, made it part of the middle-class church experience, and established revival ministry as a new profession of specialists. Opponents and proponents alike attributed the term "new measures" to Finney's revival practices. The term "new measures" was comprehensive, characterizing both the distinctive features of "religious enthusiasm" at a revival meeting and the techniques used to work up and manipulate that enthusiasm (such as the anxious bench and particular prayer or the prayer of faith) with the goal of conversion. Many of Finney's "new measures" were in fact "old measures," adapted from the revival practices he found when he began his evangelistic career in western New York.

Born in Connecticut in 1792 and brought up in western New York State, Finney was a lawyer who converted to Presbyterianism. He was licensed to preach in 1824 and became an itinerant evangelist in western New York, which at that time was still considered very much a part of the frontier. Finney helped to institutionalize the revivalism of New York's western frontier as part of the denominational church system of that region and then in eastern cities, replicating practices strongly characteristic of revivalism on the Appalachian frontier. The settlers of western New York were "go-outers," transplanted Yankees from the hills and mountainous regions of western New England, notably Vermont, western Massachusetts, and northwestern Connecticut. They were people still profoundly affected by the split in the Congregational church during the Great Awakening, and represented the more "enthusiastic" or emotional, "heart religion" strand of the "New Light" side of that religious movement.

"The winter of 1799–1800 was in western New York long called the time of the Great Revival, just as it was in Kentucky," wrote Whitney R. Cross, although the expressive worship experiences recorded there were overall not as intense as those on the Appalachian frontier.[6] Two years later, the Methodist itinerant Lorenzo Dow first visited the western New York village of Western, where Finney would launch his revival career in 1825. "Crazy" Lorenzo returned four more times to Western, up to 1817, preaching revivals and drawing converts. Dow also traveled deep into the Appalachian region, as far as what is now Boone County, West Virginia, where the 1860 census listed several persons named Lorenzo and Lorenza,[7] and local preachers long imitated Dow's asthmatic preaching style.

Small sectarian groups who emigrated from New England played a large role in western New York State "in the development of the distinctive mentality of the region."[8] Christians, whom Cross described as "Unitarian Baptists" (not to be confused with the people called Christians of the Christian Church founded in 1804 as a direct result of the Great Revival in Kentucky), and Free Will Baptists were descended from the Separatists in New England during the Great Awakening. These Free Will Baptists were Benjamin Randall's group, founded in New Hampshire in 1780. However, an earlier group calling themselves the Original Freewill Baptists, identifying themselves with Helwys's congregation of seventeenth-century England, were organized in 1727 in Virginia and North Carolina. "Their peculiar emphases were footwashing, anointing the sick with oil, plural eldership, and the regulation that only male members could hold church office."[9] Appalachian Free Will Baptist churches today are traceable not to Randall's New England group, which is generally much better known in American religious history, but to the Virginia-North Carolina group. What Robert G. Torbet called "their peculiar emphases" have long since been generalized throughout mountain church traditions—plural eldership, footwashing, and anointing with oil.

The New England Free Will Baptists and Christians were strongly in sympathy with each other and provided a large portion of the settlers in western New York, locating primarily in isolated rural areas. Quakers or the Society of Friends also emigrated in large numbers to western New York from the hill country of New England and contributed to many of the religious trends of the region by lending a strong, nonsectarian, pietistic strand of influence. This area of New York State came to be called the "burnt district" or "burned-over district," because of recurrent revivalism up to the time of Finney, who gave wider currency to the expression. Today the southwestern counties of this area bordering on Pennsylvania are included in the Appalachian region by the Appalachian Regional Commission.

When Finney began his career in a series of revivals in and around the village of Western, he was not alone. For two years, from 1825 to 1827, his constant companion was Daniel Nash, Sr., called by all who knew him "Father Nash," the "praying man." Cross wrote, "Old Father Nash had helped Charles Finney distill the desires of backwoods folk of the pioneer era into the measures of the Western Revivals."[10] Nash was the key figure in helping to lay the foundations for Finney's larger reputation in the history of revivalism, not in terms of theology but in terms of the revival practices that initially drew attention to Finney.

Finney first saw Nash at the presbytery meeting which examined Finney for licensing. Nash was himself licensed by the same presbytery and was already an itinerant evangelist. "In 1824, he [Nash] served a congregation of poverty-stricken squatters in the town of Orleans between excursions afield."[11] Nash would maintain his identification with plain, simple people until his death. Finney recorded of their first meeting, "I got in a little late, and saw a man standing in the pulpit speaking to the people, as I supposed. . . . As soon as I reached my seat and listened, I observed that he was praying. I was surprised to see him looking all over the house, as if he were talking to the people; while in fact he was praying to God."[12] This remarkable style of prayer is quite common among mountain people still today. Moreover, when Father Nash prayed privately, he prayed in a loud voice, as many, many mountain people continue to do today. Some claimed you could hear Father Nash half a mile away when he was "alone in secret prayer."[13] When you approach Sister Edna Alexander's home today and she is in private prayer, you can hear her from the road. Lillard G. Rouse, an early Church of God (Cleveland, Tennessee) minister, recorded in his autobiography that police were often called to his home when he lived in towns because he and his family prayed so loudly that it disturbed the neighbors.[14]

Asa Mahan, professor of theology at Oberlin College during Finney's tenure there and principal theologian about the Holy Spirit for the Holiness movement, wrote in his autobiography, "It is hardly presumptuous, I judge, to express the belief that the world now feels, and ever will feel, the influence of the prayers of father Nash, that holy man, who was at last found in his closet, on his knees dead before God; a very fitting place and condition for such a man to die in."[15] Mahan's tribute underscored the respect widely accorded Father Nash, "that holy man," and the regard—indeed, deep affection—many had for him. Moreover, Mahan's words indicate that, above all else, Nash was known best and appreciated most for his gift of prayer, to which Mahan accorded "wide influence," something that "the world now feels, and ever will feel."

Luther Myrick, Nash's companion in the last years of his life and by some designated heir to Finney on the New York western frontier, presented in his letter to Finney about Nash's death a different account from Mahan's, but stated nonetheless that "His praying killed him. He prayed more & far more before he died than he ever did before" (1832).[16] It was Nash who promoted the revival practice of "particular prayer" or the "prayer of faith"—speaking in prayer to God very specifically about people and events, needs and joys—one of the "new measures" almost universally attributed to Finney. Finney himself relied heavily on Nash's prayers once he left western New York for his revival career in eastern cities. As but one instance, in the fall of 1828, Finney requested that Nash pray for his work in Philadelphia and the campaign planned for Washington, D.C. In his letter of reply, Nash protested that since he no longer traveled with Finney, he did not know the specifics of what needed to be prayed for. Nonetheless, he gave assurances that he would pray as best he could for Finney and his work.[17] In all of his letters to Finney after 1827, Nash repeatedly assured him that he would continue to pray for him, often expressing a strong desire for them to be together again so that Finney could preach while Nash prayed: "Charles, I am a feeble old man, & have not more than half the strength that I had in Gouverneur. I need you to do the preaching, & let me stand by, & pray" (1828).[18]

Both Mahan and Finney recorded Nash's practice of keeping "praying lists" for people and mission stations throughout the world. Mahan even went so far as to claim that dates and places Nash recorded in his journal for specific prayer for revival in fact resulted in revival: "In turning to the *Missionary Herald*, it was found there recorded, that at the time and day specified [in Nash's journal] a revival of religion actually commenced in each station in succession; the date of the prayer and the commencement of the revival being, in every case, exactly coincident."[19] Nash's practice of keeping what Finney described as "'a praying list,' as he called it, of the names of persons whom he made subjects of prayer every day, and sometimes many times a day"[20] is highly reminiscent of particular or specific prayer practices characteristic of many mountain people today. Like Father Nash, Brother Charlie Bry Phillips (d. 1975), an independent Missionary Baptist preacher from Rabun County, Georgia (home of *Foxfire* magazine), was renowned for his praying and was called upon for prayer far and wide by ordinary people and religious leaders alike throughout his ministry. He went daily to a large rock on his property for intensive prayer. Instead of a "praying list," he used pebbles as markers for the people for whom he prayed.[21]

One contemporary (and unsympathetic) account of how Father Nash actually prayed is especially revealing:

> This Mr. Nash, by way of pre-eminence, was called *Father Nash, the praying man.* We ought, therefore, to notice him a little. He was indeed wonderful for praying; and perhaps exceeded all others in the frequent repetition of, "O, God Almighty.—Come, God almighty—come down—break in upon them." After continuing these strains, sometimes for a whole hour, alternately upon his knees, but more frequently sitting back upon his heels; and writhing in agony, throwing himself as far back as he could, and recover; and then bringing his head forward into his chair, rising and bringing the weight of his fists to bear upon it, and give emphasis to his expressions; after continuing thus *agonized* in prayer, as he called it, for a whole hour, he would, sometimes, pitch forward into his chair, sometimes throw himself backwards—sometimes rise and walk as though hurried with a restless impetus, and cry "O! God! O! God! O! God!" Thus much for the praying man.[22]

J. Brockway, the author of this 1827 account, offered examples of his own staid prayers at prayer meetings in Troy, New York, as a specific rebuke to such seemingly emotional extravagances. Impassioned, physical prayer is

reflected in their worship lives, universally mountain people strongly anticipate that "holy happy meeting" where they will be united again with their
friends and loved ones and where, true to their worship practices here on
earth, they too will "soar, & shout, & sing, & make the arches of heaven to
ring."

Father Nash's lyrical language was appreciated by others, who nonetheless also voiced reservations. P. H. Fowler quoted the words of a Dr. Aiken,
who described Father Nash as having a stronger personal identification with
the laity than with the profession of the ministry: "'Father Nash,' Dr. Aiken
writes, 'was more of a layman than a minister. His forte lay in the prayer
meeting. Of deep piety, but little education, his language was sometimes too
familiar and apparently irreverent and repulsive.'"[27] This assessment of Nash
is characteristic of the assessment of many ministers in the Appalachian region, but most especially of mountain preachers, including those with some
sort of credentials such as being licensed or ordained by a legally incorporated church. This strong identification with the laity is a product of the leveling influence of ministry in the mountains where preachers and pastors
are on a par with those to whom they minister; it is a product of resistance
to ministry as a profession set apart. That Father Nash, licensed to preach
by a presbytery and a faithful attendee of presbytery and synod meetings,
was perceived as more of a layperson than a minister is extremely telling
about the way he conducted himself and about the people with whom he
identified. Indeed, in one of his last letters to Finney he invited Finney to
come stay with him in the home of "some of my old country folks" (1831).[28]

Fowler then added his own assessment of Nash's importance in
Finney's earliest work: "Father Nash became a companion of Mr. Finney
in his revival services *and was largely relied upon by him for their effectiveness.*"[29] Fowler's judgment that Finney relied on Nash for the "effectiveness"
of his "revival services" is extremely telling about how widely Nash was
regarded as being integral, if not indispensable, to Finney's earliest work.
Indeed, it is a contemporary assessment that some twentieth-century scholars such as Cross concur with. However, most Finney scholars, notably
McLoughlin, overlook or ignore Nash's influence and significance in the
western New York revivals that led up to Finney's confrontation with New
Haven Theology ministers at the 1827 New Lebanon Convention, which
set Finney on the path to his larger reputation in the history of revivalism.
But it was the revival work in western New York with Father Nash that
brought Finney to that confrontation.

Cross observed that Finney's principal contribution in the western New
York campaigns was not a theology but a set of practices that came to be
called "new measures." The new measures identified with Finney's work
would soon meet the needs of revivals in larger towns and cities and would

be instrumental in helping to popularize the New Haven Theology. As Cross pointed out, these new measures were a product of frontier revivalism and could be attributed no more to Nash than to Finney. They were the tools for increasing the excitement and intensity thought necessary to vital religion, especially in the conversion experience, the object of revivalism. These practices were extremely similar to those of the eighteenth-century Great Awakening that troubled the better-educated and more sophisticated because of the emotional vulnerability they encouraged. Moreover, the Great Revival on the Appalachian frontier had developed and intensified these practices, not the least of which was the sanctity of common people's speech when under the influence of the Holy Spirit. Women and men alike, ordained or not, were allowed to testify, a practice that was often very close to, if not indistinguishable from, preaching. In the Nash-Finney campaigns, women were permitted and encouraged to testify during prayer meetings, a practice, also characteristic of mountain religion throughout its history, that would be challenged in particular at the New Lebanon Convention. Cross wrote about these "new measures" in the Nash-Finney campaigns, "Essentially, they rose from experience. But the likelihood is that Finney learned more from this old veteran of the backwoods than he taught in return. Father Nash served as lieutenant and interpreter of experience, the chief instructor."[30]

Whereas Nash was the interpreter of experience, "the chief instructor," Finney was the preacher who was the principal focus of attention in the western New York campaigns. Finney's eloquence and his training as a lawyer served him well. As the Nash-Finney revival campaigns gained rapid momentum, opposition began to arise strongly and quickly, opposition that focused almost exclusively on Finney. Protests were lodged with ecclesiastical authorities and other leading ministers of the day. When Finney's reputation reached such a point that it not only caught the notice of New Haven Theology ministers but alarmed them, he was called to a confrontation to defend the right order and propriety of his "new measures." This was held in New Lebanon, New York, in July 1827, and became known as the New Lebanon Convention. The meeting had to do less with a confrontation over theological principles, about which all parties involved were actually in fundamental agreement, than with concern over revival practices or "techniques." A group of "western" ministers of some standing came to uphold Finney's position, and New England ministers, notably Asahel Nettleton, came to oppose him. Lyman Beecher also was of the New England group, but apparently he came prepared to compromise.

All parties at the New Lebanon Convention were in agreement with one resolution in particular: "The idea that God ordinarily works independently of human instrumentality, or without reference to the adaptation of means to ends, is unscriptural."[31] The demise of evangelical Calvinism with regard

odists" in Appalachia that Frank Richardson of Holston Conference had written about: "Revivals among the early Methodists were spontaneous. . . . [T]hey never set a time for the Lord to revive his work. They would have considered such a suggestion sacrilegious. They esteemed that the prerogative of the Lord, and were constantly praying that *God's set time* to favor Zion might come."[37]

Apparently the sinners appealed to in Rome still held to the revival tradition centered on grace, on God's initiative in the experience of salvation, that was quite pronounced throughout the United States east of the Mississippi River until the early years of the nineteenth century. The pamphlet recounted that these sinners were "often" protesting, "We cannot change our own hearts," clearly intimating that they understood that only God could change their hearts, that only divine grace was the operative factor in the experience of salvation. But they were told to "submit," to "repent," to "believe on the Lord Jesus Christ, or be damned." Human initiative through self-assertion, taking control over their own salvation, indeed, actually *willing* their way to salvation as an act of personal decision—with "no allowance given to wait God's time"—had become the accepted norm for their religious leaders. These sinners' understanding of grace was viewed by the new revivalists as a "false dependence [which] was torn away as soon as possible." Evangelical Calvinism was now totally displaced by the New Haven Theology of fully Arminianized Calvinism upholding free will and rational decision in the experience of conversion. These new theological developments Finney wed to western New York revival practices, given initial form on the Appalachian frontier, which he mastered with the guidance and example of Father Nash. Accommodating these practices to the new theological worldview and its concomitant model of humanness—and also of divinity—gave new meaning to the question of who God is and who people are in relation to God and to each other.

In the years before his death, either in December 1831 or January 1832, Nash continued his correspondence with Finney. His letters from the late 1820s showed his initial expectation that Finney's revival work for the salvation of souls was gaining an even firmer footing as it reached outward beyond the land of its planting, only to cool when Nash became aware that Finney preferred to distance himself from the revival work that had launched his reputation, and from his prior relationship with Nash, while still relying on Nash's prayers for his work. Nash was able to warn Finney against his growing pride in ways other correspondents did not dare or would not think to, calling him back to the time when his intentions as a rural itinerant evangelist—tending the needs of villages, hamlets, and small towns—were uncluttered by the foibles of ambition and self-satisfaction. While continuing to call on Finney to preach while he prayed, Nash invited Finney back to conduct revivals on his old turf, as much for Finney's own good as for the region's: "I hardly think you would find it as difficult to breath[e] here, as it is in 'the great city.' I think if God should give you leave to spend six months in this region, it would increase your spiritual strength" (1828).[38] But Finney had already gone too far by this time to consider retracing his steps.

While Finney was becoming known and imitated for techniques such as the handwritten sermon "skeletons" which he used from the pulpit, Nash cautioned against his using them while actually preaching: "By the by—as a friend of Jesus Christ, I should advise you to be careful about using skeletons in preaching. Whatever may be the effect on you I am persuaded they would injure my spirituality; & if I be not spiritual, I am worse than nothing. If you choose to write them, for the sake of digesting a subject, write. If you wish to look at them at home, to refresh your memory, do it; but, when you preach, throw yourself entirely on God" (1831).[39] Nash's standard was spontaneous preaching from oral memory and the inspiration of the Holy Spirit ("throw yourself entirely on God"), like mountain preachers of his time and today. He saw great harm to Finney's "spirituality" and to the effect on his listeners if his sermons did not come directly from the Spirit's inspiration. Preparation was not the issue. The act of preaching under divine inspiration—unencumbered by "skeletons," notes, outlines, or completely written-out texts taken into the pulpit as a means of predetermined control over the preaching event—was what concerned Nash. Nash's warning was without effect. In Finney's memoirs, in the 1908 edition, a facsimile of one of his sermon "skeletons" was included. Finney was now totally committed to an Arminian-based model of preaching and revival ministry, a model which he, more than anyone else, was the most responsible for consolidating, and which was now far removed from Nash's grace-centered, Holy Ghost-guided model.

Because of the giant shadow Finney cast over nineteenth-century church life and denominationalism—which reaches well into the twentieth century through his equally tall progeny, culminating in the unparalleled revival work of Billy Graham—little has been written about Nash by scholars other than Cross. Here it has been important for us to explore Nash's correspondence and contemporary accounts in order to create a sense of his work and his spirituality, and of how he was perceived on his own account as well as in relation to Finney. Other material by and about Nash, notably a popular series of columns he wrote anonymously about prayer in the *New York Evangelist*, awaits examination. The subjects scholars choose to focus on, and the obscure records that escape their notice, do not reflect or determine actual historical importance. The overall absence of a scholarly portrayal of Nash in relation to Finney mirrors precisely the seeming obscurity of Appalachian mountain religion in relation to the giant shadow cast by American Protestantism on the national landscape.

Nonetheless, in many important aspects the relationship of Nash and Finney represented a critical juncture in the history of revivalism through the clear emergence in their relationship of the features that divided mainstream American Protestantism from Appalachian mountain religion. Father Nash remained to the end of his days among his "old country folks" in western New York, basically unnoticed in the history of that period, although his impact on those who knew him, including Finney, was apparently great. Finney went on to bigger and better things in the history of nineteenth-century Protestantism, and his impact and reputation are writ large today in a significant body of scholarship.

Perhaps the symbolic key to the primary differences between Appalachian mountain religion and what became the dominant religious culture of the United States is found in one of the letters Nash wrote to Finney. Recall that Nash invited Finney back to conduct revivals on his old turf: "I hardly think you would find it as difficult to breath[e] here, as it is in 'the great city.' I think if God should give you leave to spend six months in this region, it would increase your spiritual strength." It is very striking that Father Nash had no doubt that "this region," the western frontier of New York still so similar to the environmental, social, and religious characteristics of the Appalachian frontier, could only be a source of spiritual renewal for Finney. The land itself, "this region," harbored a nurturing religious ethos.

In later letters, Nash continued to encourage Finney to hold a series of revivals once again in western New York. However, Finney never returned to the region where his career began. How could he return? Finney had appropriated, adapted, and ultimately transformed the traditions of revival religiosity he had learned through and with Father Nash on New York's western frontier. He was now the apostle of a mode of revival religiosity no longer suited to the region that had birthed it. Instead, Finney's revival religiosity and the urbanized church people to whom it was directed were wedded to the religious values of the New Haven Theology. The traditions of the doctrines of grace and the Holy Spirit that had galvanized the revivalism of the eighteenth century expressed a vision of God's initiative and human cooperation, and with it a very specific understanding of who people are in relation to God and to each other. Finney's revivalism, centered on human initiative and God's cooperation, expressed a different vision of humanness, one of more fragmentary individuality within the context of community and one of more immediate and direct individual control both in this world and the next.

The mountain religious emphasis upon the centrality of grace in the conversion experience sums up within itself an affirmation of the autonomy of the individual within the context of community, but equally so the centrality of community in the life of the individual. Grace is present in all places, but it is maximized in the communal setting of worship. All the individual threads are an inseparable part of the fabric they help to create, both in the church house and in the everyday life of the larger community. This social construct is as much a product of the religious values defining the uniqueness of the regional religious tradition that is Appalachian mountain religion as of any other factor we might take into account. Those values are embodied in mountain religion by the particular worship practices, belief systems, religious experiences, and church traditions that define it.

With the New Lebanon Convention of 1827, where Finney won his credibility with the leading eastern theologians and churchmen of his day, the path toward the institutionalization of revivalism was assured and with it the institutionalization of the nature of the conversion experience itself. The energies of the conversion experience were now channeled into church-based social action, from temperance to abolitionism, embodying the denominations' institutional constructs created to promote their ideal moral vision and ideal social order, not only for themselves but for all Americans, indeed, for all the world. Through Finney-esque revivalism, the New Haven Theology had found its perfect vehicle for transmitting into the practical framework of church order and worship its evangelical Arminianism, in which theological emphasis on grace and humility took a back seat to individual merit and achievement. As Nash commented to one correspondent, "As to the convention, I was always opposed to it. I think now that it had its foundation in carnal policy. . . . I do not think the prospect for revival is as good now as it was before that meeting." Now that revivalism had been adapted to the needs of denominational development, the pietistic radicalism of mountain religious life would continue to see its own long-lived traditions of revivalism—centered on the communal setting of the conversion experience understood to be a gracious act of God rather than a human achievement—as basically incompatible with denominationalism.

Mountain religion's revivalist religiosity had been normative in the earlier awakenings that defined and directed the religious culture of much of the nation before the denominations of American Protestantism consciously and aggressively moved toward the organizational institutionalism that would consolidate their national role in determining the social order for others. With it they embraced an accompanying shift in their basic system of values. Like Nash in relation to Finney, mountain religion's foundational difference in values was a product not of stagnation but of active choice, an autonomy of self-determination that has continued to thrive. Along with those values have continued to wax the loudly reverberating historical echoes of earlier emphases in American Christianity that mountain religion now uniquely affirms through its characteristic church traditions and religious life.

The relationship of Old Father Nash and Charles Grandison Finney represented a critical juncture in the history of revivalism because it symbolically embodied the historical relationship of Appalachian mountain religion with what became the dominant religious culture of the United States. Indeed, the years 1825–27, when Nash and Finney worked together, culminated in their parting of the ways, a moment of signal importance in the history of American Christianity because of what it represented in microcosm. Although superficially it was Finney who left behind Nash and the frontier of western New York, Nash also declined to follow, which again was a choice, a decision he made not out of a willful parochialism but because Finney's religious values were now contrary to his own. Nash, however, continued to love Finney and to pray for him, offering words of caution as he saw fit in their ongoing correspondence. Indeed, Nash was Finney's radical sign of contradiction. Finney listened, but he did not heed.

On a far larger scale, Nash's actions paralleled at exactly the same time mountain religion's choices and the decisions it made in contradistinction to the directions chosen by the nation's dominant religious culture. The invisibility of Nash in terms of historical prominence once Finney moved on to the fields that would make his national reputation also paralleled mountain religion's own invisibility in the historical record once American Protestantism made theological and institutional choices that were fundamentally contrary to mountain religion's basic identity. Like Nash and Finney, mountain religion and American Protestantism have also had an "ongoing correspondence," one that has lasted nearly two centuries and made up of the history of their interaction with each other. And, like Nash with Finney, mountain religion was and continues to be American Protestantism's radical sign of contradiction.

The Nash-Finney revival campaigns of 1825–27 mark the point by which Appalachian mountain religion, now a fully developed regional religious tradition, had completely differentiated itself from what was so quickly becoming the dominant religious culture of the United States. Indeed, McLoughlin stated that American Protestantism was "the national religion of the United States" by 1840, grounded in the evangelical consensus achieved by that time, ushered in especially by the earlier work of Taylor, Beecher, and Finney.[40] Both Old Father Nash and Appalachian mountain religion were relegated to a tunnel of silence in the writing of American religious history, despite the unimpeachable indebtedness to them of both a personage such as Finney and the national religious culture he came to represent.

PART 2

Roots of Mountain Religiosity

"Religiosity" is a term fixed in many people's minds as meaning "excessive-ly, obtrusively religious." Indeed, one Congregationalist home missions of-ficial in the late nineteenth century, who was otherwise sympathetic to moun-tain religion, nonetheless chastised it for having too "much of religiosity" (1891). At the same time, for many the primary meaning of religiosity, ac-cording to the *Oxford American Dictionary*, is "the state of being religious," expanding religiosity to include "religiousness, religious feeling or sentiment," according to the *Oxford English Dictionary*—religious life. Mountain religious life is characterized by an anti-organizational or anti-institutional outlook that stands in contrast to denominationalism. This does not make "denom-inationalism" a dirty word in the study of Appalachian mountain religion. But it does make the point that denominationalism as the most distinctive institutional tradition of American religious history is not particularly use-ful in understanding mountain religious life, except as a point of contrast. It is, however, indispensable to understanding the nearly two hundred year history of interaction governing the relationship between mountain religion and American Protestantism.

Sidney Mead called denominationalism the child "living in the house of religious freedom."[1] All vestiges of any earlier intention to preserve reli-gious uniformity at the national level disappeared with the enactment of the Constitution (1787) and the First Amendment (1791). New types of church organization were needed to accommodate the requirements of religious free-dom. In traditional European terminology, a church was primarily confes-sional and territorial (state established), whereas a sect was an exclusive re-ligious group set over against the establishment as dissenters. The presence of more than one establishment in the American colonies and the fact of religious pluralism weakened the distinction between church and sect, left and right wings. In the northern colonies all but Congregational churches were dissenters, be they Anglicans (right wing) or Baptists (left wing). In the southern colonies all but Anglican churches were dissenters, be they Pres-byterians (right wing) or Quakers (left wing). As a result, a historical merg-ing of organizational forms or patterns took place. Together with such dis-tinctive features of the American environment as the "frontier," these mingled into different configurations. "The result was a complex pattern of religious thought and institutional life that was peculiarly 'American,' and is proba-

half of the nineteenth century. But we have presented aspects of plain-folk camp-meeting religion in preceding chapters (unlike the other three streams of religious movements explored in this section), and will continue to do so throughout the rest of the book, giving it special attention in "Mountain Religion and the Holiness-Pentecostal Movements" in part 3.

The contrast between mountain religion and denominationalism comes full circle in the concluding chapter of this section, bringing us into the last decade of the twentieth century. A West Virginia Methodist minister's 1992 characterization of mountain religious culture as "Indian headdresses," quaint but not in the least representative of what "religion in Appalachia" is actually like today, gives a vivid illustration of how American Protestantism continues to view the religious life unique to Appalachia's mountain regions, taking into account the distinctive twist added by those who are both Appalachian born and bred and part of the leadership of the Protestant mainstream in Appalachia.

Mountain Religion and Denominationalism: Campbell, Hooker, and Albanese

Olive Dame Campbell prepared for publication the notes her husband, John C. Campbell, left upon his death in 1919 for the creation of the first and what many still consider the best comprehensive survey and portrait of the Appalachian region, *The Southern Highlander & His Homeland* (1921). John C. Campbell had been a Congregationalist home missionary assigned full-time to the Appalachian region beginning in 1896 by the American Missionary Association. Later he became secretary of the Southern Highland Division of the Russell Sage Foundation, which funded his social survey work for the creation of *The Southern Highlander & His Homeland*. As Rupert Vance states in his foreword to the 1969 reprint, "This was a period when many felt that unless home missions, private church academies, and outside philanthropy were adequate to save the mountain people from stagnation and isolation they could not be saved."[1]

Denominational home mission literature on Appalachia and the mission to "mountain whites" had been extensive before Campbell began his survey work and he himself was frustrated by the parochialism of these efforts.[2] In 1913, he founded the Conference of Southern Mountain Workers, later called the Council of the Southern Mountains. The purpose of the conference was to coordinate the uplift endeavors of competing benevolent agencies— church and secular alike—and minimize their duplication of efforts, to channel information to field-workers who frequently were quite ignorant about the people and the region they sought to assist, and to provide outreach to national agencies during the time of America's burgeoning philanthropic activity and the move toward "federation" for collective efforts. But this forms another part of the history of Appalachian mountain religion which we will explore in part 4, "The Home Mission to 'Mountain Whites.'"

Campbell's own religious sensibilities most likely were a significant factor in his pronounced awareness of the importance of mountain religion for mountain people. The home mission literature had devoted material not so much to religious life and traditions unique to Appalachia as to the perceived social and evangelistic needs of Appalachian people, the assumption being

For one so little versed in reading he [the mountaineer] has a remarkable knowledge of the Scriptures. He "loves" to "read after" them, and to "study on" them. Even when nearly illiterate he often has a real appreciation of the beauty of their language and of human nature as revealed in their pages, as well as ingenious interpretations or deductions to draw from the context. (p. 177)

Visions, dreams, and omens have a part in the life of the people, especially in the life of the older women. (p. 180)

. . . special reference should be made to these older men [native mountain preachers], not only because of their numbers through the rural sections but because they represent one of the strong links with the past which here in the Highlands have not yet been broken.
    Most of the older ministers have an extremely limited education; very few have received any scholastic training for their calling. They are usually older men of native ability who still have much influence over the older people—influence which they exercise by reason of the fact that they have received what they themselves, and their people as well, believe to be a divine call to preach. Their mission is not that of the priest but of the prophet, serving often with little or no pay. (p. 181)

Among these preachers are many who have grown tender through experience and have a firm hold on the deeper things of life. They have, too, keen insight and a knowledge of human nature, dramatic power, and an ability to touch responsive chords in the hearts of their hearers—a combination of endowments which makes them leaders not to be ignored in any effort for betterment. (p. 182)[6]

Like other sensitive observers, Campbell picked up on the central place of the "heart" in mountain religion and the pronounced role of intuitive discernment and nonrational religious experience. He also resoundingly affirmed the ministry of traditional mountain preachers, be they literate or not—as did the Presbyterian Hamilton W. Pierson when writing about his work in the Appalachian wilderness of the 1850s (see chapter 16, "In the Brush")—stating that they are "leaders *not* to be ignored in any effort for betterment." Campbell's admonition continues to be ignored.
    Campbell gave particular attention to the distinctive music traditions of mountain worship life, writing, "The congregation sways to and fro, in part from the rhythm of the music, in part to express the inner surge of feeling aroused by the exhortations of the preacher and the tense emotional atmosphere. It is but a step from this to sobs and tears, to shouting, screaming, jumping up and down, and even to more violent manifestations" (pp. 183–87, quotation on p. 187). Like Emma Bell Miles describing Brother Absalom's service, Campbell also made clear that strong, physical-emotional worship traditions in mountain religious life were in no way limited to Holiness-Pen-

tecostal churches (p. 172).[7] Instead, he confirmed the central place of ecstatic and expressive behavior in the worship environment, echoing Pierson, who also observed in the worship life of the Appalachian wilderness in the 1850s this "swaying to and fro" to the music and the preacher's exhortations, and the shift it triggered to vibrant emotional expression in worship. Campbell then quoted Miles, "herself a mountaineer," and the quotation he chose was one of Miles's most revealing when she wrote about how "we of the mountains are becoming more sensitive year by year. It ought not to be so—God knows what the old ceremonies mean to those who take part in them" (pp. 187–88).

Campbell noted the compelling impact of mountain religious culture on mountain churches belonging to mainstream Protestant traditions such as the Methodists and Southern Baptists, stating that these churches "are *not* to be taken as the measure of the denomination in more accessible regions within and without the Highlands" (pp. 188–89, emphasis added). The religious life of larger towns, urban centers, and broad valleys could not, and should not, be equated with mountain religious life, even for mountain churches affiliated with prominent denominations. Campbell called American-born ministers not native to the region who came to serve their denominations' churches in the mountains "foreign ministers," picking up on the vocabulary mountain people used to characterize them. Campbell declared, "A too general tendency prevails on the part of both pastors and teachers to force upon the mountain people modes and methods natural in other regions but unnatural to the mountaineer. . . . If foreign ministers would follow so far as they conscientiously could the practices that have through long association become somewhat sacred to the mountaineer, and beautify rather than abolish these, there would be an increase in church membership and prestige" (p. 190). Here Campbell was making a direct appeal for denominational ministers and church workers to take seriously, and to esteem, mountain religious culture as a valid regional religious tradition of paramount importance to mountain people with its own historical integrity and "beauty." Only then could they hope for "an increase in church membership and prestige" in Appalachia's mountain regions.

Campbell used baptism by immersion as one example of mountain worship practices of which "foreign ministers" needed to be especially respectful. Perhaps as a model of what Campbell had in mind, one autobiography by a Methodist minister who recalled his four years of work between 1933 and 1937 in the Gauley River area of Nicholas County, West Virginia, gave an account of what he termed "A Most Un-Usual Baptism":

"No, I can't wait until next third Sunday, and I don't want to be baptized by sprinkling, either. I want to be baptized by immersion right today!"

It was the voice of Mr. Asa Stull. He had started long before day-break and had walked the eight miles from Nettie to the Parsonage at Canvas, and for no other purpose than to be baptized. I tried to reason with him that it would be better to wait until my appointment at his church on the next third Sunday of the month, and that others would go with us to help with the service. Perhaps there would be others desiring to be baptized by immersion along with him. But he insisted that it was urgent, and he quoted some passages of the Bible that he had been thinking about. He would have no part of any procrastination.

Without further debate, and deeply appreciative of Mr. Stull's sincerity, we started to Deepwell, on Deer Creek, where I had noticed a deep hole of water as I rode that way on my horse to Beckley Chapel.

The minister baptized Mr. Stull by immersion. "A more happy person I have never seen. He shouted for joy and thrashed about in the water for some time before we changed our clothing and continued on to his home in the Nettie community." Worrying about what he would have told law officers had one of them drowned, "Our story of how we had gone there alone to that most desolate spot for baptism would have seemed an unlikely story, which is to say the least."[8] In point of fact, it would not "have seemed an unlikely story," given the widespread ethos of mountain religious culture in Appalachia beyond the doors of the mountain church house. Even though it was an "unusual baptism" to this Methodist minister, his sensitivity and respect for the urgency of Mr. Stull's religious sensibilities—baptism by immersion in a natural body of water when the moment of conversion was ripe and immediate—marked him as one of the ministers who in his own heart understood the wisdom of Campbell's words to "foreign ministers" in the mountains.

Campbell wrote also of "Another stumbling block . . . placed in the way unintentionally, by supporters at a distance. . . . The natural reaction of the Highlander, accustomed to a ministry which derives its support mainly from labor like his own, is to look with suspicion at these efforts for numbers and support from the field, and it usually culminates in active antagonism" (p. 191). This factor would not be understood very well by "supporters at a distance" whose intentions and techniques they would feel should be above question to people in such obvious need of their assistance. But feelings of antagonism did indeed focus on missionary ministers and church workers in the mountains who were supported by the centralized agencies of their denominations, in contrast to mountain preachers who supported themselves by their own efforts in the tradition of Pauline tent ministry. Mountain people had especial antagonism toward "these efforts for numbers," utterly contrary to their own religious values yet a quantifiable, materialistic goal of paramount importance used by many denominational agencies as the measure of their workers' success in the home missions field of Appalachia. We have noted that this antagonistic predisposition was already more than a century old in the mountains, first recorded in writing by John Taylor in his 1819 pamphlet, *Thoughts on Missions.*

Campbell observed that denominational goals promoting what the mainstream Protestants of his day considered to be progressive changes were short-circuited in large part because the ministers trained and sent into the home mission fields had such a short tenure, making it impossible for them to integrate themselves fully and effectively into mountain life and culture. This elemental observation would be sidestepped in home mission literature and training for ministry in the mountain regions of Appalachia up to the present day. Late twentieth-century minister-scholars such as the Presbyterian James Cushman also caution that, for ministry in any area of rural, small-church Appalachia, staying put should be considered a lifetime commitment if one's ministry in the region is to succeed.[9] For many denominations which encourage high mobility of their clergy, and for many clergy who would find Appalachia more than they could chew and swallow, or a lovely setting to spend their last few years before retirement, or simply one more step on their career ladder, or, worst of all, as a place to work out their messianic impulses, Cushman's injunction, like Campbell's, is still unacceptable.

Finally, Campbell hesitated to proffer what he knew would sound like undue criticism, but he noted that there had been up until his day a pattern of sending ministers who had not succeeded in the cities to the mission field in Appalachia: "Their missionaries are failures because the men the church sends were failures before they came" (p. 192). Campbell added, "A live native minister, though illiterate, wields a wider influence than learned, dead imported ones" (p. 193). Given his theological schooling (Andover Theological Seminary) and his Congregationalist background and professional spheres of activity, it is striking that Campbell's sympathetic observations of mountain religious life would lead him to align himself with what was essentially a traditional position expressed by many revival proponents during the Great Awakening, especially among the Baptists in the mid-South, and during the Great Revival on the Appalachian frontier. In fact, such a position had earlier led to the schism within the Presbyterian church that gave birth to the Cumberland Presbyterians during the Great Revival, one of the denominations indigenous to the Appalachian region.

Of perhaps greater importance, Campbell recognized that despite what the denominations perceived as a void in the religious history of the Appalachian region, apart from themselves, there had been an unbroken chain of religious life unique to the region, the integrity of which must be recognized and honored by all who take it upon themselves to establish home missions for the benefit of mountain people, especially those whose principal activity is evangelization and the founding of home mission churches. Campbell identified this unbroken chain especially with the mountain preachers, "because they represent one of the strong links with the past which here in the Highlands have not yet been broken" (p. 181). The religious culture which the mountain preachers were especially responsible for helping to transmit was passed on from generation to generation and from person to person orally, through their worship lives and the belief systems their worship embodied.

Mountain religious life and history would not receive such a thorough treatment again until 1933, with the publication of Elizabeth R. Hooker's *Religion in the Highlands*. The subtitle of her work, *Native Churches and Missionary Enterprises in the Southern Appalachian Area*, made clear that her purpose was to inform the national, denominational home mission interests which had sponsored her study about the state of religious life in Appalachia, both indigenous to its mountain regions and the product of home mission and benevolent efforts. Devoting two-thirds of her text to "native churches," Hooker also came to see qualities and features that Campbell had tried to communicate. Like Campbell, Hooker's hands-on field research had led her to recognize and appreciate the importance of mountain religious life and traditions that had continued to develop on their own, quite apart from the active involvement of nationally constituted denominational bodies. Like Campbell, Hooker understood that any attempt at home mission work in the region had to be deeply aware and respectful of the distinctiveness, continuity, and integrity of mountain religious life.

In her effort to show how mountain religion was deeply woven into the fabric of the lives of mountain people, and how this of necessity affected any efforts at home mission work in the region, Hooker was the first to attempt to trace the religious roots of mountain people back to Europe and the British Isles. In the first chapter of her work, titled "Antecedents," Hooker identified the three predominant groups who settled the region, the Scots-Irish, English, and Germans, where and when they settled in the region, and the religious traditions they brought with them, such as those of the fourteenth-century Lollards in England, Anabaptist polity and pietism, and the sacramental meetings (large communion services which lasted several days) of the Scots-Irish, along with their conventicles or field preaching. Hooker did not develop such key clues about the antecedents of mountain religious life and traditions, but simply made note of them. Since Hooker, no one has attempted to elaborate on her insights, except for Catherine Albanese, who looks at pietism and Anabaptist groups in the mountains, and Loyal Jones, who explores the influence of early Welsh Baptist traditions on the Old Regular and Primitive Baptists.[10] Several articles do assume the influence of the Great Awakening and the Great Revival on the development of Appalachian mountain religion, but, for the most part, these repeat what has already been covered in denominational literature or look to standard themes in American religious history not specifically focused on mountain religious life. My primary purpose here is to explore—or at least suggest—some of the major religious movements that are the historical roots of mountain religiosity, a religiosity that has crossed over ideological or theological lines of distinction throughout Appalachian mountain religion.

The first and only work in American religious history to examine Appalachian mountain religion as a regional religious tradition is a path-breaking chapter Catherine Albanese includes in her *America: Religions and Religion* (1981), titled "Regional Religion: A Case Study of Tradition in Southern Appalachia."[11] Albanese is the first scholar since Campbell and Hooker to present an abbreviated yet comprehensive portrait of mountain religious life and history, understanding that the church traditions most characteristic of mountain religion are not the same as what she terms "organized religion" or denominationalism. Albanese writes, "By the twentieth century, as we will see, this intensely religious people would have the least need for official church structures of perhaps any people in the United States."[12] Campbell's assertion, "In no part of our country will one find a more deep and sincere interest in matters of religion than in the Southern Highlands," reverberates in this statement. Albanese was also the first scholar in American religious history to bring a religious studies perspective to the exploration of Appalachian mountain religion, rather than approaching it from an exclusively church history perspective, which concentrates on the more accessible topics of main events, institutional developments, and prominent individuals.

The recognition and acknowledgment by Campbell, Hooker, and Albanese that Appalachian mountain people were an "intensely religious people" who, by the twentieth century, "would have the least need for official church structures of perhaps any people in the United States" not only highlighted the fact that Appalachian mountain religion was clearly distinct from the denominationalism of Protestant church traditions in the United States but raised many questions: How does mountain religion "organize" itself, if it rejects the institutional models of denominationalism? Where is its "coherency," if not in institutional expressions? If it is a style or mode of worship practices, belief systems, and religious traditions, what allows us to see how mountain religion "makes sense" as a regional religious tradition? The following chapters begin looking into these questions by exploring some of the most basic religious movements that were indispensable to the creation of mountain religiosity—pietism, Scots-Irish sacramental revivalism, and the Baptist revival in colonial Virginia. This section does not pretend to be comprehensive. The profoundly significant influences of Welsh Protestantism and English Baptists, along with other traditions yet to be identified, await investigation.

Pietism, Pietists, and Holiness People

The influence of pietism on mountain religious life and history may well have been as profound as the influence of revivalism. The Radical Reformation was a diverse movement producing a vast array of groups, the Anabaptist traditions representing only a part.[1] It is unclear whether the tradition of church polity that is normative for mountain religion has its roots primarily in Anabaptist or early Baptist traditions that came into the region during its formative stages of religious development. As Torbet states, "Baptists can be understood best by seeing them as a part of the expression of the Free Church movement in Christianity. While evident from time to time in the centuries prior to the Protestant Reformation, the movement became most articulate in the sixteenth century in the Anabaptist-Mennonite tradition of the Continent and in the Puritan Separatist and Non-Separatist tradition of England."[2]

The effects of religious traditions on each other in the mountains of Appalachia have been extremely fluid from the first years of settlement up to the present. Mountain religion's traditionally anti-institutional, nondenominational character has been a constant, allowing for a broad mixing of influences. This mix has not only created variety but distilled many worship practices, belief systems, and religious traditions into features that defined mountain religion as a regional religious tradition. Although they may vary from church to church, these features have at least as an undercurrent something that is very much in common with each other. Free church polity is one of those features, and one of the most broadly applied. The extent to which Anabaptist or continental free church traditions of the Radical Reformation, and the extent to which pietism in particular, have influenced mountain religious life can only be alluded to at this stage of research.[3] The following paragraphs seek to explore through allusion, illustrated by the lives of Brother L. L. Bradley and Sister Edna Alexander, some of those influences and similarities in mountain religious life. But first we begin with a brief historical summary of pietism and the appearance of major pietist traditions in the Appalachian region.

Pietism was a product of the Radical Reformation, which began to take clear shape in the late seventeenth century and was often seen as the second phase of the Reformation. In the first phase, reformers had focused on the areas of doctrine and polity. In the second phase—the pietistic phase—

reformers focused on applying reformed principles to Christian life. The term "pietists" was first used to describe the followers of Philip Jakob Spener (1635–1705), although evangelical pietism had been developing on the Continent and in Great Britain a century before Spener. Considered by many to be Luther's successor, he became the leading pastor of Germany and the central symbol of pietism.[4] Spener's colleague and successor to leadership of the pietist movement on the Continent was August Hermann Francke (1663–1727). Francke was the major institutionalizer of European pietism's educational and social outreach, founding Halle University in 1694, as well as such eclectic enterprises as an orphanage, a home for widows, a farm, a bookstore, a hospital, a bakery, a brewery, a library, and an art museum.[5]

The year before his death, Spener blessed his godchild, Nicholas Ludwig von Zinzendorf (1700–1760), an ardent pietist who was later educated at Halle University. The Unitas Fratrum (Unity of the Brethren or United Brethren), better known as the Moravians, took refuge on his estates in the early eighteenth century. Their devotion to missionary work soon led them to the American colonies, and Zinzendorf traveled with them to help establish Moravian mission settlements. These Moravian missionaries would be among the first of the German pietists to settle in the Appalachian region.

F. Ernest Stoeffler observed that pietism "must be seen as the major manifestation of the *experiential tradition* within post-Reformation Protestantism."[6] Above all else, mountain religion is centered on experiential religion, or religious experience, mediated by grace through the Holy Spirit. Insisting that pietism cannot be known by external forms such as the overt institutionalism in which is invested much of the individual identity of church traditions such as denominations (what he called "sect-type"), Stoeffler identified four basic or defining emphases by which pietism could be identified. The first emphasis was the *experiential,* by which Stoeffler meant "the personally meaningful relationship of the individual to God."[7] In pietist tradition, the doctrine of assurance was based upon the unassailable authority of the individual's personal experience. Concurrent with the emphasis on the experiential was emphasis upon the creative work of the Holy Spirit within the individual, perceived in the felt experience of the heart.

The second emphasis by which pietism was known was religious idealism or *perfectionism.* This centered upon the experience of conversion and subsequent striving for sanctification or perfection (what John Wesley later called the second blessing or second work of grace), without which the Christian life was dead. As such, justification—or the movement from prevenient (anticipatory) grace to saving grace within the conversion experience, leading toward assurance—was, Stoeffler noted, more than a mere "forensic" or legal act of God; instead, it too entered directly into human experience. The influence of pietism's emphasis on perfectionism is clear in

"decisive confrontation" for his own spirituality and for the emergence of Methodism.[13] Wesley had also been deeply impressed by the Moravian "love feast," which he appropriated into the Methodist tradition. The "love feast" was originally a tradition of testifying at a common meal about what saving grace meant in your life, a tradition that, very early on, would become a staple in the worship services of Appalachian mountain churches. It probably first came into mountain worship life through pietist influences rather than through the Methodists, though the latter strongly reinforced the practice. Early revival Baptists of the Great Awakening in the South, centered in colonial Virginia and North Carolina, also knew and practiced the love feast. Indeed, David Benedict listed it in his 1813 Baptist history as one of the "nine Christian rites" observed at least into the early 1770s by Sandy Creek Association in North Carolina, parent of all Separate Baptist associations in the South.[14] Sandy Creek's traditions or "rites," so characteristic of German pietists in the region—especially "washing feet," "anointing the sick," and the "kiss of charity," along with "love-feasts"—became regionally specific to Appalachia and its mountain church traditions soon after.

Moravian missionaries traveled throughout the Appalachian region, especially the Blue Ridge area, and their diaries provided the earliest outside recorded accounts of the Mennonites in the Shenandoah Valley of Virginia.[15] The Mennonites settled heavily in the Blue Ridge area, especially on what would later become the border of West Virginia and Virginia. They were among the first white settlers in the Shenandoah Valley, arriving in 1727, and include today among their congregations in the Blue Ridge area the Beachy Amish, Old Order Amish, Conservative Mennonite, and Old Order Mennonite, as well as less traditional congregations of Mennonites. These Mennonites emigrated from Pennsylvania, along with the German Baptist Brethren and Seventh Day Baptists.

The German Baptist Brethren or Dunkards (also called Dunkers) first immigrated to America in 1719 and gathered their first congregation four years later in Germantown, Pennsylvania.[16] Soon they were located wholly in the United States, and began to migrate south, especially into Virginia and West Virginia. The worship practices for which they were known were footwashing and baptism by immersion. German Baptist Brethren practiced "trine immersion," immersion face-forward three times to represent the three Persons of the Trinity—hence the name "Dunkards." Catherine Albanese wrote of the German Dunkards, "Following the Anabaptists of the Radical Reformation, they brought two profoundly moving rituals to the people of Southern Appalachia. The first was baptism, which they sought to perform usually in a running stream. . . . The second was footwashing. . . . With the coming of the German Dunkers, both of these practices had been in the mountains since the first decade of settlement."[17] Other important practices associated with pietist groups that settled early in Appalachia, such as the holy kiss and the refusal to take an oath, would also find their way into practices in many mountain churches, especially among Holiness churches.[18] In 1728 the Seventh Day Baptists were formed by a member of the German Baptist Brethren, who formed the semimonastic Ephrata community in Ephrata, Pennsylvania, four years later. Although this community disappeared soon after its founder's death in 1768, Seventh Day Baptists persist in Appalachia today, especially in West Virginia.[19]

The Anabaptist heritage in the earlier history of the United States was heavily represented by settlements on the Appalachian frontier. Early settlements extended from southeast to southwest Pennsylvania (which the Appalachian Regional Commission includes today in Appalachia), to eastern and especially southeastern Ohio (also officially included in Appalachia), as well as Virginia (encompassing what later became West Virginia), and the Carolinas.[20] Indiana was the only region of their early settlement not included in what the goverment designated in the mid-twentieth century as "official" Appalachia. Regardless of these largely politically based designations today, especially on the far north and south of "traditional" Appalachia, early Anabaptist groups were clearly identified with the areas that have always been included in Appalachia, along with its immediate border areas.

The four emphases used by Stoeffler to characterize pietism are reflected not just in mountain church traditions but in basic sensibilities representing much of popular religious culture throughout the Appalachian region, whether church attendance is involved or not. In fact, pietists have likely had far greater impact on the religious life distinctive to the mountains of the Appalachian region than on the religious life—other than, of course, their own—of any other region in the United States, large or small.

The study of pietistic influences on mountain religious life is truly in a rudimentary stage. Moreover, it is dependent on evidence found almost exclusively in oral tradition and material culture, rather than in a body of literature. Mountain people today bear in their own lives the clearest living chronicles, the loudest historical echoes, that allow us to begin to see pietism's extraordinary impact on their religious life and history. And so, we shall conclude this abbreviated exploration of pietism by looking briefly at the lives of Brother L. L. Bradley and Sister Edna Alexander. Brother Bradley is an independent Holiness preacher in southern West Virginia. His family on his mother's side were Old Order Dunkards, and he attended their worship services during his growing-up years. Sister Edna Alexander of eastern Kentucky has always been independent Holiness. Her extremely simple lifestyle reflects pietist emphases on living a Christian life. For the past few years, Sister Edna has been drawn to spend a few months out of the year living in a traditional Mennonite community in south-central Tennessee.

Brother L. L. Bradley

A little over halfway from Lewisburg to Peterstown in southern West Virginia is Dunkard Church Road. Two or three miles down Dunkard Church Road, when the road has become dirt and gravel, far out in the countryside with few houses in sight are two churches on opposite sides of the road and well within a stone's throw of each other, separated by less than a tenth of a mile. The first is the newer Dunkard church, established in 1954, called by the name the more progressive Dunkards took for themselves, Church of the Brethren. The other church building is unmarked, a much more traditional whitewashed structure with two separate entryways, one for men and one for women. Both churches are still in use. A large population of German Baptist Brethren settled in this area of West Virginia. I do not know their provenance. But the people of the Dunkard community who settled in this part of West Virginia are connected to another church in nearby Peterstown, an independent Holiness church.

Just before you enter Peterstown from Lewisburg, to the right is a large, faded yellow sign with black lettering: "Peterstown House of Prayer, Pastor L. L. Bradley, Services Thurs. 7:30, Sat. 7:30, Sunday School 10:00, Sunday 7:00." Frequently independent Holiness churches have a Sunday morning Sunday school, but the only Sunday service, if any, is held in the evening. The sign for Peterstown House of Prayer is posted by a dirt road that enters into a trailer park that goes straight up a steep hillside. At the base of the hill to the right is the House of Prayer, designed and constructed solely by Brother Bradley, friends, neighbors, and worshipers. Loudspeakers are attached above the front entry and on the left side of the building. Next to the church building and slightly to the front is an open shed. Attached to the shed is a large white sign, hand-lettered in red: "Campmeeting July 30–Aug. 7, 7:30 P.M." Underneath this sign is another white sign with red lettering: "Used Trailers for Sale or Rent, Call: . . ." and then a telephone number. The telephone number is that of Brother Lawrence Bradley, pastor of Peterstown House of Prayer, who lives directly across from the church on the dirt road going into the trailer park. His home is a small, white, single-story house, the only permanent structure in the trailer park.

Brother Bradley says that the New Testament Church of God is called a House of Prayer: "Is it not written, My house shall be called of all nations the house of prayer?" (Mark 11:17). Now in his mid-seventies, Brother Bradley has pastored the church which he built on his own property for twenty-five years. He sold chain saws for twenty-eight years. Today he preaches and hears other preachers full-time. In his church worshipers practice footwashing every two to three months. Saturday evening is the main service of the week. Musical instruments for services include mandolins, banjos, guitars (both acoustic and electric), and a piano. A food bank is housed in the church basement. The Ladies Prayer Room on the main floor off of the sanctuary holds used clothing for those in need. Over the years Brother Bradley's church and the people who attend it have worked and worshiped with other churches, including the Fire Baptized Holiness Church, the Pentecostal Holiness Church, and the Independent Bible Church of God. Members of a local Church of Christ had been teaching in his House of Prayer on Sunday afternoon at 2:00 for the past several months when I met him. Prior to that Baptists and Methodists have also taught in his church. Brother Bradley states, "The Bible says, 'We're helpers one to another.' We never get so strong along the way not to need help. Only thing that brings us to one is the Word."

Before he became an independent preacher and pastor, Brother Bradley was a member of the Church of God (Cleveland, Tennessee). He made the transition to independent Holiness when he studied with an independent Holiness preacher in Marion, Virginia, not too far from Peterstown in the southwestern part of Virginia. This preacher had memorized verbatim fifty-six chapters of the Bible, and helped Brother Bradley to memorize verbatim twenty-eight chapters. Brother Bradley's conversation is laced with lengthy, rapid quotations from the Bible. He says often, "Study and see. Studying makes us perfect." His injunction is one backed by an ecumenical spirit and humility, rather than the certainty of rationalism and scholasticism. The interaction of his church with other churches and church traditions in the Peterstown area attests to the sincerity of his words.

Brother Bradley has lived in the Peterstown area "off and on" his entire life. When he was little he attended an Old Order Dunkard church. His mother was an Old Order Dunkard from age thirteen until her death at age ninety-seven. In the front room of his home hangs a photograph of his grandparents, Elisabeth (d. 1921) and John (d. 1924) Bowers. They too were Old Order Dunkards all of their lives. In the photograph his grandmother is wearing a traditional Dunkard bonnet and his grandfather has a traditional Dunkard beard and dark coat with no collar or lapels. Brother Bradley has no explanation why he became a Holiness preacher and pastor rather than staying with the Old Order Dunkards of his mother's family. He sees the independent Holiness mountain tradition of which he is a part today as a natural continuation of the religious sensibilities he was exposed to as a child in the Old Order Dunkard church community in southern West Virginia.

Sister Edna Alexander

Many, many years ago Sister Edna Alexander had a "dream or vision" about how she should dress. A few years later she carefully printed out her account of that dream/vision and its consequences for her life:

God's will for her and her family. She believes that such a lifestyle is God's manifest will, not for all people but for most, if they would but listen to the voice of the Holy Spirit in their lives. Close ties to the earth open wide channels to God. Her understanding soundly contradicts the stereotype of a stagnant attitude expressed in the narrow logic of "That's the way we've always done it, and that's good enough for me." Most of Sister Edna's days are spent in prayer, even though she is constantly working. A simple lifestyle is no easy thing to maintain. It entails continuous, hard work that is quickly backbreaking for those not conditioned to it, usually by upbringing. But Sister Edna retreats on a regular basis to a small cabin on top of the ridge of her property that she uses for private prayer when she needs to be alone with God.

A few years ago one of Sister Edna's sons discovered a Mennonite community in south-central Tennessee, one that engaged in the simple living which he had known all of his life and which had so separated him from most of the people he encountered. He moved his own family to this community and has since been joined by two other brothers and their families. For the past few years Sister Edna has spent several months out of the year living in the Mennonite community with her sons. Devona has photographs of her mother mixing lye soap outdoors in a large black kettle, surrounded by grandchildren in the Mennonite community where her three sons now live. One of her sons supports himself by making rocking chairs entirely of wood, pegs and all (no nails). In this community the homes have no electricity or running water. Cavelike overhangs going straight up from the rich river bottom are used as barns and winter storage for food. There are in fact two communities ten miles apart, each with a church house, one of which is used for the school (the children are required to learn both German and Dutch). Church services alternate between the two church houses each Sunday. Horse-drawn wagons and buggies rather than cars are used to commute the distance. The Mennonite community in south-central Tennessee is now about fifty years old, stemming from the west-central Kentucky Mennonites, who in turn emigrated from Pennsylvania.

Sister Edna was as delighted as her children to discover the Mennonites. She says that they are "living the life, but they don't have the faith. They're searching." To Sister Edna, she is "living the life," meaning a simple lifestyle, because the Holy Spirit called her to it, and her "faith" is a product of her intimate responsiveness to the Holy Spirit in her life. She sees the Mennonites as living the life because they are searching for the Holy Spirit. She sees their gifts as being more in the material world, even though she admires their ability to separate from the world and not depend on it, for the most part. Nonetheless, unlike Sister Edna, these Mennonites go to medical doctors when in need, whereas Sister Edna has for decades now relied entirely on God and traditional healing arts for all of her medical needs. She says that the Mennonites don't know about the Spirit and about healing. She also says that the Mennonites are attracted to her primarily because of her experiential knowledge of the Spirit and healing. "They sure welcome me. They call on me to come pray with them when somebody's sick." Sister Edna says that she has her tradition (mountain Holiness) and they have their tradition (German–Dutch Mennonite), both of which are very similar apart from obvious cultural differences. For Sister Edna, the only dissonance between them is their understanding and experience of the workings of the Holy Spirit.

Since the above paragraphs were first written about Sister Edna Alexander, she has experienced several life changes. Sister Edna is now in her early sixties. In December 1989, Vincent, her husband, had a ruptured appendix and died of peritonitis. Vincent held to the same healing tradition as his wife. For nearly a week he stayed in bed, refusing all medical treatment, preferring to receive only the prayers of his family and neighbors, a constant flow of whom poured in from all around. Nonetheless, someone in the Red Lick area called the sheriff to report that a deathly ill man was being denied medical attention. The sheriff came out to investigate. Sister Edna told the sheriff that it was not their practice to "go against the law" and they would do whatever he said. The sheriff ordered that Vincent be taken to a hospital where he died a few days later.

Within a few months, Carl, one of Sister Edna's sons who was living in the Mennonite community in south-central Tennessee, moved back home with his wife and children to help out his mother, taking residence in the cabin atop the mountain on his family's property line that Sister Edna had used for private prayer. Pat Parker Brunner calls them "Holiness-Mennonite people," for Carl and his family are a product first of mountain religion's independent Holiness tradition, yet are very influenced by the culture and piety of the "plain people" as he calls them and, indeed, as they are commonly called. Even though living back home again, far from his Mennonite community, Carl and his young son continue to dress in pants that have only buttons and wear flat, broad-brimmed black hats. His daughters and spouse also wear traditional Mennonite bonnets and long-sleeved dresses. Carl has expressed to me a strong hope—actually an intense excitement—about the prospect of learning to read so that he can read the Bible for himself, continuing in a long path taken by innumerable mountain people for acquiring basic literacy.

Yet another major change has occurred in Sister Edna's life. The longtime family acquaintance who owned the cabin she and Vincent had lived in since moving back from southern Ohio, along with the small patch of land they had farmed, unexpectedly reclaimed it for his daughter's residence. Sister Edna now lives a quarter-mile back, where she grew up, in the two-story log house her father built earlier in the century, thus coming full circle in her life.

＝

9

Scots-Irish Religiosity and Revivalism

The single most important piece of religious art in mountain churches and homes, and by far the most common, is the *Last Supper* by Leonardo da Vinci. It appears in churches most often on black or blue velvet tapestry. Even in churches with some other picture behind or on the pulpit—such as Jesus the shepherd leading his flock, which you'll find in Sister Lydia Surgener's New Church at Mill Creek in Cranks, Kentucky, and in the Smoky Mountain Full Gospel Church near Cosby, Tennessee; or a black velvet tapestry of the head of Jesus wearing a crown of thorns in Rex Church, an independent Holiness mining community church just outside of Harlan, Kentucky—there is still a color reproduction of Leonardo's *Last Supper* near the pulpit. Leonardo's *Last Supper* is also found in many Old Regular Baptist churches, independent Missionary Baptist churches, Free Will Baptist churches, and in the church houses of other mountain church traditions. I showed a few of the dozens of photographs Warren Brunner and I had taken of the *Last Supper* in mountain churches and homes to a psychiatrist acquaintance who got very excited about the repetition of this picture and asked, "Yes, but why *that* picture?" I had no answer, but her question got me to thinking about it.

What is the picture about? It is about the Last Supper, certainly, but more than that it is about the communion service. It is also a community piece. Other religious pictures found in mountain homes in particular, such as Jesus praying in the Garden of Gethsemane, are more often solitary portrayals. Mountain homes tend to have more religious art about Jesus being singled out, or alone, than churches do. Mountain churches have more art where Jesus is in a social setting, a community setting. In Becky Simpson's home are found the fourteen Stations of the Cross on the wall above her television set. Becky Simpson is half-sister to Sister Lydia Surgener and the founder of Cranks Creek Survival Center. Their mother was a Presbyterian who became independent Holiness and for a time in her life handled serpents. In Sister Mae June Hensley's home, Sister Lydia's New Church at Mill Creek, and Cumbo United Methodist Church near Rose Hill, Virginia, is found the Sacred Heart of Jesus. Roman Catholic religious art is very popular in mountain homes and churches. Mountain people are especially fond of the Sacred Heart motif, given their heart-centered religion, and do not identify it as Roman Catholic. But Leonardo's *Last Supper* remains preeminent in mountain churches and homes today. Sister Hassie

Miser, spouse of Brother Coy Miser, gave a large framed picture of the *Last Supper* that had been in her family for some time to Sister Mae June when she married a few years back. We shall explore clues as to why Leonardo's *Last Supper* is so important, other than as a symbol of community worship, in this chapter on Scots-Irish religiosity.

When I began to wonder about the importance of the *Last Supper* in mountain religious life, I pondered the fact that communion services do not take place very often in mountain churches, except in the Church of Christ where communion is received on a weekly basis. In many, many mountain churches communion and footwashing take place together, and footwashing is usually considered the more important of the two. As Albanese observed, there is a strong sacramental quality to these celebrations in mountain churches. "Protestant in their attachment to a religion of the biblical Word and the felt experience of the heart, they wove their Protestantism with a new sacramentalism which spoke to their condition. Yet, perhaps because it smacked too clearly of Roman Catholicism, the communion service was not nearly so powerful a religious ritual among the mountain people as baptism or foot washing."[1] Perhaps so, perhaps not. There may well be other, more pronounced historical reasons for the ascendancy of baptism and footwashing, and the apparent receding in importance of the sacrament of communion in relation to them.

Dorgan has observed in his field studies of communion-footwashing services that the communion part of the service tends to be "extremely sedate and dignified." Emotional release is reserved primarily for footwashing. For many of the churches where Dorgan has attended footwashing, "Throughout this part of the service there was considerable crying, shouting, singing, praying, and even preaching,"[2] while in a much smaller number of churches the response was limited to quiet sobbing. For Old Regular and Primitive Baptists, the annual communion-footwashing service is often simply called "footwashing." Yet the communion part of the service is called "sacrament." The entire communion-footwashing service is accorded the title "sacramental meeting." This would seem to be distinctly liturgical, "high church" vocabulary for such nonliturgical, "low church" people. As we shall see, it is a major clue to mountain people's religious history and their religiosity.

For Old Regular and Primitive Baptists in particular, and for other mountain church traditions not adhering to Calvinist doctrinal traditions, the communion-footwashing service is a communal conversion experience. In Old Regular and Primitive Baptist churches, it is carefully prepared for by the ritual of declaring the church at peace, a practice of cleansing the community as a whole by requiring its individual members to search their hearts and minds. It is a communal practice quite similar to what came to be called "falling under conviction" in the classic revivalism that took clear shape during the Great Awakening. It is far removed from the perfunctory "confession of sin" in liturgical traditions. Declaring the church at peace in these mountain churches may well be a tradition with strong Scots-Irish connections from several centuries earlier.

I have often wondered about the strikingly revivalistic features of the worship practices of Calvinist-based groups such as the Old Regular and Primitive Baptists who do not embrace the revivalism that evolved out of early nineteenth-century Arminianized evangelization because of their doctrinal heritage. Yet, their emphasis on the Holy Spirit moving within individuals in the communal setting of worship has resulted in emotionally charged piety and practices so often associated with revivalism. The revivalistic piety of mountain religion's most doctrinally conservative church traditions, centered firmly on the movement of the Holy Spirit, characterized and dominated Scots-Irish worship life of the early seventeenth century, also staunchly Calvinistic.

As we shall come to see in the following pages, today Old Regular and Primitive Baptist worship practices reflect the community-building features of revivalistic piety, as they did for early Scots-Irish Presbyterians in their focus on the Lord's Supper. The Lord's Supper for the Scots-Irish was also a communal conversion experience, like communion-footwashing meetings throughout Appalachia's religious history. What the Scots-Irish called their "sacramental meetings" or Lord's Suppers—the same term common throughout mountain religion, from Old Regular Baptist to independent Holiness, for communion-footwashing services—laid the foundation for revivalism in Scots-Irish communities in seventeenth-century Ulster and western Scotland. The emotionally charged piety of revivalism is focused on the conversion experience, and revivalism itself is essentially a communal experience.

Yet another major point of intersect connects mountain religion to the worship life of the early Scots-Irish. Albanese noted about the core of mountain religiosity, "[T]he episodic conversion experience became the mainstay of Southern Appalachian religion."[3] The key word in Albanese's statement is "episodic." Throughout mountain people's religious history, conversion is a religious experience renewed time and time again. As we shall see, mountain religion's distinctive heritage of "the episodic conversion experience" continues the bedrock tradition of conversion and renewal of conversion in a communal setting that was the hallmark of early Scots-Irish worship life centered on celebrating the Lord's Supper. Moreover, it is simultaneously strongly tied to the community-building emphasis of Scots-Irish religiosity.

From what has been outlined in the preceding paragraphs, it is clear that revivalism has not always been a tool of aggressive evangelization or rooted in the assumption that salvation is a rational, free-will decision. Revivalism has gone through many transmutations over the centuries, reflecting different types of religiosity. Its earlier traditional expressions among the Scots-Irish appear to continue in the Calvinist traditions of the Old Regular and Primitive Baptists, as well as in many other mountain church traditions. The Scots-Irish of seventeenth-century Ulster and western Scotland were evangelical Presbyterian Calvinists. Later in the United States they would exchange their strict Calvinism for the modified Calvinism of the Baptists or Baptist and Methodist Arminianism when they settled in the Appalachian region, taking with them their revivalist piety. The episodic communal conversion experience of the early Scots-Irish sacramental meetings or communion services, the careful preparation of community cleansing that preceded them, and how this developed into a very specific tradition of revivalist piety for the Scots-Irish have extremely strong echoes in mountain religious life today. These echoes may well account for the symbolic importance of the image of Leonardo's *Last Supper* in mountain churches and homes, even as we near the conclusion of the twentieth century.

It has long been a matter of debate in Appalachian studies whether or not mountain people are primarily Scots-Irish or English ("Anglo-Saxon").[4] In the earlier years when Appalachia was emerging as a distinctive region in American consciousness, its Anglo-Saxon heritage was emphasized, especially at the turn into the twentieth century. Richard B. Drake summarized "the general outlines of the story of Appalachian settlement" as follows:

> 1. The first group to settle in the Southern Appalachians were the Germans—in the Shenandoah in the 1720's.
> 2. Perhaps the most important single European immigrant group to people the Appalachian area were the Scotch-Irish; and
> 3. A group sometimes referred to simply as "the English" comprised a very substantial part of the ancestry of the Appalachians. Made up of Welsh, French, Dutch, English and others, this group were usually drawn from the established areas of the colonies, persons who may have been second- or even third-generation "Americans" then. Probably this group was as large as the Scotch-Irish.[5]

Drake's summary is what is most widely agreed upon today for the populations settling the Appalachian region. It is generally accepted that by far the single largest ethnic group to settle in Appalachia was the Scots-Irish.

The Great Migration of Scots-Irish to the colonies began in 1717 and continued for fifty-eight years. They came mostly by way of Philadelphia, Chester, and New Castle in Pennsylvania and Delaware and settled in a seven-hundred-mile arc stretching from Philadelphia to the upper Savannah River.[6] The original three major areas of concentration of Scots-Irish people were in southeastern Pennsylvania, the Valley of Virginia (the upper part of the Greater Appalachian Valley), and the Piedmont of the Carolinas. After 1725, the Cumberland Valley of Pennsylvania was the center of Scots-Irish settlement for decades. By 1776, nine-tenths of the Scots-Irish were living in Pennsylvania, Virginia, and North and South Carolina. From these areas the Scots-Irish settled in the more mountainous regions of Appalachia, reaching on into Kentucky and Tennessee in significant numbers by the 1780s and 1790s.[7]

In my study of the roots of mountain religiosity I became especially interested in the Great Awakening in the Middle Colonies, home to the largest settlements of Scots-Irish at the time and principally a Scots-Irish Presbyterian phenomenon. Accounts such as that of Samuel Blair, a Presbyterian minister whose congregation was Scots-Irish, of a revival in his church at Faggs Manor, Pennsylvania, in 1740, were particularly arresting: "In the beginning of March I took a journey into East Jersey, and was abroad for two or three Sabbaths. A neighboring minister, who seemed to be in earnest for the awakening and conversion of secure sinners, and whom I had obtained to preach a Sabbath to my people in my absence, preached to them, I think, on the first Sabbath after I left home. . . . Under that sermon there was a visible appearance of much soul-concern among the hearers, so that some burst out with an audible noise into bitter crying; a thing not heard in these parts before." Even though the emotional piety of the hearers was "a thing not heard in these parts before," was it a *new* "thing" to them? Blair went on to write, "The news of this very public appearance of deep soul-concern among my people met me a hundred miles from home. I was very joyful to hear of it, in hopes that God was about to carry on an extensive work of converting grace among them."[8]

Blair had described his guest minister as being "in earnest for the awakening and conversion of secure sinners," suggesting to modern ears aggressive evangelization. However, if we look at Blair's following statement, we see that at this time in the history of revivalism, conversion was still dependent foremost on "grace," God's own "work" of immediate salvific presence in church communities which maintained an active "*hope*" that it was always imminent. The flowing waters of what Blair called "converting grace" were God's initiative. Human cooperation through conversionist preaching and the people's own "deep soul-concern," grounded in "hope," only primed the well. We see the steady persistence of this tradition in the mountains of Appalachia today reflected in the titles of Dorgan's *The Old Regular Baptists of Central Appalachia: Brothers and Sisters in Hope* (1989) and Sovine's "A Sweet Hope in My Breast: Belief and Ritual in the Primitive Baptist Church" (1978).

After his return from East Jersey in the spring of 1740, Blair met the same sort of response to his first sermon.

> The number of the awakened increased very fast. . . . Our Sabbath assemblies soon became vastly large, many people, from almost all parts

around, inclining very much to come where there was such appearance of the divine power and presence. I think there was scarcely a sermon or lecture preached through that whole summer but there were manifest evidences of impressions on the hearers; and many times the impressions were very great and general; several would be overcome and fainting; others deeply sobbing, hardly able to contain; others crying in a most dolorous manner; many others more silently weeping; and a solemn concern appearing in the countenances of many others. And sometimes the soul-exercises of some (though comparatively few) would so far affect their bodies as to occasion some strange unusual bodily motions.[9]

What drew "vastly large Sabbath assemblies" was "such appearance of the *divine power and presence*" that made "impressions on the hearers." The "evidences" of these "impressions" were spontaneous and highly emotional, and Blair described them as "soul-exercises." This description is a key. By this time, expressive and ecstatic behavior in worship such as "fainting," "deeply sobbing," "crying," "silently weeping," and "strange unusual bodily motions" were understood to be "soul-exercises" coming from the very core of the individual, yet having their source in the "appearance of the divine power and presence" that drew people from all around. Such spontaneous yet ritualized conduct, so wide in its range and so outwardly emotional, was associated directly—indeed, it was equated—with revival.

These powerful expressions of emotional piety have characterized, since Appalachia's first settlements, what eventually became mountain religious life. For the uninitiate even today, after nearly three centuries of revival tradition on American soil and the emergence of the Holiness-Pentecostal movements, such emotional expressions in worship are very frightening. Apparently they were not frightening to the Scots-Irish Presbyterian community in southeastern Pennsylvania in 1740. Indeed the outbreak of highly emotional expressions in worship at Blair's church drew Scots-Irish people "from almost all parts around" like a magnet. Evidently there were antecedents familiar to the people, a strong tradition for such expressions of emotional piety during worship, focused as it was on the experience of conversion and identified with revival.

When I read the following statements in Leonard J. Trinterud's *The Forming of an American Tradition* (1949), the best available study of the development of the Presbyterian church during the Great Awakening in the Middle Colonies, I found other indirect indications of antecedents for the strong emotionalism associated with revival religiosity. Trinterud wrote, "The Log College revivals were not sudden outbursts. Such momentary movements were called 'stirrings,' or some such name, to indicate that they had not developed into a real revival. A true revival was one that carried on for sev-

is the only venue in the United States in which the religiosity of the Scots-Irish first characterized by the Great Awakening in the Middle Colonies continues to flourish. If the Great Awakening "was one episode, albeit a magnificent one, in the life and growth of a religious tradition," Appalachian mountain religion continues that "religious tradition" today, and has throughout its history. We find significant clues in the history of Scots-Irish religiosity as to why mountain religiosity is characterized primarily by an anti-organizational or anti-institutional outlook. We see strong hints in its history for why religious authority resides in the laity to the extent that religious leadership is characterized by a leveling influence that puts ministers on a par with those to whom they minister, rather than viewing the ministry as a profession set apart. The history of Scots-Irish religiosity also begins to explain why the rituals associated with revivalism can be found among the Old Regular and Primitive Baptists as well as among independent Missionary Baptists, independent Holiness churches, and other church traditions characterizing mountain religious life—despite the strict Calvinism of some and the free-will Arminianism of others.

While Scots-Irish religiosity may provide a predominant matrix of interpretation, the influences of other traditions with very similar features such as Welsh Protestantism and the pietism of the Radical Reformation have long intermingled in mountain religiosity. In the following pages, with the help primarily of Westerkamp and Schmidt, we will explore the history of Scots-Irish religiosity. We will begin with seventeenth-century Ulster and western Scotland, then cross the Atlantic to the Middle Colonies during the Great Awakening, followed by the Great Revival on the Appalachian frontier, and conclude with a "sacrament meeting" in an independent Holiness church in eastern Kentucky held during the final hour of the last day of the 1980s.

The Six-Mile-Water Revival and Sacramental Meetings

By 1625, Scots from the Lowlands of western Scotland had been settled in Ulster less than twenty-five years and Scots missionaries had been ministering in Ulster less than ten years. In 1625 Ulster experienced the Six-Mile-Water Revival, a momentous occurrence in the religious life of that region. Outbreaks started around the town of Antrim and spread throughout counties Down and Antrim, the first recorded revival of its kind in the British Isles. Moreover, Irish church historians marked this revival as the beginning of the Irish Presbyterian church. The revival soon spread from Ulster to western Scotland. The towns of Stewarton and Shotts, among the closest points to Ireland, became revival centers by 1630.

The revivals of the 1620s and 1630s were the direct products of large, multi-day sacramental meetings or communion services. Indeed, the communion services laid the groundwork for revivalist piety, for these sacramental occasions were combined with the revivalism of the Scottish and Ulster Scottish evangelical Presbyterians. According to Schmidt, the sacramental revivalism—conversionist preaching combined with the sacrament of communion—of the Lowlands of western Scotland (the traditional bastion of evangelical Presbyterianism) and of the Ulster Scots made the communion "festival" a point of distinction separating out the core expression of their evangelical Presbyterian tradition from others in the transatlantic community.[16] This is a key insight, for it shows that the Scots-Irish who would populate Appalachia in such large numbers had at the core of their religious identity a unique form of religiosity, sacramental revivalism.

The initial divisions of the early seventeenth-century "sacramental season" or communion meeting were a penitential fast on Thursday, preparatory sermons on Saturday, distribution of the communion elements (which could continue for up to twelve hours) on Sunday, and a thanksgiving service on Monday. A sacramental meeting came to average, then, at least three to five days, extending well before and after the actual serving of the communion elements. In addition, sacramental meetings maintained "a seasonal focus on summer" since many people traveled significant distances to participate, for people from more than one church community would take part. The sacramental meeting also included distribution of communion tokens, fencing of the tables, and the reception of communion, which participants sitting at long tables distributed among themselves. Three or more ministers from various churches cooperated in the three to five days of preaching and distribution of the elements. Moreover, preaching was held from an outdoor pulpit called the "tent."

Schmidt identified the features of the sacramental meeting that became particularly characteristic of revivalism:

> Such things as preparatory services, sitting to receive the elements, self-examination, careful fencing of the tables, and communion tokens were all evident in one form or another from the early years of the Reformation in Scotland. . . . What separated the festal communion from earlier sacraments were such characteristics as outdoor preaching, great concourses of people from an extensive region, long vigils of prayer, powerful experiences of conversion and confirmation, a number of popular ministers cooperating for extended services over three days or more, a seasonal focus on summer, and unusually large numbers of communicants at successive tables.[17]

Indeed, the three-to-five-day sacramental meeting was "intertwined from the first with revival."[18]

Within Scottish tradition centered on the Lowlands of western Scotland

and on Ulster, the sacramental meeting had nearly a two hundred year history before reaching its peak in America on the Appalachian frontier of the Great Revival period. Soon the same revivalistic features of traditional sacramental meetings became integral to mountain religious life: revival meetings lasting no less than three days (earlier Baptists called them "great meetings" and mountain people called them "big meetings"); revival services stretching past midnight; "long vigils of prayer" at revival meetings and other religious gatherings often lasting until dawn; "a seasonal focus on summer" as mountain religion's "high days" of the year; many people traveling great distances to attend religious events of all sorts, as well as revivals; participants (whether in revivals or communion-footwashing meetings or homecomings or memorial meetings or other religious gatherings) drawn from more than one church community; several preachers from different churches participating in a local church's regular worship service or other periodic religious events, as well as revivals; preaching out of doors from what was by the time of plain-folk camp-meeting religion called the "stand"; and finally, ecstatic experiences of conversion or, for others, the ecstatic reaffirmations of their experiences of conversion (what Catherine Albanese called "the episodic conversion experience") in these communal gatherings.

Theological heritages emphasizing either personal or communal conversion combined to give expression to conversion as the foundational religious experience undergirding all of Appalachian mountain religion. English Independents and especially New England Puritans emphasized individual conversion and a church composed of "visible saints"—those who were visibly converted, that is, had undergone conversion as an individual, personal experience and were added to the church one by one, based upon their personal testimony of how they "came to grace."[19] Scots-Irish Presbyterians rejected the notion of a visible saint church. Instead, all but the overtly notorious were permitted to become church members since it was impossible to distinguish the converted from the unconverted, according to the Augustinian tradition of conversion most Calvinists shared. The New England Puritans' "visible saint" tradition, based on their federal or covenant theology, was a radical variant of this model.

Not being able to distinguish the converted from the unconverted meant that, for the Scots-Irish Presbyterians, each parish had "unsanctified members" and that each parish community had to be purified before the communion service. The community itself, through the collective religious experiences of its individual members, must undergo conversion on behalf of the impure members in its midst and in order to nourish the spirituality of its individual members within that collective setting. Although, as in later revivalism, the individual's personal conversion was a goal, the larger purpose was to promote the conversion of the church community as a whole.

Individual members shared a strong communal identity, a predominant characteristic in mountain church traditions today, especially those combining the "visible saint" model with the communal conversion model of church life.

Since a church community's collective experience of conversion was attained only through its individual members, at its earliest stages Scots-Irish sacramental revivalism made little practical differentiation between individual conversion and the communal conversion experience, for individual conversion typically occurred within the revivalistic context of the sacramental meeting, the locus of the church community's collective experience of conversion. As we have seen with the Old Regular Baptists, for the Scots-Irish the communal conversion experience was not the experience of individuals "getting saved" in a church service; it was the collective experience in worship of what heaven must be like, an experience that informed worshipers of what social relationships should be like in the here and now. This communal conversion tradition crosses theological lines of distinction within Appalachian mountain religion. Unlike Calvinist traditions, church traditions such as independent Holiness emphasize the conversion experience of the individual especially in the context of worship; but the worship life of such church traditions cannot be understood apart from their defining heritage rooted in the communal conversion experience.

The communal cleansing preceding the Scots-Irish Presbyterian sacramental meeting thus involved the process of individuals falling under a form of conviction that was communally centered; the individual's personal conduct may have weakened the fabric of the church community's life, which needed to be repaired through the individual's own concrete actions of repentence and reconciliation with others. Only then could the church community's collective experience of conversion take place. The conviction/conversion pattern, whether individual or communal, would characterize classic revivalism, first emerging with the Great Awakening in the American colonies. With the evolving emphases in Calvinist tradition influenced by rationalism, the revivalistic focus soon centered on the individual within a collective setting—contrary to the earlier Scots-Irish communal model—culminating in the nineteenth century's definitive shift toward Arminianism and the ascendancy of Finney-esque revivalism. The main exceptions to this shift during the nineteenth century in the United States were the revival traditions characterizing Scots-Irish religiosity that were now regionally specific to the upland South, geographically dominated by the Appalachian region.[20]

For the English Puritans, conversion was "intensely personal"; for the Scots-Irish, it was "vibrantly communal."[21] Appalachian mountain religion has carefully blended both aspects of personal and communal conversion,

tic" verbal genres—preaching, singing, praying, and testifying—that are the vehicles for spontaneous oral compositions and for spontaneous actions (expressive and ecstatic behavior) within the context of the worship service.[39] For Lawless, traditional religion is essentially oral, passed on through oral transmission and oral interpretive traditions. For the Scots-Irish laity, their traditional religiosity persisted through the "beliefs, behaviors, practices, and rituals" defining the long, transatlantic heritage of their multi-day sacramental meetings and revivals, a heritage that was imparted through oral transmission and oral interpretive traditions, and was creatively galvanized anew in each generation by their emotional piety and spontaneity in worship. In Appalachia today and throughout its history, mountain religion is characterized by its orality and its traditional features, which, as seen in analyses such as Westerkamp's and Lawless's, go hand in hand.

As Lawless points out, "folk churches" which are characterized by worship practices and belief systems that are grounded in oral tradition and are, therefore, "performed orally by the collective group involved . . . do tend to be autonomous."[40] This autonomy allows for variety and variation, rather than a codification yielding nearly identical expression in churches of the same tradition. At the same time, the nature of oral tradition creates similarity and replication, given the integrity of the transmission process. The oral character of Appalachian mountain religion is both a product and a cause of the overall autonomous character of mountain church life—even among church traditions steeped in a strong creedal heritage—thus eschewing any overtly controlling institutionalism of church life, from individual church communities to church traditions. This oral character is also a product and a cause of the shared features—whether they are strong or less pronounced—found in the worship practices, belief systems, and religious experiences unifying the variety of church traditions largely comprising Appalachian mountain religion as a regional religious tradition, apart from what are otherwise professed ideological or theological distinctions.

The Scots-Irish may have had their Westminster Confession, their Directory, and their Longer and Shorter Catechisms labored over by divines and transmitted by the clergy as the summation of Protestant reformed tradition for the Presbyterians. But they also had their traditions of emotional piety and spontaneity in which were grounded their revivalistic religiosity, their own religious ideology for which the vehicle was oral tradition.

James McGready and the Great Revival on the Appalachian Frontier

Long before the Great Awakening began to wane, large numbers of Scots-Irish had settled in Virginia and in North and South Carolina. The sacramental revivalism distinctive to them set the stage for what would become key elements in the foundation of mountain religious life. Soon the traditional religiosity of these Scots-Irish Presbyterian laity was blending into other denominational and theological movements in the region, influencing and being influenced by the revival Baptists and later the Methodists, and by modified Calvinism and Arminianism. By the very last years of the eighteenth century, the time was fully ripe for the combustive force of these commingling religious sensibilities and traditions to explode, creating the Great Revival on the Appalachian frontier. Almost simultaneously, these religious sensibilities and traditions quickly converged into—and thus generated—a regionally specific framework made up of land, people, history, and traditions through which the characterizing features of Appalachian mountain religion would develop and define themselves. But first we need to rehearse briefly the standard account of this period.

The camp meetings or large multi-day field preachings that characterized the height of the Great Revival in the Old Southwest were initiated during the revivals that broke out under the preaching of James McGready, a Presbyterian minister. McGready was born in Pennsylvania to Scots-Irish parents, grew up in North Carolina, was licensed to preach in 1788 by the Redstone Presbytery in southwestern Pennsylvania, and was assigned to work in North Carolina. His revivalistic preaching style in North Carolina resulted in many converts, several of whom were young men (including Barton W. Stone) who would go into the ministry and follow him to Kentucky when he received a call in 1796 from three congregations in Logan County, very near the Tennessee border.[41]

After weekly praying and fasting by McGready's Kentucky congregations for nearly a year, a revival broke out in 1797 and spread in 1798 and 1799. Prior to McGready's coming to Kentucky, Presbyterianism had converted few frontierspeople. In July 1800, McGready held a four-day revival meeting at Gasper River. People traveled forty, fifty, up to one hundred miles to participate. Since the crowds needed local accommodations, it was suggested that a regular encampment be formed around the center of the grounds, which was set up for worship. Thus the camp meeting was born under Presbyterian auspices. Soon the revival effort was interdenominational, involving "general" camp meetings and including the Baptists and Methodists. In 1800 ten camp meetings were held in Cumberland and Green River settlements. In upper Kentucky, between May and August 1801, six camp meetings were held.

In August 1801 the general camp meeting at Cane Ridge in Bourbon County, Kentucky, marked the peak of the Great Revival on the Appalachian frontier. The crowds numbered in the thousands. Eighteen Presbyterian ministers were present at Cane Ridge, including McGready; Barton W. Stone, whose enthusiasm for revival religion would soon lead him and others to form the Christian Church (1804), a new denomination indigenous to Appalachia; and Richard McNemar, who would become the leader of the Shaker movement in the West. John Lyle was also present, an "anti-revival" contender who would be instrumental in provoking the conservative reaction of the Synod of Kentucky and later the General Assembly in their response to the crisis in the Cumberland Presbytery generated by the Great Revival. This crisis resulted in the founding of the Cumberland Presbyterian Church in 1810, yet another new denomination indigenous to Appalachia.

The above sketch reflects the customary account of the camp meetings that swept the Appalachian frontier at the turn into the nineteenth century. What is missing is the central role played by Scots-Irish religiosity, which Schmidt is at pains to demonstrate: nearly all of the most celebrated camp meetings marking the height of the Great Revival started as Presbyterian sacramental meetings. The 1780s and 1790s saw a series of Presbyterian revivals in western Pennsylvania, Virginia, and North Carolina, now among the major centers of Scots-Irish settlement. McGready himself was born in Pennsylvania around 1758 and grew up in Guilford County, North Carolina, a stronghold of Presbyterianism. His training in western Pennsylvania placed him in the heart of sacramental revivals sweeping the area in the 1780s. He returned in 1788 to Guilford County to pastor the congregations of Haw River and Stoney Creek, and under his ministry there were a series of sacramental revivals. Departing in 1796 to Logan County in the Cumberland region of Kentucky, he took up the pastorates of the Muddy River, Red River, and Gasper River congregations. The Great Revival was quickly ignited through the communion seasons of these tiny churches. In his journal McGready wrote what Schmidt called a "standard litany" of the marvels of the communion season. "Repeatedly he related how 'a most remarkable season of the out-pouring of the Spirit of God' was connected with these communion occasions."[42] The huge gathering at Cane Ridge in August 1801 was also initiated as a Presbyterian sacramental meeting. At least one thousand people came forward to the tables. The crowds, swollen to around twenty thousand, surpassed Cambuslang in fervor. McGready wrote of eighteen revivals held between 1797 and 1800; sixteen were directly ignited by Presbyterian sacramental meetings.

Both Guilford County and Logan County today are immediately proximate to "official" Appalachia. Logan County in Kentucky is just two small counties removed from where the ARC identifies the boundary of Appalachia in that state. Guilford County in North Carolina borders Forsyth County, included within Appalachia in western North Carolina by the ARC. Bourbon County in Kentucky, the site of Cane Ridge, borders four very small counties included in Appalachia by the ARC. When the Great Revival broke forth, the geographic and especially the cultural and environmental boundaries of the Appalachian frontier—which steadily shrank in upon themselves over the next two centuries—encompassed these locales.

McGready's repeated description of sacramental meetings on the Appalachian frontier as "a most remarkable season of the out-pouring of the Spirit of God" was not simply a stock phrase. Like the Old Time Baptists of the region (who were not yet considered "Old Time"), McGready equated people's ecstatic religious experiences during these extraordinary occasions with the tangible presence of the Holy Spirit. In addition, revivals were not yet a product of scheduling and organizational advance planning as they would be in Finney's day, less than thirty-five years later in the East. Instead, McGready and his congregations prayed and fasted for a year in 1796, waiting on God to act in a movement of grace through the Holy Spirit. Only then did a series of revivals "break out," creating the Great Revival on the Appalachian frontier. This tradition of prayerful expectation and alert readiness for the uncontrollable and unpredictable quickening of the Holy Spirit remains a dominant trait of mountain religious life today.

In 1803 McGready published the following account in the new Presbyterian-sponsored *Western Missionary Magazine,* issued out of Pittsburgh:

> I HAVE the happiness to inform you, that the Lord is yet doing wonders in our country. Our Sacramental occasions are days of the Son of Man indeed, and are usually marked with the visible footsteps of Jehovah's majesty and glory. . . . [A]t the Sacrament in the Ridge congregation . . . [t]here were upwards of five hundred communicants; and at the tables, through the evening, and during the greater part of the night, the people of God were so filled with such extatic raptures of divine joy and comfort, that I could compare it to nothing else than the New Jerusalem coming down from heaven to earth.[43]

Here McGready "could compare it to nothing else" than the communal experience in the here and now of what heaven must be like, an ideal that became foundational to mountain worship life. A little over a century later, W. F. Bryant of the Church of God (Cleveland, Tennessee) would offer similar reports about communion-footwashing meetings in small mountain cabins. McGready's succinct yet full account, "A Short Narrative of the Revival of Religion in Logan County," appeared serially in *Western Missionary Magazine* during its first year of publication. In addition, McGready sent out shorter versions of his "Narrative" in letter form to several friends, and many of these shorter versions appeared in a number of eastern evangelical magazines. As Paul Conkin observed, "No simple description of religious events, save possibly Jonathan Edward's *A Faithful Narrative* [*of the Surprising Work of God in the Conversion of Many Hundred Souls in Northampton* (1737)], had as profound and lasting an effect."[44]

Schmidt concluded that "The Great Revival was the grandest display of the powers of the Scottish sacramental occasion that America would witness. . . . Though changes would come and new measures replace old, the frontier regions—western Pennsylvania, the valley of Virginia, backcountry North Carolina, Kentucky, and Tennessee—would be the places where the sacramental practices of the evangelical Scots and Ulster Scots would be best preserved."[45] Like Westerkamp, Schmidt grounded the "preservation" or perpetuation of the sacramental revival traditions that were the religiosity distinctive to the Scots-Irish laity almost exclusively within what became Appalachia, and soon localized in its mountain regions—"though changes would come and new measures replace old."

Growing numbers of Scots-Irish settlers of these "frontier regions" were becoming Baptists, intermingling their evangelical Presbyterian heritage of revival religiosity with the revival culture of the Baptists, principally from Virginia and North Carolina. By the time of McGready's earliest sacramental revivals in the Kentucky-Tennessee area, Baptist revival culture, which centered in the more private setting of worship in church houses as well as in their "great meetings" lasting over an extended weekend, had also been well planted in these less-settled parts of the region. At the same time, with the apogee of Cane Ridge, Scots-Irish sacramental revivalism had all but died out in the East, where soon Finney would wed classic revival practices to new theological developments, transforming revivalism itself and divorcing it from the religiosity now normative to the Appalachian frontier. Indeed, New England Presbyterian and Congregationalist travelers to the Appalachian frontier, such as John F. Schermerhorn as early as 1812–13, would find it necessary to explain these multi-day communion meetings to the readers of their written accounts—readers who were themselves Presbyterians and Congregationalists. Scots-Irish sacramental revivalism and its distinctive religiosity were now regionally specific to Appalachia. With the advancing decades of the nineteenth century, that sacramental consciousness and the revival religiosity it defined soon limited themselves—now transformed by other religious traditions that also became regionally specific—primarily to Appalachia's mountains and small valleys.

From the blending of Scots-Irish religiosity especially with Baptist revival culture (although not exclusively, for pietist influences were also extremely significant) emerged a form of sacramental revivalism that became unique to the mountains of the Appalachian region and was the normative tradition of mountain religiosity. This religiosity would characterize the numerous, doctrinally diverse church traditions making up Appalachian mountain religion, emerging as a regional religious tradition without parallel in the history of American Christianity. Nonetheless, the integrity of mountain religion as a uniquely American and Protestant tradition, created within and delimited by the Appalachian region, was all but invisible to the prevailing national religious culture. That invisibility was due, in part, to the cloaking devices of oral transmission and oral interpretive traditions within the predominantly oral culture of mountain religion. It was also due to the "isolation" issue. As a consequence, mountain religion historically was disregarded by the dominant religious culture of denominationally based American Protestantism. American Protestantism itself represented and reflected a larger society that knew how to acknowledge and respect only bureaucratically entrenched institutions and the authority it invested in reams of written documentation and expository material—legitimizing requirements that were the antithesis of Appalachian mountain religion. The overall absence of the features necessary to legitimate mountain religious culture in the eyes of the national religious culture was the primary reason—along with the overwhelming presence of the "corrupting" influences of expressive and ecstatic worship practices—that the first large wave of home missionaries dismissed mountain religion as not a "real" religion, or, at best, a "folk" religion made up of innumerable, incoherent "sects."

Mountain religion's revivified form of the "sacramental/sacrament meeting," from Old Regular Baptist to independent Holiness, perpetuated not only the Scots-Irish laity's traditional religiosity of the communal conversion experience but even their vocabulary. Today in many Appalachian mountain churches, "sacrament" or the Lord's Supper is combined with footwashing, a transformation of the Scots-Irish sacramental meeting stemming from the Baptist revival in colonial Virginia and North Carolina. The revivalist religiosity of the early Scots-Irish and their sacramental sensibilities firmly undergird communion-footwashing, a worship event of extraordinary power now unique to mountain religion. Scots-Irish sacramental revivalism, beginning in early seventeenth-century Ulster and western Scotland, profoundly shaped the religious history of the Appalachian region, and continues today as a living lineage in mountain religious culture where it found its home.

A "Sacrament Meeting" in an Independent Holiness Church

On December 31, 1989, I attended a "night watch" service for praying in the New Year at Cranks Holiness Church in Harlan County, Kentucky. ("Night watch" is a common word-order inversion for the tradition of the "watch night" service going back most recently to plain-folk camp-meeting religion and earlier still to Baptist revival culture.) This was to be a special occasion, for Brother Coy Miser had called a "sacrament meeting" for the night ser-

Although sociology has been one of the biggest culprits in making popular stereotypes of Appalachian mountain religion academically legitimate, it also offers a helpful alternative interpretive framework. Recent scholarship in historical sociology of the Baptist revival in colonial Virginia is extremely pertinent to understanding how the religiosity characteristic of Appalachian mountain religion, rooted as it is in revivalist traditions in particular, has created within the structure of mountain religious life a very specific power of self-definition. The power of self-definition for individuals within their church communities, as well as for individual church communities and the church traditions of which they are a part, directly contradicts interpretations of Appalachian mountain religion rooted in functionalist notions of compensation for alienation and powerlessness.

The following discussion is based on the work of J. Stephen Kroll-Smith in the field of historical sociology, which does a very good job of not reducing revival religion—and religion itself—to the function of social systems only. Kroll-Smith saw revival religion as a religious solution to a religious problem. He also saw it as having a relationship to or "point of intersect between" social structures where problems intrinsic to social systems were translated into religious issues.[14] Kroll-Smith identified the revival religion of colonial Virginia Baptists as a "status movement." Before we proceed further, it is best to introduce now rather than when they first occur thumbnail definitions of several tightly interconnected terms that appear repeatedly in various combinations over the next few pages. This somewhat technical yet brief discussion will provide the groundwork for understanding the power of self-definition embodied in the worship practices, belief systems, and church traditions making up mountain religious culture.

> *Status* has to do *not* with economic or psychological indicators such as class or levels of prestige, but with a distinct lifestyle.
> *Style of life* intertwines social identity and social action (conduct) and is built around criteria that are, in Kroll-Smith's words, "personal and meaningful" (p. 29).
> A *status group* is a community or membership group bound together by a distinct style of life.
> A *status order* is the specific set or system of values expressed in a distinct style of life.
> *Status authority* is the right to assign identity and regulate conduct within a status or membership group.

The two key terms for our purposes are "status power" and "status movement."

> *Status power* is the power of self-definition, or control over the means for creating a distinct style of life.

A *status movement* allows people to *gain* control over the means for creating a distinct style of life.

Our focus on Kroll-Smith's insights about revival religion as a status movement will set the stage for a fuller discussion of the religious rituals and organizational structures that he also identified as embodying Baptist revival culture in eighteenth-century Virginia. These religious rituals and organizational structures translated into features that became extremely characteristic of Appalachian mountain religion in general and served most of the same purposes, especially with regard to mountain people's power of religious self-definition through the creation of their own religious culture. Moreover, these rituals and structures of Baptist revival culture intermingled with the sacramental consciousness and revival religiosity of the Scots-Irish as they migrated south and west into Appalachia, together creating the larger framework making up what was by the mid-1820s a distinctive regional religious tradition.

Kroll-Smith began by observing that today denominations such as the Southern Baptist Convention, Church of God (Cleveland, Tennessee), and Church of the Nazarene (one of the largest and oldest Holiness denominations) are "institutionalized variants of revival religion." Generically, and apart from notable historical variants such as the Scots-Irish represent, revival religion is based in a pietistic-puritan or pietistic-ascetic tradition of "personal conversion and moral conduct," that is, conversion or *salvation by experience* and *assurance by conduct* (p. 9). This twin aspect of salvation and assurance in revival religion was the key to shifting *status authority*—"the right to control conduct and assign identities" (p. 14)—from the prevailing or dominant status group of the gentry in colonial Virginia, who claimed hereditary privilege, to the burgeoning agrarian-based middle class, who identified themselves with revival religion at the same time they achieved economic autonomy through the introduction of slave labor in place of indentured servants. Control of labor and land controlled the economy. Until the early eighteenth century, the Virginia gentry controlled both. Slave labor widened the base of economic opportunity and "life chances" beyond the exclusive control of the gentry (p. 85). The revival Baptists were mostly a "highly mobile middle class" always in pursuit of land (p. 91), a pursuit that would take many of them into the mountains of Appalachia. Although many of the original revival Baptists achieved their economic autonomy and middle-class standing through participation in the South's "peculiar institution," mountain people, with few exceptions, historically were not slaveholders.

As they gained self-sufficiency through ability rather than privilege, the eighteenth-century Virginia middle class also wanted control over social

more likely than not prepared to call the combustion of sounds and actions a "melody." A "heavenly confusion among the preachers" and a "celestial discord among the people," not just at great meetings but at the annual meetings of associations too, may not edify the understanding, but "raise great emotion in the heart."

Highly emotive, nonrational religious experience centered on the heart rather than the head: not only did ritual ecstasy displace rationality but it was fundamentally a religious leveler, the great equalizer of all the participants, regardless of background or communal standing, that carried over into the ordinary aspects of church life. Moreover, as Kroll-Smith noted, "In the context of this ecstatic milieu participants were moved to commit themselves unconditionally to the ideology of the revival movement" (p. 201). Ecstatic expression in mountain religious life still serves as a means of committing oneself to the shared ethos of the church community. It is not simply "fun" or "have-a-good-time" religion, or a desparate release from life's travails, as it is so often portrayed. Whether at great meetings or in the privacy of local church houses, ecstatic expression encouraged and reinforced transition. Indeed, it was both transformative and confirmative, the difference in emphasis determined by its settings.

If the public rituals of baptism and the great meetings were transformative, Kroll-Smith observed that the rituals that occurred in the more private setting of worship in church houses were confirmative, and may more appropriately be called "revival ceremonies." Indeed, revival ceremonies were worship practices designed to integrate revival religiosity into that private setting to make it part of the ordinary occasions in people's religious lives, as well as the extraordinary. In the private life of individual church communities, revival ceremonies served to represent and reinforce or confirm a new social reality—both as it was and as people wished it would be. Revival ceremonies thus served, in Kroll-Smith's words, as a principal "means of value integration" (p. 206). This is certainly the function of the worship practices most characteristic of mountain church life today. They serve to integrate the values of mountain religiosity into the ordinary occasions of worship. Mountain religion's own "revival ceremonies," worship practices originally grounded in revival religiosity, give people an experience in the immediacy of the moment of what heaven must be like, the ideal social reality. They also inform how people are to conduct their daily lives, how to bring a part of that ideal social reality into the here and now. They are mountain religion's principal "means of value integration."

The actual revival ceremonies of colonial Virginia Baptists were often identical to the worship practices found in mountain churches today. David Benedict (1779–1874) recorded about Sandy Creek Association, the mother of all Separate Baptist associations in the South:

This Association held many sentiments formerly, and it also holds some now, which are of a peculiar nature, and which do not prevail among their brethren elsewhere. Many of its members were formerly thought to lean considerably towards the Arminian system; but they have now become generally, and some of them strenuously Calvinistick. . . . They formerly held nine Christian rites, viz. *baptism, the Lord's supper, love-feasts, laying-on-of-hands, washing feet, anointing the sick, right hand of fellowship, kiss of charity, and devoting children.* They also held to ruling elders, eldresses, deaconesses, and weekly communion.[27]

The "peculiar sentiments" of this foundational association in Baptist history in the South had to do with a shift from Arminianism to Calvinism.

From Benedict's statement, we can see what many mountain church traditions have confirmed in their own histories and ongoing presence in the region: there could be as much of a movement from Arminianism to Calvinism as there had been almost everywhere else a movement from Calvinism to Arminianism. Arminianism was not simply higher up the evolutionary ladder of theological development. Many mountain church traditions, though "general" or "universal" in their atonement doctrines, nonetheless would make a wide berth for Calvinist traditions of grace and the Holy Spirit, which firmly tamped down the rational-decision/human-initiative aspect of fully developed Arminianism. By the time Benedict published his history of Baptists in America (1813), the "peculiar sentiments" of Calvinism did "not prevail among their brethren elsewhere," and by "elsewhere" Benedict meant throughout the rest of the United States. The "peculiar sentiments" of Calvinism had become regionally specific.

Benedict also wrote that the "greatest part of the nine Christian rites, and especially those of them which were of a peculiar nature, together with the offices of eldresses and deaconesses *have fallen into disuse.*"[28] Nonetheless, all of the "formerly held nine Christian rites" of the Sandy Creek Association are found throughout mountain churches today, although not all churches practice all nine rites.[29] This suggests the intertwining of theology with ritual, where Calvinist traditions uplifting the values of grace and humility found embodiment in communal worship practices that were a "means of value integration" representing a social reality both as it was in the worship environment and as the worshipers hoped it would be in their daily lives. Footwashing in particular became the premier symbol of humility or "humbleness" in mountain religion, an interpretation fully developed in the theological traditions of the Primitive[30] and Old Regular Baptists and representative of mountain church life generally wherever footwashing continued to be practiced.

Along with Sandy Creek Association, Free Will Baptists—organized in North Carolina in 1727 and originally located in North Carolina and Virgin-

vidual within that community and revivifying the community as a whole. The original purpose of these "revival ceremonies" in the worship services of revival Baptists during the Great Awakening in the South was to break through people's social distance. This alone made it possible to build up a community of faith that strove to embody in its worship life the ideal social reality of what heaven must be like. To that end, the worship practices of the revival Baptists conveyed profound intimacy and affection; they expressed what the people themselves understood Christian love to be by affirming in the context of worship itself the rightness and appropriateness of emotional, physical, and psychic vulnerability to each other that was personally risky. Willingness to be at personal risk through such worship practices was the key to creating the type of worship environment that was the hallmark of Baptist revival culture, and later mountain religious culture.

The experience of what heaven must be like in mountain worship services today is also grounded in the experience and understanding of what is Christian love for each other. Expressions of tender-heartedness—profound intimacy and affection—are paramount in mountain religion, located especially in tears and tactility. They are meant to "raise great emotion in the heart," as John Leland put it, and express what is Christian love for each other—a love that is translated into community-based social action or what Ron Short called "a cooperative spirit" outside the doors of the mountain church house. For observers of mountain church services open to such expressions, it is impossible not to recognize that the worship practices are extremely successful in tenderizing the hearts of the worshipers, which carries over to a greater or lesser extent into their everyday lives. This emotional focus of mountain worship practices on people's tenderheartedness to each other within the context of worship makes these practices the most important and the most potent "means of value integration" within mountain religion.

Perhaps the most striking aspect of such emotive practices in revival Baptist worship life was the individual autonomy that underlay them. As Benedict stated about Sandy Creek Association, "It must not be understood, that all the churches in this body were strenuous, or even uniform, in the observance of this long list of rites, all of which, however, appear to be suggested by the Scriptures; nor did those who maintained them, refuse communion with their brethren, who neglected a part."[44] As in mountain religious life today, it was for each church—and especially each person within a church—to decide what actions were appropriate to engage in within the context of worship: for churches whether it be some or all "of this long list of rites," and for individuals whether it be crying, shouting, running, and other physical motions, silently weeping, spontaneously praying out loud or singing, going from person to person shaking hands and embracing, testifying, and even preaching. The fluidity of individual spontaneous action was built into and affirmed by revival ceremonies in private worship life—and this is probably the most profound and heart-touching aspect of mountain worship life today.

Individual spontaneous actions—expressing ecstatic religious experiences or "blessings" (as Brother Coy Miser called them) centering on the individual—were not simply a product of self-indulgence or total self-absorption fragmenting the worship service. Instead, such actions—individuals shouting, dancing, being slain in the Spirit, and so on—had the effect of being appreciated as "a blessing" also to those who witnessed them. In Brother Coy's words, such individual blessings "edify the church" (that is, the people gathered for worship) because they were understood to have their source in the power of God through the Holy Spirit. Individuals as well as the community as a whole were a conduit for the presence of the Holy Spirit during worship, with neither assuming greater importance than the religious experiences of the other. Indeed, for mountain people today and the eighteenth-century revival Baptists, such expressive and spontaneous behavior on the part of the individual was affirmed by the worshiping community as a whole because it marked the immediate presence in the worship environment of the "divine power" (as the Scots-Irish Presbyterian Samuel Blair said in 1740), identified in mountain religion as the power of God through the immediate presence of the Holy Spirit.

In the egalitarian ethos of revival culture that affirmed individual autonomy, individual churches could choose what revival traditions they engaged in, and individuals within a church community had a further right to choose what actions they would engage in, what actions they considered sacred and appropriate to their public expression of their experience of salvation. This ethos and affirmation are especially true today for independent Holiness churches, which have great variety and total autonomy in the particulars that shape their worship lives but draw from a common base of oral tradition. As for the individual, Kroll-Smith summarized succinctly the purpose of such expressive, intimate rituals or ceremonial acts in worship: "[T]he ceremonial life of the revival Baptist movement was organized so as to dramatize the autonomy of the person" (pp. 210–11).

Personal autonomy and individual recognition within the framework of intimate face-to-face communities, both in the setting of worship and in everyday life, were paramount and were the very focus of the revival ceremonies. Baptism, footwashing, the Lord's Supper, laying on of hands, devoting children, the kiss of charity, anointing the sick with oil, the right hand of fellowship, testifying through the love feast (and later within the context of worship itself)—along with their catalytic traditions of spontaneity and emotional piety (expressive and ecstatic behavior)—the center of attention

Semple wrote that "impressions were made upon the minds of many" that had a profound, motivating influence on them to seek out conversionist preaching or revival preachers. This parallels, if not connects, accounts such as Samuel Blair's of the 1740 revival among the Scots-Irish in his church in southeastern Pennsylvania. Blair wrote that there were "manifest evidences of impressions on the hearers." Blair identified the "appearance of the divine power and presence" with the "*evidences* of impressions" such as "fainting," "sobbing," "crying," "weeping," and "strange unusual bodily motions," which he called "soul-exercises," that is, ecstatic expressions specifically identified with Scots-Irish religiosity and their revival culture. In comparison, Semple wrote that "meeting at private houses on Sundays for the purpose of singing and praying and reading the Scriptures" triggered "impressions . . . made upon the minds of many," what Blair had called "impressions on the hearers." "Impressions" were more than mental categories. They were accompanied by "evidences" in Blair's account. Although Semple made no mention of "evidences," nonetheless specific "impressions" led those holding house meetings to seek out the first of the double prong of Baptist revival culture, conversionist preaching. As Semple wrote earlier about Baptist revival preachers, "Being often deeply affected themselves while preaching, correspondent affections were felt by their pious hearers, which were frequently expressed by tears, trembling, screams, shouts and acclamations." While conversionist preaching and communion made up the double prong of Scots-Irish sacramental revivalism, the central place of the Lord's Supper was superseded in Baptist revival culture by the sacramental practice or rite of baptism as the point of entry for full incorporation into that culture. Both Scots-Irish sacramental revivalism and Baptist revival culture employed most of the same common behavior patterns of expressive and ecstatic behavior—emotional piety—making up their nearly identical revival religiosity. The primary difference between them was the shift in sacramental focus.

In Semple's account of Smith's Creek Church, local Baptists held meetings "at private houses," a long-standing and ongoing tradition of mountain religious culture underscoring the distinction mountain people make between a "church" (the people) and a "church house." Smith's Creek Church's participants also traveled "greater distances to hear preaching and to invite preachers" to their house meetings. They were not sent preachers by a larger ecclesiastical body, but had "preachers raised up among them" through the "divine mercy." Mill Creek itself was a mother church from which Smith's Creek Church was "constituted off." Mill Creek Church was formed by the efforts of a revival Baptist named John Koontz who began to preach in his own neighborhood soon after his baptism, later moving on to Mill Creek where he had family: "Rev. John Koontz was the first that preached a pure gospel within the limits of Mill Creek. Having been baptized in Fauquier

December, 1768, and living at the time in Frederick county, near Front Royal, he began in a few months after his baptism to exhort and preach in his own neighborhood. So he continued until November, 1770, when he resolved to go up to Shenandoah, into the neighborhood of Mill Creek, where his brother George lived."[49] Semple's accounts about Smith's Creek Church and Mill Creek Church show how revival culture spread through itinerant preachers—who often began preaching and exhorting soon after baptism in their own face-to-face neighborhood communities of family, friends, associates, and acquaintances—and through the constitution of individual churches that would send out "branches or arms" until they too became self-sufficient as individual churches.

As Kroll-Smith observed, individual churches were constituted on the basis of a church community's competency in revival culture. Sandy Creek Association illustrated the interweaving of Calvinist theology with the "rites" or worship practices associated with Baptist revival culture. The interweaving of Baptist revival culture with Calvinism at the institutional level of constituting churches was illustrated by the Kehukee Association, whose mother church of the same name in Halifax County, North Carolina, was organized in 1742 as General Baptist and became Particular Baptist in 1755, just before the Baptist advent of the Great Awakening in the South. Indeed, Morgan Edwards stated that the Kehukee Church "was the first to become calvinistic,"[50] a harbinger of the Kehukee Association's central role in galvanizing the anti-mission controversy, the counterresponse to the American Benevolence movement, culminating in the Kehukee Declaration of 1827.

The 1803 history of the Kehukee Association (and "the Virginia Portsmouth and Neuse Associations, which were formed out of this") summarized the process of institutionalization by which revival Baptist churches were traditionally established:

> A church of Christ is a congregation of men and women, publicly professing faith in Christ Jesus, and being regularly baptized by immersion, who have covenanted together, given themselves up to one another in the Lord, to be governed by his word, and to be guided by a regular and proper discipline, agreeably to the Holy Scriptures.
>
> .   .   .   .
>
> The newly-constituted churches in this Association are such as have been constituted out of the old churches, being branches or arms of the same. Being gathered, baptized, and received members of such churches: and, when ripe for constitution, usually petition the body for dismission thereto. . . . The ministers inquire whether it is their *desire* to become a church, whether their *habitations* are near enough to each other conveniently to attend church conferences [monthly business meetings]? Whether they are so well acquainted with each

other's life and conversation as to coalesce into one body, and walk together in love and fellowship? . . . These things being answered in the affirmative, then a covenant is produced, . . . and being read, consented to, and subscribed, the ministers pronounce them a church, in some such words as these, "In the name of our Lord Jesus Christ, and by the authority of our office, we pronounce you . . . a true *Gospel church.*"[51]

When "ripe for constitution"—in other words, churches were made up when the time was right, when there were a sufficient number of people who had been "gathered" under the wing of revival culture and "baptized by immersion," the public rite of social transition. Local access to a church meeting house or common gathering place and a knowledge of one another "as to coalesce into one body, and walk together in love and fellowship" were paramount.

Churches were also required to "*keep up a regular discipline* agreeably to the Scriptures," a product of moving private morality into the public sphere.[52] Churches regularly disciplined members at the monthly church conferences, when on the testimony of more than one witness charges of public drunkenness, profanity, slander, quarrels, fighting, infidelity—anything that would disturb the peace of the church community—were proven. Salvation by experience of conversion initiated the individual into the new status order of revival culture. However, assurance through conduct determined appropriate behavior within the new status order. The local church community assumed the task of regulating social conduct not just within but outside the doors of the church house. The local church's involvement in the social conduct of its members would remain formidable in Appalachian mountain religion, especially in the traditions of the Old Regular and Primitive Baptists.

As the Kehukee account indicated, "the old churches" or mother churches would form "branches or arms of the same," often called daughter churches, by which means revival culture was transmitted to other locations. When an arm or branch had acquired its own stability and sufficiency, it would "petition for dismission" to "arm off" as a church community independent of the mother church. Many churches armed off in this fashion would themselves become mother churches, in turn forming their own arms or branches as daughter churches. Mother churches were thus churches that not only attended to the needs of their own members but would send out individuals to evangelize throughout the immediate area until daughter churches were constituted. This process of local evangelization was the original meaning behind the term "home missionary" in the Baptist movement in the mountains. Associations functioned and were formed the same way. When a sufficient number of churches were grouped in a geographic area, they would petition the mother association to arm off as their own independent association. Thus Mates Creek (org. 1849) and Union (org. 1859) associations armed off from New Salem Association (org. 1825) of Old Regular Baptists, Mates Creek later becoming Regular Primitive Baptist and Union remaining Old Regular Baptist. From these strategies for institutionalization, we can now see that, like a vine stretching forth a tendril, which puts down roots and sends out tendrils of its own, the status movement of Baptist revival culture grew throughout Virginia and North Carolina and into the mountains of Appalachia.

This highly localized and locally controlled tradition for planting revival culture is today normative in mountain religious life and has determined its institutional history, both formal and informal. Like the umbrella term "evangelicalism" in American Protestantism, the regional religious tradition of Appalachian mountain religion is also an umbrella under which are found many church traditions. Mountain religion has general yet highly pronounced distinguishing features, but the features differentiating its various church traditions are more specific. The differentiation of these church traditions is rooted principally in variations on revival culture, variations that have to do with different emphases. Throughout the history of their strong doctrinal heritage in the region, Primitive and Old Regular Baptists have emphasized the prescribed institutional aspects of revival culture much more so than have other mountain church traditions. Formal constitutions and dismissions of churches and associations, establishing "church covenants," agreeing to live by a "regular and proper discipline," "church conferences" (monthly business meetings), the prerequisite of being in "love and fellowship" before the monthly worship service can take place, annual meetings of associations where questions of doctrine and polity and basic lifestyle are addressed, as well as other features of institutionalization continue to characterize the highly traditional Old Regular and Primitive Baptists. Status or style of life is tightly intertwined with their institutional structures at both the local and associational level. Indeed, for the Old Regular and Primitive Baptists, these institutional structures embody major aspects of their own status orders or systems of values marking their distinctiveness within Appalachian mountain religion.

But for mountain religion generally, the rituals or common behavior patterns making up its revival religiosity, transmitted primarily through oral tradition in its broad variety of settings for worship (from the most private to the most public), have had much greater impact overall, certainly for independent Holiness and even for the Old Regular and Primitive Baptists. The status or style-of-life delimitations determined by emphasizing the formal institutional features of revival culture as mountain religion's most traditional groups have done, even their creeds (which had characterized their Regular Baptist ancestors), have had less impact. Again, ideology and institutions, although major factors, have less influence on mountain religion than the symbolic activity or common behavior patterns that are the principal means by which revival religion manifests itself. The transmission of revival culture thus continues in Appalachian mountain religion almost entirely through oral tradition,[53] from its worship practices and the belief systems they embody (emphasizing grace, the Holy Spirit, and the centrality of religious experience), to its organizational base through local itinerant preachers and the local formation of churches. The nature or type of institutionalization is the principal variant. For nearly all mountain church traditions, their institutionalization—no matter the type or the extent—does not reach beyond the local or at most the subregional level (including mountain church traditions with a scattering of individual churches now located beyond the cultural-geographic bounds of Appalachia through out-migration). Among the exceptions are those individual mountain churches belonging to the denominations of American Protestantism, but whose cultural and religious identity are far more regional than institutional or national.

As Semple stated about Smith's Creek Church, when a local area established regular preaching, often in a home, either by an exhorting lay member or a local preacher, other preachers would soon begin to visit that location for regular preaching and it would become ripe as an area for organizing a new church. This tradition thrives in mountain religion today and is especially strong among independent nondenominational churches. The process itself among these churches is much less formalized and much less strictly regulated than it was for the revival Baptists of colonial Virginia or for the Old Regular and Primitive Baptists today. For example, Brother Coy Miser would autonomously establish a church, usually in a "dwelling house" (a term he used to distinguish it from a "church house"), when he saw a need in a neighborhood where he was living or working. Brother Coy says that often he would get permission from the house's owner to knock out walls to allow sufficient room for people to gather. Brother Coy would then tend to that church as a preacher and pastor until sufficient numbers were gathered and someone came forward to take over as preacher and pastor, with many local independent preachers drawn to the new location where they would exercise their gifts. Brother Coy would then continue to worship in the new church community until he moved on.

In this way Brother Coy has established independent Holiness churches—by his estimation eleven to date—throughout southwest Virginia, eastern Kentucky, northeast Tennessee, and southern Ohio. Brother Coy has no possessiveness about these churches. He does not call them "his" churches. Instead, in his understanding, his efforts have been a response to the hand of God on his life in the transmission of the Gospel. At the least, his work is a genuine offspring of the tradition of planting churches and transmitting revival culture first established by revival Baptists in eighteenth-century Virginia. Brother Coy himself as a preacher and pastor is also a genuine offspring of that tradition. In his life's work as a mountain preacher we see clearly an example of the "native ministers found in the mountains" whom Campbell identified as "one of the strong links with the past which here in the Highlands have not yet been broken."[54] We also see in Brother Coy's life's work "the native Church" Campbell wrote of at its most basic and, if one dares to use the word, "indigenous" expression in the mountains of the Appalachian region today.

Baptist revival culture (conjoining the Regulars and Separates) was planted in Kentucky by the earliest years of the 1780s, and thence throughout the mountains of Appalachia. While moving to Kentucky, Gilbert Craig helped to constitute a church in September 1781 at the farthest southwestern settlement of Virginia at the Cumberland Gap, the traditional heart of central Appalachia where Tennessee, Kentucky, and Virginia meet. During these years, and earlier still in Virginia and North Carolina, the sacramental revivalism of Scots-Irish people—as growing numbers of them became Baptists—intermingled with Baptist revival culture. This reconfigured the original sacramental focus on the Lord's Supper of Scots-Irish revival-based ritual practices, at about the time of the Great Revival. As the evangelical Scots-Irish Presbyterian sacramental meeting or "communion season" of the Lord's Supper receded almost totally into memory, the early and highly circumscribed Baptist tradition of practicing together communion and footwashing during what Benedict also called the "communion season," along with the universal Baptist practice of baptism by immersion, gained ascendancy as the sacramental focus of revival religiosity. Scots-Irish sacramental consciousness was now wedded to these two ritual traditions—the sacramental meeting combining communion with footwashing, and baptism by immersion ideally (and usually) in a natural body of flowing waters—creating a transformed sacramental revivalism now unique to Appalachian mountain religion.

Oral tradition shaped the revival religiosity normative to mountain religious culture that came from numerous complementary sources that had integrated themselves into the region during its earliest years of settlement. Highlights ranged from the unique preaching traditions of the Welsh Baptists, who were also in the forefront of introducing to Baptists in America the practice of laying on of hands beyond the context of baptism, to Anabaptist baptism practices and the Anabaptist groups—particularly the German Baptist Brethren and the Mennonites—that conjoined communion with footwashing. Of particular importance, pietism's emphasis on the primacy of the Holy Spirit moving within individuals through spontaneous emotional expression in the communal setting of worship had worked its way deep into

churches were particularly concentrated, so today are independent Holiness churches, although Holiness churches were never limited to the range of Methodist churches. Hooker noted that "Methodist churches are peculiarly liable to be weakened by the Holiness services in the vicinity."[6] In terms of many mountain Methodists' traditional religiosity, a religiosity that was principally revivalist in practice and centered on religious experience, Holiness churches through their worship services met people's needs. The Holiness movement on the eastern seaboard, officially inaugurated at Vineland, New Jersey, in 1867, had been a direct response to the loss of the centrality and vitality of religious experience and revivalist religiosity in Methodism. Mountain people never lost that spirituality, and so never needed a separate movement to reactivate it. It remained at the core of their religious lives.

The term "Holiness" was adopted by Baptist churches, as well as by Methodist churches usually not tied as tightly to the connectional system; however few or many is not known. Baptist-Methodist-Holiness was a common transition in the religious journey of mountain people within a single lifetime. Except for the term itself, "Holiness" was not so much brought into the mountains as already present, although theological influences certainly had an impact as the national Holiness-Pentecostal movements developed and defined themselves. Baptist and Methodist people who had long embodied in their worship lives the traditions of plain-folk camp-meeting religion, deeply planted in mountainous Appalachia, also identified it with their traditional religiosity. Their shift in self-identity to Holiness beginning in the late nineteenth century, many founding new churches, was a logical transition. One of the most important values of the traditional religiosity stemming from plain-folk camp-meeting religion that was incorporated into independent Holiness churches were the egalitarian norms its worship life embodied, norms now contradicted by the highly developed hierarchical institutionalism of the Methodist church as a denomination.

Many of Methodism's small mountain churches also created an exception to the ambitious goals of "modern Methodism" in Appalachia as a result of the pervasive influences of mountain religious culture and their particular affinity with the mountain church tradition of independent Holiness through which they heard loudly reverberating historical echoes from their not so distant past. Many of them still today remain much closer to the traditions of mountain religion than to modern Methodism—especially the "high church" Methodism found in some Appalachian urban centers. The traditions making up mountain religion and especially independent Holiness churches were a radical sign of contradiction that created a conflict over Methodist self-identity in Appalachia: proud of their tradition's long frontier heritage in the region, nonetheless much of Methodist leadership in Appalachia and even much of the laity into the last decade of the twentieth century chose to overlook or discount the fact that Methodism in Appalachia was surrounded by a religious culture still perpetuating religious emphases and values it had long ago abandoned. Typically, many even went so far as to insist that the surrounding culture of Appalachian mountain religion was "marginal" to the overall religious life of the region—meaning the religious life that really mattered to them—thus artificially placing the United Methodist Church at the forefront of religious life in Appalachia because it was the region's second largest denominational presence.

In the summer of 1992, one West Virginia native, a Methodist minister of a large urban church in his home state, told me that the traditions making up mountain religious life that were distinctive to Appalachia were "Indian headdresses," quaint but not in the least representative of what "religion in Appalachia" was really all about today. Ironically, he and several of his colleagues in the West Virginia clergy expressed great pride in the fact that West Virginia was the only state included in its geographic entirety within Appalachia. Moreover, he and his colleagues were also firm in their intent to "lift up Appalachia" into a "position of leadership" at the national level within the United Methodist Church. But the Appalachia they were intending to "lift up" most certainly did not include the religious culture that was special and unique to the Appalachian region.

This minister meant to convey by his "Indian headdresses" analogy that the worship practices, belief systems, and church traditions making up Appalachian mountain religion as a regional religious tradition had no significance to his church life today and but little (he assumed) to Methodist history in Appalachia. He perceived Methodism in Appalachia to be more insular than expansive, a bringer of religious influences but not significantly influenced by the surrounding religious culture during its long history in the region (a surprising perspective given Methodism's historical flexibility and the fact that its celebrated frontier heritage was located largely in Appalachia). Throughout my research on Appalachian mountain religion, I have continuously interacted with the presence of American Protestantism in Appalachia. The attitudes toward mountain religious life expressed by this minister were extremely representative not just of Methodism but of nearly all of American Protestantism in Appalachia. In fact, I have encountered widespread and strong resistance to any serious, sustained focus on mountain religion, be it academic or not. As I have argued, a basic conflict of religious values was at the heart of this resistance, masked by labels such as "Indian headdresses." For many of the Appalachian churches of American Protestantism, as we shall see with the Methodists, that conflict was intensified by issues of self-image.

Today some Native Americans of the Cherokee Nation in Cherokee, North Carolina—now a tourism center—model "Indian headdresses" and

mance of the Amish and "Pennsylvania Dutch Country." An entire industry totally out of the hands of the Amish had been created around them, from hex signs to little dolls and figurines crudely approximating Amish garb to cookbooks purporting to record the traditional recipes of the "plain people," and "Amish cheese" that had not a scrap of Amish input in its production. Although none of these commodities related directly to religion, nonetheless their appeal had to do with what had become gross stereotypes of a "fascinating" people set apart by a highly distinctive, long-lived religious culture that permeated every aspect of their daily lives. The Amish may have their own religious integrity, but they were quaint and marginal to the overall religious life of Pennsylvania. What entrepreneurs and the Pennsylvania Department of Commerce did with them was exploitative, focusing on stereotypes about the strange and different, yet old and traditional, that had marketable appeal.

Promoters of the "Indian headdresses" analogy argued that the same applied to Appalachian mountain religion, which in their view was also quaint and marginal to the overall religious life of Appalachia. When attention was drawn to the church traditions and religious culture perpetuated by mountain religion's "small minority," they served as showpieces of a strange and different, yet old and traditional, religious culture. Indeed, any focus on mountain religion was inherently exploitative, promoting a fantasy made up of stereotypes with marketable appeal about "religion in Appalachia" that was ludicrous at best, and slanderous at worst. The vestiges of Appalachia's "old-time religion" laced with the "spectacular" were trotted out in (a very small number of) commercial publications such as *Foxfire 7: Ministers, Church Members, Revivals, Baptisms, Shaped-note and Gospel Singing, Faith Healing, Camp Meetings, Footwashings, Snake Handling, and Other Traditions of Mountain Religious Heritage* (a perfectly fine oral history published in 1982). Mountain religion was also exposed in (a smattering of) documentary-type films like Kevin Balling and Howard Dorgan's *While the Ages Roll On . . . A Memorial* (a 1990 release that is one of the finest of this extremely tiny film genre). Moreover, Appalachia's "hillbilly religion" was put on display when small groups were occasionally herded into an Old Regular Baptist worship service one Sunday morning and perhaps a Holiness night service a few days later during an "Appalachia immersion experience" (periodically sponsored by a very few regional, noncommercial organizations, usually academic). The primary result of these endeavors was only to entertain cultural tourists and sightseers curious about what "traditional" religion was like in Appalachia, having nothing to do with what "religion in Appalachia" was actually like today.

This "marketed" portrayal of an unrecognizable and nearly nonexistent "traditional" religion in Appalachia, so the argument went, clashed violently with the overwhelming realities of the world of Appalachia today and was an insult to its people—meaning, of course, the people making up the Appalachian churches of American Protestantism who felt the most betrayed by what they perceived to be caricatures of religious expressions (about which most of them, native or not, knew precious little) that were deemed to be especially authentic and largely indigenous to Appalachia. This attitude suggested that there was a "betrayer" in their midst, and that the betrayer was mountain religion itself and those who took it seriously, from mountain people who gave it life to historians who sought to hear and understand its historical echoes. The assumption that mountain religion was only marginal to Appalachia's general religious culture today was especially revealing when it was voiced by the Methodist minister who originated the "Indian headdresses" analogy and who also pastored one of the largest Methodist churches in West Virginia. What accounted for his selective sight, not at all unique to him? How could he not be aware of the overwhelming presence of mountain church communities and expressions of mountain religious culture surrounding his urban center and large urban church? Perhaps issues of power and self-identity? If I do not see it, recognize it, and acknowledge it, then I do not have to grapple with how it challenges my own values and worldview?

The fundamental flaw in the analogy of "Indian headdresses" was that the North Carolina Cherokee were, like many tribes, trying to eke out a living by playing up to gross stereotypes of generic Native Americans and their "traditional" culture outside of any particular time or place ("authentic Indian" jewelry and rugs and pots abound, like "Appalachian" quilts and brooms and dulcimers). These economic endeavors stood quite apart from who the North Carolina Cherokee themselves actually were today as Native Americans. If the tourists did not come to Cherokee, North Carolina, there would be no "Indian headdresses" modeled on the street corners. In contrast, Appalachian mountain religion, unlike many other aspects of "traditional" Appalachian culture from clogging competitions to moonshine festivals, had not been appropriated by commercial interests that quantify, standardize, and sell a romance by marketing a generic "Appalachian" product. The overall paucity of academic and noncommercial material on—let alone any marketable commodities of—mountain religion attested to this. Like the Amish and the overwhelming majority of Native Americans, mountain people fiercely guarded the autonomy of their worship lives from any hint of commercialization, occasional recordings by the Library of Congress and the Smithsonian Institution notwithstanding. Moreover, entrepreneurs, academic or free-market, had not exactly beaten on the doors of mountain religion, unlike the Amish of Pennsylvania or the Cherokee of North Carolina. There were only a very, very few loosely connected exceptions related

also a lifelong native of West Virginia, said to me, such values "convicted" his colleagues and they felt "threatened." In this particular group of Methodist clergy, he stood alone in his affirmation of mountain religious culture, but then, unlike his colleagues, he had had intimate personal association with that culture over a lifetime. In the sweep of Methodism in Appalachia, ministers such as this who recognized and felt comfortable with mountain religion's firm presence in their midst—even to the level of deep appreciation and a strong sense of spiritual kinship—were not entirely alone, but neither were they prevalent. The group of West Virginia Methodist clergymen who declared that they wanted to "lift up Appalachia" to a "position of leadership" within their denomination at the national level, while at the same time rejecting outright what was special and unique to Appalachia's religious culture, engaged in a clear contradiction of meaning and purpose. Their contradiction pointed to other motivations.

Methodism in Appalachia is a case in point, but it does not stand alone. Other denominations making up the Protestant mainstream and long established in the region, especially the Southern Baptists, have had the same conflicted relationship with mountain religious life. As we shall see, the home missions movement beginning in the 1880s would attempt to defeat mountain religion's challenge to its system of values by defeating mountain religion itself. Mountain religion made that challenge by simply being what it was and by its refusing to disappear, go away, or be controlled and bullied into submission in order to become a "real" religion with which the nation's dominant religious culture could identify and be comfortable.

Since mountain religion could not be subjected to the controlling interests of American Protestantism, either in the 1880s or today, the alternative strategy for dealing with Appalachian mountain religion has been equally potent and long-lived. Try to take away mountain religion's own power of self-definition and broad authority over social identity and social action throughout much of the Appalachian region by trivializing its significance, marginalizing its scope, and demeaning its values in the lives of rural and small-town people dominating the mountainous and small valley areas of Appalachia. Declare that mountain people who do not belong to churches you are willing to recognize and interact with—and be influenced by—are unchurched or have almost no religion at all other than the sorry, embarrassing remnants of a self-absorbed little world gone by that somehow persists as the "Indian headdresses" of "religion in Appalachia." Mask this alternative strategy by arguing that efforts to highlight and appreciate the contributions of mountain church traditions and their central place in the religious life and religious history of the Appalachian region are irremediably tainted by the status you assign to these traditions. Insist that this status simply makes them susceptible to exploitation in the realm of generalized perceptions—namely, personifying negative stereotypes about "religion in Appalachia"—that will only paint with a broad brush the Appalachian churches of American Protestantism. Assert that, apart from mountain religion, the Appalachian churches of American Protestantism are otherwise proud of their Appalachian "flavor" (an appeal to the "romance" of Appalachia in the American consciousness) that distinguishes them within their own denominations and the prevailing national religious culture—to which they are, in fact, far more tightly bound in identity and purpose.

PART 3

The Independent Holiness Church

The current state of research does not yet permit an adequate overall scholarly interpretation of mountain religion and the Holiness-Pentecostal movements in the Appalachian region. Thus far the bulk of attention on Holiness-Pentecostal traditions in Appalachia has been centered on serpent-handling mountain Christians and has come overwhelmingly from social scientists. Many people consider serpent handlers to be the most spectacular and aberrant of Holiness-Pentecostal traditions in the region, despite the fact that serpent-handling services differ little from the Holiness tradition of independent nondenominational churches except for the addition of serpent handling as a sacramental part of their worship practices. As I stated in the introduction, serpent handling has been seen by "outsiders" as the church tradition synonymous with Appalachian mountain religion, because it is a practice that occurs in the United States only within the Appalachian region, except through out-migration. There is deep resentment in the Appalachian studies community about this nearly exclusive focus on serpent handlers and the amount of attention that has been paid to them by social scientists and the popular press. Serpent handlers are certainly a part of the landscape of mountain religious life, representing one aspect of the independent nondenominational church tradition, but the practice of handling serpents is not common in Holiness church communities.

Sufficient research has been done, however, to provide clear evidence for the claim of this study that the independent nondenominational church, be it Baptist or Holiness, stands at the center of the spectrum of mountain religious life. The spectrum model is linear or two-dimensional, and so is useful only for purposes of description. Perhaps a circular, three-dimensional model is more appropriate, for the left-right aspects of the spectrum image create difficulties unresolved at this time. It is best to view the spectrum model as bands of color, each merging into the other, for which there is no left or right, only variations of refracted light. On either side of the spectrum's independent, nondenominational center are mountain church traditions at the subdenominational level, a level marked by membership in subregional organizations such as Baptist associations, or some form of loose fellowship, but not in national, denominational, organizational structures. Immediately proximate to the spectrum's center we find mountain church traditions such as Old Regular Baptists, Primitive Baptists, Free Will

Baptists, United Baptists, Regular Baptists, and Church of Christ (although it is the only one that is firmly and significantly established outside of Appalachia), to name some but certainly not all. The associations are not hierarchical structures. Membership is primarily for fellowship, not for the deferral of authority over local church matters. (However, as Howard Dorgan observes, "[T]here is some evidence that the strength of Old Regular Baptist associations in particular may be growing, to the detriment of that local church autonomy.")[1] These church traditions, along with that of the independent nondenominational church, most fully embody the heart, the unique identity of mountain religious culture and are overwhelmingly regionally specific to Appalachia.

Nearer the ends of the spectrum encompassing the range of mountain religious life are denominational traditions that had their origins in the Appalachian region and still maintain much of their strength in the region—denominations such as the Church of God (Cleveland, Tennessee), Christian Church, and the Cumberland Presbyterians. Approaching very close to the periphery of the spectrum are mainstream denominations long established in the Appalachian region—ranging from the Church of the Brethren to the Southern Baptist Convention and the United Methodist Church, which are the two largest denominations in Appalachia. Setting the ends of the spectrum are mainstream denominations that are present primarily in Appalachia's valleys and larger towns, and are very sparsely established in the mountains, almost exclusively as home mission interests—Presbyterians, Congregationalists, Disciples of Christ (despite the identification of their earliest years with the Church of Christ and Christian Church), Reformed Church, Episcopalians, Lutherans, Roman Catholics, and so on. These are groups marked almost entirely by a national identity, a national purpose, whose churches are much less affected by regional influences. Some of their individual churches within the mountains of Appalachia may well have features in common with mountain religious life, but that depends upon location and historicity. At the heart of the spectrum defining mountain religion remains the independent nondenominational church tradition. This section is devoted to the independent Holiness church as the most wide ranging yet least considered part of that church tradition.

In all writings about Appalachian mountain religion, the independent Holiness church has been the most ignored, even though it distills many of the defining features of mountain church life in Appalachia. It has been the most ignored largely because its churches are extremely small and radically autonomous with an anti-organizational structure, and an almost complete absence of a clearly defined doctrinal tradition, making them amorphous, difficult to pin down and examine. However, mountain religion's large host of independent Holiness churches have a great deal in common with each other in worship practices and belief systems, even though they are marked by their own freely determined individuality or particularity. Indeed, they form their own unique genre within mountain religion, one with common roots going back to the era of plain-folk camp-meeting religion during the first half of the nineteenth century.

The first chapter in this section, "Mountain Religion and the Holiness-Pentecostal Movements," proposes a tradition history for mountain religion's nondenominational church tradition of independent Holiness in relation to the nationally based Holiness-Pentecostal movements. My contention is that plain-folk camp-meeting religion serves as the basis for most independent Holiness churches and many independent Baptist churches strongly influenced by mountain Holiness traditions, instead of the Holiness-Pentecostal movements per se and their unique theological contributions. This chapter also argues that the worship practices, emphasis on nonrational religious experience, and centrality of the Holy Spirit identified with the initial defining features of the Holiness-Pentecostal movements were transmitted without interruption by Appalachian mountain religion, keeping them continuously in place in American religious history as no other tradition did, thus profoundly influencing the prehistory of the Holiness-Pentecostal movements.

The second chapter of this section is "How an Independent Holiness Church Became a Major Denomination." A little-contemplated fact is that the Church of God (Cleveland, Tennessee), the second largest Pentecostal denomination in the South today with a major part of its membership now outside of the continental United States, had its immediate origins in an independent Holiness church in the mountains of western North Carolina. This chapter looks back at the mountain roots and earliest history of the Church of God (Cleveland, Tennessee), providing much new material on Richard Spurling and Richard G. Spurling, in whose personal religious history the Church of God traces its initial origins.

The concluding chapter of this section is based on excerpts from an oral history interview with Brother Coy Miser, whose voice and work as an independent Holiness preacher has added much richness and insight to this book. Oral history is one of the primary tools in the study of mountain religious life and its history, since Appalachian mountain religion is principally an oral religious tradition. Much of the material in the interview with Brother Coy confirms many of the descriptions, analyses, and interpretations I have made throughout this study about the nature and features of mountain religion. In addition, I use this chapter, in the voice of a single individual, to conclude the first three sections of this book, which have attempted to look at mountain religion on its own terms. That single individual voice leads directly into part 4, which traces the nearly two hundred year history of American Protestantism's concerted home mission efforts to Appalachia and mountain people, and the history of its response to mountain religion which confounded its purposes.

12

Mountain Religion and the Holiness-Pentecostal Movements

In the first part of this chapter I propose a tradition history for mountain religion's nondenominational tradition of independent Holiness churches in terms of their relationship with the Holiness-Pentecostal movements. But this tradition history poses larger questions about basic assumptions in much of contemporary Holiness-Pentecostal scholarship. I respond to those questions in the second part of this chapter, in which I offer support for my claims with the help of an extraordinary book called *Shouting,* self-published in 1859 by George W. Henry, a Methodist intimately involved in the worship life of the emerging Holiness movement. Henry's book was an American history of expressive and ecstatic worship practices which he located as reaching their zenith and normative form on the Appalachian frontier, attributing them to a variety of sources, Arminian and Calvinist, not exclusively tied to Wesleyan tradition.

These worship practices and the beliefs they expressed assumed their form long before their suppression in the Finney-esque revivalism embodying the New Haven Theology in the East beginning in the late 1820s, channeling the energies of the conversion experience into church-based moral reform and social benevolence. They assumed their form, then, long before their later revivification and re-formation outside of Appalachia in the worship behaviors that were associated with the Holiness-Pentecostal movements' perfectionist theology. That theology was the conduit for how Holiness-Pentecostal people came to understand sanctification, the Holy Spirit, and finally the ideological capstone of Spirit-baptism theology, including initial evidence of speaking in tongues that came to distinguish the Pentecostal movement from the Holiness movement by the early twentieth century.

The broad spectrum of ancient, common behavior patterns of revival religiosity and the popular beliefs to which they gave voice that was the clay, the primary material, with which the Holiness-Pentecostal movements sculpted themselves is epitomized by the uninterrupted history of this broad spectrum in mountain religious culture that in turn provides major clues to the prehistory of the Holiness-Pentecostal movements. Indeed, it can be argued that this broad spectrum is far more encompassing of the ordinary and extraordinary occasions of Holiness-Pentecostal worship life, as moun-

into "moral reform and social benevolence."[1] This transformational process significantly altered the nature of revivalism in the broader national culture.

But the revival traditions wed to New England theology—appropriated and transformed by practitioners such as Charles G. Finney who localized them in the urban settings of the East that were themselves being transformed by the industrial revolution and the shift in values it compelled—were, only a few years before, consolidated in the Great Revival on the Appalachian frontier. Earlier traditional features informing this first stage of the Great Revival continued to flourish through Appalachian mountain religion, unaffected by how they were transformed in the East, and later became identified with the characteristic religiosity of the Holiness-Pentecostal movements. These traditional features stood apart from major theological definitions uniquely identified with the Holiness-Pentecostal movements, such as the Pentecostal movement's own Spirit-baptism theology, with initial evidence of speaking in tongues that expressed what Harold Hunter called "the fully developed American Classical Pentecostal position"[2] by the earliest years of the twentieth century. Long before that "fully developed position," there was a distinctive type of religiosity that was the emerging Holiness-Pentecostal movements' primary impetus and was also nearly indistinguishable from the religiosity not only energizing but defining Appalachian mountain religion.

We find in shared historical echoes an earlier, common heritage for worship practices ranging from ritualistic ecstatic behavior to anointing with oil, and for popular belief systems focusing on the catalytic presence of the Holy Spirit in the worship environment. That common, earlier heritage illuminates the fundamental similarities uniting later variations in worship practices and beliefs identified with a normative tradition in American religious history centered on religious experience—most significantly at the ground level of conversion itself. Mountain religion consolidated and transmitted much of that earlier heritage which the Holiness-Pentecostal movements called upon in various ways to help give form to the substance of their defining religiosity. The historical echoes of that earlier heritage are much less resonant—indeed, they are muffled—in the theological hairsplitting found in the breadth of written documentation assumed to be the basic (and only reliable) primary sources for understanding the emergence and early development of the Holiness-Pentecostal movements in the United States. To what extent and in what ways mountain religion influenced, directly and indirectly, through its oral and material culture the Holiness-Pentecostal movements—especially in their formative years—remains a question mark. To what extent mountain religion, at the level of popular religious culture, continues to inform the development of the Holiness-Pentecostal movements—especially as they are manifested within Appalachia itself—is yet another area awaiting exploration.

Geography and Methodist-based theological contributions of perfection-ism or sanctification were integral to what initially distinguished the religiosity of the Holiness-Pentecostal movements from mountain religion. Nonetheless, mountain religion's groundwaters of earlier religious movements nourished many of the defining features of that religiosity—from pietism and Scots-Irish sacramental revivalism to early Baptist revival culture in the mid-South, all of which were infused by a strongly pronounced and thriving Calvinist heritage emphasizing grace and the Holy Spirit. That Calvinist heritage created the specific theological cast for the central role of religious experience in the normative revival religiosity crisscrossing mountain church traditions, despite ideological distinctions that otherwise served to differentiate them within mountain religion. Mountain religion's normative religiosity conjoining its variety of church traditions came to be further reconfigured in the regionally specific movement of plain-folk camp-meeting religion that dominated much of early to mid-nineteenth-century popular religious culture in the upland South, most of which Appalachia embraced. These earlier, defining religious movements—pietism, Scots-Irish sacramental revivalism, Baptist revival culture, plain-folk camp-meeting religion—and the extent to which they are relevant to the most distant echoes still to be heard in the Holiness-Pentecostal movements introduce historical and theological components yet to be taken into account in understanding the tradition histories and symbol systems of Holiness-Pentecostal culture. Given the myriad of sociocultural, ethnic, and geographic variations on the Holiness-Pentecostal movements' basic building blocks in American religious history, the question arises, "Where might they still be best 'preserved'?"

The later influences of the Holiness-Pentecostal movements are today most pronounced in mountain religious culture in the nondenominational tradition of independent Holiness churches. However, we find especially in mountain Holiness churches the ongoing transmission and development of that earlier heritage of worship practices and belief systems—and the religiosity they embodied—that preceded the actual emergence of the Holiness-Pentecostal movements and their restructuring of that heritage. Although independent Holiness churches continue to remain rooted primarily in traditional mountain religious culture, they provide a wealth of insight into the Holiness-Pentecostal movements' basic building blocks prior to their theological (and later sociocultural) transformations. Through loudly reverberating historical echoes that strongly persist today in their worship life, mountain Holiness churches provide major clues to the tradition histories and earlier symbol systems of many of the most important worship practices and the beliefs which they expressed that became identified with the Holiness-Pentecostal movements—often in the crudest terms—in the national consciousness. These carefully nurtured clues point most immediately to an earlier (and little recognized) heritage crystallizing in the predominantly oral culture of plain-folk camp-meeting religion whose influences did not remain confined solely to the large expanse of the upland South where it ostensibly "died out" by the mid-nineteenth century.

The heritage of plain-folk camp-meeting religion—germinating in the piety of a popular religious culture outside of denominational or official institutional church structures—continued to thrive in the mountains and to extend, in less apparent ways, far beyond their ridges and valleys into the national religious culture. That popular religious culture enshrined the centrality of religious experience energized and defined by the strong emotional piety of a very specific type of revival religiosity already normative to Appalachian mountain religion. Plain-folk camp-meeting religion, as a religious movement, was simultaneously incorporated into mountain religious culture of which it was, in reality, already a part from its inception, unlike mountain religion's earlier defining movements. Together their distinctive religiosity, found throughout the sweep of American religious history, now had such a large and decisive presence nowhere else in American Protestantism. Though submerged for some time throughout the rest of the nation's Protestant religious culture and later reconfigured in other theological terms by the Holiness-Pentecostal movements, the centrality of a type of religious experience defined by the emotional piety of expressive and ecstatic worship practices would not be thwarted. What had been predominantly and for some time a regionally specific religiosity, centered on religious experience itself, began to reemerge elsewhere, asserting itself far beyond the Appalachian region where the heritage of that religiosity had not only persisted without interruption but would continue to thrive; indeed, it defined a large and theologically diverse regional religious tradition.

The "hidden" quality of what are today—located all over the American landscape—innumerable nonaligned or only loosely aligned church communities of the Holiness-Pentecostal movements, as well as their many submovements and even their established denominations, mirrors the "invisible" status of mountain Holiness churches in the eyes of the world beyond the reaches of Appalachia's cultural-geographic periphery and confuses their provenance. We put the cart before the horse if we identify the emergence and development of mountain religion's nondenominational tradition of independent Holiness churches as a direct product—primarily, if not exclusively—of a later perfectionist theology (making up most of the important theological spadework of the Holiness-Pentecostal movements) that came into the Appalachian region through the Holiness-Pentecostal movements in their early years. We also grossly misrepresent by such an identification of their origins the normative—and the historically deep and regionally rooted—theological orientation of a significant number, if not a majority, of mountain Holiness churches, which they still share with nearly all mountain church traditions. That normative theological orientation long preceded the presence of the Holiness-Pentecostal movements in the mountains of Appalachia. It already characterized established mountain church communities that may have come to identify themselves as "Holiness" in the late nineteenth century, as well as mountain people of that era who would create new church communities—as soon became the pattern—which they would call "Holiness." The nondenominational tradition of independent Holiness churches was not merely the mountain adaptation of the Holiness-Pentecostal movements which otherwise "created" it; its defining religiosity was integral to mountain religion from the first.

Although we lack clear evidence at this time, it is probable that, in the mountains of Appalachia, the appellation "Holiness" was appropriated by Baptist churches of various backgrounds, as well as by Methodist churches less closely aligned to Methodism's connectional system beginning no later than the 1890s. At the least, it was a term applied to newly created church communities by people who came out of Baptist and Methodist churches that had perpetuated the traditions of plain-folk camp-meeting religion. Many churches had institutionalized in their worship life the revival traditions distilled in plain-folk camp-meeting religion which, though a religious movement, had quickly established itself as a nondenominational church tradition of popular piety. As a church tradition, plain-folk camp-meeting religion had characterized the worship life of numerous mountain Baptist and Methodist churches since the camp-meeting days of the Great Revival. For the members of these churches who either remained with their churches because they took on the name Holiness or parted to form new ones, "Holiness" served better to describe their traditional, customary worship identity and that of their churches, clearly distinguishing their worship life for the first time within mountain religious culture.

It is likely that the term "Holiness" was thus appropriated in the late nineteenth century as a fitting description of a long-popular variant of mountain religion's normative revival religiosity. That variant embodied a style of worship life now fully differentiated from other and more theologically conservative Baptist church traditions (from Old Regular Baptist to Free Will Baptist) which were in turn differentiated by their own variants of mountain religion's normative religiosity. "Holiness" also served to distinguish the churches of former mountain Baptists and Methodists steeped in the heritage of plain-folk camp-meeting religion from the now fully "denominationalized" Methodist and Southern Baptist churches, also found throughout Appalachia, especially in the valleys and in county seats, larger towns, and urban centers. Although they were themselves once an integral part of plain-folk camp-meeting religion, which had given them their biggest boost in numbers in the very early nineteenth century, the Methodists and the church-es that would be identified as Southern Baptist after 1845 had eschewed, soon after the ebbing of the Great Revival on the Appalachian frontier, the center place of religious experience for the national institutionalism of denomina-tionalism, and by the 1890s they had been separate from mountain religious culture for many decades.

The appropriation of a name should not confuse our understanding of the origins of the nondenominational tradition of independent Holiness churches. My thesis is that a well-established movement in the mountains of a popular religious culture, present long before the clear emergence of the Holiness-Pentecostal movements, quickly took on the name "Holiness" to characterize itself once the term had been elevated to such prominence in the Holiness-Pentecostal movements. If so, this would strongly indicate that mountain people perpetuating plain-folk camp-meeting worship life in their churches themselves recognized the fundamental similarities between their distinctive variant of mountain religious culture and the Holiness-Pentecostal culture emerging outside of Appalachia.

"Holiness" was likely deemed by a significant segment of mountain people to be a useful heuristic device that revealed or led to the discovery of what set them apart along with their churches—be they Baptist (proba-bly a majority) or Methodist—within mountain religious culture as the on-going, church-based presence of a long-established, popular movement that scholars would later identify as "plain-folk camp-meeting religion." This process was identical to what became in Virginia and North Carolina dur-ing the Great Awakening the "confirmative" church-based presence that in-stitutionalized, in the more private setting of the local church house or a local residence, the worship practices and emotional piety characterizing the broader "transformative" religious movement of Baptist revival culture. Ear-ly Baptist revival culture, as we have already seen in some depth, was one of the cornerstones of Appalachian mountain religion. It established within mountain religious culture patterns of transmission and institutionalization that were directly applied to plain-folk camp-meeting religion. Thus, as a popular and regionally specific religious movement, plain-folk camp-meet-ing religion possessed its own variant of the revival religiosity already nor-mative to mountain religion. "Holiness" brought to the conscious level how that variant differentiated so many churches, whose worship lives embod-ied it, from other mountain church traditions. Those churches perpetuat-ing plain-folk camp-meeting religion which did not choose to sever ties with their Baptist and Methodist identities saw many of their members, galvanized by a new conscious awareness of their distinctive yet long-standing identity within mountain religious culture, depart to form independent churches that went by the name Holiness.

The emergence of the nondenominational tradition of independent Holiness churches, like the earlier emergence of other mountain church traditions, is a testimony to the vitality and ongoing development of mountain religion as a regional religious tradition. Mountain Holiness churches are, in many respects, set quite apart from the larger Holiness-Pentecostal movements outside of Appalachia, belonging much more to mountain religion than to these larger national movements. Indeed, they belong to mountain religion first—apart from which they cannot be understood—and to the Holiness-Pentecostal movements only secondarily. "Holiness," and thus the Holiness-Pentecostal movements, initially reached into the mountains of Appalachia in such an instrumental way in the late nineteenth century *not* by introducing into mountain religion a new tradition that reconfigured it. Instead, the Holiness-Pentecostal movements provided a term that created a consensus of self-recognition and gave mountain people perpetuating in their church life the traditions of plain-folk camp-meeting religion the means to "name" and thus clearly set apart the tradition that had, over time, come to differentiate them within mountain religious culture. This consensus of self-recognition, identifying Holiness with a variant of mountain religion stemming from the camp-meeting days of the Great Revival, reinforces the premise that the traditions consolidated and transmitted without interruption almost exclusively by mountain religion helped to shape the foundations of the Holiness-Pentecostal movements, despite their later, more self-defining theological formulations.

If a large segment of mountain people recognized at an early point that their distinctive variant of mountain religious culture shared fundamental similarities with emerging Holiness-Pentecostal culture, a variant they came to call by the name "Holiness," there are also indications in the early literature of the Holiness-Pentecostal movements that this recognition of a shared religious culture and history was mutual. In *Shouting* (1859), George W. Henry (1801–?) produced a remarkable lineup of authorities testifying to the validity of expressive and ecstatic worship practices as a clear demonstration of the immediate presence of the Holy Spirit in worship. *Shouting* was published, appropriately, in Oneida, Madison County, New York, the stomping grounds of Finney and Nash in the last moments before traditional revival culture outside of Appalachia was transformed into fodder to stoke the engines of denominational development and the promotion of social and political causes. Henry charted the course of the history of very physical and strong emotional piety from the Bible to the early Church, then drawing extracts, as his extended subtitle states, from the writings of Wesley, Evans, Edwards, Abbott, Cartwright and Finley. The purpose of these extracts (and Henry's effusive commentary) is, as his subtitle continues, to give "a history of the outward demonstrations of the

Spirit, such as [in bold type] Laughing, Screaming, Shouting, Leaping, Jerking, and Falling under the Power, &c."

Henry's book—as a product of the earliest stages of the Holiness movement in Methodism—was not a defense but a historical justification for what had become, to the dominant religious culture of American Protestantism (including the Methodist church, now far removed from such worship expressions), the most deeply disturbing and frightening manifestations of an earlier revival religiosity it devoutly hoped had died out altogether. Henry's argument was that expressive and ecstatic behavior was not aberrant, that in fact it was a piety extremely appropriate to an ancient tradition of "heart" religion ("heart" is a continuously repeated motif in *Shouting*) that hungered for and celebrated God's initiative in the worship environment through the immediate presence of the Holy Ghost clearly manifested in such physical and emotional expressions. Henry also counterargued that a rigid, programmatically predetermined worship setting, allowing for only a narrow range of highly controlled behavior, simply—and unavoidably—snuffed out any sign of the Holy Ghost's presence as lack of oxygen would snuff out a flame.

Henry's inclusion of the "Views of John Wesley" and the "Views of Jonathan Edwards"—an Arminian and an evangelical Calvinist—in numerous brief chapters is understandable enough. What is especially revealing is his selection of supporting material, all of which points directly to the consolidation of the American heritage of strong emotional piety (and its transatlantic heritage in the British Isles) in the religious culture of the mountain regions of Appalachia. Sandwiched between Henry's material drawn from Wesley and Edwards is a brief chapter on "Welsh Jumping," as "the manner of religious rejoicing so remarkable among the Welsh"[3] was derisively called by the English, taken from the work of Christmas Evans (1766–1838), whom Henry accurately described as "a Calvinist Baptist, who figured in Wales about forty or fifty years ago. He was to the Baptists in Wales what Wesley was to the Methodists" (p. 291). After reprinting a lengthy extract from Evans's 1829 diary entry on "Welsh Jumping"—written as a continuation of a dispute Evans had had with several English clergy who derided the practice as an affront to rationalism—Henry concluded, "We have conversed with aged Welsh Baptist saints, who said they had witnessed hundreds of men and women, leaping as does upon the mountains, and shouting at the top of their voices, under the preaching of Mr. Evans. . . . O, that the Baptists of the present day in America had such men,—aye, and the Methodists, too" (p. 302).

As regional scholars such as Loyal Jones are well aware, the Welsh Calvinist Baptist heritage is quite pronounced in Old Time Baptist traditions in the mountains, such as the Old Regular Baptists.[4] Evans's account, as reproduced in *Shouting*, was a clear reminder of the indisputable presence of expressive and ecstatic worship behavior among groups long thought, because of their Calvinist doctrinal heritage, to be more taciturn than emotive in their worship after the passing of the Calvinistic revival era of Jonathan Edwards in New England and the Scots-Irish Presbyterians of the Middle Colonies. As we have seen throughout this book, such emotional religiosity, still present to a greater and lesser extent throughout most theologically conservative mountain church traditions, strongly characterizes Old Regular Baptist churches especially.

After Christmas Evans's account, Henry turns to Jonathan Edwards, who is in turn followed by Benjamin Abbott (1732–96), "who blasted out of the mountain some where in Pennsylvania, by the prayer of his sainted mother, as her feet were in the waters of Jordan" (p. 332).[5] Abbott's own account of his conviction, conversion, and sanctification tells of his journey to the satisfactions he found in Methodism and the second blessing, following his earlier embrace of Presbyterianism, where, Abbott writes, "I . . . went often to meeting, and many times the Spirit of God alarmed my guilty soul of its danger; but it as often wore off again" because he found there no "heart work" (pp. 333–34). Abbott's account goes on to tell that he became a Methodist preacher whose ministry—centered in Pennsylvania, New York State, and Maryland—was steeped in the heritage of expressive and ecstatic worship practices, his descriptions of which illustrate that they anticipated the worship traditions of the Appalachian frontier during the Great Revival, where Methodism found such affinity.

Henry turned next to Peter Cartwright (1785–1872), Methodist trailblazer extraordinaire who, for more than half a century, "rode wilderness circuits from the Appalachians to the Mississippi."[6] Cartwright was born in Amherst County, Virginia, on the crest of the Blue Ridge Mountains, and moved at an early age with his parents to Logan County, Kentucky, where the Great Revival ignited on the Appalachian frontier. Again, Henry's thematic focus is unambiguous. As with his preceding material, Henry wrote, "We will take from 'Uncle Peter,' an account of the 'jerking spirit,' one which has frequently made its advent, in different ages of the Church." Henry quoted as his first sentence from Cartwright, "From 1801, for years, a blessed revival of religion spread through almost the entire inhabited parts of the West, Kentucky, Tennessee, the Carolinas, and many other parts, especially through the Cumberland country, which was so called from the Cumberland River, which headed and mouthed in Kentucky, but in its great bend circled south through Tennessee, near Nashville" (p. 367). Cartwright rode circuits in Kentucky, Tennessee, Ohio, Indiana, and Illinois, but his *Autobiography*'s record of his work in Kentucky and Tennessee has been called upon endlessly in secondary scholarship to document the consolidation of the very specific type of revival religiosity that exploded as the Great Revival and the camp-meeting tradition it birthed.

Henry concluded his record of ecstatic worship life in America by drawing on the autobiography of James B. Finley, writing, "Mr. Finley commenced his career as a minister in the West, about sixty years ago, and entered upon his everlasting rest in the year 1858. His father was a high-toned Calvinistic preacher, who endeavored to thrust down into the heart of his son, election, reprobation, and kindred doctrines; but not having powers to digest such spikes and irons, he cast them up and turned to better things. . . . He stowed away, in his great heart, the blessed doctrines of a free and full salvation" (pp. 376–77). Finley recounted the earliest history of Methodism in Appalachia in his *Sketches of Western Methodism* (1855), beginning with William Burke, the oldest "pioneer preacher" still living when Finley wrote. (Burke was born January 1770 in Loudoun County, Virginia, bordering what are today West Virginia and Maryland.) What Henry drew upon first from Finley's writings was his account starting with his marriage in March 1801, which prompted him, as Finley wrote, "to move and take possession" of the land his father had bought "in what is now Highland country" (that is, the Southern Highlands). It was at the momentous Cane Ridge camp meeting that Finley's "pride" was broken and his "heart" (again, Finley's word) was made tender and vulnerable enough to allow himself to respond within his own body through physical manifestations to the power of the presence of the Holy Ghost. But we may observe an irony here. In a very direct sense, Finley was going home. According to Henry, Finley wrote, "In the month of August, 1801, I learned that there was to be a great meeting at Cane Ridge, in my father's old congregation" (p. 381). Finley provides one of the most subtle and detailed descriptions of what ecstatic worship is like on such a massive scale, as well as for the individual in the midst of such a gathering, calling upon his own struggles and perceptions in that meeting.

Henry began with Wesley and Edwards, but then drew squarely on the history of ecstatic expressions in the lives of a Welsh Calvinist Baptist, a preacher from the mountains of Pennsylvania, and the firsthand accounts by Cartwright and Finley (themselves born and reared in what became the Appalachian region) of the legendary 1801 Great Revival meeting at Cane Ridge. *Shouting* makes very clear that, at least for Henry in 1859, the recognized lineage for such practices reached its definitive form in the Great Revival on the Appalachian frontier and the camp-meeting culture that emerged there. That definitive form thus preceded the revivalism that was thoroughly transformed ideologically and institutionally in the East (a transformation symbolically and decisively demarcated by the publication of Finney's *Lectures on Revivals of Religion* in 1835), and became the norm—now clearly distinct from that of the Appalachian frontier—for the Protestant mainstream at that time. Numerous segments of the Holiness-Pentecostal movements would initially embrace the very distinctive type of revival religiosity that worship life in the Appalachian region had crystallized. Inevitably, such spontaneous and strong emotional piety was thoroughly tempered with the passage of time and the unremitting and increasing pressure on these movements to institutionalize and "legitimize" themselves, especially in what emerged as their largest denominational manifestations.

As an American history of expressive and ecstatic worship practices prior to their suppression in the "new" revivalism of evangelical Protestantism and their revivification outside of Appalachia in the later Holiness-Pentecostal movements, Henry's book makes clear that he understood them as manifestations of the immediate presence of the Holy Spirit and as upholding the centrality of a type of religious experience mediated by grace and not by the direct human manipulation central to the "science" of Finney-esque revivalism. His interpretation of such practices was not a backward look to a lost era awaiting resuscitation through the Holiness-Pentecostal movements. It was an account of the same worship practices and beliefs that were normative to Appalachian mountain religion and that, by no later than the mid-1820s, clearly and decisively *differentiated* it from the otherwise dominant national religious culture—well before the Holiness-Pentecostal movements laid hold of the moorings of worship practices, strong emotional piety, and emphasis on the Holy Spirit that mountain religion had kept continuously in place in American religious culture.

On this note of separating themselves out—Appalachian mountain religion and later the Holiness-Pentecostal movements—from what McLoughlin described as "the national religion of the United States" by 1840,[7] Henry made a revealing side remark in his excitement over James B. Finley's account: "We were converted and sanctified wholly at camp-meeting. Well would it have been for our Presbyterian brethren, if they had continued their feast of tabernacles" (p. 388). Henry is, of course, referring to the profoundly influential revival tradition of the evangelical Scots-Irish Presbyterian sacramental meetings, or multi-day communion services, that sparked the Great Awakening in the Middle Colonies and were carried south and west into Virginia, North Carolina, and western Pennsylvania. The Scots-Irish carried their sacramental revivalism one step farther, into the heart of the Appalachian frontier, where it reached its zenith in American religious history, beginning in 1797 with the sacramental meetings held in the tiny Presbyterian congregations of Muddy River, Red River, and Gasper River under James McGready and culminating in Cane Ridge in 1801.

By including the spontaneous and strong emotional piety of what was originally a staunchly Calvinistic tradition of sacramental revivalism, Henry made clear that his *Shouting* was not simply a paean to the Methodist theological cornerstone of perfectionism or sanctification which could be read back, in revisionist manner, into such ecstatic expressions as though this theology was assumed to be the means by which they were best interpreted. Henry, after all, included Jonathan Edwards as well as Brother Christmas Evans, and a brief aside recognizing the role played, especially on the Appalachian frontier, by the Scots-Irish Presbyterians through "their feast of tabernacles" and its centuries-old heritage of powerful revival religiosity centered on the Holy Spirit.

Henry was instead celebrating what he saw as an uninterrupted tradition in the history of Christianity embodied by a very specific type of religiosity that is extremely emotional and physical, as well as psychically risky—and at its most powerful when it is communally experienced. It is a religiosity that is centered on religious experience itself, its history in no way confined—as Henry's book attests, beginning with the Bible and the early Church—to the theological vagaries of passing church traditions and religious movements. As both Marilyn J. Westerkamp and Leigh Eric Schmidt observed in their histories[8] of sacramental revivalism, that religiosity would withstand both theological and denominational transmutations; and the only place on the American landscape where it would continue unabated was the mountain regions of Appalachia.

Indeed, Schmidt concluded that this religiosity did not die out with the waning of the Great Revival in the coarse wilderness of the Old Southwest. Instead, "Though changes would come and new measures replace old, the frontier regions—western Pennsylvania, the valley of Virginia, backcountry North Carolina, Kentucky, and Tennessee—would be the places where the sacramental practices of the evangelical Scots and Ulster Scots would be best preserved."[9] The term "new measures" was the catchword associated with Finney's consolidation of classic revival techniques with the new theological developments defining his era in the East and transforming revivalism in the broader national culture—but not in the mountain religious culture of Appalachia. Like Westerkamp, Schmidt grounded the "preservation" or continuation of the sacramental revival traditions of the Scots-Irish in the religious life distinctive to what became the cultural-geographic borders differentiating Appalachia as a regional entity. That revival religiosity persisted in reinvigorated form in the mountain regions of Appalachia, where it merged with other religious movements, from pietism to early Baptist revival culture, and ultimately with plain-folk camp-meeting religion.

Henry's book would continue to serve its original purpose into the twentieth century. Two Holiness organizations—the Metropolitan Church Association (1894–), organized out of Chicago, and the Holiness Movement Church (1895–1959), organized throughout nearly all the provinces of Canada—even reissued *Shouting* to legitimize expressive and ecstatic worship practices by proving their historicity. Charles Edwin Jones listed Henry's *Shouting,* separately republished by these two organizations in 1903 and 1908, under "authoritative sources," meaning "[w]orks by non-members published by the group to support its teaching."[10] Jones noted about the Metropolitan Church Association in particular, "[T]he Metropolitan churches early placed great stress on emotional display in public worship and ascetic standards in personal behavior."[11]

Many Holiness-Pentecostal people would come to Appalachia and have direct impact on the intermixing of Holiness-Pentecostal culture with geographically scattered pockets of mountain religious culture, especially (but not exclusively) through mountain religion's highly individualistic independent Holiness churches. In 1876 George O. Barnes,[12] an Englishman and former Presbyterian missionary to India, came as an independent evangelist to eastern Kentucky where, preaching to "several thousand" over a period of a few years, he promoted "healing by faith" and anointing with oil, practices already well established in mountain religious culture since its inception. Some people would found small, subregional submovements. In 1924, Lela G. McConnell (1884–?),[13] a Holiness Methodist, came from Honey Brook, Pennsylvania—midway between Ephrata and Philadelphia—to eastern Kentucky, where she founded the Kentucky Mountain Holiness Association and spent the rest of her life promoting that work through educational institutions. That Holiness "took" when it entered into the domain of mountain people and their religious culture in a way that the home missionary efforts of American Protestantism never achieved, even though it breached the mountain ranges of Appalachia at about the same time, also points directly to the fundamental similarities shared by mountain religious culture and the Holiness-Pentecostal movements, similarities that were indispensable to their evolving cross-pollination.

The proposed tradition history developed in these pages for mountain religion's appropriation of the term "Holiness" and for the emergence of its nondenominational tradition of independent Holiness churches thus asserts that the flow of religious influences in Appalachia did not simply go up the valleys and into the mountains, where they congealed in forms peculiar to "mountain culture." Although its actual role is not yet clearly laid out, the claim can be made that, at the least, mountain religion was as much active in the primal history of the Holiness-Pentecostal movements—at the "primal soup" level where it is far more difficult to achieve a satisfying historical precision—as it was later acted upon by them after they had fully emerged and entered into the mountains, where their contributions to mountain religious culture were limited primarily to unique theological formulations (such as Oneness or Jesus Only theology) that built on mountain religion's own solid foundations.

Mountain religion, especially through its independent Holiness churches, did not trigger the Holiness-Pentecostal movements in the United

States or determine in a decisive manner what they eventually became. It did provide the groundwaters of many of their earlier and earliest religious heritages, which never dried up and did not simply flow parallel but fed them at the level of basic nutrition. Scholars do not claim that the Holiness-Pentecostal movements jump-started or created themselves de novo, but they have yet to recognize what was already long and continuously in place in these movements' very midst. The historical continuity mountain religion provided was indispensable not to what they later became but to what initially, and formatively, distinguished these movements as a "new thing"—in terms of their worship practices, spontaneity and strong emotional piety, and emphasis on the Holy Spirit—within the much larger setting of American Christianity.

That highly emotive, nonrational religious experience—found in expressive and ecstatic worship practices and in fact present throughout American religious history—remained at the core of the religious predispositions of so many people in every generation points far beyond functionalist interpretations of lower-class status, economic deprivation, alienation, and powerlessness so many scholars and church people in every era of American religious history have assigned to them with varying degrees of sophistication. Their persistence has generated the ongoing conflict between piety and reason—the heart and the head—that has been the thematic focus of most of the defining periods of American religious history. Like Henry's leitmotif in *Shouting,* the most important and recurrent theme in mountain preaching, from independent Holiness to Old Regular Baptist, is that of the broken heart, tenderness of heart, a heart not hardened to the Spirit and the Word of God. "God speaks to the heart. The Devil speaks to the head," says Brother Coy Miser, a mountain preacher in the independent Holiness church tradition. (I have never heard Brother Coy use the term "sanctification.") Again, his admonition is not peculiar to him but is highly representative of the basic orientation of mountain people in terms of how they conduct their lives and understand the world about them. This one theological theme, crystallized in the symbolic image of the human heart and how its spiritual condition translates into everyday living, most comprehensively expresses the religious values embodied by Appalachian mountain religion.

Mountain religion is a very deep canyon in the history and ongoing drama of "the heart versus the head" in American Christianity and American Protestantism in particular. How that drama plays out in the history of the interaction of Appalachian mountain religion with American Protestantism may well put into an entirely different light the history of the condescension, propelled more by fear than by pity, of the predominantly nonemotive, highly rationalistic, and much more rigidly structured American Protestant culture toward the Holiness-Pentecostal movements. The lessons we learn from the history of mountain religion as a regional religious tradition in relation to American Protestantism may also ground the more public, and better known, ongoing "debate" between American Protestantism and the Holiness-Pentecostal movements, both possessing nationwide identities, where it more appropriately belongs—at the level of a fundamental conflict between their very different sets of religious values expressing who they are and how they choose to live in relation to God and to each other in the world God created for them to cherish and to help bring them to salvation.

13

How an Independent Holiness Church Became a Major Denomination

A little-contemplated fact is that the Church of God (Cleveland, Tennessee)—hereafter referred to in this chapter simply as the Church of God—had its immediate origins in an independent Holiness church in the mountains of western North Carolina. The Church of God is the second largest Pentecostal denomination in the South today, with two-thirds of its membership now outside of the continental United States. The first General Assembly of the Church of God was held in a small mountain cabin in January 1906 near Murphy, North Carolina, and represented only four small mountain church communities in southeastern Tennessee, southwestern North Carolina, and northwest Georgia (a tri-state area). The following year, "Church of God" was adopted as the name by which the group would be known. Prior to that, what became the Church of God had been a single independent mountain church known since 1902 as the Holiness Church at Camp Creek, with services held mostly in the cabin home of William F. (W. F.) Bryant (1863–1949). Later in Church of God historiography, four different theories developed, each with its own influential proponents, for the origins of the Church of God. Each was valid, depending upon the perspective from which the church's history was considered: (1) January 26–27, 1906, with the first General Assembly—F. J. Lee; (2) the May 1902 founding of the Holiness Church at Camp Creek—W. F. Bryant and M. S. Lemons; (3) the August 19, 1886, founding of the Christian Union—Richard G. Spurling; (4) June 13, 1903, A. J. Tomlinson's personal revelation from God on what is now called Prayer Mountain in Fields of the Wood—A. J. Tomlinson. Tomlinson also embraced the other three points of origin for the Church of God.

The Holiness Church at Camp Creek in Cherokee County, North Carolina, was an outgrowth of the Christian Union, a nondenominational, loose association of covenanting individuals organized in 1886 near Turtletown, Tennessee, just twelve miles away, by the Baptist elder Richard Spurling (1810–91),[1] who reunited with his home church, Holly Springs United Missionary Baptist Church, a few months later. The work was continued by his son, Richard G. (Green) Spurling (1858–1935), also a Baptist minister and in fact ordained by his father. Richard G. Spurling and W. F. Bryant, also of Baptist background, worked together over the years, especially after the 1896 revival in Cherokee County, when Spurling felt emphatically the need to "set a church in order," as he put it—a phrase reflecting his strong Baptist background—the result being the Holiness Church at Camp Creek in May 1902.

Spurling, Bryant, and Frank Porter were the first three ministers of the Church of God, Bryant receiving his ordination from the hands of Spurling and Porter. M. S. Lemons, a schoolteacher from Bradley County, Tennessee (the county seat is Cleveland), came into the mountains and joined their work in 1903 as the fifth minister ordained by the Holiness Church at Camp Creek.[2] Earlier in 1903, A. J. Tomlinson (1865–1943) joined the Holiness Church at Camp Creek as its fourth ordained minister. A Quaker from Indiana who had worked as a colporteur for both the American Tract Society and the American Bible Society in the mountains making up the tri-state area of North Carolina, Georgia, and Tennessee, Tomlinson had been deeply involved in home mission work to mountain people. Tomlinson would become general overseer "for life" in the Church of God, until his forced departure in 1922–23 over a scandal that prompted him to found a competing group in Cleveland, Tennessee, also called the Church of God, that legally became known as the Church of God of Prophecy in 1952, yet another significant Pentecostal denomination in the South today. Because of Tomlinson's literacy, zeal, and charisma, he served first as clerk of the small group, keeping the written records. It was Tomlinson's ambitions for founding what he called a worldwide "movement" that brought the Holiness Church at Camp Creek out of the mountains of western North Carolina into the valley town of Cleveland, Tennessee, and developed the Church of God from a small cluster of independent mountain churches into a major denomination based on an episcopal authority structure.

The symbolic import of moving the Church of God out of the mountains of Appalachia into a valley town and developing it into a large, international denomination from its roots in a tiny handful of independent Holiness churches should not be lost. Of equal importance, historians such as Charles W. Conn, official church historian of the Church of God and general overseer during the 1960s, recognize that were it not for Tomlinson—who was not native to Appalachia and who had come into the region originally to do home mission work—the Church of God would never have left the mountains, nor would it have developed as it did. One faculty member at the Church of God School of Theology, the denomination's seminary in Cleveland, Tennessee, has called the Church of God "Appalachia for export," stating that Church of God ministers native to the mountain regions of Appalachia have very specific ideas about appropriate worship practices and religious traditions that are more characteristic of Appalachia than they are of the Holiness-Pentecostal movements generally. When such ministers are transferred to churches outside of the Appalachian region they tend to make their church members uncomfortable by their insistence upon expressive and ecstatic worship practices and religious traditions specific to mountain religion's independent Holiness churches.

In an interview, Brother Conn discussed the Appalachian influence on the Church of God:

> DVM: For me, at the heart of the spectrum [of mountain religious life], at the dead center, is the independent nondenominational church, the invisible church, almost. They are everywhere throughout the region.
>
> CONN: I dare say that is the most predominant church in Appalachia.
>
> DVM: [One faculty member] is of the opinion that the [Church of God] is what he calls "Appalachia for export" in many ways.
>
> CONN: I hadn't heard that idea phrased in that way. . . . I still have to deal very much with that Appalachian culture in my travels and in my work. And, it's still there. It is still a part of it and the "I'm not giving an inch" attitude—the hard-bitten, rather crusty self-sufficiency. Therefore [mountain people] go into religion the same way, it's all or nothing. When you get religion, you really get religion. You live it with great commitment.
>
> DVM: [A. J. Tomlinson] was doing home mission work in the mountains in western North Carolina. But, when he came in, because he was searching in himself, he was open to the religious life he saw and was pulled into it. If it hadn't been for an Appalachian "outsider," there would have been no Church of God.
>
> CONN: There would have been somewhere, maybe a small independent congregation. That would have been it, yes. . . . See, the Appalachia of those days was the world [to mountain people], and if [not for] Tomlinson, nudged slightly by Lemons, . . . Bryant and Spurling would have never opened up the mountains. . . . The Spurlings didn't [leave the mountains]. Now, you have to understand about Bryant. He left the mountains because he became so attached to Tomlinson, but really he never did. He was mountain through and through. . . . In other words, to have a Northerner speaking well of you, to have a Northerner really accepting you was the highest compliment and here comes a Hoosier and he loves them. He cares for them and he's a right smart man, as they referred to him. Right smart, meaning that he read, he wrote, when many of them, I could almost say most of them, did not. Not until the 1930s did they really begin to open up Appalachia.
>
> You know, there is something I hope you discover that has bounced around in my mind. I have never had the occasion nor the

motivation to look at it. These independent congregations, now it seems to me that they are largely of the Holiness or Pentecostal variety. Largely, I say, and that's an impression. Did, prior to the Pentecostal awakening, were there so many independent churches?
DVM: I want to know that, too.
CONN: In other words, have we encouraged the rise of the independent congregation, or is it just typical of the mountains and has always been there?

This question about how far back the tradition of independent nondenominational churches goes in the mountains of Appalachia has puzzled others, too. In a little self-published book titled *The Forgotten Church* (1962), Brother Joe Abbott of Bridgeport, Alabama, stated, "We have gone over Mountains Creeks Hills and Hollows to find the answer to the Question, where did the Free Holiness Church Start; I am convinced that I have found the place the time and People."[3] Independent nondenominational churches in Appalachia's mountain regions often identify themselves as "Free Holiness," not as the church's name but as the designation of the church tradition and religious movement of which they are a part. Such churches are truly independent, belonging to no organizational structure, only to the casual, loose network that is formed by the people who attend such churches and may be moved to start their own. Brother Abbott wrote,

> We have been told some of the old members of the Barney Creek Church of 86 [1886], was among those that was Organized in the year 1906 and the Organization was called the Church of God and it was moved to Cleveland Tennessee,
> However, many of the Holiness Church, remained in their homeland, built a Church house on Ka-Tas'ka mountain later it was burned by the enemy it is supposed they then moved to a water Grist mill, The Grist Mill and dam of water was on Steer Creek, below the Holly Spring Baptist Church.
> There they continued to Preach Holiness and among the Boxes an[d] Barrels some repented, and were Baptized in the Cold blue Waters in Steer Creek washing away their sins Calling upon the name of the Lord, acts, 22–16,
> Then they Built on Paul's Mountain, and moved there kept mov[ing] and sometime devi ding like other places through-out our Country, Still carrying on sometime under Different Names;
> It might sound strange and untrue, but the true Holiness Church in our day according to all land marks and testimonys of the old and older ones, started with less than a dozen members, men and women in the Unicoi Mt, of East Tenn, 1886.
> Today 75 years later, there are multiplied millions, who profess Holiness under hundreds of different names.[4]

BRYANT: I can't remember his name—I believe his name was Albert Pingleton, a Baptist preacher.

CHESSER: After you were saved how long was it before you received the baptism of the Holy Ghost?

BRYANT: I don't know, but quite a while. I was married and we had a family coming on. I was about twenty-five years old then.

CHESSER: Who was conducting the meeting when you got the baptism?

BRYANT: I was.

CHESSER: You had not at that time heard about the Holiness church?

BRYANT: No.

CHESSER: Where did you get the Holy Ghost?

BRYANT: I got the baptism in the same county. When I got the baptism they turned twenty-nine of us out [over the years 1896–1900] of the Baptist Church [Pleasant Hill and Old Liberty] for claiming that we were living free from sin.

CHESSER: How long was this before the Holiness people came along, or did you twenty-nine who were turned out form a band?

BRYANT: We kept our prayer meetings up and formed a band ourselves.

CHESSER: Where did you learn about the Holy Ghost?

BRYANT: I just knew about Sanctification then. I didn't know about the Holy Ghost.

CHESSER: Did the Baptist church teach Sanctification at that time?

BRYANT: To some extent, but they turned us out for claiming we were living free from sin [Bryant was exluded from Old Liberty in 1899].

CHESSER: It was not long after this until you received the baptism?

BRYANT: Soon after that I got the baptism. Billy Martin, of Coker Creek, Tennessee, a Methodist preacher, came in there preaching entire Sanctification and the Baptism of the Holy Ghost and talking in tongues.

CHESSER: That was after you received the baptism?

BRYANT: About the same time. I hate to tell you, but you see, back there I couldn't hardly read my name in box-car letters.

CHESSER: Then Billy Martin came through and—

BRYANT: Yes, and my cousin, Milton McNabb, and Billy Hamby and Joe Tipton came in. All four of them worked together.

CHESSER: Where were they preaching?

BRYANT: Around Coker Creek.

CHESSER: Was Coker Creek the Post Office?

BRYANT: No, that was just a creek there. Turtletown was the Post Office.

[The period of time Bryant is discussing began in 1896 when William Martin, a Methodist layman (not an ordained "preacher," as

Bryant's account seems to indicate), came from the Coker Creek area of Tennessee over to Cherokee County, North Carolina, where Bryant's group of twenty-nine who would be turned out of Old Liberty and Pleasant Hill were well primed for a revival based on preaching the doctrine of sanctification. Martin traveled with Milton McNabb and Joe Tipton, both Baptist laymen. They may have known Richard G. Spurling and his Christian Union. The "Coker Creek" area in Tennessee was the location of Spurling's Barney Creek meeting house, on the juncture of Barney and Coker creeks in Monroe County, Tennessee, near Turtletown, just two miles from the Tennessee-North Carolina border. The 1896 revival involved hundreds of participants, and Spurling joined his efforts with those of Bryant after the Barney Creek church died out, as Bryant recounted in the following.]

CHESSER: What church did these men represent?

BRYANT: It wasn't a church—they were just Holiness.

CHESSER: Do you know where they got their experiences?

BRYANT: Right there on Coker Creek.

CHESSER: You do not know where the first one of them got the blessing?

BRYANT: No. Billy Martin said that the Holy Ghost fell on him. He was Methodist.

CHESSER: At this time no church had been set up?

BRYANT: No. We had not thought of a church yet.

CHESSER: How long did you travel on like this, without a church?

BRYANT: We had prayer meetings and kept the people going until Brother R. G. Spurling came in on Coker Creek. He started a meeting. He was from Turtletown, Tennessee, and he went over there and started a preaching a little. . . . He organized a church over there with five or six members [the original members of the Christian Union at Barney Creek meeting house]. He was a good man. He came over [to Cherokee County, North Carolina] and wanted me to help him in his meeting, but I told him I could not because, to be fair, I did not care about this meeting, because I thought I had the Holy Ghost, but I didn't have it all then, but I went with him, but the meeting went dead.

CHESSER: What did he call that church?

BRYANT: I do not remember, but the history book gives it [Christian Union, at Barney Creek meeting house].

CHESSER: What church did Spurling belong to?

BRYANT: Baptist. He set that church in order [Christian Union]. He had been ordained by his father, a Baptist preacher. He organized that church and traveled along until it went dead. The rocks that

CHESSER: Where did you worship?

BRYANT: We built a brush arbor, and in the winter we had services in my house. I had a big house—four or five rooms—and I threw it open to them.

CHESSER: People were receiving the Holy Ghost all along?

BRYANT: Yes. One lady got up speaking in tongues without going to the altar. She had never been to a Holiness meeting before.

CHESSER: Where was Brother Spurling living at this time?

BRYANT: At Turtletown, just across the [state] line.

CHESSER: Was he farming?

BRYANT: No, he was a kind of a millwright.

CHESSER: When and where did you change the name from the Holiness Church at Camp Creek to the Church of God?

BRYANT: Not until the first Assembly was held there. [Bryant amended this statement later in the interview by saying it was around the time of the second assembly.] Brother Lemons says he was the first man that suggested the name Church of God, and Brother Trim said he was the first. I don't remember for sure, but I think maybe Brother Trim was the man.

CHESSER: At the time the church at Camp Creek was changed to the Church of God, who was the leader? Brother Tomlinson was the pastor.

BRYANT: I think Brother Spurling was considered the leader. He was right with us all the way. When he wasn't there I was there. It was either one or the other of us at that time—that was R. G. Spurling.

Official Church of God history is replete with hagiography about "Richard G. Spurling, Sr." and "Richard G. Spurling, Jr.," to whom it traces its initial origins in Spurling "Sr.'s" Christian Union, which he established in 1886 in Monroe County, Tennessee. In 1902 Spurling "Jr.," along with Frank Porter and W. F. Bryant, went on to found the Holiness Church at Camp Creek in Cherokee County, North Carolina, out of which soon emerged the Church of God. In fact, the standard historical account of the Spurling family and their religious background is flimsy and full of errors, from names to birth and death dates, even to religious affiliations and family lineage in the United States. The Pentecostal scholar Wade H. Phillips offers for the first time a solid reconstruction of the origins and migration of the Spurling family, tracing them to their probable English origins.[8] Phillips's account presents much new evidence, filling in large holes by directly addressing the mountain roots of the Church of God through the Spurling family, opening wide the doors to clear identification of the initial mountain Baptist influences on a denomination that has long since dismissed any consideration of its religious roots that did not directly affirm Wesleyan-Holiness tradition.

Phillips offered the following account of the religious and family history of Richard Spurling and his son Richard G. Spurling as "evidential, with no speculation." His reconstructions are based on census data, wills, marriage records, deeds, court records, newspaper accounts, and church minutes and records. As a starting point, Phillips stated that in no official documents was Richard Spurling ever listed as "Richard G. Spurling" or "Richard G. Spurling, Sr." Moreover, the proper name of Richard Spurling's son was Richard G. Spurling, with the initial G. standing for "Green," and he too was not known legally as "Jr.," except as a term of convenience. On this basis, I have broken with the Church of God "Sr./Jr." tradition and have referred to the father as Richard and to his son as Richard G.

The Spurling family in the United States is directly and conclusively traceable three generations before Richard G. (b. 1858) to John Spurlin (b. ca. 1740–d. 1822), father of twenty-three children and the family's patriot during the Revolutionary War. Somewhat less conclusive evidence seems to point back two more generations to Jeremiah and his father, also named Jeremiah, who made his will in 1726 in Westmoreland County, Virginia, where there were two large families of Spurlings, then spelled Spurlin. Richard Spurling added the -g ending to the family name. The Spurlin family moved in the late eighteenth century from Virginia to western North Carolina. Around 1823, the Spurlin family, headed by James, moved from North Carolina to Anderson County, Tennessee, and then around 1828 to Fentress County.[9] In 1832 James's son, Richard, married Nancy Jane Norman in Anderson County (where later he would die while traveling). Both had attended New Salem United Baptist Church when the Spurlin family lived there.

The Spurlins sold their property in Fentress County around 1847 and moved one county over to Morgan County, approximately fifty miles due west of Knoxville and seventy-five miles southeast of the area on the Kentucky line where the earth-shaking and history-shaping camp meetings took place in the Green River Valley. Richard's father, James, was recorded as eighty-one years old in the 1850 census, in which his wife, Frances ("Frankie") Hicks, was also recorded. Both were living with Richard at the time. James and Frances were United Baptists, listed on the books first for Union Church and then for Clear Creek Church in Morgan County. Like his father and mother, Richard and his family belonged to Union Church (est. 1846), a United Baptist church and the second oldest church in Morgan County. In August 1852 Union Church armed off Clear Creek Church, also United Baptist. Richard, his wife Nancy, son James J., and his parents, James and Frances, were all charter members of the new church, where Richard was ordained a preaching elder.

Richard sold his property in Morgan County near the time his son, Richard G., was born (1858) and in 1859 moved his family just southeast of Morgan County to the Holly Springs area of Monroe County, Tennessee, which bordered Cherokee County, North Carolina. Richard had over twelve hundred acres in Morgan County, but Phillips stated that "he left in a hurry." As a probable cause, Phillips proposed that Richard may have been antislavery and a pacifist, and thus took refuge in Monroe County from the imminent outbreak of the Civil War. His mother, Frances, was in large part Cherokee. Twenty-one years after the Trail of Tears, the 1838 removal of the Cherokee Nation by the federal government, Richard moved his family to Monroe County, much of which is included today in the Cherokee National Forest.[10] In 1859, Cherokee land was almost being given away for settlement.

Set far back in the mountains, the Holly Springs area of Monroe County had at least 125 families. Richard helped to organize on Steer Creek the Holly Springs United Baptist Church of Christ on August 19, 1859. "Richard and Nancy, his mother and father, Frances and James, and several children, brothers, nephews and nieces, were added to the church by 'acknowledgment' or 'experience' by 1860."[11] The Holly Springs Church quickly developed into a large church with over two hundred members. The church house had two stories with the Odd Fellows given the upstairs. Richard was a preaching elder and the church's first moderator, which Phillips surmised meant that he had probably organized the church and, if so, likely through a revival. Richard was sent by Holly Springs Church as their delegate to the association's annual meetings, moderated services, performed marriages, and was also called upon as a "special messenger" to help arbitrate problems in other churches.

Richard had been a member of Holly Springs Church on and off (1859–63, 1875–86) over a twenty-seven-year period when he organized the Christian Union on August 19, 1886. Oral tradition says that the church met in a room Richard had added on to a grist mill he owned on Barney Creek, also in Monroe County. The very next month Holly Springs Church, which Richard had helped to organize, also on an August 19, excluded him for what the church minutes recorded as "heresy." At this point the reasons can only be speculated upon. From his study of Richard G.'s *The Lost Link*, written mostly between 1895–1900 but not published until 1920, Phillips discerned the influences of Landmarkism and the Spurlings' rejection of its exclusivism, successionism, and dogmatism, while continuing to embrace other aspects such as its interpretations of free church polity, which had strong Anabaptist overtones. "For this reason Landmarkers have been called 'Church equality Baptists.'"[12]

Phillips proposed that the Holly Springs Church had been swept up into Landmarkism, a movement in the Baptist tradition that originated in mid-nineteenth-century Tennessee and became more and more dogmatic, with an exalted ecclesiology promoting the succession of Baptist churches directly from New Testament churches. The Landmark movement wedded its successionist theory to an extreme exclusivity, limiting fellowship and preaching to Baptists, recognizing no other Christian fellowship, and eventually becoming exclusive even of other Baptist churches. By creating the Christian Union, Richard had violated both the successionist and exclusivist principles of Landmarkism, to which he also gave affront by directly challenging its dogmatism. His conduct was, in fact, "heretical," according to the principles undergirding Landmarkism. His struggles, noted Phillips, were not with the Baptist tradition per se, but with the harsh, aggressive Landmark movement especially characteristic of east Tennessee at that time.

Indeed, Clear Creek Church, where the Spurlin family had been charter members, "was one of the earliest churches influenced by Landmarkism."[13] Although United Baptist, which was loosely interpreted at the time in the religious life of the Appalachian mountains, Clear Creek Church soon went by the name Clear Creek United *Missionary* Baptist Church. The first time the modified name was entered into the church minutes, "Missionary" was inserted by a caret between "United" and "Baptist." "Missionary" was a term applied to the "more strict and distinct tradition" of the Landmark movement within the nineteenth century's broader distinction between Missionary Baptist churches and the Southern Baptist Convention.[14] Indeed, churches self-designated as Missionary Baptist in this area were overwhelmingly Landmark in orientation and influence. By founding the Christian Union on the basis of a creed, but one not to be held dogmatically, Richard gave priority to the liberty of conscience of all of its members, thus returning to the full tradition of consensus-based, Holy-Spirit guided, priesthood-of-all-believers, free church polity that had shaped the church life of his noncreedal Separate Baptist ancestors who had united with the Regular Baptists in Virginia in 1787. Indeed, Phillips detected in the Christian Union strong influences discernable in Richard G. Spurling's *The Lost Link* "more keenly identifiable with the Anabaptist tradition"[15] with which free church polity was so closely associated. By leaving the Holly Springs Church, "The Spurlings left the Landmark tradition and organized the Christian Union."[16] In fact, Phillips deduced, "It now seems safe to conclude that Christian Union was for the most part a reformation of Landmarkism."[17]

For some years Richard Spurling had been trying to bring a reformation to Holly Springs Church, attempting to move it away from the exclusivity and dogmatism of "men-made creeds" and "doctrines" (as Richard G. put it in *The Lost Link*) promoted by Landmarkism, and thus away from an emphasis on faith as right belief, moving it instead toward a covenanting community based on the New Testament only and an emphasis on the "law of love." Richard had little success in his efforts and so, in 1884, he and his son, Richard G., began two years of self-study in the Bible and church history, looking closely at other traditions such as Alexander Campbell's Restoration movement and Methodism. Their study resulted in Richard's founding the Christian Union on Thursday, August 19, 1886. As we can glean from *The Lost Link*, Richard Spurling envisioned it as the restoration of the Bible church, in keeping with Anabaptist restorationist emphases, rather than as the founding of a new church. "But," Phillips observed, "even more than the doctrinal and theological differences, the Spurlings were reacting against the generally uncharitable and harsh spirit that tended to characterize Landmarkism."[18]

Richard issued an invitation to membership in the Christian Union to those attending its inaugural service: "As many Christians as are here present that are desirous to be free from all men made creeds and traditions, and are willing to take the New Testament, or law of Christ, for your only rule of faith and practice: giving each other equal rights and privilege to read and interpret for yourselves as your conscience may dictate, and are willing to set together as the Church of God to transact business at the same, come forward."[19] Eight people responded to the invitation. On September 26, 1886, Richard ordained his son, Richard G. His original ordination certificate reads that Richard G. Spurling was "an ordained minister of, 'The Church of God,'"[20] a standard phrase of the period. June Glover Marshall, in an interview, explained that "Church of God" "was not in as a title, but I don't know how to say it, it was not the name, but was a designation." We have noted earlier that "Church of God" is one of the most popular names for independent Holiness churches throughout the Appalachian region, having no formal or informal connection with the Pentecostal denomination of the Church of God (Cleveland, Tennessee). What Richard G.'s ordination certificate and the original Christian Union invitation to membership both illustrate is that at least by the mid-1880s "Church of God" was already in use as a common expression among mountain churches.

When Richard Spurling returned to the Holly Springs Church in November 1886, Richard G. continued the work of the Christian Union, developing further his own theological thinking, especially his emphasis on the "law of love," New Testament government, and rejection of "men-made creeds" and "doctrines." He was known for his motto, "Love is the law on which Christ built the church." He called the "law of love" the "lost link" in church history, and the basis for any latter-day reformation of the worldwide Christian community of believers. Brother James Marshall of Cleveland, Tennessee, a Church of God minister, and his spouse, Sister June Glover Marshall, have devoted their lives to a study of the earliest years of the Church of God in the mountains of Appalachia, pastoring in several church com-

munities associated with its earliest history. The Marshalls used their own
money to republish Richard G. Spurling's *The Lost Link,* first published in
1920 by the authority of A. J. Tomlinson, then general overseer of the Church
of God. Brother Marshall said of Richard G.'s emphasis on love, "[Spurling's]
little book, even on the back of that book, his motto in his messages, and
his motto in the main messages of his sermons, was love is the law on which
Christ has built his church and the lost link itself means that love is the lost
link in the church. That's what he promoted from the very beginning, so the
whole message of the early church doctrine was based on love. . . . [Spurling]
denounced creeds of men . . . because he realized that this is how the church
made the mistake in the early beginning. See, the church has tried to reform
their doctrines, instead of having the basis of love."[21]

During our interview, Brother Marshall had me read out loud an excerpt
from *The Lost Link* that accounted for the beliefs of the Christian Union in
1895, the year before the 1896 revival at Shearer Schoolhouse in Cherokee
County, North Carolina:

> We here give the agreement or basis of union as it stood in 1895. First.
> The new Testament is the only infallible rule of faith in practice, so we
> reject all other articles of faith and men-made creeds, and for the basis
> of our union we accept the law of love instead of faith [right belief],
> faith in Christ being the only faith required in the gospel and love be-
> ing the commandment of Christ, by which we should know each oth-
> er as His disciples.
>
> We further agree that the New Testament contains all things neces-
> sary for salvation and church government. So all dealings must be on
> gospel principles. Baptism, the Lord's supper, the feet-washing, as
> taught in the Scriptures and that each member shall have equal rights
> and privileges to read, believe and practice for themselves in all mat-
> ters of religion that may not prove contrary to the law of love or the
> true spirit of Christianity. We invite to union and fellowship all persons
> who avow faith in Christ and love to God and His people and a will-
> ingness to live a Christian life so as not to dishonor the cause of Christ,
> and we exclude only for known violations of God's Word or commands.
>
> Whereas each member shall give an account to God for themselves
> and a christianized conscience is the basis of purity we do reject all con-
> science binding creeds as being contrary to Scripture, also to religion
> and love, and are in open rebellion against the constitution of our na-
> tion. Against such we do protest.[22]

Richard G.'s emphasis on the law of love, rejection of conscience-binding
creeds and doctrines, commitment to the autonomy of the individual believer, and insistence upon the New Testament as the only guide and rule for
church government combined what are most characteristic of the independent nondenominational church tradition in the Appalachian mountains, in

so and I was again called to account for disobeying their rules. Now I must forever quit preaching or leave my church, so I left them, choosing to obey God rather than man. . . . *I was turned out* of what I once thought was Christ's only true church" (p. 48, emphasis added). Phillips pointed out that this last sentence only underscored the influence of Landmarkism on Richard G. ("what I once thought was *Christ's only true church*"), against which he and his father finally rebelled in their founding of the Christian Union after they failed to "reform" their home churches.[23] As for the fundamental problems with creeds themselves, Richard G. wrote, "For centuries we have been under creeds or doctrines and instead of unity it makes division; instead of peace they make strife; instead of unity they bring discord; instead of love they bring hatred" (p. 26). In a parallel passage more concrete at the level of the local church house, especially in the mountains of Appalachia, he wrote, "See the little preacher in the stand [pulpit area] riding some hobby, branding all others as heretics or devils. So he wounds someone or more and breaks the unity of the Spirit and brings division instead of unity, hatred instead of love" (p. 37).

Richard G. developed in *The Lost Link* the metaphor of "trying to run a broad gauge engine on a narrow gauge railway" (p. 48) to describe the source of the conflict between him and his Landmark church. Indeed, he placed this analogy in the sentence immediately preceding the one where he stated that his Landmark-influenced church "demanded my license." As Phillips concluded, "They were confining him with institutionalism." *The Lost Link* bears out Phillips's interpretation. Here Richard G. used the railroad metaphor for his ecclesiological model of the church. God had laid down the two "golden rails" which were "the great law of love. . . . Next come the great drive wheels, the law of liberty and equality." The two "golden rails" were "the first and second commandment of God with double force, 'Thou shalt love the Lord thy God will all thy soul, mind and strength.' The second is like unto it, 'Thou shalt love thy neighbor as thyself.' . . . These are the golden rails . . . on which every wheel must roll" (pp. 13, 14). Creeds were the antithesis of the golden rails "on which every wheel must roll," wheels driven by "the law of liberty and equality." Richard G. wrote that first the Church of Rome and then the Protestant denominations "took out" the "golden rails," "the golden link of God's law and set in the wooden rails" which he identified with "men-made creeds" (p. 16).

The railroad metaphor was also a metaphor for "the lost link" itself: "Where is the lost link of the golden chain of God's law? Oh, where did the Church sidetrack? Oh, where did they leave the golden rail and set in the wooden rails of creedism?" (p. 20). For Richard G., "the lost link" of "God's law" was threefold: *love* ("I have said many times that love is the law on which Christ built the church" [p. 12]); *fellowship* ("Therefore fellowshipping each other by the law of love is the lost link" [p. 22]); and *unity* ("The lost link is seen as the law of unity" [p. 44]). Fellowship and unity embodied "the law of liberty and equality," none of which was possible unless founded on "love . . . the law on which Christ built the church." In these words Richard G. encapsulated the ecclesiology normative to so much of mountain religious life.

Richard G. traced the problem with creeds beginning with the Council of Nicaea in 325 C.E. and the formulation of the Nicene Creed, which eventually led to splitting the Church into eastern and western Christianity. "This change gave birth to creeds and every creed has made a sect or denomination," a change soon followed by the unification of church and state (p. 23). Creeds and creedism also gave birth to "political ecclesiasticism" (p. 18), the engine that drove religious institutionalism, which the Spurlings, father and son, rejected as utterly contrary to "God's law of love." Given Richard G.'s thematic emphases, Phillips's identification of his priorities is not unexpected at this point. Phillips stated that Richard G.'s ecclesiology was "strong on inner discipline and moral community, but loose on polity and institutional government." Also it does not seem surprising that Richard G. would be squarely at odds with the ever-increasing institutionalization and centralization and "political ecclesiasticism" of the Church of God and then the Tomlinson Church of God. According to Phillips, the nondenominational Christian Union, marking when the history of the Church of God first began, was far more the "passion and legacy" of Richard G. than of his father.

Richard G. Spurling founded independent churches wherever he settled, as Brother Abbott's *The Forgotten Church* recounted[24] and the unpublished account left by Richard G.'s eldest son, G. P. (Goldsberry Pinkney) Spurling, corroborated:

> Father furnished his own lumber and built a small church house and how people would fill this church every night and pray and how God would bless and save, but still it was hard for people to give up their church creeds. But Spurling never became discouraged.
>
> About this time Spurling went over near the center of Monroe County, Tennessee, to a place called Piney and set a church in order and this church is still in function. Years later they choosed to be independent. I cannot say they have accomplished much because I visited there about six years ago. They are mostly just one family church. After organizing the Piney Church, Spurling went to a place in Polk County and bought a farm. In 1889, we moved to Polk County where Father had organized a church sometime before. While we lived there this church did good and prospered well. But school facilities were bad here for us children, so Father knowing this went to Turtle Town, in Polk County [in 1893] and bought a farm where schools were convenient. He still kept watch over the work even though it was small, taking nothing from them for services, but he helped them.

tist advisory council, but Tomlinson made it more and more centralized and authoritative. Phillips wrote,

> Even the early "General Assemblies" were more or less fashioned according to Baptist association meetings and purposes. The local churches were still considered independent, and Assembly decisions and recommendations were held to be only advisory and informational. Everything—including missions—fell back to the local churches as a matter of principle. Not until A. J. Tomlinson gained preeminence in the organization (1910–14) did changes begin to occur that little by little transformed the churches of God from Baptist-type independent republics into an authoritative and highly centralized episcopal system.
>
> . . . Thus, through Tomlinson, primarily, the original Baptist-type concept of an Associational Moderator metamorphosed from 1906–1914 into the popish-type office of General Overseer; the Baptist practice of the Introductory Sermon was institutionalized in the prestigious Annual Address; committees became static authoritative councils, and councils ecclesiastical tyrannies. Pastors, once called by the churches (in the tradition of the Baptists), were soon appointed by the General Overseer, and later by state overseers when that office was created. As this episcopal hierarchy was little by little built down from the office of General Overseer, commensurately, the Baptist roots and legacy in the Church of God disappeared.[31]

Spurling had a prominent role as a speaker at the 1913 General Assembly; but after that he was less and less involved until finally he was not even listed as a minister in the General Assembly minutes after 1917, even though he had been a bishop in the Church of God. Spurling may have withdrawn his name from the rolls, making a protest against the latest step in centralization.

A Council of Elders (officially called still today the "Council of Twelve") was recommended and accepted at the 1916 General Assembly. "[T]he affairs of the Church of God" were now entrusted "to the hands of these twelve choice men," wrote Charles W. Conn.[32] Its first members, appointed in February 1917, made moves to curb Tomlinson, especially during 1918, the year of the influenza outbreak when the annual General Assembly was canceled, giving the Council of Elders more leeway to maneuver. Not only were they trying to curb Tomlinson but also to ensure their own power in what would soon be an oligarchical church government that in later decades would evolve into a form of episcopalism. Other forms of encroachment on the liberty of individual congregations, one involving the centralized collection and distribution of tithes and offerings, were also afoot at this time among the Church of God hierarchy.

Spurling's *The Lost Link,* written around 1895–1900, included a "Supplement" composed sometime in 1919–20, which Phillips suggested Spurl-ing added as a protest against "the very drift of the church at that time." A composite of key statements from Spurling's "Supplement" makes clear that his thematic focus was steeped in the values and worldview of mountain religious life. His reproach to the ¿overnance of the Church of God during this period was also unambiguous. Spurling wrote,

> Oh, preachers, do not scatter the flock and make infidelity. Do not make the people to abhor their offerings as did the sons of Eli. 1 Sam. 2:17. Don't ask more than God has provided. Do not be a hireling, do not look after pay instead of the flock. . . . Where is the meek and humble bride of Christ [biblical metaphor for the church] whose adorning is of the inward man of the heart and not of the putting on of gold and costly apparel. . . . [W]e see this kingdom ["the visible church"] is set up in the hearts of His people. So every child of God has the kingdom of heaven in them while the church is a union of three or more per-sons. Matt. 18:16, 17. . . . Some think Christians ought not to be unit-ed in any bond of fellowship while others are not satisfied with the law and government of Christ and the Holy Spirit but must have a great many more laws and governments. . . . Liberty is what God's people want and must have it at any cost or hypocrisy will soon invade the church. (pp. 37–38, 41–42)

Spurling even challenged in *The Lost Link* the distinguishing beliefs and worship practices of Pentecostal denominations identified with the gifts of the Holy Spirit as not enough in and of themselves, writing about 1 John 4:20–21, "Verses 20, 21 forever settle the fact that love is the infallible rule to know a man's religion. St. Paul says though I have the gift of tongues, even to speak the language of angels, and have not charity, it is a failure. Neither is the gift of prophecy or knowledge of faith without charity sufficient to know God's people. God's Word puts it beyond all dispute as to the apostol-ic church being established on the law of love" (p. 22).

Spurling markedly distanced himself from the church organization when the Church of God did centralize its members' tithes in 1920 (which was later reversed) and the next year instituted a constitution that authorized an oli-garchical form of government to try to curb Tomlinson's ever-increasing, near-totalitarian power. The constitution of 1921 also for the first time took away the authority of local churches (which was later restored). Concurrently, Spurling fell out of fellowship and friendship with individual members of the Council of Elders. During this time J. L. Scott, a prominent church leader, and Sam C. Perry, a member of the Council of Twelve, resigned from the Church of God and formed the (Original) Church of God in Chattanooga.

"Spurling remained in warm friendship with Tomlinson" to his death, said Phillips, but otherwise distanced himself from the now highly centralized church which would continue to characterize both the Tomlinson group and the Church of God after their split in 1923. The ten years following the split saw more confusion and disputation, with the U.S. Postal Service not knowing at times where to deliver the mail. Tomlinson's group also went by the name Church of God, later distinguished as the Tomlinson Church of God until May 2, 1952, when a court decree settled the nearly thirty year old legal battle between the two denominations over entitlements to properties and the name "Church of God." At that time the Chancery Court of Bradley County, Tennessee, with Cleveland its county seat, ruled that the Tomlinson group would be officially and legally known as the Church of God of Prophecy "in its secular affairs (not religious or spiritual affairs)."[33]

Throughout most of the first decade of the split, some members associated themselves with the Tomlinson group while remaining members in good standing of churches belonging to the Church of God. Spurling fit this common pattern during the first three years of the split. He associated himself with the Tomlinson group at least by 1925–26, while maintaining membership in the Church of God. Tomlinson sent him in as a pastor to Okeechobee, Florida, in 1925–26, though he stayed less than a year. Tomlinson was such an opportunist that he knew the symbolic value of hanging on to Spurling. But he was also canny enough to heed the measure of the man whom he had known for many years. Tomlinson never required Spurling to be obsequious and deferential to church power and authority, like his other ministers.

Spurling was as independent as both the Church of God and the Tomlinson group would allow him to be as part of their Spirit-system of church life. But the Church of God did eventually disfellowship him. In 1926, Spurling was a member of Copper Hill Church of God near Ducktown, Tennessee, fifteen miles from his home in Turtletown, where he apparently caused a fair amount of disruption, although the specifics are in no way clear. It is highly probable that he held the Lee/Llewellyn faction of the divided body responsible for the acts that led to centralization and disruption. This faction, made up of powerful members of the Council of Twelve (J. S. Llewellyn was a particularly influential member) moved to surreptitiously challenge Tomlinson's autocratic authority after he was made general overseer "for life" at the tenth annual assembly in 1914. Gleaning from correspondence and church records, Phillips reconstructed why Spurling was probably dropped that year from the rolls of the church. Phillips recounted that John C. Jernigan, then pastor of Copper Hill (and later general overseer of the Church of God), wrote an appeal to Church of God General Overseer F. J. Lee (who was elected to take over the position when Tomlinson was removed) to deal with Spurling, which most likely meant pulling Spurling's license as a Church of God minister in order for the local church to be able to exclude him.

Phillips noted that, apart from appealing to the general overseer to deal with members who were licensed ministers, which the local church could not do, in order to clear the path for the local church to take actions against them, there was no other apparent reason for Jernigan to turn to Lee about Spurling. If, on the other hand, Spurling had earlier resigned his ministry with the Church of God (namely, after 1917) to protest assembly resolutions which centralized the government and operation of the church, Jernigan may have appealed to Lee simply out of respect for Spurling's former standing and the high esteem in which so many people held him. Whatever the case may have been, the divorce between Spurling and the Lee/Llewellyn faction is certain.

In the late 1920s, Spurling was listed as a member of the Wildwood Church of God [of Prophecy] in Cleveland. He was in fellowship with Tomlinson and his followers (known since 1952 as the Church of God of Prophecy) from 1926 until his death. Spurling died at his home in Turtletown, Tennessee, in 1935.

In 1910 the Church of God began publication of *The Evening Light and Church of God Evangel*. By this time work in the mountains was again objectified to home mission status, reflecting Tomlinson's original work in the mountains and despite the mountain origins of the Church of God. During this time W. F. Bryant was the recognized "home mission" evangelist to the mountains, as he was called, for the Church of God. But he functioned as a mountain preacher. Many of his reports reflected the predominance of the traditions of plain-folk camp-meeting religion in mountain worship services, then influenced by the more developed traditions of Pentecostal theology. Of equal importance, Bryant's accounts and the accounts of those who traveled with him gave a portrait of life and conditions in the Appalachian region that was highly reminiscent of the accounts left by Hamilton W. Pierson in *In the Brush*, describing religious life in the Appalachian wilderness of the 1850s.

In the very first issue of *The Evening Light and Church of God Evangel*, Bryant wrote in a piece titled "Work in the Mountains of Tennessee,"

> The Church of God at Hillview, Tellico Mountains, have chosen me again as their pastor, which will make my fourth year with them. The first Saturday and Sunday of this month was my regular time for services there. On Saturday night the Lord helped us to preach from 1 Cor. 15:55–57 in the power and demonstration of the Spirit. At the close of the service some began to cry out in the congregation for mercy, a number got blest, and one restored and sanctified, and on Sunday came back to the altar seeking her Pentecost. Sunday God greatly blessed the preaching, from Heb. 6:4–6, at the close of which six or seven penitents fell at the altar calling for mercy. Among that number were fathers,

writer also reported, "The people do not believe in government,"[38] a comment upon attitudes toward the then highly centralized government of the Church of God.

In 1914 Bryant wrote that Tomlinson was trying to get him to give up his work among mountain people: "Bro. Tomlinson and some others have been thinking I ought to give up my missionary work in these mountains and go into new fields, but I have been waiting before the Lord and there are so many of these people calling me to come, it looks like I will have to keep it up, as they are saying if I don't they will have no one to preach for them."[39] While Bryant continued his mountain ministry, he commuted by rail from Cleveland, Tennessee, into the back reaches of Appalachia where most travel was by either foot or horse. Bryant struggled with the poverty that beset his mountain pastorates, appealing repeatedly in print for boxes of clothing to be shipped to his Cleveland address for distribution among mountain people. Bryant even organized an orphanage for mountain children in 1911, though it was disbanded after a few months as "impractical."[40] Bryant was, nevertheless, tapped for higher offices, being made state overseer for Tennessee in 1911–12, and then for Kentucky from 1914 to 1918. After 1920, due to advancing age, Bryant became much less visible in the Church of God, although he continued to preach until his death in 1949. W. F. Bryant had been the stalwart partner and colleague of Richard G. Spurling in the mountain church tradition of independent Holiness that gave birth to the Church of God, coming out of strong Baptist roots shaped uniquely to the contours of mountain religious culture. Said Bryant of their early years together, "Me and Brother Spurling were standing shoulder to shoulder." Bryant was also the last solid link with the denomination's mountain origins.

The overriding influences of plain-folk camp-meeting religion continue to be found in small mountain churches of the Church of God throughout Appalachia. Indeed, even today Conway Church of God, on Route 25 near Berea, Kentucky, has much more in common with traditional mountain worship life than does North Cleveland Church of God, the mother church of the denomination in Cleveland, Tennessee. The congregation of North Cleveland Church of God is distinctly middle- to upper-middle-class. Its staid, brief (one hour), tightly orchestrated Sunday morning worship services, replete with a robed choir, would make any urban evangelical Protestant comfortable.[41] The "church complex" of interconnecting buildings and a large satellite dish making up North Cleveland Church of God takes up an entire city block. It is very much a throwback to the "super church" era of the early twentieth century, like John D. Rockefeller's Riverside Church in Manhattan. In contrast, Conway Church of God is housed in a converted gas station out in the country. Its revival services, which last for at least two to three hours, are at the most ecstatic end of the scale. People leap over pews, shout all at once, kneel on the floor at their pews and up at the altar while praying loudly all at the same time their own personal prayers. They also get the "jerks" and are slain in the Spirit. All of these traditions go back to the region's plain-folk camp-meeting religion of the first half of the nineteenth century. Like many of the mountain churches of the Methodists and Southern Baptists, the mountain churches of the Church of God are generally much closer to the worship traditions characterizing Appalachian mountain religion than are its urban and non-Appalachian churches.

We glean the greatest insight in Richard G. Spurling's small book, *The Lost Link,* about the contrast between his heritage in mountain religion and the highly centralized denomination that claimed his and his father's religious efforts as its own initial origins and patrimony. Phillips stated that Richard G. "had an acute sensitivity to the spirit of the Gospel" which he manifested throughout *The Lost Link.* Said Phillips, "*The Lost Link* is almost completely preoccupied with the basis for Christian fellowship and, by the power of Divine love, in breaking down the walls of denominationalism. That is why Spurling called 'love' the 'lost link.' He desired to build a fellowship that was more of a manifestation of people's hearts than their heads. Spurling said that creeds break down unity. Short definitive statements on doctrines could not express the spirit of the Gospel,"[42] but locked people in while locking out the spirit of the Gospel. Phillips's remarks about the essence of *The Lost Link* could not better summarize the essence of mountain religious life that I have proposed throughout this book, including the creedally based church traditions nearest the center of the spectrum delimiting mountain religion's range; for indeed, Richard Spurling's Christian Union was also founded on the basis of a creed. It was the intertwined priorities of "love," "fellowship," and "unity," together making up "the lost link," that determined for the Spurlings—and mountain people generally—the role and the power of a creed in church life, rather than the other way around that inevitably opened the door to what Richard G. Spurling described as "division," "strife," "discord," "hatred," and "political ecclesiasticism."

Finally, the Holy Spirit itself could not be subjected to creedalism. In *The Lost Link* Spurling wrote, "It is impossible to set up a creed for a man to preach and the Holy Ghost guide into all truth. Where can you lead an ox that is tied to a stake? It is impossible to teach the doctrines and commandments and not insult the Holy Ghost" (p. 25). Like the Old Time Baptists of Appalachia such as the Old Regular Baptists, about whom John Wallhausser wrote, "This creedal faith is the historical backbone that has given these communities their tenacity, resilience, and theological toughness,"[43] Spurling argued in his words about the Holy Spirit that a community of faith's understanding of their creed must always be directed, first and foremost, by their submission to the leading of the Holy Spirit, rather than subjecting the

Holy Spirit to the requirements of their creed. His argument, grounded in the normative tradition of free church policy and reflecting the ethos of mountain religious culture, required flexibility and adaptability, rather than the iron restraints of dogmatism.

Phillips located Richard G. Spurling's preoccupation with how to form a Christian fellowship based on the law of love in the Spurling family's strong Separate Baptist heritage and in Anabaptist influences, to which I wish to add one additional point: Richard G. Spurling's life and emphases, especially as demonstrated in *The Lost Link,* were a product of the all-pervasive mountain religious culture in which his family was immersed since the eighteenth century. I have already spoken about Separate Baptist and Anabaptist influences on mountain religious culture. Phillips, who stated that his own investigations have been confined to a more narrow focus than mine, concluded, in words he chose without any prompting, that Spurling's *The Lost Link* "is almost completely preoccupied with the basis for Christian fellowship and . . . in *breaking down the walls of denominationalism.* That is why Spurling called 'love' the 'lost link.' He desired to build a fellowship that was *more of a manifestation of people's hearts than their heads.*"

Indeed, in *The Lost Link* Spurling summed up the normative goals of mountain church life in his own era and still today, despite his and his father's struggles with movements such as Landmarkism that only galvanized these two mountain preachers into a stance of resistance: "Dear reader, ask the Lord to help you to know the truth and to obey it. If we have right to anything in this world, it is to read God's Word. He has promised to give His Spirit to His people and what we want is perfect love to God and each other and perfect liberty" (p. 42). The primary components for mountain church life—which Spurling thought of in universal terms, believing that they would reform all churches and denominations everywhere—were personal access to the Bible and the right to interpret it for oneself as the Holy Spirit leads, seeking and upholding the gift of the presence of the Holy Spirit in the community of faith, and finally wanting "perfect love to God and each other and perfect liberty." With these words, Spurling had summed up the foundational parameters of free church polity as we first explored them in chapter 3, including in those parameters specifically Anabaptist emphases on the laity and the Bible, and especially on heart religion, which we looked at in "Pietism, Pietists, and Holiness People." "Creedism" killed the life of the churches, according to Spurling; "thousands today. . . fail to see that God's law wasn't a creed system" (p. 21). On this point, Spurling singled out the Methodists for particular mention, "It is no wonder the once powerful Methodist Church has lost so much power with God and man. Her twenty-nine articles are enough to drive the Spirit filled saints from her fold" (p. 25).

Given Phillips's own summary of *The Lost Link* and the words we have heard from it, Richard G. Spurling, like his father Richard, epitomized the values and worldview of mountain religious culture which, within the framework of their serious historical study and sustained theological reflection, were the earliest unambiguous foundations of the Church of God. Such values initially compelled the Spurlings to rebel against the Landmark movement, with its exalted ecclesiology in their own churches which they otherwise loved very much (recall that Richard G. wrote in *The Lost Link* about his home church which "I once loved so dearly"). These foundations in mountain religious culture contradicted and were a source of internal resistance to the episcopal authority structure and the much larger worldly ambitions of the Church of God and the Tomlinson Church of God, sometimes challenging directly, but usually indirectly, the "political ecclesiasticism" eagerly engaged in by many of the leaders of these two denominations, who wanted a piece of the power their institutional structures had concentrated and centralized, even though they were compelled to have it within a shared but elite context.

Brother Callaway of Avery County in western North Carolina and Richard G. Spurling were both born in 1858. Though they traveled in different circles, they shared a fundamental commitment to mountain religion's normative independent nondenominational church tradition. In 1907 Brother Callaway built "with his own hands" the structure housing the Independent Church of God which he founded on his own property where "he spent his whole life"; Spurling built and founded independent churches wherever he settled, culminating in his manifesto, *The Lost Link*.

The irony here is "evidential, without speculation," to borrow Phillips's words about his data and reconstruction of the religious and family history of the Spurlings. Richard G. Spurling's *The Lost Link*—ironically published under the authority of A. J. Tomlinson, without which it would probably have never appeared in print because of Spurling's own modest resources—made explicit his evident position as the ongoing radical sign of contradiction in the midst of the Church of God and then the Tomlinson Church of God, denominations that had evolved initially and largely out of his personal religious history and that of his family in the Appalachian mountains. Finally, we see an overarching irony in the mountain roots of these two denominations, epitomized by the life of Richard G. Spurling, that were the antithesis of what they so quickly became. Here we have a paradigm extraordinaire of the fundamental incompatibility of mountain religious life with denominationalism in terms of their opposing religious values and worldview about who God is and who people are in relation to God and to each other.

This fundamental incompatibility stands regardless of whatever debt of history various denominations may have owed a slice of mountain religion, as the Church of God and the Tomlinson Church of God owed the religious history of Richard G. Spurling and his family. Other denominations' debts to mountain religion and its history might also be mentioned. But like the Church of God and the Tomlinson Church of God, these other denominations were now very far removed from mountain religion and its history, regardless of the historical debt they rarely acknowledged; indeed, they almost never looked back, except to capitalize on the value of a romanticized past, be it to justify or to glorify.

14

Brother Coy Miser

Brother Coy Miser has graced the pages of this book throughout with comments, observations, and illustrations. It is highly appropriate to conclude this section on the independent Holiness church with an opportunity to hear Brother Coy speak about his life as a mountain Holiness preacher. In the introduction I observed that mountain religion is essentially an oral religious tradition. Worship—the preaching, singing, and praying—is the "text," the primary source document of mountain religious life, along with the conversion narratives and testimonies, the visions, dreams, and trances of religious experience. Oral history is one of the primary tools in discovering the contours and features of mountain religion. The independent nondenominational church tradition, which stands at the center of the spectrum of mountain religious life, and its preachers—people like Brother Coy Miser—have been rendered invisible in nearly all previous, and usually abbreviated, written accounts of religion distinctive to the mountains of Appalachia by those who were not part of it. People like Brother Coy have also rarely been allowed their own voice in the quite limited number of scholarly investigations of Appalachian mountain religion. Given the central place of the church tradition Brother Coy represents, how it crystallizes features normative to mountain religion, concluding this section with the voice of Brother Coy Miser will lend insight and descriptive detail that will illumine even more the independent nondenominational church tradition and mountain religion's characterizing features—especially in basic attitudes shared by mountain Christians.

On October 16, 1989, I recorded a three-hour oral history interview with Brother Coy, covering many topics we had discussed in the past. The interview is roughly divided into three sections: (1) personal and religious background; (2) religion in the mountains and especially in independent Holiness churches; and (3) the Holy Ghost and the religion of the heart. What follows is a summary of the interview with excerpts from the transcript and some interpretive commentary.

Brother Coy Miser was born June 1, 1918, in Lee County, Virginia. Lee County is the very southwest corner of the state, bordering both Harlan County in eastern Kentucky and Hancock County in northeastern Tennessee. His mother and his father, subsistence farmers, moved from near Sneedville, Hancock's county seat, to Lee County before he was born. Brother Coy was a coal miner in southwest Virginia for twelve years in the 1940s and early

1950s, after which he went into construction work, "laying block and brick" for prefabricated houses. He lived in Miamisburg, Ohio, for twenty-one years doing construction work. Like so many mountain people who out-migrate to areas still within a long day's drive to their homes in the Appalachian region, Brother Coy returned on the weekends to Lee County, driving hundreds of miles in each direction and going without sleep, to visit family and friends and to replenish himself.

Brother Coy was ordained in 1948 at Harber's Chapel, an independent Holiness church in Pennington Gap, Lee County. Harber's Chapel was the church where Brother Coy's parents first took him as a child of five or six years of age. His parents had been Missionary Baptists, but Harber's Chapel was the church closest to their home. Harber's Chapel was started through the influence of Mollie Burkhart Harber, the church matriach, whose son was the first pastor. A plaque above the entryway reads:

Harber's Pentecostal Holiness Church
God is love.
Built for the people.
Mollie Burkhart Harber

Harber's Chapel has no connection with the Pentecostal denomination called the Pentecostal Holiness Church, the third largest Pentecostal denomination in the South today with headquarters in Franklin Springs, Georgia. Instead, Pentecostal Holiness Church, like Church of God, is a very popular name among mountain people and is commonly chosen for independent Holiness churches, having nothing to do with the denomination by the same name. A common conflation of the two names found among many independent Holiness churches is Pentecostal Church of God, the name Brother Coy used for his church work when he incorporated it in 1961.

Brother Coy's public education went only to the second grade. He is totally illiterate, unable to read for himself. His children's education ended with the fifth grade. He had two sons. George Edward drove heavy construction equipment and died several years ago. His younger son, Dewey, worked in the coal mines and was a subsistence farmer. Brother Dewey began preaching at the age of thirteen and is also an independent Holiness preacher. Like his father, Dewey is in poor health, both of them suffering the ill effects of coal mining. Brother Coy has heart disease, black lung, and emphysema. He is on oxygen twenty-four hours a day, carrying a portable tank when he leaves the house. Both of Brother Coy's parents and his two sisters, his only siblings, have all died. Brother Coy has had three wives. The first two died while married to Brother Coy. Sister Hassie Miser has been Brother Coy's spouse for the past fourteen years as of this writing.

Brother Coy estimates that he has started eleven independent Holiness churches in southwest Virginia, eastern Kentucky, northeast Tennessee, and southern Ohio. Most of these churches began in what he calls "dwelling houses," to distinguish them from "church houses." Brother Coy would start up a church and, once it was strong, hand it over to another pastor. In the interview I asked him why he did that. Brother Coy replied, "Well, seemed like I had a calling to be, to build them up. To get them to go. To get them started. It was my job to get out there and get them in, you know. That's the reason, that's the way I worked."

In spite of a strong instinctive distrust for legal intrusions into matters of faith, or perhaps because of those intrusions, in 1961 Brother Coy legally incorporated his work as the Pentecostal Church of God. He had ordination certificates and wallet-size identification cards printed up for the mountain preachers he ordained, which he stamped with the seal of incorporation. Brother Coy's sole purpose was to license other independent preachers so that they would have legal recognition as ministers to baptize, marry, and minister in hospitals or in emergency situations such as the scene of an accident. Brother Coy never had the intention of founding a small denomination or parachurch called the Pentecostal Church of God. None of the churches he has "started up" goes by that name; all are independent. Once a preacher is licensed by Brother Coy, he or she is fully autonomous, liable only to themselves and to God.

In reading the interview, it is important to be aware that Brother Coy usually begins speaking in short phrases, often somewhat repetitive. His difficulty breathing is the cause of much of this. It is only when he starts to "get the Spirit" that his narrative becomes stronger and clearer, his sentences more fully formed. Brother Coy begins the interview with his own definition of Holiness as "a clean life," not as a series of do's and don'ts in delineated Holiness codes of conduct that prevail in much of Holiness-Pentecostal culture.

DVM: Why did you become Holiness?
MISER: Well, it was just because I read the Bible, or heard the Bible read, I can't read myself but I heard it read and I, my understanding of the Bible was I had to be holy before I could make it through to heaven. The Father said without Holiness no man could see the Lord, so I realized it was just a clean holy life. Holiness is not what a lot of people preach it to be though [i.e., Holiness codes of conduct]. Holiness just means cleanness. To be, in other words, to be cleaned up and get ready to go up. When the Lord comes or when Death's Angel comes, whichever way you go first, you know, we could be here when the Lord comes, be called up to meet him in the air but if not we go by the way of the Angel, we still got to be

cleaned up inside and be living a holy consecrated life before God. So, that's why I went Holiness. I realized it was a clean life and I realized that's what it took to be a child of God, is to be clean.

It is common in Appalachian mountain religion for someone to attend a church for many years and eventually be converted, if at all, moving from the "sinner" state to that of a "saint" of God. Conversion is not simply a matter of placing church membership, but concerns the status of one's heart and soul. Answering the call to conversion pulls the individual's whole life into change, change that is not limited to one's "faith" or "religion." In mountain religion, many conversions do not happen in church or even at a revival (the more common setting for the experience of conversion in non-Calvinist traditions), but happen instead in the setting of everyday life, often in times of crisis. This lack of separation between "church life" and "home life" is part of the very fabric of Appalachian mountain religion. It is not unusual to stop by to visit someone who is bed-bound or sick and have that visit turn into a healing session of prayer and witness, with neighbors and friends pouring in from all around. Brother Coy gives a narrative of his conversion experience which is quite similar to Brother John Sherfey's in Titon's *Powerhouse for God,* centered upon the life-threatening illness of his child. According to Brother Coy, "I was about twenty years old. And, I got saved at the house. I didn't get saved in the church. I got saved in my own kitchen. At 10:31 at night." It is very common for the actual date and time of conversion to be clearly remembered, often written on the fly leaf of a favored Bible.

DVM: Would you tell me about that?
MISER: Well, my oldest son was sick.
DVM: What was his name?
MISER: George Edward. We called him Eddie all the time. George Edward was his name and he got sick. He was just a little bitty thing, about two and a half, three years old and I worked at Kingsport [in Tennessee] at that time, construction work for the government, you know on a government project. And, I come home, I was having to board over there cause I didn't have no transportation to get back and forth and I come home when I got my pay check to bring them some money so they would have something to live on, and he just has a little cold and it didn't seem to be bad, you know. And, but when I got ready to leave he hung onto me and screamed and cried and his mother begged me not to go. I told her I got to go cause I got to work. It's the only way we got to live. And, I went on and I was working on a [?] and when I went to the job there was a telegram for me there that if I wanted to see my child alive I better come back home.

So, I rushed back home and caught the bus out that night and come back home and when I got back home he didn't even know me. He didn't know anything and he was sick for twelve days and nights and I had a doctor with him every day. The doctor said he couldn't find what the problem was, what the trouble was, and, of course, I started out, I started praying for him which I wasn't fit to pray for him. I needed to pray for myself and on the twelfth night he just went wild. He tried to come out of the bed, you know, and all that stuff. I went to the kitchen and went to praying and, then I was praying for myself and I got saved there in that old kitchen that night. When I got saved, by the time I got back into the room, he up and was doing alright and was up talking and wanted to be put back to his bed.

DVM: What was it like getting saved? What did it feel like?

MISER: I just got such a blessing, there was just something come down over me, you know, and I felt so good. Back then they didn't have cabinets and refrigerators and all that, you know, to put your pots and pans in. Had them hung up around the wall around the stove, and I was getting such a blessing, I was knocking the pots and pans off the wall. They run in to see what was the matter and it was me getting a blessing from the Lord. But, that was the best feeling I ever felt in my life, you know, because it was something different. It was really a good feeling. It's just something that you can't really explain. I just had a good feeling because it's unspeakable, untalkable. You just can't tell it, but anyway that's when I changed and started living rightly.

Love for his son played a key part in Brother Coy's conversion. Although he was "not fit" to pray for Eddie, because he was not yet saved himself, he poured all of himself into that prayer, and in doing so made room for the saving grace of the Holy Spirit to move in. When Brother Coy describes his experience of the Holy Spirit, "a blessing from the Lord," he says that it is "unspeakable, untalkable, you just can't tell it." A very popular saying among mountain Holiness people for their experience of the Holy Spirit is "better felt than told," echoing the title of Troy Abell's *Better Felt Than Said: The Holiness-Pentecostal Experience in Southern Appalachia* (1982).

Brother Coy Miser and Richard G. Spurling are both in agreement that love is the law on which Christ has built the church. Throughout the interview Brother Coy makes clear that love of God and love of neighbor are at the heart of his religious convictions, and this love makes a person a "child of God," in his words.

DVM: What do you think the difference is today?

MISER: Well, people has, they're loving the world more and more, more than they love God. They've got away from the love. They're after their own lust and such and it's really, really let down on God. Because, back years ago, if somebody got sick, why, we had neighbors back then. What I mean by neighbors was people would come in and help, you know, set up and do what they could do, and if a man got down sick and he was a farmer, people was farming, why they'd go ahead and plow and put out his crop for him. That's what I call love, what I call a neighbor. But, today you can't get nobody to do that. They won't do it. They are all for theirselves and nobody else. Seems like they don't care. The Bible says, we need to get that love, be concerned for one another, have love for one another, care for one another, even the sinners we's supposed to care for them as we care for ourselves. See, that's where they've got away from their love because they don't do it anymore. We got churches that they won't go to no other church except their own, they won't fellowship. They won't try to have love one for another, so it means a great deal to have love.

Fellowshiping is an extremely important part of mountain religious life. Not only does it show support for neighboring churches, but it also gives preachers and churchgoers a chance to hear different ideas, share news about people in the community, and go to church every night without placing an unreasonable burden on any one person or group, as well as helping to build and strengthen relationships through healing and renewal. Fellowshiping takes an enormous amount of caring and sensitivity on the part of church leaders. A pastor who changes a service schedule into a time slot already occupied by another local church is understood to be challenging that church, opening the door to strife and distress. The fluidity and comprehensiveness of church meeting schedules is a major problem in the mountainous rural areas for mainline denominations which expect all churches to schedule services on Sunday morning with a possible prayer meeting or Bible study group on Wednesday nights. What is not understood by most mainline clergy coming into Appalachia's mountain regions is that although Sister So-and-So may claim Cranks Holiness Church as her home church, she also always attends Red Hill Holiness Church and gets to Harber's Chapel and the Highway to Holiness Pentecostal Church as often as she can find a ride. Sister So-and-So does not belong to Cranks Holiness Church in a formal, institutional sense; she belongs to God. The "church" is truly made up of the individuals who worship there, with the church house owned by an individual or family who may not even attend its meetings (worship services). Fellowshiping is the embodiment of belonging to a Christian community of faith much larger than one's home church.

> MISER: Without that love we're nothing. We ain't got the love of God in us, and care for people, I'm afraid we're not going back with him when he comes because we're going to have to be perfect in the eyes of God. People says you can't live perfect, which we can't in the eyes of people, but in the eyes of God we better be perfect in here [gestures toward his heart].

Brother Coy's words loudly echo those of Old Father Nash, who wrote in 1831 that Christians cannot hope to reach heaven unless their hearts are broken: "O Dear! What miserable things christians are. Love this world more than heaven—love money more than souls—love themselves more than God, good christians to[o] good to be reproved—offended at a word of blame. How they will look in heaven. Do you think they will get there? I do not think they will unless they get their hearts broken before they go."[1] Like Brother Coy, for Father Nash heart religion, which he had no doubt was the path to salvation, was inextricably grounded in recognizing and embracing the Holy Ghost whose task, among others, was to tenderize the human heart, making it receptive to the love of God and all the work in the world that receptivity entailed.

"Without that love we're nothing," says Brother Coy, giving voice to the most elemental value infusing mountain religion's normative ecclesiology, which Richard G. Spurling articulated so well in *The Lost Link* (1920), in which he says, "Love is the law on which Christ built the church."[2] For Spurling love is "the lost link" in church life. That lost link Brother Coy assumes as an unquestioned given, but, as we have heard in his words about "neighbors," he sees it dissipating. The fullness of life which is brought by "that love" has led him to commit his life to the service of God which, for Brother Coy, means love of neighbor through spiritual expressions (such as prayer) and direct social action, or what he calls simply "helping out." Brother Coy also makes very clear that the life of religious commitment he has led has given him unspeakable joy ("it's just untold"), so much so that *it does not matter to him if there is an afterlife*, despite the great hardships he has suffered. His attitude puts mountain Christians' characteristic "hope of heaven" in a different light, confounding the popular label of "fatalism" applied to the religion of people like Brother Coy. Unequivocal joy is an integral part of his life as a Christian:

> MISER: I was about twenty-one when that happened [his experience of saving grace] and I've been going ever since for the Lord. Of course, I've not done, I've not been perfect all that time. I've made

mistakes but I've made my mistakes right, you know. I didn't let them hang. I've grown cold on the Lord. I've been cold on the Lord. During them years that I got all this, I never got so far away from the Lord what I didn't feel his presence, feel him dealing with me, you know. But, still I got cold. You know, you will do that when you fail to pray. So, its, but it's a wonderful life. It's just something that you just can't explain, you can't tell it when the blessing that God gives you, why it's just untold. You can't tell it all. It's, but I really enjoyed my life. I told my wife last night that I really thank God for my life because I've had a lot of heartaches and a lot of bad things through life and I've had a lot of troubles but I thank God for my life because I learned, through these heartaches and these hard times, I learned something from it and through my mistakes I learned a lot. It helps us because if we don't make mistakes, or if we don't do something for the Devil to get after us, then we're not doing much, you know. I've had hard times and I've had good times, and through them all I thank God for all my life because I've en-joyed it. I used to walk six or eight miles a night, one-way, just to get to go to church, carried a kid on my back, and I enjoyed it. I didn't think nothing about it, you know.

. . . I wouldn't take nothing, I wouldn't change, wouldn't go back for nothing in this world and to the world, you know, cause they's nothing like serving God. Now, when I was a sinner I thought I was having a good time, but when I found the Lord I found out I wasn't having no good time. Because, the best time I've ever had is serv-ing the Lord because there is much more joy to it. It's worth living for if there wasn't no hereafter. The feeling that we have and the blessing that we get is worth living for just here in this world, you know. It really means something.

Brother Coy's declaration, "[I]f we don't make mistakes, or if we don't do something for the Devil to get after us, then we're not doing much," is about risk-taking, about not being afraid to fail or "make mistakes" in the service of God through the conduct of our lives, a radical, nondefensive stance built on intense faith and trust in God. It is also extremely significant that Brother Coy says of his Christian experience, "It's worth living for if there wasn't no hereafter. The feeling that we have and the blessing that we get is worth living for just here in this world, you know." Brother Coy thus de-bunks the popular notions of structural functionalism (focused on adapta-tions to environment) that the religious life and traditions of people like himself are compensatory for extreme deprivation and powerlessness, a sad pie-in-the-sky hope of the hereafter that somehow negates the hardships and sufferings of the present world by ignoring them or explaining them away as much as possible.

It is also key to Brother Coy's beliefs that individuals must take on the responsibility of righting the wrongs they do: "I've made mistakes [wrongs he has committed] but I've made my mistakes right, you know. I didn't let them hang." This is vital not only for the sake of your own holiness but also to give the space and support to others on their own paths to God.

> MISER: Now, you take Pauline. Pauline's a backslider. She got hurt in the church and she quit praying and cause she sung in this church, she's got in a pulpit for two or three years down there and just out of the blue, they asked her to sing but they told her she'd have to sit in her seat. She couldn't come to the pulpit anymore. Well, that hurt her and she left that church. And, so, she didn't go back any more and she still hasn't went back. They still haven't made right with her, so they need to go to Pauline and talk to her and fix that up because if Pauline was to die, why her blood is liable to be on their hands, you know, because they'd be the cause of her being lost maybe and would cause them to be lost too.

In this story, Brother Coy declares it is the duty and responsibility of the church, the "saints," to make right their wrongs against "backsliders" like Sister Pauline, and against "sinners" too. Accountability knows no divine dispensation. Here Brother Coy makes very clear that he does not believe, as some mountain preachers do, that once God has fully entered your heart you can live a life without sin and without temptation. To the contrary, he believes that if we are truly doing God's work, we will be targeted all the more for temptation and even suffering, for the Devil is like all who turn love into lust: that which is already in your grasp you despise, and that which is farthest from your grasp is what you most desire, the biggest prize. Indeed, we have already heard from Brother Coy a variation on one of his oft-repeated expressions, "If the Devil is on your tail, you must be doing something right!"

Brother Coy also talks about the experience of "going under the Spirit" when he first started preaching. Once he discovered that God would fill his mouth if he opened it, he stopped making excuses "like Moses" why he could not preach. Especially in mountain religion, genuine preaching is done not just by the preacher but by the Holy Spirit. The Holy Spirit brings scriptures to mind and leads the preaching when a preacher is "anointed." This is one reason why many Holiness people will take very seriously the words of a person who is "under the Spirit," but might not otherwise trust the same person's ability to get across the road unharmed. It also provides one of the major reasons, one promoting egalitarian values, why women and even children are not excluded in speaking and leading in independent Holiness churches, a tradition well established through plain-folk camp-meeting religion.

I asked Brother Coy how he became a preacher, which, in mountain religion, is synonymous with "minister."

DVM: When were you called into ministry?

MISER: About a year after I got saved. I fought it for a long time. I made excuses to the Lord, you know, uneducated and that kind of thing. I wouldn't be able to preach, and I wouldn't be able to tell the people, you know, what I need to tell them, but he kept dealing with me. And there was a couple preachers give out an all day meeting at a home over in Loughton Hollow and I went over to that meeting and the preachers didn't show up and, the big crowd, the house was full, and the yard full with people and they kept waiting and waiting. It was over thirty minutes past time, you know, for services to start. Finally I told the people, we ain't going to let the Devil completely cheat us. We're going to have a few songs and a prayer anyway. I realized, you know, what to do about that. Anyway, they sung three or four songs and we had a prayer. I took a prayer request and we had a prayer and when I went to my knees that was the last thing I remember. God just completely took my whole body over, my mind and everything. I mean he just really took over. And, when I come to myself I had preached for about forty-five minutes. There was three or four that got saved while I was preaching and they was out in the yard shouting. They was in the house shouting. They was in, running in the house and out, you know, out in the yard and back in the house and old people that wore bonnets back then, and them old bonnets was going through there, you know, and we was just having a wonderful time.

People got saved *not* through Brother Coy's preaching but because God preached through Brother Coy, who did not "come to myself" until it was over.

Brother Coy does not read, but he has a comprehensive oral memory of the Bible. He knows the Bible as oral literature. In other interviews he described his oral memory as a gift of the Holy Spirit. Throughout this interview Brother Coy quoted scriptures and summarized Bible stories as points of illustration, which demonstrated his ability in this area.

DVM: You don't read, do you?

MISER: No.

DVM: So, do you have a good oral memory of the Bible?

MISER: Yes, I can remember the Bible when I hear it read or hear a

preacher preaching. If he gets out of the Bible I can tell you right
when he gets out and they read and misquote scripture I can tell
you.

DVM: Do family members or friends read the Bible to you?

MISER: My wife reads it to me, you know, a good bit.

DVM: Do you have favorite parts?

MISER: Well, yes. I like it all. I have her to read all down through it,
you know. From different scriptures, different books, I even have
her sometimes go back in the Old Bible and start in Genesis and go
right on back into the New Bible cause it all links up, you know. I
go to picking out scriptures [?], you can read some over in the Old
Bible and do over to the New and pick it up and it's the same thing
only just the words are a little different but it all means the same
thing.

The oral tradition of allowing biblical texts to interpret each other by following the lead of a text's embedded literary structures we have discussed
in "Brother Callaway of Avery County." Here Brother Coy describes this process of text interpretation in the barest, briefest terms.

Brother Coy Miser reinforces many observations made throughout this
book about the characterizing features of mountain religious life and its
representative church traditions. For example, Brother Coy speaks frequently about building up churches by having meetings or worship services in people's homes and in their yards where "hundreds" (his term for
large numbers) of mountain people would gather. He talks about starting
churches in "dwelling houses" by tearing out the partitions and putting in
seats or "benches," and then building up the church and handing it over
to another preacher, rather than possessively hanging onto the new church
community as his own. Starting, building up, and handing over churches
has been a pattern throughout his life, as it was for itinerant revival Baptist preachers in colonial Virginia.

Brother Coy talks about Holiness people in the mountains as well as
others upholding the belief that the baptism of the Holy Ghost comes after
conversion or the experience of salvation, rather than the common Baptist
belief that the Holy Ghost comes when people are saved. Nor does he hold
to the belief stemming from Wesleyan-Holiness tradition and represented
by the Church of God (Cleveland, Tennessee), as well as by some mainstream
Pentecostal denominations, that sanctification, following after conversion,
is an intermediate step separate from and preceding the baptism of the Holy
Ghost. Instead, for Brother Coy, as for many mountain Holiness people, there
are two steps—salvation or conversion and the baptism of the Holy Ghost.
Sanctification is not a noticeable part of his vocabulary, suggesting strongly

the predominance of Baptist-influenced traditions about the Holy Ghost stemming from plain-folk camp-meeting religion prior to the late nineteenth- and early twentieth-century Holiness-Pentecostal awakenings. In the interview Brother Coy spoke of how he received the baptism of the Holy Ghost about a year after he got saved.

Brother Coy's mention of the churches' fundamental need to fellowship with each other is something which he has also lived out personally. In the course of the interview, Brother Coy demonstrates his own ecumenism. Throughout his life he has worshiped in "just about all" church traditions and denominations present in the mountains, among them Baptist (Missionary, Primitive, Free Will), Methodist, Presbyterian, Church of God (Cleveland, Tennessee), and Roman Catholic.

> DVM: When you were a child, were you aware of any other types of churches other than the one you went to?
> MISER: Well, yeah, some of them. I went to other churches.
> DVM: What were they?
> MISER: Baptist and Methodist and went to the Church of God. I didn't go the Church of God too much, however I went some.
> DVM: What kind of Baptist churches did you go to, because there are Primitive Baptist, Old Regular Baptists, Free Will Baptists.
> MISER: Well, I've actually, I've been to just about all churches.
> DVM: And, you've done that as an adult, too?
> MISER: I've been to all churches since I've been growed up, come to be a man. I've been to the Catholic churches. I've been to the Presbyterian churches. All of them. I, all but, I haven't been to the Jehovah's Witness yet. So, I'm going to slip in on them one of these times and see what they do. They might throw me out but I'm going to go find out, you know. I love to visit different churches and, it helps you to learn. It teaches you a lot of things.
>
> .   .   .   .
>
> DVM: Have you been a part [a member] of any other church besides Holiness churches?
> MISER: I've worked in Baptist churches.
> DVM: In what capacity did you work in them?
> MISER: I preached in them.
> DVM: But, you didn't become a Baptist?
> MISER: No, I just preached for them.
> DVM: What kind of Baptist churches were they?
> MISER: Different ones.
> DVM: Could you name a few?
> MISER: Well, the Missionary Baptist, and the Primitive Baptist, I

preached in there and I preached a little bit in a Free Will Baptist. But, I've preached for them. I went to one Free Will Baptist and asked them for a revival and the deacon told me, I was talking to the deacon of the church, he told me he said Coy if it was just you, I'd say the church would go along with, but the bunch that runs with you he said I don't think the church would approve of it.

As is clear from the Free Will Baptist deacon's comments, not all mountain preachers or church communities have beliefs and attitudes as open and tolerant as Brother Coy's.

Unlike many mountain people, Brother Coy holds no antipathy toward Roman Catholics, staying in a priest's rectory in Harrisburg, Pennsylvania, when he was in the military and attending Mass (the eucharistic Catholic worship service) with the priest. He talks about his second wife's healing through prayer when she was in the hospital with a paralyzing stroke, and how a Roman Catholic woman in the bed next to her also received healing and "got saved" at the same time. By this Brother Coy does not mean to suggest that because the woman was Roman Catholic she was not a Christian. In mountain church traditions, many people go to church throughout their lives on a regular basis until late in adulthood before they can profess an experience of saving grace, a norm which Brother Coy applied to this "Catholic sister" (a revealing designation in and of itself). As Brother Coy states later on, "I think everybody more or less is Christians." In gratitude for her healing, this woman tried to have him live next to her, taking him "just like her priest." Here Brother Coy makes a clear distinction between God the healer and people's prayers for healing.

> DVM: And, you didn't feel prejudice against the Catholics, in particular? Because a lot of people do.
> MISER: No, I didn't. I went in Harrisburg, Pennsylvania, I went to a Catholic church.
> DVM: What were you doing in Harrisburg?
> MISER: I was in service there. And, I stayed all night on the weekends, I'd stay all night with the priest. I had a key to his house. I'd go there and when I got sleepy running around over town, I got tired and I'd go there and go to bed and he'd get me up and take me to church with him. He was awful nice. He was good to me. Just as good to me as he could be. Treated me nice in his home. They are awfully friendly people. There was a Catholic sister got saved up there in the hospital. She tried to get me to move in the house with her. She had a house sitting right beside of hers.
> DVM: When you say a Catholic sister, do you mean a nun or just a regular person?

to people showing them what power that God has and so that really made believers out of them and after that they got to come.

We have heard Brother Coy use the terms "backslider" and "sinner" or "sinner man" more than once. It is important to recognize that these terms are not pejorative but descriptive and stem from the history of plain-folk camp-meeting religion. Dickson D. Bruce delineates three categories of people at early camp meetings—sinners, mourners, and converts, that is, people who had passed through different stages of the conversion experience. As we see with Brother Coy, "sinner" is still part of the vocabulary of mountain churches today, especially in independent Holiness churches. It is an inclusive term for all who are not converted or, as Brother Coy said, "has never been a Christian." "Mourner" has slipped from mountain church vocabulary, being covered under what is now the more encompassing term "sinner." But in the early nineteenth century the distinctions were clear. Sinners in a camp meeting were those in the preconversion condition, who were appealed to by the exhorters. Mourners were the awakened who were under conviction, which meant that they were acutely aware of their sinfulness or brokenness and accepted the responsibility of it. Penitent but not yet converted, they were in the transitional stage. Converts were those who had completed the transition to conversion that enabled them to experience the love and mercy of God in the form of God's forgiveness for their sins, responding by taking the steps necessary to change their ways from brokenness to oneness with God and the community of faith. Converts had experienced assurance, the spiritual, emotional, and physical feeling of uniting with God's love, acceptance, and immediate presence in their lives.

One other category of people was also extremely important: backsliders were those who had come to the camp meeting to reexperience conversion, what Catherine Albanese called mountain religion's "episodic conversion experience," which was also the norm in Scots-Irish sacramental revivalism. Backsliders were old converts or church members who needed a renewal of their faith through a renewal of conversion as their primary religious experience. As with the revivalistic religiosity of the early Scots-Irish Presbyterian laity, conversion was an experience that was renewed time and again throughout their earthly pilgrimage in the communal setting of revival. Today this tradition of the conversion experience strongly persists in the revival meetings of non-Calvinist mountain church traditions, or in the night services of small, independent Holiness churches like Brother Coy's that are camp-meeting night services in miniature, maintaining many of the worship practices and the spontaneous emotional behavior belonging to that earlier heritage.

Traditional camp meetings would have morning, afternoon, and night services. But it was at the night service, which would go at least to 10 P.M., often until midnight, with exercises continuing in the tents long after the service had closed for the evening, that sinners were awakened and converted. It was at night meetings that the power of God would fall and all of the expressive and ecstatic worship practices for which camp meetings were best known would manifest themselves. The power of God could not be evoked (no more than could God's grace); it simply "came down" and ignited the meeting. The power of God was equated with the Holy Spirit. How Brother Coy speaks about the Holy Spirit throughout this interview, especially when he describes how the Holy Ghost as the power of God comes into a worship service and how it expresses itself, makes clear that this earlier tradition for understanding the Holy Spirit in the worship environment, a tradition regionally specific to Appalachia, is very much alive today and that it is representative, in no way unique to Brother Coy. Moreover, plain-folk camp-meeting religion is the immediate explanation for the normative role of night services, rather than Sunday morning worship, in mountain church traditions such as independent Holiness and not a few independent Baptist churches.

Brother Coy explains in some detail how he conducts a "sacrament meeting," combining communion with footwashing, which in many of his churches was held once a month, unlike the annual sacramental meetings of the Old Regular and Primitive Baptists. He declares that his practices are the same as Old Regular Baptists, meaning not codified rubrics but fundamental commonalities. Brother Coy also talks about how many people will not participate in sacrament and footwashing, and why he believes their refusal to partake is unscriptural. He identifies the Bible basis he upholds making communion-footwashing a practice for all churchgoers today "so that we can have a part with the Lord," despite some people's scruples about their own worthiness to partake.

> DVM: I've only been to Old Regular Baptist footwashings. I'd like to go to a Holiness one. I'd like to go to one of yours.
> MISER: Well, we have the same way. Now, what I do, and I've got Bible for it, I take a table and set it out here in front of the Bible stand [pulpit], I use three chairs, I use one, a chair at each end of the table and I use one here at the side, and spread something white over this, it's a side that's recommending that Jesus is gone, that's his chair, you know, but these chairs, I let the women take the sacrament first and I have one to come sit down and sit down in these chairs and then let one come in behind them and kneel down and pray while these two is taking the sacrament. When these two's a praying then they get up and get in the chair, two more comes in behind them kneel down praying. That's the way I carry that out.

we have come to recognize throughout this study as a common practice, especially so among independent nondenominational churches. Indeed, Brother Coy summarizes succinctly his understanding of what is distinctive about the independent status of so many Holiness churches, "You go independent, they can't take your church away from you." Brother Coy believes that independent Holiness churches are the same as other churches in the mountains, "The only thing, they just got a different name, just under a different head, that's all the only difference is then," echoing Emma Bell Miles, who in 1905 wrote about the variety of mountain church traditions, Calvinist and non-Calvinist, "[B]ut at the bottom they are very much the same."[3]

Brother Coy's declaration of the shared base, the fundamental unity of mountain church traditions through which mountain religion exists as a regional religious tradition, leads into his discussion about the difference between religion in the mountains versus religion in the larger valley towns. Although he is not an isolationist, nor does he uphold this orientation for others, he feels that those who are not distracted by worldly things have a better chance of remaining lively in their faith.

> DVM: Do you think that has anything to do with religion in the mountains versus religion in the valley?
> MISER: Well, I think it would have. I think it would have a bearing on it, in a way.
> DVM: What kind of a bearing?
> MISER: Well, where people is willing to obey the Lord instead of trying to do something theirself. See this man [the independent Baptist preacher who built a large yet isolated church house "back in the mountains"], he knew who was talking to him and he obeyed the voice. If people would obey what God would tell them, they would find and see that it would be a lot more done.
> DVM: Well what has that got to do with being in the mountains more than in the valley? Are you saying that people in the mountains obey the voice of the Lord more than people in the valley?
> MISER: It seems that way. It seems that there are more of them and they have got a hungry to go to church and they got a hungry to serve God and these in the valley, they just take it for granted. They go to church once a week or once a month and that's all right, you know. They think that's all they got to do and these in the mountains they believe in getting in there and working and they do it.

Here Brother Coy contends that mountain people are far more committed to an active religious life rather than a passive one where "they just take it for granted" like "these in the valley." In contrast, "[T]hese in the mountains they believe in getting in there and *working* and they do it."

In an illustration of mountain people's "hunger for the word of God," Brother Coy also confirms the role of grace in matters such as revivals, and the given norm in mountain religion of human cooperation with divine initiative, regardless whatever change in plans or inconveniences it involves.

> MISER: That's just like years ago, I don't know just how many years its been, I went over in Tennessee, that's just a little while after I started preaching, as a matter of fact, it was the first revival I ever preached. I went over in Tennessee to have a meeting for just one night in a hall. Ended up having a three weeks revival in a man's yard, and people come out of those mountains. You could see that they had what you call possum lanterns, I guess you heard of them, and you could see them lights coming swinging out of the mountains. It was so dark they would have their lights on coming to church and they would be two-and-three hundred people there in that yard at night for church. See they was hungry for the word of God.

Brother Coy's one-night meeting became a three-week revival, illustrating the grace-centered tradition of revivals based not on organizational advance planning and set scheduling (the revival tradition of human initiative and human control that assumes divine cooperation) but on spontaneity and a willingness to let go of plans, a flexibility that is required in order to respond appropriately and for however long to the unpredictable and uncontrollable quickening of the Holy Spirit. Brother Coy's three-week revival was the result of responding to the perception of God's initiative of converting grace through the experience of the explosive power of the Holy Spirit in those open-ended revival meetings, requiring people's cooperation and adaptability. Perhaps this premier theological value of grace, this rock-bottom norm in mountain church traditions indispensable to their identity, best encapsulates what distinguishes mountain religion historically and today from American Protestantism.

Brother Coy expresses the major aspect of the upside to Appalachia's famous "isolation" factor when it comes to matters of religion, due largely to the absence of distractions from a focus on God.

> DVM: That's very interesting the difference you see between people in the mountains when it comes to religion versus people in the valleys. Do you consider yourself a valley dweller?
> MISER: Well, I am still a mountain preacher but I am associated more with valley people, you know like I say, if I was back in the mountains like a lot of the other people like they are down in Tennessee and downstate in Hancock County and all down in there, people

might. That's doing the work. He's the one that's causing you to shout. He's the one that's causing you speak in tongues. He's the one that's speaking. It's really, it's, and he's the one that does the preaching. It's not the man or not the woman, it's the Spirit of God preaching through him. They're standing up there and their mouth is working, their mouth is going, but it's the Spirit of God, the Holy Ghost is the one doing the speaking. If they've got anointed. If they ain't got anointed, they are just standing up there talking just like I'm talking now, you know. It don't edify the church. Now, if they've got a good anointing then it edifies the church. The church will get something out of it. They will get a blessing.

Brother Coy also explains that people help the Holy Ghost come into a worship service by having an active "hope" for its presence, "having hope that he will be there." This tradition is normative throughout mountain religion, reaching back to the era of the Great Awakening, as we saw in the comments of the Scots-Irish Presbyterian Samuel Blair about the revival at his church in southeastern Pennsylvania in the summer of 1740. Blair said he "hoped God was about to carry on an extensive work of converting grace among them," a work he identified with "the divine power and presence," or what people understood to be the immediate presence of the Holy Spirit that produced what Blair also described as "soul-exercises." Such "exercises" were expressive and ecstatic worship practices, ranging from "fainting" and "deeply sobbing" to "strange unusual bodily motions," which became the hallmark of plain-folk camp-meeting religion on the Appalachian frontier and its regional progeny, mountain religion's independent Holiness churches.

DVM: Is there a way of helping the Holy Ghost come into a worship service?
MISER: Well, I think everybody more or less is Christians, I think when they go to church I think they have a hope that the Holy Ghost will take over, you know, and really speak and really do the things that they want to see done. I know I do. If I go to church, I go expecting the Holy Ghost to do something for me, to bless me or help me that I can be a blessing to someone else, or something like that, you know. Because, without that I wouldn't even go if I didn't have a hope that he was going to do something for me, or let me be a blessing to somebody or get a blessing, why I've got that hope that he'll be there. That he will work in some way or some how to bless someone. If I can't get a blessing, I pray that other people will get a blessing, see what I mean.
DVM: Yes. So a way people can help the Holy Ghost come into a worship service is basically by hoping.

MISER: Yeah. Hope, having hope that he will be there and ask the Lord, Lord you let the Holy Ghost take over. You let the Holy Ghost rule and you let the Holy Ghost bless somebody. If you can't bless me Lord, you bless somebody else and that's the way I pray. I pray that if there's not a blessing for me, because if I see somebody else get a blessing, I'm going to get one too. It's a blessing to me to see somebody else get a blessing. That makes me feel good inside. In other words, if God was to move on you right now, and start you a shouting or start you a running or start you dancing, that would make me feel good. See what I mean?

Brother Coy makes clear that the galvanizing influence of the Holy Spirit in a worship service is made manifest in strong emotional and physical behaviors that he calls "a blessing," behaviors that are the indisputable evidence that the Holy Spirit is "there," as Brother Coy says, and has "taken over." Samuel Blair in 1740 called such behaviors "soul-exercises," the "*evidences of impressions on the hearers*" caused by "such appearance of the *divine power and presence.*"[4]

Finally Brother Coy talks about the heart as the place where God lives and works in the individual. Moreover, Brother Coy claims that preaching about the heart is a special emphasis in mountain religion and he explains why:

DVM: My impression is that mountain preachers focus a lot of attention on the condition of people's hearts. Do you think that they do?

MISER: Yeah, I know they do.

DVM: Why is that?

MISER: Well, that's because God lives in the heart and that's why they preach as much mention the heart so much. Because, that's where God lived. What comes out of the heart is from the Lord and what, so, about all the churches and about all the preachers preaches about the heart. The soul lies in the heart and what comes out of the mouth comes from the heart. That's the reason preachers, Brother Underwood was preaching last night and he was preaching about the heart. So, I think all preachers does that more or less.

DVM: In the mountains in particular?

MISER: In the mountains in particular.

DVM: So, do you think that emphasis on the heart is a special emphasis of mountain religion?

MISER: Well, yes, I'd say it is. Because, in order to have religion, we've got to have him in our heart and that's the only place he's got to live. Of all, as big as the world is, as big as, as many people as there are, that's the only place that God has got to live in this world is in the hearts of people, men and women. He's big enough to fill the universe but yet he is small enough to live in our hearts. And, therefore, he's, and that's the only place he has to live in this world because he can't set foot on this world until it's purified and when it's purified, purified and cleansed then God can set his foot back on the earth. But, the only place right now he's got to live is in the hearts of the people and that's just the ones that will let him come in.

"But, the only place right now [that God has] got to live is in the hearts of the people and that's just the ones that will let him come in." Brother Coy's sensitivities about God and the human heart encapsulate mountain religion's most prominent and descriptive thematic motif identifying the nonrational as the deep well of religious experience and spiritual knowledge, distinguishing it from the reason-centered worldview of America's Protestant mainstream. They are divided by fundamental differences not only in anthropology but in an ecclesiology that successfully embodies mountain religion's heart-centered theology.

Brother Coy identifies mountain people's physical landscape as instrumental in nurturing their religious devotion and in shaping their distinctive religiosity.

> DVM: Why do you think that mountain religion would emphasize the heart more than other places?
> MISER: Well, take the mountains, just like I was talking about Tennessee, about the people living back in the hills, as far back as they can get out maybe once a month. The people in the hills is, I don't know, I think they are still trying to stay close to the Lord where people out in the cities, they've got, as I said a while ago, the Devil has got so much to offer them, that they are not really praying like they should, not getting as close to the Lord as they should and I think that has a lot do to with it, has a lot of bearing on it.

"Praying," "staying close to the Lord" are encouraged for "people in the hills" by their physical landscape, "the mountains." The religious influences of a physical landscape, in this instance a chain of mountains called the Appalachians that are among the oldest in the world, is a subliminal force of extraordinary power on mountain people, an area yet to be explored in studies about Appalachian mountain religion. Brother Coy firmly believes—indeed, he knows as a matter of fact—that mountain people have a distinct religious advantage over "people out in the cities."

Brother Coy concludes the interview with a prayer, thanking God for the interview and "for your great love and your mercy that you send out to us. Praise you Lord for your love and for caring."

Throughout the interview Brother Coy Miser makes clear that, for him, Christianity is a matter of the heart, not of doctrine. He asks, "Do you love God? Do you love your neighbor?" Not, "Do you believe in the right precepts?" Although not all mountain preachers are as tolerant and loving as Brother Coy, he is still highly representative of a type of posture among mountain preachers and their church traditions that is generally accepting of differences as long as the Holy Spirit is not hindered in its work. Brother Coy's itinerancy and autonomy as an independent Holiness preacher are also highly representative of mountain religion's defining church traditions and their unique history in the Appalachian region, making him an outstanding model of the traditional mountain preacher, one of the most important carriers of mountain religious life and, as John Campbell wrote, "one of the strong links with the past which here in the Highlands have not yet been broken."

Even though, in the last few months of my revising the book manuscript, Brother Coy Miser has been called by "Death's Angel," marking the end of a generation, Campbell's observation from more than seventy years before still stands true today. Although Brother Coy has been called home, mountain preachers and mountain religion continue to persist, indeed, thrive, in innumerable coves and hollows, on mountainsides and in small valleys. A thread may come to an end, but the cloth won't come apart. Brother Coy was a bright and lovely thread, but a thread nonetheless—and he never wanted to be anything else. Younger men and women continue to carry on mountain religious life; they too are "strong links with the past"—bright, lovely threads like Brother Coy—yet creating and re-creating through their cultural landscape and their own cultural self-consciousness, especially through their shared values and worldview, what has been and continues to be unique and special about their religious culture in the geographic region with which it is indelibly identified. We make way for them by giving Brother Coy Miser the final word, indeed, a flowing stream of words, on mountain religious life "from within" that the first three parts of this book have attempted to address.

With the juxtaposition of this section on the independent Holiness church with the following nearly two hundred year history of American Protestantism's home missions presence in Appalachia, we go from the very center of the spectrum defining the range of Appalachian mountain religion as a regional religious tradition to beyond the outer limits of the spectrum's reach. We look now to the nation's dominant religious culture and its unremitting historical quest to objectify Appalachia, its people, and its mountain religious culture. Even more to the point, in Brother Coy Miser we hear the voice of a single individual who is the personal embodiment of mountain religion's independent, nondenominational church tradition that distills to their essence many of mountain religion's normative, defining features. From Brother Coy we move to the largely impersonal world of nationally based, organized religion that stands as the antithesis of the religious world of a great host of people like Brother Coy in Appalachia's mountain regions. The national institutional church constructs and the national identity defining the denominations of American Protestantism predetermined their stance in Appalachia, whether as established churches or home mission interests. Brother Coy provides the most radical and yet the most appropriate bridge possible to the concluding section chronicling American Protestantism's home mission to "mountain whites"—to people just like Brother Coy Miser.

The original caption reads, "A Log Church-House in the Mountains," in this book on home missions by the Council of Women for Home Missions of the Reformed Church in America. From Edith H. Allen, *Home Missions in Action* (New York: Fleming H. Revell, 1915), p. 144.

Climax Church, a now-dormant independent Holiness church in Climax, Jackson County, Kentucky, 1987. Note how closely it compares with the preceding log church house, down to the single shutters for windows. Photograph by Warren Brunner.

Sister Mae June Hensley, mother of Cranks Holiness Church, 1988. Photograph by Warren Brunner.

Night service at Cranks Holiness Church, Harlan County, Kentucky, 1987. Photograph by Warren Brunner.

River baptism by Brother Coy Miser, Pennington Gap, Virginia, 1987. Photograph by Warren Brunner.

Sister Lydia Surgener, 1987. Photograph by Warren Brunner.

New Church at Mill Creek, owned and pastored by Sister Lydia Surgener. Cranks, Kentucky, 1987. Photograph by Warren Brunner.

Sister Lydia Surgener's weekly half-hour Sunday radio program on WSWV, Pennington Gap, Virginia, 1987. Also shown are Sister Mae June Hensley and Sister Lydia's nephew, Junior. Photograph by Warren Brunner.

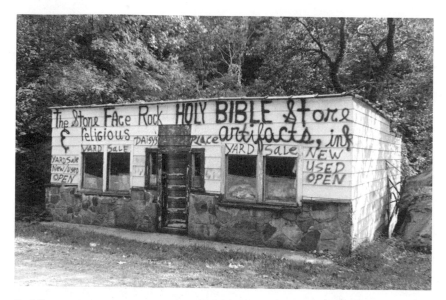

Building on Route 421, on the Virginia side of the Kentucky-Virginia border near Stone Face Rock, 1987. The property has since been turned into a used car lot and the building repainted. Photograph by Warren Brunner.

Church house sign above a separate entry way in a private dwelling on the outskirts of Harlan, Kentucky, 1988. Photograph by Warren Brunner.

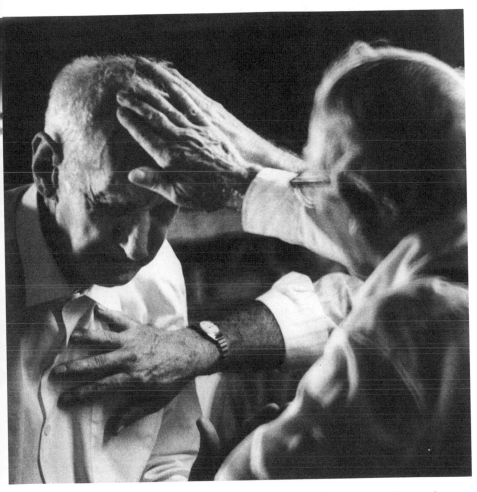

Laying on of hands during a meeting at Red Hill Holiness Church, owned by Brother Lee Crider, in Pennington Gap, Virginia, 1988. Brother Crider is being prayed over by Brother Coy Miser and Brother Loyd Haskell Underwood. Photograph by Warren Brunner.

W. F. Bryant standing in the doorway of Hillview Church of God. Tellico Mountains, Tenn., ca. 1909. Wade H. Phillips Collection. Used by permission.

Church signs on Scaffold Cane Road, near Berea, Kentucky, 1987. Scaffold Cane Holiness Church is in the background, set on the property of Scaffold Cane Cemetery. Photograph by Warren Brunner.

Becky and Bobby Simpson, holding matchstick religious folk art created by their
deceased son, Rick, 1988. Becky and Bobby founded and operate Cranks Creek
Survival Center, a local self-help effort. Photograph by Warren Brunner.

This photograph in *American Missionary Magazine* ([Oct. 1921], p. 266) is attached to an article titled "The Highlanders," celebrating the American Missionary Association's educational endeavors among mountain people: "Gradually the educational standards have been lifted up, thousands of the best young people of the mountains have been educated and moved out."

The Home Mission to "Mountain Whites"

Loyal Jones has written, "No group in the country, in my estimation, has aroused more suspicion and alarm among mainstream Christians than have Appalachian Christians, and never have so many Christian missionaries been sent to save so many Christians than is the case in this region."[1] "Appalachian Christians" have "aroused" so much "suspicion and alarm among mainstream Christians" because of a basic difference in religious values, summed up in a very different perception of the nature of religious experience. The extent to which these differences have upset and confounded American Christians, principally Protestant, is demonstrated by the extent to which denominations representing mainstream Protestant groups—from Presbyterians to Methodists to Southern Baptists—have felt compelled to evangelize and "uplift" through education and social services mountain people of the Appalachian region. Home mission efforts have been principally and historically among nonwhite and immigrant populations. The home mission to "mountain whites" was unique because mountain Christians were in the vast majority a "white" population and long-settled in the Appalachian region; indeed, their families were among the original settlers of the area in the eighteenth and early nineteenth centuries. Part 4 attempts to trace the home missions movement to the Appalachian region and its interaction with—primarily in terms of its perceptions of—mountain religious life.

The first chapter of this section looks at the published statement on "religion and morals" west of the Allegheny Mountains of John F. Schermerhorn, who toured as a missionary in 1812–13. Schermerhorn provided the earliest clear recognition of the distinctiveness of religious life in "the West," what historians today call the Old Southwest, a region that was identified largely with what soon became known as Appalachia. His descriptions of Old Southwest Baptist worship life and beliefs are particularly revealing, consistent with observations on mountain religious life made throughout this book. Indeed, Schermerhorn found his descriptions of "Baptists" applied also to other church traditions characteristic of the Old Southwest. The key belief and the core of spirituality that Schermerhorn claimed was shared by all church traditions of the Old Southwest, Baptist or not, was the centrality of the Holy Spirit, about which Schermerhorn provided extensive statements. Baptists of the Old Southwest would be regarded, in a few years, as "Old Time" Baptists, from Free Will and

oramic history of American religion: it was a manifesto for a worldwide reformation of Christianity that took American Protestant voluntaryism as its model. To Baird the religion in America simply *was* revivalistic evangelicalism—though he did include a brief, condescending section on the unevangelical bodies. His basic value judgment is suggested by the mere two pages he allotted to the Roman Catholic church, which was in 1850 the largest denomination in America.[3]

The Christian America movement representing the norms and goals of mid to late nineteenth-century mainstream American Protestantism—self-characterized as evangelical and unabashedly nationalistic—continued into the early years of the twentieth century, when it was greatly enhanced by the Social Gospel movement (ca. 1890–1920). Though the Social Gospel, wrote Robert T. Handy, "had roots deep in history and had many direct continuities with the evangelical Protestantism of the nineteenth century," it "broke significant new ground in this period"[4] that would adjust the course of home missions in Appalachia well into the mid-twentieth century.

The earlier Christian America movement saw the religious life and social conditions of Appalachian people as standing in the way of progress, the national good, and the universally recognized goal of creating "a complete Christian commonwealth" (in the words of the mid-nineteenth-century Protestant reformer Horace Bushnell). The Christian America movement defined all home mission work to Appalachia throughout the latter half of the nineteenth century and into the early twentieth, and determined how mountain religion was portrayed in home mission literature. The foundational church traditions that were already solidly established in the region in Schermerhorn's day and the firmly rooted images home missionaries had of religious life in the region had become stereotypical by the early 1850s. These stereotypes were further developed and given wide currency with the onrush of home missions to Appalachia that began in the early 1880s. Home mission literature became the primary source of information about mountain religion until the advent of social science writing on the Appalachian region beginning in the 1930s.

When Elizabeth R. Hooker published in 1933 her social science survey, *Religion in the Highlands,* on mountain churches and home mission efforts in the Appalachian region, it was the first effort since Pierson and Campbell to take seriously the reality and importance of what Hooker designated the "native church" in the lives of mountain people. Two-thirds of Hooker's text were devoted to religious life that was now indigenous to the mountains of the Appalachian region. Chapter 18 examines Hooker's conclusions about mountain religious life and the impact of home missions.

Instead of simply reiterating Hooker's conclusions about the "native church," we will make a close examination of Brother Terry Galloway's history of Wolf Creek Baptist Church, an independent Missionary Baptist church on Wolf Mountain in the Blue Ridge of Jackson County, North Carolina. Galloway's history ranges from 1886 to 1987, and Galloway himself has been a member of Wolf Creek Church since 1936. Galloway's history highlights what Hooker called the "common characteristics" of "native churches" in rural Appalachia, especially in the mountains, most of which persist still today. Following the history of Wolf Creek Church, we look at Hooker's conclusions about the home mission denominations operating in the mountains of the Appalachian region. Hooker made an important distinction between denominations "long-established" in Appalachia and what she called "foreign denominations" known in the mountains primarily as a home missions presence—including the Presbyterians, despite the extent of their history in the region—mirroring in her use of the term how such denominations were (and are still) perceived by mountain people, who themselves used the term "foreign" to designate them.

The concluding chapter considers home missions today, although many Protestant and Catholic workers in the region would eschew such an identification of their efforts. We will look at some denominational and interdenominational organizations that have taken over home missions in the Appalachian region since their heyday between 1880 and 1940. We will also look at the factors that have transformed their mode of discourse and programming in terms of the helping posture they continue to assume in relation to Appalachia and mountain people. That helping posture—rooted deep in the history of liberal values and their tradition in American Protestantism—one colleague of mine and student of American religious history has called a "social work" posture, set in motion by the Christian America movement and reinforced by the Social Gospel. The two most significant transforming factors for home missions among mountain people today were the War on Poverty of the 1960s and the emergence of liberation theology in the 1960s and 1970s.

agents of error in need of rightful correction. The earliest stages of the home missions movement as a national effort were set by Congregationalists and Presbyterians of the eastern seaboard, who acted out of many motives banked on one side by a narrow, sectarian, partisan spirit and on the other side by a genuine concern for the gospel demands of disinterested Christian benevolence, a profound part of New England theological heritage.

By the outbreak of the American Revolution the frontier line of settlement had not yet pushed west beyond the Appalachian mountains. This "Old West" or Southwest consisted of land between the Allegheny Mountains and the fall line of the rivers flowing into the Atlantic. Even at the time of the Revolution the frontier of settlement was shifting to the Greater Mississippi Valley. The West doubled in size in 1803, with the Louisiana Purchase. Soon the frontier line shifted to the lands of the Old Northwest territory, pushing on to the Great Plains and finally the Pacific Ocean by 1850. But the expanse of the Old Southwest, made nearly impenetrable by mountains, forests, and the inability of steam engine technology to access its recesses, made this area of the United States a continuing "frontier" even after the lines of settlement had pushed far past it.

Home missionaries from the East followed these lines of settlement. Appalachia would remain basically untouched by a focused, concerted home missions effort until just before the official "close" of the frontier in 1890 and the advent of the industrial revolution in Appalachia with the discovery of exploitable commodities—timber and coal—also around 1890. At that time Appalachia and its people were identified by home mission boards in the East as an "exceptional region" with an "exceptional population," along with Native Americans, African Americans, Eskimos in Alaska, Roman Catholics, Mormons, and newly arrived immigrant populations settling mostly in urban areas. There was, however, always some form of home missionary activity in the Appalachian region before it was identified in late nineteenth-century popular local-color writing as "A Strange Land and Peculiar People."[3] Reasons for this go back to how the "Old West" was perceived by its religious benefactors in the East, who would develop a national home missions movement by the end of the first quarter of the nineteenth century.

Attitudes that would come to characterize how Appalachia and its mountain people were viewed were established early on by easterners meeting what Timothy Dwight called "*foresters* or *Pioneers*" close to home. Dwight wrote in his *Travels; in New-England and New-York* (1821–22) that while such people may "*begin* the cultivation of the wilderness, . . . [t]hese men cannot live in regular society. They are too idle; too talkative; too passionate; too prodigal; and shiftless; to acquire either property or character. They are impatient about the restraints of law, religion, and morality. . . . [T]hey are usually possessed in their own view, of uncommon wisdom; understand medical science, politics, and religion, better than those who have studied them through life."[4] Dwight saw it as a "mercy" that "Providence" had opened up the "Western wilderness" to draw such people "away from the land of their nativity."[5] Dwight's elite stance was compounded by his position as president of Yale College and as one of the early leaders of the Great Revival in the East, known especially for his resistance to post-Revolution deism and "infidels." Although Dwight was writing about the "wilderness" of western New England and western New York, his highly representative attitudes about "*foresters* or *Pioneers*" would be honed and refined at the latter part of the century, this time applied to Appalachia's mountain people. Dwight's statements gave evidence to a long-standing distrust and misapprehension within and between regions that would prevail wherever easterners traveled "West" to evangelize newly settled populations or populations whose ways and traditions seemed closer to "*foresters* or *Pioneers*" than to the ways of Old New England.

Goodykoontz enumerated four basic motives for home missions in the earliest stages of the growing national movement,[6] all of which were centered on how religious life and conditions were perceived in the Old Southwest. Easterners were especially concerned that "*foresters* or *Pioneers*" were in danger of worshiping false gods, promoted by well-recognized denominations, notably the Baptists and Methodists, who had had far more success in the Southwest than the Congregationalists and Presbyterians. All of them were concerned about the rising "New Light" movement of Barton W. Stone and later Alexander Campbell. As such, denominational rivalries were a first and primary motive for home missions in the region. Since the New Englanders had known only an overall type of religious uniformity in their own region, they were thunderstruck and alarmed by the diversity of religious life and church traditions they found in the Southwest.

Of probably equal importance were eastern denominations' concerns over the strong emotionalism of religious life in the Old Southwest, the revivals and camp meetings, and the extremely physical and noisy character of these events and the self-abandonment of the individual in the worship environment, all embodying a style of religious life centered not on eastern denominations' premier values of "good order" and rationalism and self-control but on a profoundly emotional conversion as a crisis experience of faith. The religious traditions of the Old Southwest and New England were in fundamental conflict with each other. That conflict manifested itself in religious values that were totally contrary to each other and crystallized in their diametrically opposed worship lives. Perhaps much more so than denominational rivalries, the overpowering revulsion for strong emotional traditions of religious experience and the equally firm belief in the utterly deluded character of such traditions was an impetus

At the end of his report, and just before his final recommendations, Schermerhorn provided thumbnail sketches of the various religious groups he and Mills encountered in great numbers in the Old Southwest. In addition to Presbyterians (under which heading all Presbyterian, Congregational, and Reformed bodies were included, making up the bulwark of American Protestantism at that time), he described the Baptists, Methodists, Cumberland Presbyterians (which Schermerhorn saw as standing apart from the otherwise encompassing category of Presbyterians), and New Lights (Barton W. Stone's Christian churches). His sketches were of those religious groups, other than "Presbyterians," most characteristic of the Old Southwest at that time. Schermerhorn's portrayals of the core religious groups that would continue to be most characteristic of the Appalachian region generally—indeed two had their origins in the region—were the earliest outside descriptions encompassing a wide geographic range on the Appalachian frontier.

Schermerhorn's sketch of the Baptists is perhaps the most significant, for he discerned features of traditions that were already lost to Baptist worship life generally throughout the United States, as David Benedict attested (1813), including most of the South, but would become the mainstay of mountain people's religious life. Schermerhorn saw above all the influence of traditions about the Holy Spirit that would come to characterize almost all church traditions distinctive to the mountains of the Appalachian region. Of all the groups he discussed, Schermerhorn went into greatest depth about the spirituality of Baptist worship life—from the criteria guiding how preachers were selected and ordained; to preaching styles and their content emphasizing the sensate, the world of visions and dreams, and the heart; to how people placed church membership by making these same emphases, which they identified, said Schermerhorn, with "the *Spirit within*" (his emphasis). In his sketch of the Baptists, Schermerhorn thus talked about matters he did not even approach, let alone touch, in his sketches of other religious groups.

It would appear from the attention he gave them and from what he said that Schermerhorn found Baptist religious life in the Old Southwest the most disturbing, perhaps because it challenged most directly his own background's understanding and experience of religiosity. Goodykoontz's four motives for home missions applied especially to Schermerhorn's statement on the Baptists, but with a distinctive twist: very different understandings about who is the Holy Spirit and how it presents itself in worship life and in the life of the believer were at the heart of Schermerhorn's critique. Even though the Baptists were not the first religious group he discussed in his "Statement" (the Presbyterians as an inclusive group of reformed bodies were accorded that courtesy), it is useful—indeed, important—to look first and at some length at Schermerhorn's summary about the Baptists of the Old Southwest.

Schermerhorn did not discuss, likely because he did not find, Baptist groups moving toward or already committed to missions and denominational development—quite pronounced in the East for some years—that fully emerged with the General Missionary Convention of 1814, held in Philadelphia "because it was more centrally located."[9] The 1814 convention was the foundation for nationally organizing the Baptists into a denomination, convened the same year Schermerhorn's statement was published in Hartford, Connecticut. Instead, the Baptist groups who overwhelmingly dominated the region of Schermerhorn's survey in 1812–13 would, by the mid- to late nineteenth century, be under the umbrella of "Old Time" in the national consciousness and associated almost exclusively with the Appalachian region, including churches and associations that were now independent Missionary Baptist. Schermerhorn's report made clear that, among the established churches of all the groups he took into account, missions—as the new denominational Baptists formulated it, as well as the Presbyterians and Congregationalists—were still a nonissue. Baptists of the Old Southwest, whether Calvinist, Arminian, or somewhere in between, were far removed from these developments geographically and ideologically, and fundamentally opposed to the hierarchical institutionalism that simultaneously became entrenched in the newly constituted missions organizations and various religious societies of the East that Schermerhorn promoted and that were the earliest institutional manifestations of the American Benevolence movement.

In his sketch of the Baptists, Schermerhorn first addressed how preachers were called and accepted by a church community. As Schermerhorn observed, the centrality of not trying to second-guess the Holy Spirit in terms of whom the Spirit may call was foremost, as it is today in mountain religious life and has been throughout its history. The gift of discernment, of trying the Spirit, was paramount. The tradition Schermerhorn outlined here for the rising up and subsequent recognition of preachers whom the Spirit called is especially prevalent today in Old Regular Baptist church communities as well as in independent Holiness churches:

> The preachers of this denomination are generally illiterate . . . and while they pretend to despise all human knowledge, they profess to be led and directed by the Holy Spirit, both in desiring the office of an elder, and in their public performances. The power of licensing lies wholly with the church, of which the person is a member, and the church are the only judges of the necessary qualifications. The common practice on the subject is this, the person makes a statement to the church, that he feels an inward call to preach the Gospel.—on this the church, for fear lest they should be found fighting against the Spirit, generally permit him to exercise his *gifts*. If he is approved by them, he is soon ordained by the elders of the church.[10]

Schermerhorn explained that by illiteracy he meant preachers who did not possess a command of standard English grammar, and in some cases were not able to read the Bible and write their own names. It is notable that Schermerhorn picked up on the vocabulary of the region, calling Baptist preachers "elders," a term, as David Benedict recorded, that had generally died out among Baptists elsewhere in the United States by that time.

As Schermerhorn stated, the call of the Spirit was foremost in the call to preach, with the power to confirm that call lying solely with the local church community in whose midst a called preacher would "exercise his *gifts*," an expression that is still part of the nomenclature today. This ordination tradition was a manifestation of free church polity affirming no higher oversight by centralized authorities at any level than the local church itself, unlike the denominations of American Protestantism in Schermerhorn's day. Schermerhorn's presentation made clear that he thought this tradition of autonomy in ordination at the local church level was a manifestation of the degeneracy of the ministry in the Southwest, one of the four reasons Goody-koontz identified for why the East felt compelled to send home missionaries in order to evangelize the "West." In contrast to the model of a learned ministry, these illiterate, poorly prepared, and unsupervised preachers were not true ministers of the Gospel.

Similarly, in mountain church traditions today, if an individual claims to be called by the Spirit, congregations generally are loath to intrude on that call, unless the candidate's exercising of his "gifts" proves to the contrary, as even Schermerhorn acknowledged ("*If* he is approved by them"). Indeed, church communities do not passively roll over when an individual steps forward and says that he believes that he is called by the Spirit to preach. It is a two-way street. As we have seen in an earlier chapter, especially among Old Time Baptists with their highly developed institutionalism, church communities either invest or withhold preaching authority from individuals, who do not simply claim it for themselves, even in far less structured church traditions such as independent Holiness. Today a candidate for eldership, like his predecessors Schermerhorn observed, is given "liberty to preach" by his local elders, a form of licensing until he is ordained—or not ordained—as a preaching elder in his local congregation. Once a person is ordained as a preaching elder, he is permitted to preach in all churches with whom his church is in correspondence through the association.

Schermerhorn stated clearly the contrast in preaching traditions between his own rationalistic background and the highly emotive emphases of the Baptists he witnessed: "In their manner of preaching, their object appears to be to excite the passions; to terrify and raise into transports of joy, rather than to inform the mind, convince the understanding, convict the heart, and open the way to salvation through Jesus Christ" (p. 39). The emergence of the full Arminianization of Calvinism, soon to enter into the practical framework of church order and worship through Finney-esque revivalism, was on the cusp of Schermerhorn's remark. "[T]o inform the mind" in order to "convince the understanding" and thereby "convict the heart" was the means that "open[ed] the way to salvation through Jesus Christ." Salvation for Schermerhorn, as a highly educated New England clergyman, was clearly a rational exercise centered on the decision of the individual, rather than a movement of grace through the Holy Spirit over which there was no control, only an expectation, a constant watchfulness and readiness, a "sweet hope," as it was for the Baptists of the Old Southwest.

Further on, Schermerhorn talked about the "wonderful dreams and visions" that were a staple in the sermon repertoires of many preaching elders he observed. This is still very true. In the summer of 1987, I heard Elder I. D. Back preach during a service at Blair Branch Old Regular Baptist Church in eastern Kentucky about a wonderful vision that had come to him one night. It was about his finding a lamb in the brush near a river bank, picking up the lamb in his arms, and riding down a raft on the river, still holding the lamb, until he came to a place where the "saints" were standing on the banks of both sides of the river singing and praising God. It was a powerful accounting that moved Elder Back to tears, as well as most of us present in the congregation.[11] Visions and dreams continue to form a significant part not just of preaching but of testimonies and conversion narratives in many mountain church traditions. Schermerhorn wrote, "They [Baptist elders] often introduce tender stories, wonderful dreams and visions, with such expressions of countenance, and affecting tones of voice, as are calculated to excite the tender, sympathetic emotions of the heart. There is also a studied singularity in the choice of their texts, and an effort to spiritualize every passage of Scripture" (p. 39).

Schermerhorn's account of traditional Baptist preaching style in the Old Southwest underscored preaching elders' emphasis on "the tender, sympathetic emotions of the heart." Rather than seeing emphasis on the heart as a normative, defining value in the religious life and religious discourse of the region, Schermerhorn attributed it to a preaching method that was "calculated," like his own experience as a seminary student schooled to grasp the attention of his auditors. Perhaps the "studied singularity in the choice of their texts" reflected what is today an overall preference for stories and narratives, rather than legal and prescriptive texts or texts of instruction. At this point Schermerhorn reinforced the centrality of the Holy Spirit in the preaching he heard in Baptist worship life: "They pretend also to preach wholly by the Spirit, by which they mean, as the Spirit gives them utterance, in the manner the apostles were inspired." This emphasis on submitting oneself to the lead of the Holy Spirit while preaching continues as an overriding tradition in mountain worship life today. Sermons are spontaneous, "unprepared," not dependent upon preselected texts and outlines prepared in advance. Mountain preachers preach as the Spirit "gives them utterance," a difficult tradition which is particularly hard for young preachers. It takes years to learn how to listen to the voice of "the *Spirit within*" and to follow the gentle nudgings a preacher will feel throughout a sermon. Often when I have thanked a preacher for his or her words, the preachers will reply that they have no clear recollection of what they even said, only that the Spirit was "upon" them, and so they knew that they had preached well.

Schermerhorn discussed different aspects by which people of his own background would understand how the Holy Spirit functions, in contrast to how Baptists of the Old Southwest saw the Holy Spirit operating among them, especially in worship. At this point in his commentary, Schermerhorn identified "the mistaken notion of this Spirit" as the primary source of "error" not only in the religious life of the Baptists but for all church traditions distinctive to the Old Southwest:

> It is the mistaken notion of this Spirit that has caused so much ignorance, error, and enthusiasm in the West; for the *Spirit within,* as they term it, is made the guide for their actions, and rule of their faith. If, for instance, they feel a desire to be preachers, they have a call of the Spirit. If they are greatly impressed that certain practices are right, and others wrong, it amounts to the authority of the Spirit, that the course which the impressions direct, is correct. If they are highly elevated, with agreeable and pleasant feelings, under the preaching of certain doctrines and views of truth, they have the witness of the Spirit within them, that the one is true and the other false. (p. 39, emphasis in the original)

This passage is a very good description of how the Holy Spirit is seen to operate in mountain worship life throughout the religious history of the Appalachian region. It is also a very good indication of how the emerging home missions movement Schermerhorn represented stood in opposition to what was tantamount to the very heart of what became Appalachian mountain religion. For people such as Schermerhorn, "this Spirit" was seen to be the source of "much ignorance, error, and enthusiasm." What was for people of the Old Southwest, and soon mountain people in particular, the movement of the Holy Spirit not only in their worship lives but as their very "guide for their actions and rule of their faith," Schermerhorn called "desires" and "impressions" and "feelings," a distinctly rationalist response that little knew what to do with what Rudolf Otto called the "non-rational" in religious experience, the "mysterium tremendum et fascinans." Indeed, Otto wrote in 1923, "It is through this positive feeling-content that the concepts of the 'transcendent' and 'supernatural' become forthwith designations for a unique 'wholly other' reality and quality, something of whose special character we can *feel,* without being able to give it clear conceptual expression."[12]

What Schermerhorn called "the tender, sympathetic emotions of the heart" Otto called "this positive feeling-content . . . , without being able to give it clear conceptual expression." The religion of the Old Southwest, and later mountain religion, was not irrational, as the home missionaries characterized it, but nonrational. Indeed, the subtitle to Otto's *The Idea of the Holy* sums up not only this distinction but mountain religion's basic orientation: *An Inquiry into the Non-rational Factor in the Idea of the Divine and Its Relation to the Rational.* In the religion of the Old Southwest that consolidated into mountain religion, "this positive feeling-content"—that is, the highly intuitive, the nonrational, the heart—informed the rational, the head, rather than the other way around, a posture radically different from, indeed, diametrically opposed to the quickly emerging national religious culture Schermerhorn represented.

Schermerhorn continued his remarks by reiterating that what he had said about the Holy Spirit in Baptist worship life of the Old Southwest he had also found among other church traditions characteristic of the region, which he now identified as the common source and the basic error producing the Great Revival in the West: "These observations on the Spirit are applicable to several denominations. By this it may be perceived, that instead of following the doctrines of Christ, to try the Spirits by the law and testimony; they try the law and testimony by the *Spirit within.* It was from this delusion that all the fanaticism and enthusiasm sprang which overspread the western country a few years since, and produced a flood of error" (p. 40, emphasis in the original). "[T]his Spirit" that Schermerhorn had quarrel with and blamed for the upheavals in religion on the Appalachian frontier he called the "delusion" of "the *Spirit within,* as they term it," using the people's own language for where they understood the Spirit to dwell. Normative to free church polity, Old Southwest Baptists affirmed the autonomy of the individual and the priesthood of all believers within a disciplined church, governed from within and by consensus, that granted and affirmed for each individual the right to determine what was the will of God in his or her life. They located God's will in their personal and communal experiences of the Holy Spirit, tenderizer of the heart, as the primary source of all right knowledge of God's will for them and their local church communities, and the only avenue for genuine consensus within church life.

For Baptists with highly developed doctrinal traditions, rational examination was important, but discernment should take its lead not from the head but the heart, the home of the Holy Spirit. Schermerhorn was quite right about Baptists and the "several denominations" distinctive to the Old Southwest trying "the law and testimony by the *Spirit within,*" rather than

theless also upheld the primary value of "the witness of the Spirit within them" about their "doctrines and views of truth"; indeed, they claimed to be governed first by that Spirit, not by "law" and "doctrines." The Old Regular Baptists today are but one model in the mountains of that merging of the rational with the nonrational, prioritizing on the side of the heart for right understanding of the distinctive doctrinal traditions which provide their religious moorings in a world that dismisses them, said Ron Short, as "a unique sect of backwoods Christians with neither the mentality nor the spirit to survive."[13]

Near the conclusion of his statement on the Baptists, Schermerhorn discussed the centrality of religious experience among people in the Old Southwest and their verbal accounting of such experiences for admission into church life: "The term of admission into the Baptist church is a relation of their experiences. In these it is thought too much attention is paid to feelings and impressions of the individuals without examining them by the word of God. Dreams, visions, the unusual suggestion of some text of Scripture, which are very alarming and others that cause great inward joy and rejoicing, also form a great part of the experience" (p. 40). Again, Schermerhorn rejected a type of experience of saving grace already normative to the Old Southwest, which he described as being based on "feelings and impressions," something to which "too much attention is paid." Schermerhorn noted once again the preponderance of "dreams, visions, the unusual suggestion of some text of Scripture" as the basis for many testimonies of religious experience that had brought about a crisis in faith which resulted in conversion or an experience of saving grace. This tradition continues powerfully in mountain religious life today. However, Schermerhorn was likely simply wrong in concluding that church members, when petitioned for church membership, did not try the testimonies they heard "by the word of God."

As with the New England Puritans, church membership was very serious business on the Appalachian frontier. It always has been for Old Time Baptist traditions of the region, as well as for other church traditions that emerged after Schermerhorn's tour, such as independent Holiness. But the desire not to intrude on the workings of God's Spirit in the life of the individual more often than not overrode concerns about the worthiness of a petitioner, who was frequently known well by his or her auditors. What Schermerhorn astutely observed about the process of ordaining a preaching elder also applied to the process of church membership: "The common practice on the subject is this, the person makes a statement to the church, that he feels an inward call to preach the Gospel.—on this the church, for fear lest they should be found fighting against the Spirit, generally permit him to exercise his *gifts*. If he is approved by them, he is soon ordained by the elders of the church."

As in the Old Southwest of Schermerhorn's tour, for Old Time Baptist traditions today, church membership also involves individuals stepping forward out of their own volition to make a statement to the church about their experience of saving grace, and the church either "approves" them or not for church membership, inaugurated by baptism by immersion. What is mindful is that the gravity of church membership, like the gravity of the call to preach, puts its own restraints on individuals, firmly discouraging capricious or impulsive decisions by the people who put themselves forward for baptism or ordination, often late in life. The tradition in free church polity of trust in the individual's ability to discern the will of God in her or his life is widely honored—indeed, it is the norm—throughout mountain church traditions, and individuals just as widely honor the trust their church traditions place in them.

The major doctrinal traditions of the region Schermerhorn noted left many Baptist churches "[i]n sentiment . . . much divided. The better informed are Calvinists; but many are either Antinomians or Arminians" (p. 40), indicating that Calvinist and non-Calvinist Baptists alike shared the same worship practices and traditions of spirituality Schermerhorn enumerated as distinctive to them all in his encompassing sketch of "Baptists," regardless of their theological transmutations, and even those of other "denominations" ("These observations on the Spirit are applicable to several denominations"). This is consistent with the shared features of mountain church traditions today, especially with regard to the centrality of the Holy Spirit. Schermerhorn's critique of Old Southwest Baptists also indicated how far removed his own Calvinism was by this time from the Calvinism of the Southwest, his emphasizing conversion by way of right reason, in contrast to the tradition of emotional conversion mediated by grace through the Holy Spirit.

Schermerhorn concluded his discussion of Baptists of the Old Southwest by bringing up finally the topic of a paid ministry and the strong opposition to this eastern tradition in the region: "Against the salaries of ministers they are clamorous; and they denominate Presbyterian ministers *fleecers of the flock*" (p. 40, emphasis in the original). In his report on the Commonwealth of Kentucky, Schermerhorn pointed to yet another major—indeed, insurmountable—obstacle relative to the ministry itself between the denominations of American Protestantism and the church traditions defining the religious character of the Old Southwest: "They generally treat missionaries with respect; still there is not that regard for clerical order among them, which is desirable" (p. 20). Emma Bell Miles's words about mountain preachers from the turn into the twentieth century come flooding back: "You hear no cant in the mountains about respect due to the cloth; our preacher is never called a clergyman or a divine; even the term 'pastor of the flock' savors of patronage which would indicate a false relation; Brother So-and-So, preacher of the gospel, is title enough. He is not of a class set apart from life, from the labors, sins and sorrows of his world, nor does he pander to any class distinctions."[14]

But Schermerhorn in 1814 advocated his own background's model of the clergy as a class set apart, a "clerical order" evoking a "respect," a "regard" he deemed "desirable." Schermerhorn attributed the difference in attitude toward ministers of the Old Southwest to an inappropriate leveling influence that "arises from the principle of the Methodists and Baptists . . . selecting their preachers, and from the manners of the preachers themselves." Schermerhorn was again right on the mark. Like the mountain preachers soon to follow, the preachers he observed generally rose up from within their own neighborhoods and were very much on a par with those to whom they preached, the people who made up the region's overwhelming majority at that time, its plain-folk. Schermerhorn even picked up their distinctive vocabulary. His own background spoke of a "clerical order" or the clergy, but the people of the Old Southwest spoke of "their preachers."

Schermerhorn and Mills, while in Kentucky, had traveled far out of their way to meet with Elder John Taylor at his home, where they spent the night. Taylor, whom we have met before as one of the earliest and most eloquent spokespersons against missions, had been recommended to the pair as the Baptist to meet in Kentucky if they wished to know about Kentucky Baptists. Taylor was born in Fauquier County, Virginia, in 1752, of Scottish and French Huguenot ancestry. He was baptized at the age of twenty by James Ireland, licensed to preach the same year, and ordained an elder four years later by a presbytery officiated by Lewis Craig, whose famous "travelling church" of six hundred people would plant the Baptist tradition in Kentucky. After an earlier trip to Kentucky over the Wilderness Road, Taylor took his family there by river and settled first with Lewis Craig's church on Gilbert's Creek in Lincoln County.

Taylor spent the rest of his days in Kentucky, moving his family several times, clearing large tracts of land for settlement. He died in 1835, at the age of eighty-two. His autobiographical work, *A History of Ten Baptist Churches* (1827), is the best picture of frontier Baptist life and the best available portrait of an Old Southwest Baptist farmer-preacher.[15] Taylor lived on the very fringes of what is today the Appalachian region. The church life he described was normative to his era throughout the broad expanse of the Old Southwest, and a very strong link through his own personal history with Baptist revival culture in colonial Virginia that he and others brought into the region. That same church life was reflected in the Old Time Baptist traditions that came to characterize so much of religious life in the mountains of Appalachia. Indeed, a significant part of the early history of the Appalachian region is drawn from the continuing fringe that shrunk in upon itself with settlement and includes areas today that are considered to be on its immediate borders.

Taylor was strongly opposed to a paid ministry. He was just as strongly opposed to being made what he called the "particular pastor" or pastor-in-charge of the churches he helped to found and whose members he baptized. Taylor followed in the tradition of plural eldership where the church moderator's administrative role, as we have seen with groups such as the Old Regular Baptists, did not encompass the ministerial role of a "pastor." Taylor worked in all but one of his churches as a member and preacher, for more than one preacher or ordained elder was usual in his congregations, but being asked to be the "particular pastor" made him "very uneasy."[16] These sentiments were in line with his opposition to missionary societies and to Baptist associations assuming an increase in power and exercising an authority that would encroach upon what Taylor called the "liberty of thought" of individual congregations. Taylor was extremely concerned about preserving the equality of individual believers in the local church community, an equality to which he saw great violence done in the establishment of national and regional organizational structures that assumed responsibility—and control—over local churches and their members.

Taylor was well aware that one of the charges denominational Baptists and their national leadership—organized around the cause of missions—brought against preachers of his type was that they engaged in "secular" pursuits to support themselves, supposedly at the expense of their ministry. But in his *History* he countered that Baptist preachers who sought paid ministries from churches, especially those that they themselves had not established, were "buzzards sailing in the air":

> I consider, my greatest improprieties have been the active pursuits of this world; but in one sense, this is erring on the right side, for thereby, I have supported my large family, without spunging on the people, and if I mistake not, Paul at times, prefered tent making, to that of being a mean begger among the people. So that bad as my own course has been, I would prefer it to the course of some preaching men. To see a preacher, like a buzzard, sailing in the air, from one country to another, and from city to city, to hunt for churches already built, and when he smells a carcass pitch down and fall to devouring, I say, when this seems to be the object, of two evils, I will choose that which seems to me, the least. I have been in the ministry, just about fifty four years; and of the many thousands of meetings I have appointed, I do not recollect that worldly business ever stopped me from one of them, and I have been a man of such general uninterrupted health, that I do not think I have disappointed half as many meetings in my life, as I have been preaching years. Should this be called boasting, as Paul said, in a similar case, bare with me in my folly. (p. vii)

Elsewhere in the *History* Taylor wrote simply, "It never set well on my feelings to receive pay from the people for preaching, I therefore preferred my own exertions, to supply my own wants" (p. 34). Taylor attended as many as ten to twenty association meetings in a year. His collection of association minutes, with their statistics, made up the basis for Schermerhorn's statistics on Baptists in Kentucky.

In *Thoughts on Missions* (1819), Taylor wrote of the overnight stay Schermerhorn and Mills made in his home as part of their tour of the region:

> By an acquaintance of mine in Cincinnati in the state of Ohio, they were induced to travel sixty miles out of their way to see me, then living in the lower end of Gallatin county. The object of an interview with me, was to know the state of the Baptist society in Kentucky, and shape their course accordingly. They were at my house about one day and night. They were respectable looking young men, well informed, and zealous in the cause in which they were employed. They gave me a full history of the ordination and mission of Messrs. Judson and Rice [the two individuals responsible for establishing the foreign missions movement in the Baptist tradition], and the mighty effect it had on the people of New England; and particularly this good effect, that many poor ministers could scarcely get their bread before, but by stirring up the people in the missionary cause, and getting them in the habit of giving their money, it was now cheerfully communicated by thousands, so that ministers who staid [sic] at home, were now richly supplied. Was all this Priestly art? Those young visitants of mine were very sociable, and among other freedoms asked me how I had got through the world, as they saw me then well settled and old; which led to another question, what amount of supplies I had generally received from the people for preaching? After having considered it very puny indeed, and in friendly way blamed the badness of my policy; after finding that the Baptists in Kentucky were a great people (from the copies of Minutes I presented them of different associations,) now about fifteen associations in the state, and about that number of churches in an adjacent county (Shelby) they became quite impatient with my indolence, assuring me if I would only stir up the people to Missions and Bible Society matters, I should find a great change in money affairs in favor of the preachers; urging by questions like this, do you not know when the sponges are once opened they will always run? Only said they, get the people in the habit of giving their money for any religious use, and they will continue to appropriate for all sacred purposes.[17]

Taylor noted that Schermerhorn and Mills felt—and let him know in no uncertain terms—that he had been derelict in his ministerial duties in not seeking from the people of his numerous churches over the years adequate financial support either for himself or for other preachers, let alone for the new religious societies concerned with missions and Bible distribution which Schermerhorn and Mills represented.

Schermerhorn found in the statistical information Taylor supplied through associational minutes that there were far more Baptist churches and preachers in Kentucky than any other group. Schermerhorn wrote of the section between the Kentucky and Cumberland rivers, "There is no prospect of forming churches here, owing to the divisions and dissensions which exist among the people on religious matters, and a disposition, which is very common where Baptists and Methodists are prevalent, an unwillingness to support the Gospel. . . . It is possible, if a good missionary were sent among them, that he would be heard with attention" (p. 22). For Schermerhorn, a preacher's refusal either to solicit or accept payment for preaching and ministerial labors, and the refusal of the people to sustain the full financial needs of an individual who had a call to preach (for almost all the churches provided some level of financial support, however minimal), was clear indication that the people in this part of the Southwest maintained an overall "unwillingness to support the Gospel."

For the people of Kentucky as a whole, Schermerhorn applied to them a judgment he made repeatedly about people throughout the Old Southwest, and about Kentucky in particular, "The great mass of the people, however, were ignorant, poor, and vicious, and have handed to their descendants their feelings and habits" (p. 24). The religious life distinctive to the Southwest Schermerhorn reduced to "feelings and habits" that were now the religious heritage of "their descendants," holding little prospect for this earliest stage of the home missions movement that he and Mills represented. For Schermerhorn, "ignorance" in matters of religion had to do with not identifying with the religious values epitomized by the Presbyterian-Congregational denominations of the East—who saw themselves as "the exponents of the purest form of Protestantism," as Goodykoontz recounted—and identifying instead with the Methodists and especially the Baptists of the Old Southwest. Schermerhorn wrote of the country between the Kentucky and Green rivers, a region also heavily dominated by Baptists, "Some Presbyterian societies could also be formed, particularly in the county towns, for wherever you find men well informed there is a decided preference to that denomination, and rather than hear the Baptists and Methodists" (p. 21).

In the latter part of the nineteenth century and into the twentieth, Presbyterians especially would equate education with religious enlightenment in the Appalachian region, an enlightenment identified with receptivity to Presbyterianism and the values of the nation's dominant religious culture. Presbyterianism was understood to be the tradition of the better educated. Townspeople, as Schermerhorn noted, were more likely to become Presbyterians because they had access to schools. This logic would apply, well into

formed," for, as Schermerhorn had said of western Pennsylvania, "men of information and influence, are decidedly in favor of Presbyterianism."

Schermerhorn's longest account was reserved for Ohio—"New Connecticut"—with ten full pages of text in contrast to four pages for western Pennsylvania and only three pages for New Virginia. Ohio as part of the Old Northwest territory was seen as the most promising region for missionary labors, and indeed, after the creation of the American Home Missionary Society in 1826, it was given a particular focus of efforts by Congregationalists who established a firm foothold in the area. At the time of Schermerhorn's report "New Connecticut" had already been made the special field of the Missionary Society of Connecticut, which probably accounted for Schermerhorn's lengthy and detailed treatment of Ohio.

Like western Pennsylvania and New Virginia, eastern Kentucky was described by Schermerhorn as "very mountainous and broken country" (p. 22). The soil of east Tennessee, whose eastern border was dominated largely by the Great Smoky Mountains, he called "light and poor." The state of Tennessee was divided by the Cumberland Mountains into east and west Tennessee. At the time of Schermerhorn and Mills's tour, from one-half to five-eighths of the land was "claimed by the Cherokee and Chickesaw Indians" (p. 24). Most of Tennessee's white inhabitants, Schermerhorn noted, had come from Kentucky and the Carolinas, with some from Virginia and Georgia. Schermerhorn held out much greater prospects for missionary labors in east Tennessee than he did in the more fertile, less rugged land of west Tennessee or in any part of Kentucky. Initially, his hope is a surprise since it is east Tennessee that is today located within Appalachia, not west Tennessee. But Schermerhorn's hopes for east Tennessee had to do with the institutionalization of home missions in the region.

Schermerhorn wrote of east Tennessee, "The Baptists are the most numerous, and probably the Presbyterians next. The Presbyterians probably are loosing [sic] ground, for some of their most active and zealous preachers have removed to West Tennessee. . . . The ministers that have already settled here, have so scanty a support, that they have to resort to some other occupation than preaching to maintain their families" (p. 25). Nonetheless, east Tennessee had a higher estimation than west Tennessee in Schermerhorn's report because it had the distinction of possessing one of only two missionary societies that existed at that time outside of New England, a "Missionary, Tract, and Bible Society. . . . It is the first and only Missionary Body, except the Synod of Pittsburg, west of the Allegany, and promises to be a blessing to this part of the country. The Constitution is similar to that of the 'Massachusetts Missionary Society'" (pp. 25–26). However, Schermerhorn was quite right that "the Presbyterians probably are loosing [sic] ground" in east Tennessee. Today a very few lonely Presbyterian home mission stations near the

Great Smokies are surrounded by literally dozens of independent Baptist churches throughout the rural countryside.

What Schermerhorn had to say about other religious groups prevalent in the Old Southwest was almost perfunctory in comparison to his description of the Baptists. Where Methodists came from, their doctrines, system of districts, circuits, and classes, division of clergy into bishops, elders, and deacons, and how people become members of the Methodist church Schermerhorn dealt with in a few short sentences. His description of Methodist preachers and preaching is not unexpected at this point: "In general, they have very little learning; though when they begin to preach, they begin to study, and many of them improve considerably. As to their manner of preaching, it very much resembles that of the Baptists—is very controversial, and most bitter against Calvinists. They rail very much against the practice of the Presbyterians' receiving pay for preaching, calling them hirelings, but most unreasonably; for their salaries are more certain and, in general, greater than those against whom they speak." Schermerhorn, however, had nothing but praise for the Methodist circuit system, which he called a "complete system of missions," one worthy of imitation in this beginning stage of the emerging national home missions movement which his survey represented: "This denomination has greatly increased within a few years, and this must chiefly be attributed to their complete system of missions, which is by far the best for domestic missions ever yet adopted" (p. 41).

Schermerhorn next gave an account of the "New Lights." He found most disturbing the total congregational autonomy of Barton W. Stone's Christian churches and their divorce from Presbyterian hierarchical structure, given their roots in the Presbyterian church. The Christian churches (1804) were the first denomination indigenous to the Appalachian region, blasting out of the Great Revival which largely defined them until their union in 1832 with Alexander Campbell's Disciples. Wrote Schermerhorn about Stone's "New Lights":

> The first discovery which they pretended to make was that all confessions of faith and catechisms were made by fallible men, erroneous, contrary to Scripture and reason, and calculated to keep believers in bondage. They therefore renounced them all, except the Bible. Next, that all Assemblies, Synods, and Presbyteries were contrary to Scripture, carnal bonds, and stood full in the way of Christ, and the revivals of religion. . . . This sect is without order, regularity, or any bond of union; each does that which is right in his own eyes. They are as ignorant as any of the sects, and in their manner of preaching are much like those already noticed. (pp. 41, 42)

"[T]heir manner of preaching . . . much like those already noticed" was in fact like Baptist preaching, for Schermerhorn provided no other detailed

extemporaneous preaching as they found themselves plunged back into the ancient and "customary" Scots-Irish Presbyterian tradition of sacramental revivalism that was sustained and perpetuated by the laity themselves, rather than by the clergy. Indeed, it was a tradition now limited in the United States to the Old Southwest of the Great Revival and the Scots-Irish people settled there as its largest founding population.

Although Schermerhorn did not realize it when he provided his description of Old Southwest Presbyterian clergy and their biannual communion meetings, what is in evidence in his account is that the early Presbyterian sacramental revivalism of extemporaneous preaching and multi-day communion meetings had been mixing itself with other traditions in the region, especially Old Southwest Baptist groups who emphasized freely "the *Spirit within*." This emphasis had a strong natural affinity with the Scots-Irish laity's own traditional revivalistic religiosity of emotional piety and spontaneity. This cross-pollination of revival movements, and their shared Calvinistic heritage of grace mediated by the Holy Spirit as the foundation for their expressive and ecstatic worship lives, created a sacramental revivalism unique to the mountains of the Appalachian region and normative throughout mountain church traditions to a greater or lesser extent, from the most doctrinally conservative to the most free-flowing. As Presbyterianism within Appalachia very soon divorced itself entirely from the tradition of sacramental revivalism, its stronghold in the Appalachian region would always be limited to county seats and larger towns located mostly in the broad valleys, areas least affected by the traditions of mountain religious life, with only a handful of isolated Presbyterian churches—most of them established as home mission churches—scattered throughout the mountains and the more rural countryside.

16

"In the Brush"

The end of the War of 1812 was near when Schermerhorn and Mills published the results of their survey on religion and morals in the Old Southwest in 1814. The period marked the emergence of strong nationalistic attitudes that would intensify over the next three to four decades. In the decade of their missionary survey, national leaders were beginning to think more in terms of national rather than sectional needs. John C. Calhoun proposed a system of roads and canals that would unite the nation. Henry Clay was developing his "American System," an integrated national economic program initiating a broad reach for the federal government. Domestic issues of internal improvements, use of public domain, Supreme Court decisions under John Marshall with national implications, national banking and currency standards, less dependency on European markets for raw materials and sales, the issue of slavery, the acquisition of Florida in 1819 providing unimpeded access to the Gulf of Mexico, the expanse of the West beyond the Mississippi River—all of these compelled a focus on the United States as a unified country tending to its own needs as a nation, not relying on the European model of nation-states.

In the decade after the close of the War of 1812, denominations in the East were also swept into a national perspective for their own growth and development, especially in evangelizing the newly settled and expanding West. What had been regional and sectarian religious and benevolent societies were organized along national and nondenominational lines. In 1815 the American Education Society was founded for the funding of young men preparing for the ministry; 1816 saw established the American Bible Society; 1824, the American Sunday School Union; 1825, the American Tract Society; 1826, the American Society for Promoting Temperance; 1828, the American Peace Society. The preeminence of "American" in their titles underscored the nationalistic focus of their intentions; indeed, these national societies formed the front lines of the American Benevolence movement. For the home missionary movement, its national focus crystallized in the American Home Missionary Society, founded in May 1826 when Congregationalists and Presbyterians joined their regional societies into a single national enterprise. Between the second decade of the nineteenth century and 1835, Baptists, Methodists, and Episcopalians also formed national home missionary organizations on a denominational level.

Intense apprehensions over the shift in control of the nation's cultural and political life from the Atlantic seaboard to the populations of the advancing West created a large part of the impetus for the formation of national home mission enterprises. Their focus was as much on influencing the shape of westerners' national cultural character as it was on the religious enlightenment of populations otherwise perceived to be destitute of churches and adequately trained clergy. As John Maltby, a student at Andover Theological Seminary, made clear in his 1825 address on the connection between domestic missions and the political prospects of the country before the Society of Inquiry respecting Missions, the West at that time reached just over the Allegheny Mountains, but did not yet extend beyond the Mississippi River:

> The hundreds and thousands of populous towns and cities which stretch along the shores and cover the hills and vallies [sic] of the Atlantic states will soon cease to characterize our nation and sway its councils. They will soon come to be but a small minority compared with the millions that shall roll in wealth and luxury beyond the Alleghany, and even beyond the Mississippi. Already is the influence of the West beginning to be strongly felt in our halls of national legislation [e.g., Henry Clay of Kentucky and Andrew Jackson of Tennessee]. A few years and of those who represent our nation in our council chambers, the majority will come over the Alleghany:—a few years more and that majority will cross the Mississippi on their way. And with what character shall they come?[1]

"And with what character shall they come?" prevailed as the motivating question behind much of the impetus for home missions as a matter of preemptive cultural control that would circumvent the Atlantic states' loss of preeminence as the cultural and political focal point of the nation, along with concern for the religious needs of new settlers in the West. These dual concerns, debated for many years, informed—indeed, propelled—the founding of the American Home Missionary Society in 1826, the year following Maltby's address.

Daniel Boone had cut the Wilderness Road in 1775, passing through the Cumberland Gap where Kentucky, Tennessee, and Virginia meet, an area that has long been regarded as the symbolic heart of central Appalachia. After 1818 the Wilderness Road and the Cumberland Turnpike brought more and more settlers into the region and also, through their tributary routes, to parts of the Old Southwest bordering the Mississippi River outside the range of the Appalachian region, as well as to the New West extending into the territories just beyond the Mississippi. Many settlers chose to stay in the Appalachian region, which had not known much in the way of white settlement until after 1770, and then primarily in the valleys. By 1790, Scots-Irish and German immigration had slackened, and English settlers became predominant as the new settlers in the region. By 1850, Appalachia had approximately 1.6 million white people within its boundaries. A land once dominated by Native Americans, it had become through displacement an area that white people could call "home." White people long settled in the more rugged areas of the region would learn much from Native Americans whose land it was, from basic survival skills to land cultivation, healing arts, and attitudes toward the land that would shape their religious sensibilities. By the middle of the nineteenth century, new national roads bypassed the region; soon fewer and fewer migrants arrived. Appalachia was, for the first time, "closed off" in the sense that it was a distinctive region that would quickly develop a regional flavor of its own, especially in its religious traditions.

By 1850 Appalachia was referred to as the Southwest by writers in the East. Its regionally specific tradition of plain-folk camp-meeting religion had long been divorced from the worship traditions of Methodists and denominational Baptists and from the institutionalized revival movement in the East, which was incorporated into the denominational frameworks of American Protestantism. Plain-folk camp-meeting religion was now a mainstay in the churches and religious life of the Southwest, becoming a base that would support especially the development of independent nondenominational churches, the tradition that stands at the center of the spectrum defining Appalachian mountain religion as a regional religious tradition. In 1851 an article in *The Home Missionary*, publication of the executive committee of the American Home Missionary Society, illustrated very well the extent to which eastern denominational attitudes toward religious life in the Southwest had hardened and become stereotypical. This anonymously published article was also, in a backhanded way, a good illustration of how plain-folk camp-meeting religion had become a well-woven part of the fabric of religious life in the Southwest by 1851, when Appalachia's own cultural-geographic identity was coming into sharp focus.

The Home Missionary article was titled "The South West. Prejudices—Distracted Meetings." Its editorial introduction proclaimed, "Descriptions of the nature of the following may be regarded as not in the best taste; but as they are *sad*—if not sober—realities, which the missionary has to encounter in certain sections, they who undertake to sustain him by their sympathy and prayers, ought to know how it fares with him and his message, and what obstacles have to be overcome."[2] Once again, not only were the people of the Old Southwest viewed as irreligious because of the type of religion they had but descriptions of their worship life were considered to be "not in the best taste . . . *sad*." Home missionaries from the East who served in the region were seen to face particularly onerous "obstacles" erected by the religious life distinctive to the Southwest of the Appalachian frontier and, as a consequence, were in special need of sustaining "sympathy and prayers."

Given Schermerhorn's repeated insistence nearly forty years before that "men of information and influence," the better educated and socially superior, preferred the Presbyterian tradition to that of the Baptists and Methodists, this anonymous writer's complaint about a regional prejudice against Presbyterians, because "the people are made to believe that the Presbyterians think themselves above them," was at the least disingenuous. Indeed, this writer's own words testified to his strong sense of religious superiority over the ordinary inhabitants of the Southwest. He equated Presbyterian preaching with technological progress and advances in civilization, and characterized the people of the Southwest as "slothful" and "envious" in their negative attitude toward Presbyterianism, refusing its obvious advantages over their own religious traditions, like they refused all other "modern improvements," clinging instead to their backward ways in religion in the same manner they clung to backward ways in their everyday life: "The mass of the people are made to believe that the Presbyterians think themselves above them, and hence they treat us much after the same manner as they do most of the modern improvements in agriculture and mechanics. They go to hear the 'larned' preacher, and to see the new-fashioned plow, and the deep furrows which it makes; and then they return home, and partly from sloth, and partly from envy, cling tighter to the old rickety plow, and to the see-saw, hum and spit preacher, feeling, that improvements are for others."

The people of the Southwest enjoyed hearing Presbyterian preachers, the writer continued, "provided it costs them nothing." His implication was that they were unwilling to put their financial resources on the line for the sake of the Gospel, just as Schermerhorn in 1814 had equated lack of financial support for clergy in the same region with "an unwillingness to support the Gospel." This Presbyterian missionary to the Southwest failed totally to recognize the legitimacy of the region's normative tradition of Pauline tent ministry, where preachers supported themselves by their own labors, giving freely to the people as preachers and pastors of their own time and resources as a gift from God, without price or any expectation of recompense, and the highly esteemed value of the leveling influence this created between preachers and those to whom they preached. Of equal distress to the writer of this 1851 report, the people of the Southwest refused to join the church except through "a 'big meeting,'" the traditional avenue in non-Calvinist traditions leading to church membership. The tradition of a "big meeting" had an unbroken line reaching back to Baptist revival culture in colonial Virginia where it was called a "great meeting," about which the writer seemed to know nothing. It was also a tradition significantly intensified by plain-folk camp-meeting religion that emerged out of the Great Revival on the Appalachian frontier and by now was a religious movement normative to the region, as this 1851 account verified:

They seem glad enough to hear Presbyterian preaching, provided it costs them nothing; but when it comes to "jinin" the church, why, to-be-sure, that must take place at a "big meeting," where there is a great deal of shouting and "hallelujah singing going on."

And then to see the way they "get religion," as they call it! After a passionate appeal, (which is evidently intended to reach the weaker part of the congregation first,) about departed friends, and a vindication of shouting, the mourners are called for.

In many Holiness churches today such as Brother Coy Miser's, the preacher will say to those present before the power of God falls in the service, "If God's Spirit tells you to shout, well you shout! If He tells you to run, you run! If the Holy Ghost tells you to get up and dance, get up and dance! We're here to do what the Spirit tells us!" The rest of this 1851 report on Southwest plain-folk camp-meeting religion dealt with how people "get religion" at "a 'big meeting,'" and the stages of wearing down the senses by which a person would have what the writer recorded the people themselves called "the 'witness of the Spirit.'"

Expressive and ecstatic worship traditions were a large part of the "witness of the Spirit," among which this Presbyterian home missionary enumerated singing, shouting, screaming, clapping hands, "hopping about," laughing, and shaking hands:

And then the singing and shouting commences, and the mourners are brought in, and required to kneel down. In this, often painful position, they are sometimes kept for hours at a time, until wearied out, they sink down and stretch themselves upon the floor. This is considered a favorable symptom, and the news circulates throughout the country, that "they have got Mr. ——— and Mrs. ———, and Miss ——— down." After a while, through suffocation and exhaustion, a profuse sweat breaks out upon them, and they are made to feel as they "never felt before." This they conclude, is the "witness of the Spirit," and then, as it is expected, they relieve themselves from their procumbent situation, by springing upon their feet, and hopping about, and clapping their hands, and screaming out with loud percussive emphasis, "Glory, glory, glory, hallelujah, I've got it, I've got it," &c., and then all say that such a one "has got religion," and then there is a great deal of religious laughing, and shaking of hands, &c., &c.

Schermerhorn in 1814 had made abundantly clear the central role of the Holy Spirit ("the *Spirit within,* as they term it") in defining the spirituality of the region, a tradition with much precedence in the history of Christianity, including the United States (the Great Awakening was not yet too distant a memory), by which he was very troubled. But, to his credit, Schermerhorn presented an even-handed account of its manifestations in the worship en-

"Brush College," where they would "break brush for a year or two" (p. 6). Pierson explained, "I do not, therefore, in the pages that follow, speak of my travels in the 'wilderness' or 'forests' or 'hills' or 'mountains' of the Southwest, but adopt a more comprehensive term, universally prevalent in the regions explored, and describe some of my experiences in the Brush" (p. 9). Pierson was known widely for his ecumenical spirit. As the above quotation indicated, like the old veteran ministers he wrote about, he too attended the association meetings of Baptists, the conferences of Methodists, and the presbytery meetings of Presbyterians. At the conclusion of his work for the American Bible Society, before assuming the presidency of Cumberland College, the Louisville Annual Conference published a tribute to him in a local newspaper.[6]

Pierson wrote fondly of Methodist itinerants he met in the Brush that they "enjoyed their long rides to preach to a dozen or more at an out-of-the-way appointment—enjoyed preaching, praying, singing, shouting—enjoyed laboring with 'mourners in the altar' until late in the night, and they could scarcely speak for hoarseness—enjoyed seeing them 'come through' (the vernacular for conversion), hearing them shout, and receiving them into the church—enjoyed class-meetings, quarterly-meetings, camp-meetings, love-feasts, and conference" (p. 172). Pierson's account of what Methodist itinerants "enjoyed" in the Brush indicated the strong prevalence of a style of worship and celebration distinctive to the Southwest that continued for some time in the Methodist tradition of the Appalachian region, even after it had long died out in the East by the 1850s, the period Pierson wrote about.

Pierson stayed the night in small cabins scattered throughout the region of his labors, meeting hundreds of families in his work of supplying them with Bibles either for a small payment (from ten to thirty-five cents) or as gifts. He was exposed to the general religious life of households and commented at length on their traditions throughout his book. The first factor of utmost importance was the hospitality he was shown: "The hospitality extended to ministers of the gospel by the people who lived in the Brush was generous and large-hearted to a degree that I have never known among any other class of people. They obeyed the Scripture injunction, 'Use hospitality without grudging'" (p. 47). It is telling that he would claim that the hospitality extended to him was "to a degree that I have never known among any other class of people," given the compass of his travels and places of residence over his lifetime, including New York City. In my own experience, this tradition of "generous and large-hearted" hospitality has yet to fade from mountain households.

Often Pierson would preach when staying the night at a cabin, and the communications network he described was typical in the region until the advent of the wide use of telephones:

I knew that they would not only all be notified for miles around, but that the most of them would be present. I have found by experience that it is one of the peculiarities of the wilder and wildest portions of the country, that the people will be at the greatest possible pains to notify their neighbors far and near whenever a stranger will preach, whatever may be the day of the week or the hour of the day. . . .

As soon as my assent was given, father, sons, and daughters have started off in different directions to notify the nearest neighbors, who immediately abandoned their work to inform other and more distant neighbors. In this manner all the families over a wide extent of country would be notified in a short time. Nearly all would abandon their work, and with it all thought of supper until they should return, and, taking their children with them, would start at once for the place appointed for preaching. (pp. 158–59)

Pierson's account illustrated that people in the Brush placed the highest priority on taking advantage of an unexpected opportunity to hear preaching, to the extent of completely setting aside their immediate labors; it also demonstrated their enviable adaptability and flexibility, given the constant, plain hard work of maintaining a household in the Appalachian wilderness of Pierson's era. It made clear what came first in their lives—hearing the Word of God, "whatever may be the day of the week or the hour of the day," even at the expense of necessary labors to sustain themselves.

While staying in a home, Pierson would usually be asked to "take the Books," a Bible and a hymn book, and lead the family devotions of singing and prayer before retiring for the night. "It has been my happy lot to receive and respond to that invitation . . . in many hundreds of families and in some of the wildest portions of our land" (pp. 54–55). Similarly he would be asked to "make a beginning," or lead the prayer at meal times. The supposed "religious destitution" of the region lamented by so many agents of "foreign denominations" Pierson showed over and over again was simply not the case—at least not in his experience. Pierson's more informed account of people in the Brush in Kentucky during the 1850s made highly suspect the later claim of the Congregationalist home missionary Ellen Myers, who worked in eastern Kentucky in the early 1880s and represented a very different phase of home missions to mountain people, a phase infused by the Christian America movement. In diametrical opposition to Pierson, who reported that he was asked to lead prayer "in many hundreds of families and in some of the wildest portions of our land," Myers declared, "There is no family prayer in all the land."[7]

As he wrote of the hospitality second to none, Pierson also wrote about the importance of the Bible to people in the Brush. "I have never known such remarkable and pleasing results following the reading of the Bible, without any human help, as among the ignorant people I have visited, living in wild and neglected regions in the Brush" (p. 103). Pierson quoted one man as a representative of people who could not read the Bible, but who got their more literate neighbors to read it to them: "*I don't know what it is*—I never heard any such reading afore; *every time they read to me out of that little book it makes me cry, and I can't help it*" (p. 108, emphasis in the original). What St. Teresa of Avila called the gift of tears was especially prevalent in the Appalachian region of Pierson's Southwest. People still today are easily moved to cry by the reading of the Bible, or by the words of a familiar hymn, or at prayer. The tradition in the mountains of knowledge of the Bible as oral literature was writ large in Pierson's account, rooted in the intense listening skills of people in the Brush Pierson soon addressed in his book. Recall the observation Catherine Albanese made about mountain people, "Protestant in their attachment to a religion of the biblical Word and the felt experience of the heart, they wove their Protestantism with a new sacramentalism which spoke to their condition."[8] "[T]heir condition," shaped significantly by their landscape and forms of religious knowledge that placed no premium on literacy, Pierson claimed produced "such remarkable and pleasing results following the reading of the Bible," a response that Pierson had encountered nowhere else throughout his wide and varied travels in the ministry.

Since "[v]ery many of these churches were entirely satisfied if they had regular preaching once a month" (p. 255), the people in the Brush had a strong tradition of holding their own weekly meetings "conducted by themselves," once on the Sabbath, and once during the week: "Many had been induced to come long distances to attend these meetings, and had gone away saying, 'Surely this is the work of God, for only his power could enable such people to offer such prayers'" (p. 128). The tradition of holding weekly meetings—usually at night and either at a church house or some other small structure, but just as frequently, if not more often, in one's own home—where many people would travel "long distances" to gather to worship quite independently of any preachers was strong at the time of Pierson's work in the region and continues just as strongly today. The tradition of regular worship independent of ordained ministers extended back to the Baptist revival in colonial Virginia and North Carolina, and still further to the Scots-Irish holding their own night gatherings for worship, "conducted by themselves." It was part of the tradition of free church polity where clusters of individuals and small gatherings of families, guided by the Holy Spirit, laid hold of their own religious authority to worship and praise God.

When parents would go to night meetings, leaving their children at home, Pierson wrote, "I was told that even the little children had caught the prevailing spirit, and had commenced a 'play' that was entirely new in the neighborhood. When their parents were gone to night-meetings, as they often were, the children who were left at home entertained themselves by playing 'meeting'—going through with all the services as they had seen them at the meetings they had attended with their parents" (p. 128). Since people "were gone to night-meetings, as they often were," Pierson also noted the custom of deferring supper until after they had returned home, no matter what the hour (p. 24). Pierson's account reinforces the claim I have made numerous times that the tradition of night meetings so strong in the mountains today, especially among independent Holiness churches, was established as a part of the region's religious ethos at its earliest stages of settlement, stemming from its founding religious movements.

In several places Pierson wrote of the type of spontaneous prayer he heard in cabin homes in the Brush, their simplicity, power, and directness, and how deeply he was moved by the profundity of the prayer lives he witnessed. Of one man, named Jake, Pierson wrote, "We then all bowed upon our knees, and, after I had prayed, Mr. Jake G——, at my request, offered a prayer, such as he offered daily as he assembled his children around the family altar; a prayer so broken, so humble, so sincere, as to move the stoutest heart" (p. 115). People bowed on their knees in the Appalachia of Pierson's era, just as mountain people do today, gathering around "the family altar" or, more commonly, wherever there was enough space. Pierson did not simply note that Jake prayed in a family setting; it was the quality of Jake's prayer, "such as he offered daily," that arrested Pierson's attention, "a prayer so broken, so humble, so sincere, as to move the stoutest heart."

Jake's brother Dock, in whose home Pierson also stayed, was also a praying man: "It was a prayer such as I had never heard before. I did not wonder that his father had said to me in the morning, 'I do wish you could hear Dock pray now.' Though he could not read, his mind was evidently of a superior order, and the language of his prayer was not such as he had acquired by hearing others pray, but was entirely his own. It was deeply affecting to hear such familiar thoughts, uttered in language so strange and unusual." Literacy was not the avenue for effective—indeed, for the profound, extraordinary—prayer lives Pierson witnessed among the illiterate and isolated people of the Appalachian wilderness. Instead, these people were "taught of God," said Pierson, a bold claim for a minister of his background. Something other than the right reason so valued in his own religious tradition was operating among the people whose lives he shared: "Their hymns were mostly those that they had learned by hearing them sung by others, and their prayers were the simple, earnest utterances of those who seemed evidently to have been taught of God" (pp. 123–24). Apparently, mountain religion's emphasis on the "tender, sympathetic emotions of the heart" Schermerhorn first noted (and was troubled by) in 1814, and placing value foremost in the life of "the *Spirit within*," as Schermerhorn repeated several times, had cultivated the very mature worship lives, "conducted by themselves," of the otherwise unschooled people in the Brush that Pierson in the 1850s celebrated and was in apparent awe of, calling them people "taught of God."

Pierson commented elsewhere about the oral rather than written culture of the Southwest, like his remark about people learning hymns by hearing others sing them indicated. He wrote about what careful listeners his auditors in the Brush were when he preached, and how it was by the discipline of listening, giving their "closest attention," that they acquired most of their information:

> In addressing such an audience the speaker was always gratified and rewarded by the closest attention. I have never seen such listeners as the people in the Brush. They gave a speaker not only their ears but their eyes, and their whole attention. They seemed unwilling to lose a word that he uttered; they yielded themselves to his power. Their faces moved and glowed responsive to his sentiments; and his own mind was animated and enkindled by this sympathy of his audience. I suppose the chief reason of this very marked attention was the fact that the most of these people read very little, and very many of them could not read at all. Hence they acquired the most of their information on all subjects, religious and secular, by being good listeners. (pp. 160–61)

Many years later John C. Campbell wrote, "The 'foreign' preacher who looks down on his right into the attentive faces of the men, and on his left to the women, . . . little knows the critical faculty that is being focused upon his discourse."[9]

As with hospitality and love of the Bible, Pierson claimed, "I have never seen such listeners as the people in the Brush." They were people who "yielded themselves to [a speaker's] power," a product of open-heartedness and a willingness to render themselves vulnerable, which was a discipline in itself for it involved not following mindlessly whatever was said but thinking about what they heard, not trying the words spoken with critical judgment but discerning their intent, blending together the understanding of the heart with the understanding of the intellect. Highly developed listening skills are still widely prevalent today throughout the mountains, compensating extremely well for whatever lapses in literacy individuals may have, if any, and creating a different orientation to the world about them. As part of this oral culture, Pierson made special note of oral tradition in music, commenting on it more than once. Of a woman in whose home he stayed and who sang to him religious songs, "I now learned to my amazement that all the hymns and tunes she had sung that evening she had learned by rote—learned by hearing them sung by others" (p. 70).

In the churches themselves, Pierson gave detailed attention to mountain preaching style, a widespread tradition in the Brush of chanting and intoning and punctuating each short phrase with "ah!" which he reported that the people called, like the revival Baptists in colonial Virginia, a "holy tone":

> My brief address was followed by a sermon entirely different from those of the preacher I have already described, and deserves notice as a type of thousands that are preached to the people in the Brush. Scarcely a sentence in the sermon was uttered in the usual method of speech. It was drawled out in a sing-song tone from beginning to the end. The preacher ran his voice up, and sustained it at so high a pitch that he could make but little variation of voice upward. The air in his lungs would become exhausted, and at the conclusion of every sentence he would "catch" his breath with an "ah." As he proceeded with his sermon, and his vocal organs became wearied with this most unnatural exertion, the "ah" was repeated more and more frequently, until, with the most painful contortions of face and form, he would with difficulty articulate in his sing-song tone. . . .
> . . . This "holy tone" has charms for them not possessed by any possible eloquence. As the preacher "warms up" and becomes more animated in the progress of his discourse, the more impressible sisters begin to move their heads and bodies, and soon all the devout brethren and sisters sway their bodies back and forth in perfect unison, keeping time in some mysterious manner, to his sing-song tone. (pp. 73–74)

In contrast to his great awe over the sermon of "a genuine backwoodsman" we read about below, Pierson was troubled that, in this particular sermon, "I could not see the slightest evidence that he had any idea what he was going to say from one sentence to another. While 'catching his breath,' and saying 'ah,' he seemed to determine what he would say next. There was no . . . train of thought or connection of ideas." However, Pierson nonetheless had provided an outstanding description of traditional mountain preaching style—apart from this particular preacher's disjointedness in content—still heard today. More than a hundred and thirty years later, you can tune in on any Sunday to small radio stations throughout the mountains of Appalachia and hear preachers preach in this "holy tone." Even though it is ebbing in practice, it still remains a strong tradition.[10] Today Brother Coy Miser continues to preach in this manner, although more than 40 percent of his lungs have been destroyed by black lung disease, from his twelve years of working in the coal mines, and he frequently has to resort to a portable tank of oxygen.

Pierson wrote also of the preaching power and gifts of "a genuine backwoodsman" and how he was convinced, even "if it be heresy," that God trained many preachers of this type without benefit of a seminary education:

In the morning I listened to a sermon from a genuine backwoodsman. . . . I listened to his sermon with unbounded amazement, and, I
may add, delight. It was a mystery to me how one so unlettered and
so unlearned in all religious reading except the Bible—and, in the nature of the case, but poorly versed in that—could have acquired
thoughts so sensible and good. It was a greater mystery how he could
clothe them in such appropriate language. Both his thoughts and his
words flowed as freely as the stream near by, and they had great power
to arrest the attention and move the hearts of his hearers. It was the
power of undoubted sincerity and burning zeal; it was the power of
one with superior natural endowments stirred to their profoundest
depths, and, beyond all question, taught of God. . . . If it be heresy, I
am so heretical as to believe that God has other methods of training
some men—yea, many men—to be useful ministers of the Gospel than
by filling their heads with Latin, Hebrew, and Greek. (pp. 177–78)

Emphasis on the "heart" and "feelings" abounded in Pierson's accounts of
religious life in the Appalachian wilderness. Once again, Pierson felt compelled to comment on the gifts of one who was "beyond all question, taught
of God," someone who "had great power to . . . move the hearts of his hearers." Pierson's "heresy"—a word not too strong in this instance—was in recognizing and affirming that "God has other methods of training some men—
yea, many men—to be useful ministers of the Gospel" than by the model of
the learned ministry, "filling their heads," so revered in his own Presbyterian tradition that believed right reason and rational persuasion were the only
reliable avenues to a genuinely and permanently changed heart.

Like the Congregationalist John C. Campbell after him, Pierson was
unafraid to declare that mountain preachers like this "backwoodsman" were
truly preachers of the Gospel, preaching extemporaneous sermons of "great
power," expressing "thoughts so sensible and good" and "of undoubted sincerity," reaching "profound depths" and causing in outsiders open to them
"unbounded amazement"—and "delight." These preachers, said Pierson,
though they too were "so unlettered and so unlearned," were "beyond all
question, taught of God," a God who "has other methods of training some
men" that do not conform to the ministerial standards and approval—and
religious vanity—of a more sophisticated world whose values and worldview
had long since been radically contrary to the values and worldview upholding the religious life of the people in the Brush.

Pierson also explored worship practices characteristic in the Brush that
were and continued to be normative for mountain religious life. He wrote
of "basket-meetings" that were "established institutions," meetings held over
Saturday and Sunday where people traveling some distance would bring their
cooked provisions in baskets and stay overnight in nearby cabins (p. 60).

"Basket-meetings" were somewhat of a cross between "a big meeting" or a short-term revival lasting over Saturday and Sunday and "dinner on the ground" after Sunday worship.

As Howard Dorgan wrote of the tradition among Old Regular Baptists of "singing down the preacher," where the first preacher in a worship service would create such exuberance in the congregation that an elder would line a hymn and preaching, singing, and shouting would take place simultaneously,[11] Pierson wrote of the same phenomenon:

> We had been joined at the church by a "local preacher" who had formerly served in the ranks of itinerancy, but had "located" in this neighborhood, and, after years of almost gratuitous service in the ministry, was now supporting himself and family by carrying on a small tannery and store. This old itinerant preached the morning sermon. He was a man of strong muscular frame, heavy voice, and great experience and power in moving the feelings of his hearers. In the midst of his sermon a woman sitting near me sprang up to her feet, threw her arms in the air, and shouted, "Glory! Hallelujah!" and jumped up and down, clapping her hands and shouting until she sank exhausted upon the floor. Soon another and then another, until a large part of the audience was shouting in this manner. The preacher's face fairly glowed with joy, and his voice arose louder and louder as the people were more and more moved; and there was a general blending of songs, prayers and vociferous shouts. At length, with singing, prayer and a general shaking of hands, they closed what was to them a very delightful meeting. (pp. 175–76)

Pierson did not indicate to which church tradition this "local preacher" belonged "who had formerly served in the ranks of itinerancy," now giving "almost gratuitous service in the ministry." He may likely have been Methodist, or Cumberland Presbyterian, or some variety of Baptist, but this was of little import overall to those gathered for preaching. What mattered, as we have seen repeatedly throughout this book, was that "He was a man of . . . great experience and power in moving the feelings of his hearers." Pierson's failure to identify the religious background of "[t]his old itinerant" in an otherwise detailed description of his preaching and its effect on its listeners may have been mirroring people's indifference to what church tradition a preacher belonged, for, as Dora Woodruff Cope said of mountain people in her oral account of her life during the first four decades of the twentieth century, "Appalachian people were not 'joiners.' They felt no allegiance to any particular denomination so long as they felt they were preaching the Word of God."

Like Pierson in the 1850s, Cope recounted of religious life nearly a century later, "They [Appalachian people] didn't feel it necessary to designate a

four-walled structure and paint a label over the door before they could practice their religious beliefs,"[12] an observation which ties directly into the
amount of attention Pierson paid first to the autonomy and richness of worship life in private households and the local compass of residents outside
the doors of a church house or worship conducted by preachers. As we have
discussed often, people were responsible for, and took responsibility for, their
own worship lives. Like the early Scots-Irish, they did not require or "feel it
necessary" to have the formal sanctions of the institutional church of organized religion "before they could practice their beliefs" among themselves
in their immediate community of family, neighbors, and visitors.

The tradition of the love feast, testifying at a service about what God's
grace has meant in your life, and the accompanying tradition of shaking
hands, normative to all mountain worship services, did not escape Pierson's
notice. Indeed, he wrote, "Hand-shaking among brethren and embracing
among sisters formed a very prominent part in the religious services of these
people in the Brush." Pierson recounted a love feast presided over by a Cumberland Presbyterian, whom Pierson did not identify one way or another as
a preacher, strongly suggesting that he may simply have been a recognized
religious leader within the church community. About the love feast itself,
Pierson emphasized the personal vulnerability of those gathered, centering
on expressions of love and affection for one another, manifested by the ubiquitous handshake and the nearly as frequent hug and embrace, especially
among the women.

> There was nothing to me unusual and noteworthy in the meetings
> except in the love-feast on Sabbath morning. The first to speak was my
> host, a warm-hearted, earnest man, a Cumberland Presbyterian, who
> spoke of the goodness of God to him and of his love to all the follow-
> ers of Christ, and then started out and shook hands with nearly every
> one in the house, continuing his fervent remarks and ejaculations dur-
> ing all the hand-shaking. Next, a sister spoke and started in the same
> manner, shaking hands with the brethren, and throwing her arms
> around the sisters and embracing them in the warmest manner. Near-
> ly all who followed them went through these same demonstrations.
> They not only sang,
>
> > "Now here's my heart, and here's my hand,
> > To meet you in that heavenly land,"
>
> but they gave the cordial and often long-continued grasp. As the ex-
> periences, prayers, songs, and shouting became more and more ani-
> mated and exciting, the hand-shaking became more general, until near-
> ly the entire congregation, in larger or smaller groups or numbers, were
> shaking each other by the hand, keeping time in their movements to
> the wild Western melody they were singing. (pp. 183–84)

This tradition of tactility—not being afraid to touch each other in worship with genuine feeling—is still highly pronounced in mountain churches of the Appalachian region, from independent Holiness to Old Regular Baptist.

Because tactility, touching, is so important to worship services, and has such a long tradition in the mountains, mountain people have their own norms and unspoken guidelines for where individuals can touch and how, so that this loving tradition in worship that is supposed to signify a little bit of heaven in the here and now—what social relationships are supposed to be like—is not corrupted by inappropriate behavior. Its meaning is embodied in the hymn couplet Pierson recorded, "Now here's my heart, and here's my hand / To meet you in that heavenly land." By literally giving their hands to each other in worship, and by hugging and embracing with deep emotion, and often kissing, mountain people are giving their hearts, an act of profound faith boldly embodying their "hope of heaven."

Emma Bell Miles's account of the right hand of fellowship in Brother Absalom's service at the turn into the twentieth century mirrored Pierson's from fifty years before. Miles wrote, "The preacher's voice strikes through the words of the song with encouraging shouts of goodwill; the singers throng and press about him on the floor, grasping hands right and left. . . . Tears are running down seamed and withered faces now. . . . [T]he tune changes again, and yet again—they do not tire of this. . . . 'Glory to God, my soul's happy!' It is a woman's scream that rings high over all. Several break into sobbing; the woman throws herself down with her head and arms across a bench. One touches her in a friendly fashion; the rest sing on."[13] Howard Dorgan's keen field observations from the 1970s and 1980s presented in his *Giving Glory to God in Appalachia* and *The Old Regular Baptists of Central Appalachia* on the still ubiquitous tradition of shaking hands and warmly embracing (in no way limited only to women), without fear of showing deep personal affection and regard, bring us up to the present and full circle from Pierson's accounts of what was by the 1850s truly a regional religious tradition embodied by the worship services and everyday religious life of his people in the Brush.

Pierson also observed the tradition of footwashing, and remarked briefly, "We passed a church where the members washed one another's feet at each communion. I made some inquiries in regard to the ceremony, and he told me the brethren wash only the brethren's feet, and the sisters the sisters' feet. I told him that I supposed they only sprinkled water upon their feet—they did not wash much. 'Oh!' said he, 'sometimes they gets happy, and washes right hard'" (pp. 255–56). Footwashing as Pierson would imagine it from the perspective of his Presbyterian background did not factor in the ideal of a genuine joy in a worship practice embodying the highly esteemed value of humility, a value of very long heritage in the mountains where, as Broth-

work attributed to Jonathan Cross, titled *Five Years in the Alleghanies* (1863). Cross (1802–76) was born on the border of western Virginia (West Virginia) and western Pennsylvania. He was a Presbyterian colporteur for the American Tract Society who called himself on the last page of his text, "THE PIONEER COLPORTEUR IN THE ALLEGHANY MOUNTAINS."[14] Whether or not his claim was correct, the volume Cross produced was far more typical of the era. His text was very focused on a precise accounting of the number of tracts distributed and the number of conversions secured. Emphasizing a religion that highly valued quantification and quantity, Cross's account had none of the richness or insight of Pierson's and can be mined today for very few narrative details. In places his text was somewhat contentious when talking about Roman Catholics and others not in support of his work in the region.

Cross's book is mentioned here because of the contrast it provides to Pierson and the extent to which it points up the value of Pierson's contribution to understanding religious life and traditions in the mountains of Appalachia during the era when Appalachia was, for the first time, clearly a geographic region with its own integrity, marked by characterizing sociocultural features that made it and its people distinctive on a now very different, expanded American landscape. These same features, Pierson himself said at the beginning of his book, made targets out of people in the Brush who, in a later generation, would be called "mountaineers." The people of the Appalachian wilderness, said Pierson, were "largely the subjects of exaggeration and caricature" by those who had "[c]omparatively little . . . extended personal contact with, and intimate personal knowledge of, the people." This egregious pattern in popular literature, commentary, and scholarship would prevail overwhelmingly for yet another century and beyond, setting the tone and determining the conclusions consumed by the national culture about mountain people and mountain religion. This pattern would not be challenged (it has yet to be broken) until the emergence of Appalachian studies in the 1960s, and later, in the 1980s, by an emerging religious studies perspective on mountain religious life and history that is still only beginning to define itself.

Pierson's book on the Appalachian wilderness in the 1850s marked the period by which there was finally a clearly established Appalachian identity in terms of its people's cultural landscape and their own cultural self-consciousness. That internal identity clashed in two short decades with a quickly established external Appalachian identity as "A Strange Land and Peculiar People," a view based on prejudice and stereotype, created and promoted by "outsiders" as popular entertainment, junk food for the national consciousness. Pierson was not about the business of "exaggeration and caricature" that informed (if that be the word) the popular portrayal of Appalachia and its people christened in the 1870s, though its antecedents were extensive. Instead, Pierson presented the Appalachian identity that the "generous and large-hearted" people whose tables and shelter and worship he shared for many years would recognize to be true, at least in large part, to who they really were.

Pierson believed that the unique "state of civilization" of these "generous and large-hearted" people was rapidly disappearing, which was his primary motive for writing *In the Brush:* "Here I have drawn word-pictures of many scenes in the social life of a generation, and a state of civilization, rapidly passing away, never to reappear, that otherwise would have no memorial only as perpetuated in the traditions of the people" (p. 11). But with respect to mountain people's worship practices, belief systems, and church traditions that remain unique and special to the mountains and small valleys of the Appalachian region today, Pierson was wrong to assume that they were "rapidly passing away, never to reappear." His beautifully written volume is more than a "memorial" to a people and a regional religious tradition that stole his heart. Pierson's *In the Brush* is testimony to the living lineage of a mode of religious life that continues to endure, even as others persist in calling out warnings that it is in danger of immediate demise.

---------------------------------- 17 ----------------------------------

A Christian America
and the Appalachian "Problem"

By the late nineteenth century, the people of Pierson's *In the Brush* were called "mountaineers." The external Appalachian identity of "exaggeration and caricature" Pierson named, which crystallized in the early 1870s, fueled earlier denominational perceptions of the region and its people, turning missions to mountain people into a cause. "Exaggeration and caricature" thus stimulated and informed home mission efforts among the "mountaineers," who were themselves white, Christian, and of the same ethnic and religious heritages as the missionaries. One of the prevailing themes of home missions to the mountain people of Appalachia during this era was that "they are part of us, our very own, and we must bring them home. Our Christian duty demands it." That theme was defined—and justified—by the Christian America movement.

Home missionaries typically divided Appalachian people into "Two Classes of Mountaineers," as Homer McMillan of the Presbyterian Church, U.S., wrote in *"Unfinished Tasks" of the Southern Presbyterian Church* (1922)—a title that says a lot about its treatment of mountain people:

> It would not be correct to consider all the people residing in the mountains as the objects of missionary effort. . . . The population of this vast mountain region is divided into two distinct classes, as far removed in character and environment as it is possible for people to be. First, there are those who live in fertile valleys along the rivers and the railways, with the very best religious and educational advantages, and who are equal in intelligence and refinement to any people in America. . . . But the people with whom the missionary has to do, . . . do not live in these favored valleys, but far back from the main lines of travel in small clearings by the water courses, almost entirely removed from the outside world, with few advantages for learning and few opportunities for improvement. The extreme poor live "back of beyond," beyond the towering mountains, locked in narrow coves, without teachers, without physicians, without comforts and conveniences, and without any contact with outside civilization.[1]

There are no mountains without valleys, and no valleys without mountains. The valley people of Appalachia were also technically "mountaineers," according to McMillan and others, but they were now clearly distinct from—indeed, at odds with—the people of the mountains, who alone were the subjects of home missionary efforts.

Nearly a century after Schermerhorn first made the evaluation in 1814 about the divide in the Old Southwest between people living in valleys and county seats versus those occupying the outlying regions, S. L. Morris, of the southern Presbyterians, wrote in 1904 that the valley people of Appalachia were obviously "[t]he higher type, . . . intelligent, cultivated and educated people who will compare favorably with any section of the world." However, Morris went on in the same paragraph to write an archetypical home missions sketch of mountain people: "The typical mountaineer occupies his rude cabin on mountainside or sequestered cove without associations with the outside world, with no advantages of learning and no opportunities of improvement, without ambition in life, leading an aimless, careless, thriftless existence, in attainments and character on a level with the cracker of the backwoods and the factory element of towns."[2]

Morris loudly echoed Timothy Dwight's words from nearly a century before about "*foresters* or *Pioneers*" who "cannot live in regular society," expressing unabated attitudes that were grounded in a profound mutual distrust between and within regions. Recall that Dwight wrote about "*foresters* or *Pioneers*" of his own region in his *Travels; in New-England and New-York* (1821–22), "They are too idle; too talkative; too passionate; too prodigal; and shiftless; to acquire either property or character. They are impatient about the restraints of law, religion, and morality."[3] Unlike Morris's "typical mountaineer," foreshadowed by Dwight, Appalachia's valley people were "the higher type" (Morris); they had "the very best religious and educational advantages, . . . equal in intelligence and refinement to any people in America" (McMillan), meaning the home missionaries themselves. Home missionaries and Appalachia's valley people also belonged to the same denominations; they identified and were comfortable with each other. The other people, the mountain people—with their peculiar ways and even more peculiar religious culture—were expressly in need of ministrations from the Christian (meaning Protestant) churches of the outside world, ostensibly because of their poverty and isolation, but also for reasons that distinguished these white American Protestants from other population groups targeted for home missions.

A large part of the mythology enveloping mountain people that provoked strong sentiments of support for home missions to them—and which home mission agencies did not hesitate to invoke—was that mountain people were seen to be the purest of the pure in racial stock, the very essence of what it meant to be of Anglo-Saxon heritage in America, isolated by God and circumstance to be the keepers of the flame of America's colonial era. Indeed, this was the clarion call of home missions to Appalachia throughout the late nineteenth century and into the early twentieth. Contrary to his portrait of the "typical mountaineer," Morris also wrote in 1904, "Their descendants [of the Scots-Irish] still occupy their mountain home, and like a gulf stream, a distinct river in the midst of the sea, these Highlanders have kept themselves aloof from the rest of the country, *a distinct race of people*. Immigration flowing in from all nationalities have corrupted the purity of our Anglo-Saxon stock, but immigration has never touched the life of the mountaineer. These isolated mountaineers are the best Anglo-Saxon stock, of the blood and tradition of heroes, 'the only portion of our population that retains pure and undefiled the Americanism of Colonial times,'"[4] demonstrating the popularity of these claims at the time with words taken from Theodore Roosevelt's *The Winning of the West* (1900).

Presbyterians such as Morris equated Scots-Irish with Anglo-Saxon heritage—indeed, the terms were frequently interchangeable, as in this passage—rehearsing the heritage of so many mountain people in Scots-Irish Presbyterianism over and over again in their home missions literature. Morris's racial and patriotic grounds for home missions to mountain people reverberated throughout home mission writings of all denominations, North and South, as Victor Irvine Masters of the Southern Baptist Convention wrote in *The Home Mission Task* (1912), "Who are the 'mountain people' then? They are simply the descendents of the best folks who came to America."[5]

The theme of "bringing them home" cast home missions to mountain people in an entirely different light from home missions to nonwhites and non-Christians—including Catholics and Mormons. It was a matter of saving kith and kin who were "the best Anglo-Saxon stock" from the state into which they had fallen. That fallen state was identified not just with social needs and economic conditions but with religion. Mountain people's unbudging resistance to "come back home," especially in matters of religion, outraged their now-distant cousins and would-be benefactors. The extremity of the reaction to mountain people's resistance was more than that of the responsible, concerned relative watching family members once-removed persist in their self-destructive ways—although home missionaries cast it as such. Instead, it was a clash of religious values whereby seeing themselves "as they used to be" (in Dickerson's words), they were also seeing themselves as they had become through mountain people's eyes. By judging mountain people and their religion, home missionaries were forced to judge themselves and their own religion through mountain people's shared heritage with them and staunch resistance to them.

A succession of other movements determining the particular "spin" for their era of home missions to Appalachia into the last decade of the twentieth century betrayed the same underlying motivations for resolving this fundamental contradiction in their midst—despite later theological shifts in vocabulary for articulating goals that today emphasize appreciation of "diversity," in contrast to the late nineteenth-century ideal of homogeneity. All home missions to Appalachia would reiterate the same basic themes, based on the perception that the mountains of Appalachia and the cultural landscape of its people made up a unique and distinctive region in American consciousness. That core perception would be expressed through different themes promoted for public consumption, whether as the preservers of "the purity of our Anglo-Saxon stock," as home mission officials such as Morris articulated it at the turn of the century, or as a "quilt" and "an heirloom" to the nation as a whole, today a very popular motif (with strong historical echoes highlighting Appalachia's perceived traditionalism) that a publication of the Reformed Church in America employed in an article, "The Work in Appalachia," appearing in its September 1992 issue.[6]

The various strategies for resolving the contradiction of mountain people and their religion launched the process by which American Protestantism's home missions movement to Appalachia, beginning especially in the early 1880s through the defining impetus of the Christian America movement, first attempted consciously and systematically to overcome mountain people and their religion. The goal of those initial strategies was the "normalization" or absorption of mountain people into the national culture and the national religion of American Protestantism, and the "exploitation" (which this era used as a nonpejorative) or absorption of the natural wealth of the region into the national economy. This goal was to be achieved through the complementary interaction of the Christian America movement and industrialization, both of which upheld the shared value of "modernization."

In 1909 H. Paul Douglass published a book for the Executive Committee of the American Missionary Association of the Congregational Church, titled *Christian Reconstruction in the South*. In this study Douglass devoted two lengthy chapters to home mission work in Appalachia, "The Old Men of the Mountains" and "The Passing of the Mountaineer."[7] At the beginning of the second chapter Douglass wrote, "Presiding over the future of the mountains are two ominous characters, the millionaire and the missionary. . . . The mountaineer is not so much to-day the man who has been left alone as he is the man whom we will not leave alone. For the wealth of mineral and of timber which these mountains hold, but especially for the wealth of labor power, industry is fast penetrating their most inaccessible nooks and corners. The industrial exploitation of the mountains is far advanced, and with it the passing of the mountaineer."[8] In this brief statement Douglass appeared to be making a radical critique of the industrial revolution and the missionary invasion that came upon the Appalachian region beginning around 1890, when timber and coal were being discovered. Capitalist entrepreneurs quickly bought up the mineral and timber rights to the land from its native residents at unimaginable rates of less than one dollar an acre. Unlike the entrepreneurs, mountain people had no clue of the bounty beneath their feet or how it would be harvested. This spelled disaster for the region's future, but its seeds had been planted decades earlier.

By the time of the Civil War, Appalachia or the Old Southwest was seen mostly as the quiet backcountry of the South, a peripheral region paralleling the peripheralization of the Lowlands of western Scotland.[9] Western Scotland, home of the Scots-Irish who inhabited Ulster and were to populate Appalachia in such large numbers, was seen as a buffer zone between the "wild," "savage" Highlands of Scotland and the economic core of "civilized" England. The Scots-Irish of western Scotland were seen as intermediate dwellers of a peripheral region, a version of both the Highlands and England, and an objectionable version to both. The Old Southwest of the United States prior to the Civil War was seen as a similar buffer zone between the "wild," "savage" West or exterior zone occupied by Native Americans and the "civilized" economic core of the East. Mountain people were at once "dark twins" of Native Americans—savages and barbarians—and "contemporary ancestors" of the dominant society—immature yet noble.

After the Civil War, Appalachia went through a more advanced stage of peripheralization. During Reconstruction, and just prior to the region's industrial revolution, Appalachia was still seen as a buffer zone between North and South, belonging more to the South, yet not really of it. With the advent of industrialization in the Appalachian region, it became a buffer zone of a different sort, a boundary between industrial society and nonindustrial society, a "subjugated fringe." Now Appalachian people were on the entirely wrong side of the "frontier"; the stereotypes already imposed upon them only intensified. Well into the late twentieth century, Appalachia and Appalachian people, especially mountain people, continued to be stereotyped in the popular media, and consequently often in the American consciousness, as a subjugated fringe. Images have had a narrow range, from the feudism of the Hatfields and McCoys to the chilling violence of James Dickey's *Deliverance,* and from Li'l Abner and Snuffy Smith in the comic strips to *The Beverly Hillbillies* and *Hee Haw* on television—a range from the dangerous to the ridiculous—with dulcimers and quilts helping to feed the popular craving for "traditional" Appalachian crafts.

Religious sensibilities expressed in worship practices and belief systems have had a profound continuity from the time Pierson wrote *In the Brush* about Appalachia in the 1850s up to the present. This continuity has given many observers the impression of stasis, which in turn reinforces the notion that traditionalism and an unchanging milieu support mountain religious culture, resulting in yet another destructive stereotype—that mountain people and mountain religion are passive, regressive, even fatalistic. But with the advent of industrial capitalism or economic "modernization" in the region, all of mountain culture underwent permanent restructuring. Farm properties were bought up en masse by entrepreneurs from outside of the region for timber and mining companies or to be included in national forests and parks. In 1880, the mountain farm had been the sole source of income. By 1930 most mountain farms were at best, in Ron Eller's phrase, "part-time units of production," supplemented by work in industrial communities or company towns.[10] Town populations increased fourfold, nonfarm rural populations twofold, and farm populations by only 5 percent. Traditional status structures in Appalachian communities were supplanted by economic structures which introduced into highland culture rigid class systems that controlled jobs and local politics.

Eller wrote, "Behind this transition in political culture lay the integration of the region into the national economy and the subordination of local interests to those of outside corporations."[11] People were dislodged from their ancestral homes in large numbers, many relocating in mill and coal towns, paying rent to absentee landlords. Rising land values made any dreams of returning to the home place an impossibility. By 1930 mountain people had been integrated into a new industrial system on which they were economically dependent. The driving poverty of the Appalachian region, especially central Appalachia (the heart of coal country), which helped to ignite the War on Poverty in the 1960s, was not due to the region's lack of modernization. It was instead, as Eller has made clear in his *Miners, Millhands, and Mountaineers* (1982), a product of the type of industrial modernization to which the region was subjected during the years from 1880 to 1930, the era when the Christian America movement and then the Social Gospel defined home missions to Appalachia.

Home missionaries who began to come into the region in great numbers during the last two decades of the nineteenth century saw industrial modernization as their friend, and a friend of mountain people. Missionaries believed that much of their task was to help mountain people adapt to the changes in their lives brought on by industrialization. As William Warren Sweet wrote, "The most significant single influence in organized religion in the United States from about the year 1880 to the end of the century and beyond was the tremendous increase in wealth in the nation."[12] That "tremendous increase in wealth in the nation" was about the industrial revolution defining the era. Although mountain people had enormous wealth through their natural resources, it was not a wealth from which most of them would benefit. Both their wealth and its potential benefits were abrogated by outside interests which superseded mountain people in achieving control over that wealth. That control came in the guise of "modernization."

For home missionaries in the Appalachian region during this period, to modernize was to uplift, to uplift was to Christianize, to Christianize was to Americanize. Modern life was the "better way." Modernization went hand in hand with the task of creating a unified, homogeneous Christian nation, a Christian America. The strategy for achieving a Christian America was to integrate "unassimilated" populations into what was perceived to be the mainstream of American life, a mainstream that was defined mostly by the culture of the industrialized East. Mountain people were identified as an unassimilated population at the same time that industrialization was taking place in the region. Bringing mountain people "back home" was a romantic device, a wolf in sheep's clothing. It distracted from and masked the motivation of assimilation into the dominant religious culture, as well as into the socioeconomic world of "modern" America. It had to do with dominion over mountain people and their land, driven by the engines of capitalism, of money, not simply the desire to help lost cousins regain their footing in the world of today.

Both "the millionaire and the missionary" were interdependent in mountainous Appalachia during this time. The missionary exonerated the millionaire's exploitation of the region's natural and human resources by deeming necessary the "progress" the millionaire brought to the mountains. The millionaire, by bringing "progress" to the mountains, gave even greater urgency to the missionary's task of Christianizing/Americanizing mountain people as an unassimilated population. The continuity and integrity of religious culture in Appalachia's mountain regions throughout this period and reaching into the present is a statement in itself about the nature of regional religion. It is important to look at Appalachian mountain religion and understand it as a regional religious tradition because the regionalism identified with mountain religious life and history was created in large part by a difference in religious values. The values that define mountain religion today persisted despite the irreversible changes—the economic and sociocultural upheavals—in the lives of mountain people created by the advent of the region's peripheralization as an industrial "colony" beginning around 1880.

Douglass's seeming critique of the "ominous characters" of "the millionaire and the missionary" was illuminated by his concluding statement at the end of his chapter on "The Passing of the Mountaineer": "The cooperation of missionary and millionaire has hastened the passing of the mountaineer. The future, material and spiritual, was safe in the hands of their joint product, the normally equipped American. Thus, locality by locality, the mountains cease to present a national problem, needing the ministries of special nationalizing agencies. What was merely temporary backwardness in their peculiar life is left behind; the rest, bad and good, merges with the common life of the nation."[13] Douglass's earlier language about "ominous characters," about the mountaineer "whom we will not leave alone," and the passing of the mountaineer due to "industrial exploitation" was turned on its head. Douglass saw "the passing of the mountaineer" as good; the "joint product" of the millionaire and the missionary who tended to the mountaineer's "material and spiritual future" was the "normally equipped American," someone who "merges with the common life of the nation." Home mission agencies working in the region were described as "special nationalizing agencies," dealing with the mountains of the Appalachian region as "a national problem."

What was the problem? Mountain people, like the African-American Southerners to whom Douglass devoted most of his book, were, in his words, "un-Americanized" or "under-Americanized."[14] An Americanized people were a people who were assimilated into a homogeneous nation, a Christian America. In order not to be a "problem," an "exceptional population," mountain people, like black people, needed to be assimilated into what was perceived to be the mainstream of American life, a life benefited by the progress, modernization, and wealth of the industrial revolution. Douglass's concluding statement showed that his archetype of the millionaire and the missionary accepted as a perverse good the annihilation of a people's culture and natural environment and their economic oppression by outside interests not accountable for the local consequences of their actions. This perverse good never achieved the moral status of being considered a necessary evil. The millionaire and the missionary had few compelling ethical qualms about their treatment of Appalachia's land and its people. No one doubted the benefits mountain people especially were supposed to reap through their "nationalization" by realizing their ideal "future" as part of an ideal type called "the normally equipped American," thus overcoming their problematic, unassimilated condition as "the typical mountaineer" (Morris).

True to nineteenth-century American Protestantism's primary focus on moral reform and social benevolence, most of the home missionaries who came into the Appalachian mountains at the end of the nineteenth century, and even to the end of the twentieth, were committed more to social uplift through education, health care, and social services than they were to evangelization, although evangelization certainly played a large part. The immediate precursor to social uplift endeavors by home missionaries among "mountain whites" was the post–Civil War labors of home missionaries among the "freedmen" or freed slaves of the South. The American Missionary Association of the Congregational Church was foremost in these endeavors. Of all the denominations of American Protestantism active among the freedmen and later mountain people, the Congregationalists were the most nonsectarian. Yet their organizational structure and earliest history in "mountain white work" are among the most representative of how Appalachia and mountain religion were perceived by denominational home mission agencies, and so provide a useful case study.

Three agencies that before the Civil War were nondenominational became agencies of the Congregational churches in 1865—the American Missionary Association (AMA), the American Home Missionary Society (AHMS), and the American Board of Commissioners for Foreign Missions. These agencies then redistributed their work of evangelization among themselves. The American Board was responsible for foreign missions, the AHMS for the work of establishing churches and seed money for ministers among the white population in the West, and the AMA was responsible for "colored" work, mainly among African Americans of the South and Native Americans—and soon enough to other racial groups in America, from Alaskan to "Porto Rican" to Hawaiian. The American Missionary Association had been strongly abolitionist before the Civil War and maintained its work among the freedmen during Reconstruction. Prior to the Civil War, it had also been involved among the white population, especially in eastern Kentucky, promoting antislavery sentiments.

John G. Fee, an AMA home missionary in the area, founded Berea College in the late 1850s, originally as an abolitionist school for biracial education. By the turn into the twentieth century, Berea College would be committed to educating the children of mountain people in Appalachia, demonstrating in microcosm the post–Civil War shift from home mission work among southern blacks to "mountain whites." The southern work— the evangelization and Americanization of the South, white and black— shifted focus almost by necessity to encompass southern mountain work. Southern white church populations were extremely hostile to the work of northern churches among blacks and among themselves. The fact that many northern church leaders had declared after the Civil War that the South should be considered an "unchurched" area open to northern evangelization only intensified southern white alienation and resentment.

Work among the freedmen was an insurmountable barrier to the work among southern white populations. Southern mountain work provided a convenient exception to the race problem for northern churches attempting to evangelize the South. Because of what was perceived to be Appalachia's traditional antislavery posture and pro-Union support during the Civil War, work among mountain people of the southern uplands maintained without compromise the traditional "anticaste" commitment of the Congregationalists in particular. The Congregationalists soon transferred much of their attempts to evangelize southern whites to evangelization among mountain whites. The AMA's earlier work among white people in Kentucky and elsewhere during their pre–Civil War abolitionist efforts was seen as a historical precedent for the AMA to take over white work among mountain people, rather than allow the AHMS that province.[15] The AMA did take over southern mountain work and the result of this move was to place the mountain people of Appalachia among the exceptional populations of "colored" groups, unlike any other group of white Americans to whom home missions were committed.[16] Such a result put into an entirely different light the meaning behind the home missions' conceit that mountain people were "the best Anglo-Saxon stock."

Appalachia's perceived antislavery posture and anticaste commitment were a theme reiterated right up to the end of the nineteenth century by AMA officials reporting on the need for and value of their home mission endeavors in the region. How they cast that theme exemplified the norms and goals of the Christian America movement. District Secretary Roy presented an address titled "Americans of the Midland Mountains"—that is, about the mountain people of Appalachia—at the annual meeting of the American Missionary Association in October 1891. His use of the terms "Americans" and especially "midland" was strategic for his purposes. Roy expounded upon four reasons for continuing home mission work among mountain people: "1. On account of their isolation they have retained much of the heredity, of the instincts, the habits of our colonialism."[17] "2. These mountaineers are rich in the heredity of patriotism" (p. 86). "3. These mountaineers also have the heredity of anti-slavery sentiment" (p. 88). And finally, "4. These mountaineers have also had a marked religious heritage" (p. 89). Roy continued, "Now, then, a people with such heredity of colonialism, of patriotism, of anti-slavery sentiment, and of religious life, furnish the best material for the best American citizenship, and they are found to be in affinity with the best things we can take to them of the Christian Civilization." Roy's address represented an argument for the less common emphasis on the "Appalachian promise," undertoning the more common focus on the "Appalachian problem."

Appalachia's promise, a version of which Roy summarized so well, was seen to await the beneficent actions of Protestant denominations which firmly believed that they had a responsibility to "take" to mountain people "the best things we can . . . of the Christian Civilization." Roy made very clear that he found Appalachia's "marked religious heritage," which he identified with the mountains, to be lacking within the broader scheme of "the Christian Civilization," which meant the nationally dominant religious culture that the denominations of American Protestantism represented. Unlike his first three reasons for why Congregationalists should continue home mission work in the mountains, Roy qualified the fourth by declaring that mountain people "have also *had*"—in past tense—"a marked religious heritage," thus implying a devolution or deterioration, but not a continuation or an ongoing development. This implication went hand in hand with the myth of mountain people's standing still in time, which Roy voiced in his first reason for continuing home missions to mountain people by affirming their supposed preservation of the old-time values of America's colonial period made possible, he claimed, by the region's "isolation."

Roy did have praise for the positive qualities of the remaining vestiges of mountain people's "marked religious heritage," stating, "The higher criticism has never risen so high as to reach their mountain homes and churches. They reverence the Bible. A 'Thus saith the Lord' is enough for them. There is scarcely any infidelity to be found there. A man who holds such views loses caste among them." But Roy saw fatal flaws that prevented mountain people from aspiring to the more ennobling values of "the Christian Civilization" of American Protestantism, concluding, "True their piety has now come to have much of religiosity—many denominations, many spasmodic revivals, too little of intelligence. It needs more of the resultant of good character, more of an experience that is permanent and spiritually uplifting" (p. 89). Roy's address specifically applied what was at the time the most common assumptions of the Christian America movement about mountain religion. Mountain "piety" had too "much of religiosity" (sectarianism and emotionalism) and "too little of intelligence" (rationalism). Roy's statement that mountain "piety" needed "more of an experience that is permanent" was a direct hit on the conversion traditions at the heart of mountain religious life, where the experience of personal and communal conversion was episodic, renewed and strengthened time and again throughout mountain people's earthly pilgrimage. Nonetheless, mountain people were seen as "furnishing the best material," in Roy's estimation, meaning that they were perceived to be basically good raw "material" for the goals of American Protestantism. Behind it all was the commonplace opinion exemplified by Roy's remarks that mountain people were immature yet noble, bearing much potential for the greater good of the dominant society into which Appalachia and mountain people's cultural institutions must be insinuated—for their own sake as well as for the sake of the nation.

Indeed, Roy, unlike all but a few other denominational leaders, envisioned the mountains of the Appalachian region as an "example," said Roy, to the "Cotton States" and as a healing, reconciling bridge between North and South. Roy concluded his remarks on the "Midland Mountains" by saying:

> In the further South our no-caste principle as yet is not accepted, and so we cannot do much work among its white people. It has not disappeared from the mountains; but it yields more readily to reason. . . . Push on the meritorious work, and by and by you will have brought the whole into a grand alliance of the North and South, with the midway mountains [Appalachia] coalescing the whole, healing the hurt of the daughter of our people, and so combining the good elements on both sides to resist the encroachments of infidelity and destructive

socialism. Then, indeed, shall we know all parts of our dear country as one land, and all its peoples as one in the brotherhood of Christ Jesus. (p. 90)

Roy's hopeful scenario had the distinction of casting the Appalachian mountains and their people in a "healing" role, "coalescing the whole," "combining the good elements on both sides," North and South.

Roy's positive analysis of "Americans of the Midland Mountains" was a clear variation on the more negative "buffer zone" position usually assigned to Appalachia. The vision of transforming good Roy invested in mountain people of the Appalachian region, bringing the nation together as "one land," was centered on the Congregationalists' "no-caste principle," distinguishing mountain people from the white populations of the "Cotton States," even though mountain people were also rural, with their region typically identified as the mountainous variation on the South. The Congregationalists' revered "no-caste principle" was one of the most important issues of social benevolence promoted by American Protestantism in the North before and after the Civil War.

Roy's late nineteenth-century vision of Appalachia's positive contribution, indeed, its crucial role in healing a nation still divided over race relations, almost stood alone as a clearly formulated position. Appalachia and its mountain people would be seen far more commonly not as a balm but as a burr in the hide of the nation, especially at the national, denominational level where home mission policies were institutionalized, as well as by other Protestant home missionaries in the field. Ellen Myers, a Congregationalist home missionary to eastern Kentucky in the early 1880s, had already described the region as being in imminent danger of becoming "a fretting leprosy in our nation" and declared that only home missionaries were the antidote. Her warning was especially directed toward the perceived danger of religious life distinctive to Appalachia's mountain people, a danger to which Roy himself had given much milder voice in lieu of his vision of Appalachia's larger healing role in the nation connected to issues of race relations.

The earliest item in the AMA's *American Missionary Magazine* to identify potential work among the mountain people of eastern Kentucky—and hence Appalachia—for their own sake, rather than for the sake of abolitionist and later "anticaste" interests, appeared in the January 1860 issue, in a letter by J. C. Richardson of Williamsburg, Whitley County, Kentucky, near the Cumberland Gap. Richardson wrote, "There is a vast amount of coal, timber, and water power, which may yet be used to great advantage. . . . The people are *hardy, industrious, generous,* and *brave.* . . . What a blessing to the country, if people from the North—farmers, mechanics, machinists, teachers, and ministers would come and help this people build up good society, good schools, and a pure Christianity. I am thankful that a few have made the sacrifice to come into the field to labor as missionaries, without waiting for colonies. . . . *Who will come over into* THIS MACEDONIA, *and he'p us?*"[18] This missionary's call for colonization was clear and unabashed. Recognition of the region's natural resources—its "coal, timber, and water power"—and the benefits "ministers" and "missionaries" as part of the "colonies" of "people from the North" would provide mountain people was unequivocal in this early account.

Richardson combined his call for industrial exploitation of the region's natural resources and labor power with introduction into the region of "a pure Christianity," suggesting an "impure Christianity"—if Richardson recognized any at all—already present in the mountains. Richardson's letter coincided with the beginnings of the thirty-year period when Protestant hopes for the triumph of "Christian civilization in America" were rendered most fully explicit.[19] Richardson's letter was also prescient, combining the advance of industrialization with the goals of home missions, thus paving the way for the joint venture of Douglass's "millionaire and missionary" in the first years of the twentieth century. Throughout the home missions movement beginning in the late nineteenth century, Appalachia and its people were actively incorporated into the hopes and strategies of the Protestant bodies most committed to the realization of a Christian America. But for mountain people, there was a much greater downside than upside to being incorporated into such hopes and strategies. Ellen Myers was among the first to make a Christian America work against them.

Although the northern Presbyterian church began the mission school era in Appalachia in the late 1870s, Ellen Myers and her husband Rev. A. A. Myers, AMA home missionaries in Williamsburg, Whitley County, Kentucky, beginning in 1882—the same locale served by Richardson more than twenty years before—were the first to develop "a clear, systematic, mountain mission appeal."[20] In December 1882 *American Missionary Magazine* dropped "Freedmen" from its table of contents and subsumed its work among southern blacks under the rubric "The South." Just thirteen months later, in January 1884, "mountain white work" was introduced as a category in *American Missionary Magazine* with an inaugural article by Ellen Myers, "Mountain White Work in Kentucky." This four-page article provided several descriptions of religion in the mountains from a home missionary perspective, the earliest from this era of home missions in the mountains of Appalachia.

Myers wrote, "They are satisfied if their names are on the church book. I don't think they ever question their eternal salvation after they are once inside a church. If a person dies without having joined a church his friends frame some theory on which they rest their hope of his salvation. . . . They have no conception of *living* religion. They have no prayer or conference meetings. Aside from our own I doubt if there is a prayer meeting nearer than Berea, seventy miles away. There is no family prayer in all the land."[21] The vast differences between Ellen Myers's perceptions and the field experiences of Hamilton W. Pierson from thirty years before are already quite apparent. Myers characterized mountain people as having "no conception of *living* religion," meaning no programmatic engagement with their larger community outside the doors of the mountain church house, an engagement that, for many home missionaries to mountain people even to the end of the twentieth century, was the only means of validating the worship life that went on inside the church house.

Unlike Pierson, who spent many pages on household and neighborhood worship activities in the Kentucky wilderness of the 1850s, Myers simply claimed that Kentucky mountain people of the early 1880s had no active worship life other than in the church house itself, which was also a part of their having "no conception of *living* religion." The church life they did have she characterized as inadequate, stating that mountain people actually thought that all they had to do to be saved was go to church, a salvation they were guaranteed once "their names are on the church book." Myers's perception of church membership in the mountains ran totally contrary to mountain religion's grace-centered conversion tradition; rather it was based on the typical home mission, postconversion model of a busy "works righteousness" grounded in the moral reform and social benevolence activities sanctioned by American Protestantism as the only true evidence of a genuine conversion.

Myers also targeted friends and loved ones who maintained a hope, well grounded in their doctrinal traditions, for the salvation of people who died without being baptized as church members. These were the people who made up the congregations of groups such as the Old Regular Baptists, so prevalent in Myers's section of eastern Kentucky, which were swelled far beyond the numbers of church members who were accorded the privilege of being seated on the stand during worship. Myers dismissed their well-developed, popular tradition of belief in God's accommodation of saving grace beyond the grave even for faithful but unbaptized churchgoers—people who formed the congregations integral to the worship experiences that defined the very character of mountain religion—as simply "framing some theory." For Myers, matters of religion were grim indeed in the Appalachian mountains of the 1880s. The challenges facing its home missionaries of the era were daunting, especially those who, like Myers, engaged almost exclusively in the evangelization of mountain people.

Myers continued her description: "The prevailing churches are the Reform or Campbellites, the Methodists, and the Missionary and Anti-Missionary Baptists. The latter church is strong all through the mountains. They are bigoted and ignorant, and boast that their knowledge comes direct from the throne, and they have nothing to do with man-made theories, as they call education. Their preaching is a sort of canting reiteration of the text and what few Scripture verses they chance to know and some hackneyed expressions. They are great on arguing, and it would be laughable if it was not so pitiful to hear the profound questions they discuss" (p. 14). The "Reform or Campbellites" are what Barton W. Stone's "New Lights" came to be called after the union of Stone's Christian churches with Alexander Campbell's Disciples in 1832. This united group soon diverged into three streams known as the Churches of Christ, Christian churches, and Disciples of Christ. Campbell himself was Scots-Irish, having come from Ulster to western Pennsylvania and later to western (West) Virginia. He is best known as the progenitor of the "Restoration" or "Reformation" movement (hence Myers's "Reform or Campbellites"), a primitivist movement that sought to return the church of his day to the pristine conditions of the New Testament church.

By the time Myers wrote, the terms "Missionary Baptists" and "Anti-Missionary Baptists" were already long established in the Appalachian region, although these divisions were only sporadically significant elsewhere throughout the nation. Prior to the emergence of these terms, the Baptist groups which they identified had been consolidated with regard to their shared features and characteristics, especially in worship practices and spirituality, by John F. Schermerhorn in 1814 under the general heading of "Baptists." At the same time he recognized that major ideological distinctions otherwise divided them. Like Schermerhorn, Myers did not mention denominational Baptists in the region of her labors, only the Baptists most responsible for defining the region's religious ethos. And she was most preoccupied and disturbed by the "Anti-Missionary Baptists."

Myers observed that "Anti-Missionary Baptists" were "strong all through the mountains"; indeed, they had long been far stronger in the mountain regions of Appalachia than anywhere else in the United States by the time Myers encountered them. Myers, and American Protestantism in general, followed the lead of the denominational Baptists in dismissing the anti-missionary Baptists by calling them "bigoted and ignorant." She distorted the tradition of Spirit-directed preaching by claiming that such preachers "boast that their knowledge comes direct from the throne." Myers was scornful because anti-missionary Baptists rejected Sunday schools and the "education" of seminary training, believing instead that God equipped whom God called. She also cruelly denigrated their knowledge of the Bible, based largely on oral memory ("what few Scripture verses they chance to know"), and mocked as "canting" and "hackneyed" their regionally specific preaching style. Finally, Myers characterized the Calvinist theology of anti-missionary Baptists as "laughable" and "pitiful," words of stinging condescension. She epitomized the now solidly launched process of holding up Old School Baptists in the Appalachian region, notably the Primitive and Old Regular Baptists, as the quintessential expression of Appalachian mountain religion and making them a particular target of her criticism. Her account also advanced the process of setting the stereotypes by which anti-missionary Baptists were characterized in home mission literature, as well as in popular commentary, and through which mountain religion in general was trivialized.

Even though Myers mentioned several groups, the anti-missionary Baptists remained the focus of her attentions: "They [the anti-missionary preachers] do all they can to prejudice the people against our work. They call our religion railroad religion. They are great barriers in our way" (p. 14). Myers's statement revealed two primary developments. For outsiders looking in, mountain preachers such as the anti-missionary Baptists were exasperatingly stubborn and pig-headed about clinging to their grossly inadequate religion, "prejudicing the people against our work." Myers's statement also revealed that at this early stage of the aggressive evangelistic home mission work she represented in the Appalachian mountains, the preachers and religious leaders representing traditions most characteristic of mountain religion were already highly resistant to outside incursions on their religious life and culture. Those incursions were manifested as the effort to bring evangelization to "unchurched" mountain people, which Myers's account made clear very much included church-attending mountain people if their churches were under the umbrella of mountain religion. Mountain preachers knew explicitly who were the home missionaries with their "railroad religion." Railroads made up what were universally called "the *main lines* of travel" where lived the people "with the very best religious and educational advantages" (as we heard from Homer McMillan in 1922 about "two classes of mountaineers"). The common American expression "mainline religion," meaning the leading denominations of American Protestantism, was derived from this usage.

Myers was also quite antagonistic toward the casual environment of typical mountain worship services:

Another barrier to be overcome is their habits of worship. They have meetings but once a month during the summer and none at all during the winter. When they have service it is more for a visit than for worship. Their churches are rough log houses, and so small that the greater part of the congregation remain out of doors. Four or more ministers are always in attendance, and all must preach. The congregation expect a tiresome time, and from the first are restless. They go out and come in, and they keep a constant march to and from the water pail, which usually sits on the desk in front of the speaker. Several grown people at a time will be standing waiting on each other at the pail. The speaker seems to be used to such things, and not at all disconcerted. (p. 15)

The tradition of the summer season, going into very early fall, as mountain religion's high days of the year totally escaped Myers's awareness. The tradition of monthly services (services held once a month over Saturday and Sunday), continuing among many mountain Baptist and Methodist churches well into the twentieth century,[22] Myers saw as a problem. For her it was a product of irreligiousness rather than a result of a widely scattered and sparse population, rugged conditions, bad weather, and difficult transportation.

The casual environment of worship services led Myers to conclude that mountain people gathered "more for a visit than for worship." She interpreted the ancient tradition of more than one preacher at a worship service to mean that "the congregation expect a tiresome time," which she believed was manifested in the constant movement in and out of the building and to the water pail. Myers took no account or had no knowledge of the free church tradition of at-easement in worship services which, in the mountains, on average lasted at least three hours. In fact, her interpretive descriptions revealed her total lack of understanding for what she observed, showing more about her expectations as to what constituted an appropriate environment for worship than about the mountain worship environment. Her complaints about mountain worship would become normative in outside interpretive descriptions of mountain religious life, from denominational leadership to social scientists of another era.

Myers did allow that not all the people were unworthy, even though she countered her faint praise with damnation:

> These are peculiar people. What I have said of them has reference to the *general* class of society. But there are some who seem to be of better stock, who are shrewd, keen, far-sighted people. You cannot find their superiors in *native* ability in any country. . . . The majority of the people are unstable, thriftless, improvident and ignorant. . . . We never worked harder and saw less result in the conversion of sinners than while in Kentucky, and yet never more satisfied that we were where God wants us, and doing an important work. Unless these people have help they will prove a fretting leprosy in our nation. (p. 16, emphasis in the original)

Myers's "important work" was "the conversion of sinners." Mountain preachers and mountain religion were "great barriers in our way." Seventy years after Schermerhorn, who was troubled by but took seriously the religious life of the Old Southwest, Ellen Myers saw mountain religion as no religion at all but a nettlesome barrier to her work in converting mountain people to the religion of Christian Civilization, American Protestantism. She also said, "These are peculiar people" who "will prove a fretting leprosy in our nation" unless home missionaries "help" them. In a few short years, home missionaries had translated the perception of mountain people's "otherness" into an urgent need they must meet—in order to disarm a major threat. Ellen Myers located that threat especially in mountain people's religion.

In contrast to Ellen Myers, Samuel Tyndale Wilson attributed mountaineers' "problems" to isolation and natural environment instead of heredity or innate character (Myers too had echoed Dwight in her words about "the *general* class of society"). Nonetheless, in *The Southern Mountaineers* (1906), a home mission text written for the Presbyterian Church, U.S.A. (northern Presbyterians), that was the most comprehensive work on Appalachia written up to that time, Wilson repeatedly referred to the Appalachian "problem" in his table of contents: "The Appalachian Problem," "The Problem's Reason for Being," "Pioneer Presbyterianism and the Problem," "Later Presbyterianism and the Problem," "Present-Day Presbyterianism and the Problem." He did, however, conclude with "The Appalachian Promise."[23] For other denominational commentators, that promise receded into the darkness of an overwhelming problem, a threat that was identified with the "otherness" of an autonomous people marked by a regional identity who remained staunchly "unassimilated" into the larger national culture. The representatives of American Protestantism found themselves confounded by a people who were so much like themselves yet refused any part with them, especially in matters of religion.

Ellen Myers did not stand alone in her perceptions of the nature of Appalachian "otherness" that most home missionaries equated with "need" when they entered into the region during the last years of the nineteenth century, a need that they saw to be as much religious as it was physical or social or economic. The experiential traditions of the strong Calvinist heritage of grace influencing the worship life of almost all mountain church traditions—and an understanding of conversion as a gracious gift of God rather than a human achievement—strongly conflicted with the nonemotive, rationalistic, merit-based, and accomplishment-oriented Victorian Christianity of the home missionaries. Moreover, as we have seen, home missionaries closely linked conversion to their own understanding of Christian morality. A substantial part of mountain people's social behaviors conflicted outright with the narrow codes of conduct home missionaries deemed acceptable. The less-than-subtle message behind home missionaries' heavy-handed critique of mountain mores and lifestyles was that mountain people had a long way to go before they could enter into the mainstream, and that their religious traditions held them back as much as any other aspect of their lives, if not more.

One northern Presbyterian home missionary, Florence Stephenson, achieved national renown as a model for southern mountain work through her educational efforts in the Asheville, North Carolina, area. Stephenson presented an address on "mountain whites" to the 1890 annual meeting of the Woman's Executive Committee of the Board of Home Missions of her denomination. In that address Stephenson said of the children who came to her school and who had grown up in the "immersionist" tradition of mountain churches, "[S]o many of the girls who come to us unable to read a word are Church members. We must work wisely so as to not arouse their prejudices, and yet lead them to understand that they have not been made new creatures in Christ Jesus."[24] On the surface, the theological arrogance of this statement seems extraordinary. As we shall soon see, Stephenson simply engaged in the standard practice of equating mountain peoples' "illiteracy" with what was characterized as their "religious destitution."

Stephenson and others idealized education as the primary stepping-stone to salvation itself. For Stephenson, if the mountain girls who came to her school could not read, they could not be Christians, because they could not possibly have the tools necessary for acquiring the right reason indispensable to true conversion and without which they could not make an informed "decision for Christ." Her rationalistic position could not have been more contrary to the norm of the centrality of grace and religious experience in mountain religion, where the Holy Spirit on an intuitive, experiential level was the source of all genuine knowledge in matters of religion. Like the New Light revivalists and laity of the Great Awakening in the Middle Colonies—dominated by the Scots-Irish—mountain people did not oppose learning and education but rejected the rationalistic conceit that saving faith was characterized by right reason rather than emotional conversion. Unlike the Old Lights, New Lights insisted that a "true piety" came only through a nonrational experience of converting grace. This split in Calvinist tradition that crystallized in the Great Awakening—which may be loosely characterized as the split between the head and the heart—underwent progressive theological transmutations over the next century, but still persisted unabated in this fundamental conflict between home missionaries and mountain people over "real religion."

As a result, and beyond literacy itself, for many a home missionary like Ellen Myers and Florence Stephenson, conversion and baptism in any mountain church tradition was no conversion and no baptism at all. Instead, as Marcia Clark Myers observed, conversion was about "acceptance of Jesus Christ" and that meant "acceptance of and conformity to the moral and social standards of the missionaries. . . . This was the theological dimension to Appalachian 'otherness.' "[25] Mountain people had to be weaned away from mountain religion's grace-centered model of conversion, and the worldview it embraced, to the model of a rational decision for Christ whereby they could be assimilated into the norms and values—"the moral and social standards"—of the nation's dominant religious culture, and its worldview, as represented by Stephenson and her colleagues. That her attitude was typical is demonstrated by the fact that the denominational leadership considered her such a success, in direct contradiction to the assumption of Presbyterian tolerance Wilson expressed in his writings: "The Presbyterian Church is the broadest and most tolerant in Christendom. It would not re-enter the mountains with any spirit of denominational zeal or with any word of depreciation of the other Churches of the Appalachians."[26]

Wilson was either cynical or naive. S. L. Morris, Secretary of Home Missions for the General Assembly, Presbyterian Church, U.S. (southern Presbyterians), stated clearly—and stripped of any ennobling pretense—the home missions' strategy of educating mountain people in order to convert them. Morris wrote about "mountaineers" in 1904, "Noble Christian people may educate and even teach these children the Bible and fundamental principles of morality and religion, which is a step in the right direction, but unless the organized church is planted and maintained near by, most of the fish gathered in the school-net will escape again to the great sea of unregenerate humanity."[27] Morris articulated a simple, direct approach. First educate, then evangelize; "the fish gathered in the school-net" must then be directed toward "the organized church planted and maintained near by." The failure to execute this strategy successfully meant that mountain children would return whence they came, to "unregenerate humanity." It was a given that mountain children did not know about "the Bible and fundamental principles of morality and religion," meaning the "fundamental principles" sanctioned by American Protestantism, and so had to be taught them. Morris's attitudes toward mountain religion were clear: there was no real religion in the mountains (that is, mountain people had no real religion) apart from the values and "fundamental principles of morality and religion" that home missionaries in the field promoted and taught and that were the denominational goals and standards Morris represented.

Twenty years later Morris, now Executive Secretary of Home Missions, wrote about the Appalachian mountains in "The Romance of the Hills," "While we have scarcely touched the outer edges of *the problem of illiteracy and religious destitution* hidden behind vast mountain ranges, yet we point with pride to our growing churches, our great mission schools and our evangelistic activities. . . . [I]t is our purpose to establish cordons of religious forces until they meet and stretch from state to state in their beneficent influences."[28] "[T]he problem of illiteracy and religious destitution" justified

tain Mission Problem in a compact form and under unified control. The pioneer history of this Synod belongs to the several states which gave up many of their long established churches in order that this experiment in Home Mission efficiency might be tried out."[34] The language of Armstrong's statement more than seventy years later sounds violent: "[T]he Mountain Synod of Appalachia was *carved out* of the connecting mountain sections." It was a means of presenting to the church "its Mountain Mission Problem in a *compact form* and under *unified control.*" It was an "*experiment* in Home Mission *efficiency.*" Moreover, it represented a sacrifice by "the several states which *gave up* many of their long established churches," as though, with the creation of the Synod of Appalachia, these churches had been packed up and sent off like foreign missionaries to labor in the Lord's vineyard among the heathen, without their actually moving one blade of grass beyond where they had been physically, geographically "long established."

But these "long established" churches had, in a very real sense, been packed up and sent off to labor among the heathen with this radically concrete conceptualization of the region in which they were located as now "distinctively a home mission synod" (McMillan, 1937), specifically created to encompass the domain of mountain people. With Armstrong's statements, we see completed the objectification of mountain people and the rejection of mountain religion by denominational home mission interests representing the churches of American Protestantism in the "Southern Highlands," located almost exclusively in larger towns, county seats, and urban centers of the "favored valleys" on "the main lines of travel" (McMillan, 1922). These churches were very much a minority presence numerically and geographically, amid the large mountain expanses where mountain religion predominated. They were also a minority presence culturally, as well as in terms of social historical context and ultimately in terms of religious values and worldview.

By the time Armstrong wrote, Appalachian mountain religion, made up of its own white American Protestants, had long been seen as standing fully apart from the norms and goals of America's national religious culture, represented in the mountains by what were minority churches in the extreme. This was a very difficult stance for the "mainline/mainstream" churches used to being the only type of religiously dominant, white American Protestants in the nation, especially in the territory east of the Mississippi long claimed by white, non-Catholic—indeed, staunchly Protestant—settlers. Over the years, home missionaries expressed frustration and aggravation about mountain people's unbending recalcitrance, especially in matters of religion. Mountain people's obstinate defiance of the authority claimed by institutions and agencies representing the nation's dominant religious culture had little to do with what was assumed to be their "ignorance" and a stubborn refusal to see the divine light of Christian Civilization shining forth from the missionaries' lamps. It had everything to do with what had been a fully developed clash of religious values for some time. To the home missionaries, mountain religion needed to be overcome, if not by defeating it utterly by winning over its adherents (Plan A), then by ignoring it altogether and trivializing it when compelled to pay any attention to it whatsoever (Plan B).

Plan A failed. Plan B prevailed despite John Campbell's forceful, cautionary words in *The Southern Highlander & His Homeland* (1921) and Elizabeth Hooker's basic recommendation in her *Religion in the Highlands: Native Churches and Missionary Enterprises in the Southern Appalachian Area* (1933). Hooker strongly advised that American Protestantism and its home mission interests, the sponsors of her study, could no longer continue to ignore or demean the religious life and "native churches" of mountain people if they were truly serious about establishing a noncolonial, helpful presence in the mountains. Nonetheless, as we saw in chapter 11, "Methodism in Appalachia—A Clash of Religious Values," ignoring or dismissing or trivializing mountain religion continued to be the norm among the denominations and agencies of American Protestantism to the end of the twentieth century. We shall explore this pattern further in the concluding chapter of this section.

In this chapter we have focused almost exclusively on Presbyterian and Congregational writings of the home missions era of 1880–1930, an era coinciding with the industrialization of the Appalachian region. This focus has its own appropriateness. At the beginning of the nineteenth century, Congregationalists and Presbyterians were the premier New England traditions that Goodykoontz said considered themselves to be "the exponents of the purest form of Protestantism." The Massachusetts Missionary Society and the Missionary Society of Connecticut had sponsored Schermerhorn and Mills on their 1812–13 home missions tour of the Old Southwest of the Appalachian frontier to investigate its "religion and morals." A close look at religious life in what became the Appalachian region was thus the stated motive for the inaugural grand tour that launched the home missions movement as a national enterprise. The goal of this tour was to make straight the path in this earliest stage of home missions for the home missionaries who would follow. Those who did follow decades later into the mountain reaches of Appalachia discovered that the lay of the land with regard to its "religion and morals" had changed very little since Schermerhorn and Mills first assessed the Old Southwest of which it was a very large and integral part, despite the transforming impact of industrialization in the years between 1880 and 1930, when Presbyterian and Congregational home missionaries started their advance on the region in large numbers.

What Hooker called Appalachia's "long-established denominations"— Southern Baptists, Methodists, Disciples, and Cumberland Presbyterians—

by the 1880s had long been fully aligned with the norms and goals of American Protestantism and were ardent supporters and participants in the creation of a Christian America, but with their own variations determined by their distinctive histories and institutional personalities. Hooker will help us in the next chapter to look briefly at their home mission efforts in the mountains of Appalachia, the tone and practice of which differed little from the Presbyterians and Congregationalists, along with their attitudes toward mountain people and mountain religion.

To mountain people of this home missions era, their worship practices, belief systems, religious history, and church traditions had long ago come to express the heart of who they were. While continuing to change and develop as Appalachia continued to change and develop, mountain religion stayed very much the same in its essence. Its characterizing features and basic values remained remarkably constant, even as generations of home missionaries entered the mountains, whether under the banner of American Benevolence (early nineteenth century), a Christian America (late nineteenth century), the Social Gospel (early twentieth century), or liberation theology (late twentieth century).

Elizabeth Hooker and
Brother Terry Galloway:
On the Same Side of the Mountain

In 1933 Elizabeth R. Hooker of the Institute of Social and Religious Research published *Religion in the Highlands: Native Churches and Missionary Enterprises in the Southern Appalachian Area.* Her study of seventeen counties in a six-state area had been commissioned by "the Joint Committee on Comity and the Five-Year Program, representing the Home Missions Council, the Council of Women for Home Missions, the Federal Council of the Churches of Christ in America and the Community Church Workers."[1] Hooker's study was a product of the era of "cooperative Christianity," exemplified by the Federal Council of Churches, organized in 1908 to represent the denominations of American Protestantism as a collective, progressive force, and to mark the emergence of new inter- and nondenominational agencies created to focus on issues of shared concerns. Despite the muscular character of these new institutional alliances, American Protestantism was in the midst of a major upheaval that, for the first time in American history, compelled a change in its exclusive, uninterrupted leading role among American religions.

By the mid-1920s, as Robert T. Handy has identified, a "spiritual recession" had set in throughout the nation during the postwar period. Handy observed that the Protestant denominations' "special identification with American civilization was drawing to an end."[2] By the mid-1930s, "[S]ome conspicuous Protestant leaders were calling for the disentanglement of Protestantism and American civilization; they were asking for a reversal of what had long been axiomatically accepted."[3] During the period of the Great Depression, indeed, by 1935, "[T]he 'Protestant era' in American history came to a close. The voluntary effort to maintain a Protestant America had failed."[4] The nation's spiritual recession culminated in the collapse of the long-energizing vision of a Protestant America as the epitome of Christian civilization to be spread to all Americans and throughout the world. It was a product of what Handy called "the second disestablishment" when American Protestantism, which had always been the nation's dominant religious culture, was finally coming to terms with the reality that it was no longer preeminent. It had to adjust to a change in status, although it would continue to assert itself as the principal voice of Protestantism in the United States.

Still profoundly influential, as it would continue to be to the end of the century, American Protestantism could no longer claim the unimpeachable authority of being the sole arbiter of the nation's overall religious values and worldview. Other voices must also be heard, including the voices of mountain people speaking out of the values and worldview of mountain religion. The original, commissioned purpose of Hooker's study was to determine the home mission situation in the Appalachian region with recommendations for policy and future actions. Hooker's strategy, however, in keeping with the reality of the second disestablishment, was to contrast any study of home missions in Appalachia with a careful look at the "native churches" that widely prevailed throughout the mountains. In *Religion in the Highlands*, Hooker was not a champion of mountain religion, and she still saw the religious life of mountain people through the filters of her own time and background, which included the filters of the sponsors of her study. But her perspective on mountain people as a sociologist of religion was unusually clear-sighted compared to that of her sponsors, who would disregard her basic recommendation to understand and take seriously mountain people's religious culture in further home mission efforts.

Hooker certainly did not suggest that the home mission interests of American Protestantism should pack their bags and get out of the mountains when it came to matters of religion. However, *Religion in the Highlands* was a forthright acknowledgment that religious life independent of all home mission efforts, especially those of denominations in no way characteristic of the mountains, flourished quite apart from American Protestantism's longstanding efforts to absorb into itself a people whom it persisted in characterizing as religiously destitute. It was also an acknowledgment that mountain religion spoke to mountain people's condition more effectively than American Protestantism could ever hope. Hooker distinguished herself, along with John C. Campbell only the decade before, by recognizing and presenting mountain religion as an authentic, very real, and regionally based religious tradition worthy of respect—and even admiration, despite what American Protestantism saw as its flaws and insufficiencies.

The chapter preceding "Conditions Confronting Home Missionary Agencies" Hooker entitled "The General Church Situation," about the general state of mountain people's "native churches." While acknowledging that there were "wide differences among the sections of the Highlands in regard to the situation of the churches" (p. 142),[5] in "The General Church Situation" she concentrated on the "common characteristics" that convincingly demonstrated to her that "the rural church situation is uniform throughout the Highlands in many important respects" (p. 149). Hooker began this chapter with one of her most telling insights: "In this region, where ministerial service is almost entirely confined to monthly visits from non-resident ministers, *the nature of the churches is determined to an unusual degree by the standards and characteristics of the members.* . . . The standards held by Highland church members regarding church procedure are to a great extent the result of tradition" (p. 149, emphasis added). Her recognition of the role of the people in the church community is even more important than her recognition of the role of tradition. Hooker understood that it was not ministerial authority that determined the life of a church community. It was instead the people themselves who made up a church community who "determined to an unusual degree" the "nature of the churches." Hooker's study established that, for mountainous rural Appalachia, churches of congregational polity were overwhelmingly in the majority. Even mountain churches of noncongregational polity, such as the Methodists, were strongly influenced by congregational polity in their local church life.

This chapter will look first at Hooker's conclusions about the "common characteristics" that made up "the general church situation" in the mountains of Appalachia in the light of the history of Wolf Creek Baptist Church in the Blue Ridge of North Carolina, written by Brother Terry Galloway, a deacon in the church and church member since 1936. Galloway's history encompasses September 1886 through December 1987. Galloway, now in his early eighties, has supported himself by being a timber assayer for a local lumber company. Wolf Creek Church is an independent Missionary Baptist church only loosely affiliated with the local association that is part of the Southern Baptist Convention. The church is located on Wolf Mountain in Jackson County near the border of Transylvania County. Transylvania was one of the three counties in North Carolina included in Hooker's survey. This immediate geographic proximity to Hooker's areas of field research and the range in time of Galloway's history make Wolf Creek Church very much a prototype of the native mountain church in a majority of its traditions and a good illustration of Hooker's summary of "common characteristics." At the time of my visit, Wolf Creek Baptist Church was on the only major road in the Blue Ridge mountains of North Carolina still unpaved, making for an arduous commute over dirt and gravel.

This chapter will conclude with a summary of Hooker's evaluation of home missions to mountain people as of 1931, the year she conducted her field research in the region. Especially significant is the distinction Hooker made between what she called "long-established denominations" and "foreign denominations" with home mission interests in Appalachia. Hooker's study remains the best evaluation of home missions in the Appalachian region up to the time of its publication, and is the only careful survey of its kind of "native churches" of that period. The extent to which the "common

characteristics" she discerned were and remain normative for mountain religious life is born out by Brother Galloway's "History of Wolf Creek Baptist
Church." Indeed, Pat Parker Brunner, my host at Wolf Creek Church in
October 1989, whose uncle is Terry Galloway and whose family members,
the Parkers, live within sight of the church building, described Wolf Creek
Church as a classic example of what she called "generic mountain Protestants." The other branch of Pat's family, also long established in the mountains since the first years of white settlement, is but a stone's throw away (in
mountain distance), located outside Brevard in Transylvania County along
the French Broad River.

The founding pastor of Wolf Creek Baptist Church was Josiah Galloway,
a Baptist preacher born and reared in Transylvania County, North Carolina,
in the mid-nineteenth century. Brother Josiah moved to the Canada area near
Wolf Mountain, establishing preaching points within a twenty- to twenty-
five-mile radius. Brother Josiah "had been preaching for some few years at
different homes in the area." Homes often served as preaching points for local
church communities in this era, as they had the century before and up to
the present day. Brother Josiah Galloway would travel to a different preaching point each weekend, making an average circuit of four churches once a
month: "In those days, services were held once a month in a community
unless it was revival time. Once a month, a preacher would come to the
preaching point on Saturday morning; he would hold one service on Saturday and another one on Sunday. The next Saturday and Sunday he would
preach at a different place. . . . Most of these country preachers farmed for
a living and worked for the Lord without charge to the people."[6] Hooker also
observed that the majority of preachers she surveyed who served churches
based in congregational polity were farmers (pp. 163–64).

With the decline of the mountain farm as the sole source of income
during the period of her survey (1931), the occupations of mountain preachers soon included many other options. For the western North Carolina area,
working for lumber companies was one of the most common. All the pastors and preachers of Wolf Creek Baptist Church have supported themselves
through labor other than the ministry. Hooker commented on the tradition
of Pauline tent ministry in the mountains by stating that "pastoral care" suffered (pp. 164–66). What Hooker, like so many other "outsiders" we have
noted, failed to recognize was that "pastoral care" was a responsibility shared
by the entire church community, especially by the several recognized religious leaders, women and men, each church had, even though they were
often not appointed to any formal post. Brother Terry Galloway commented on the lack of pay in a poetic tribute, "To Our Humble Pastor," written
for Brother Claude Nicholson, pastor of Wolf Creek Baptist Church from

1967 to 1987—the longest tenure of any pastor serving that church community. One stanza reads,

> The challenge is great, the road is rough,
> His pay is small, just barely enough,
> To pay the expense of the Holy task,
> But for more pay, he would never ask. (p. 27)

Today, unlike during most of its history, Wolf Creek Baptist Church meets four Sundays a month. The weekly collection is taken up during Sunday school, rather than during the preaching service. One collection a month, averaging a little over one hundred dollars, is given to the pastor, the only pay the pastor receives from the church for four Sundays of preaching and additional ministerial responsibilities.

In early 1886 people decided to establish a church in the community loosely organized around Wolf Creek, which was and remains today a scattering of homes and mountain farms clustered in the area. It is not even an unincorporated town. No road marker indicates its location. In the 1880s most country churches met in the local schoolhouse, as they had for decades when not meeting in homes.[7] Wolf Creek Baptist Church was established in September 1886. Galloway notes that "They met in the schoolhouse on the bank of Wolf Creek" (p. 1). To this day elections are held each July for church officers—pastor, church clerk, secretary/treasurer, superintendent of Sunday school, and teachers for the Sunday school classes. These offices show organizational changes over the years having to do with Sunday school which, as we shall see, played a major healing role in the history of Wolf Creek Church.

Some of the most common family names in the area, filling family and church cemeteries for miles around, are found in the roster of Wolf Creek Church pastors: Owen, McCall, Cook, Burrell. All the church's pastors, except for Brother Nicholson, served only one, two, or three years. The high turnover of pastors was not at all uncommon, representing the large pool of nonresident preachers over a wide area, the willingness to travel significant distances to pastor a church, and the fluidity of ministerial appointments. The one constant was the people who made up the attending church community itself. Wolf Creek Church embodied what Hooker meant when she wrote, "In this region, where ministerial service is almost entirely confined to monthly visits from non-resident ministers [as was true for Wolf Creek Church throughout most of its history], the nature of the churches is determined to an unusual degree by the standards and characteristics of the members." Over the past century, not even the location of Wolf Creek Church was fixed, since the church met in two schoolhouses, homes, a local store, a community church house shared with the Methodists, and two small brick church houses built by Wolf Creek Baptist Church, one of which was eventually flooded out by the local power company, which bought up the property and provided for a new location.[8]

Listed among the church deacons over the years at Wolf Creek Baptist Church are other very common family names, such as Parker and Galloway. Church membership and attendance has remained steady over the decades. From the 1930s to 1989, church membership was in the upper seventies to low eighties, with church attendance mostly in the mid-thirties, even when the monthly preaching service shifted to weekly in the early 1960s. In recent decades many who attend weekly services travel great distances, some over two hours by car. Wolf Creek is their family church, even though they or the generation before them have moved away from the Wolf Creek area to Brevard, Hendersonville, or Cullowhee, the nearest major population centers in the small Blue Ridge valleys near Wolf Mountain, or to other much smaller communities scattered throughout the area.

According to Galloway, "In the early 1930s the Methodist Church proposed to build a community church at Wolf Creek." This initiative represented the financial power of the Methodist denomination in the area, for only three people in the Wolf Creek community were Methodists. The Methodists suggested that the new community church house be shared by the two church communities. The Methodists would meet once a month and Wolf Creek Baptist Church would have access to the church house the other three Sundays. At the time, Wolf Creek Church had been meeting once a month in the schoolhouse since 1886, or for nearly fifty years. The Methodist church provided the building material for the church house and the Wolf Creek community provided free labor (p. 3).

The community church initiated by the Methodists started a split in Wolf Creek Baptist Church that lasted for fifteen years. When the Methodists brought their proposal to Wolf Creek Church, its members took a vote. By nearly two to one—twenty to eleven—the church voted to accept the offer of the Methodists. The eleven members who voted against the proposal chose to continue to meet in the schoolhouse once a month, and tried to exclude from Wolf Creek Baptist Church the members who worked on the new community church house. (In his history, Brother Galloway merely stated this turn of events, discreetly refraining from outlining the reasons behind the call for expulsion, since many of the family members of the original participants in the split, and some of the surviving participants, including himself, continue to worship at Wolf Creek Church and the memories surrounding these events run long and deep.) Once the church house was built, the twenty members who supported building it met in the new structure, holding Sunday school every Sunday morning and occasional preaching services. Galloway wrote, "On the Sundays that the other [Wolf Creek Church] group met in the schoolhouse (which was one Sunday a month), [Deacon J. G. Parker] would take his [Sunday school] class and meet with them and stay for preaching. This went on for several years. At times the members who refused to go to the community church would suggest excluding the members who did."

Parker's persistent strategy to promote reconciliation was notable, but not remarkable or exceptional in mountain communities. It did bear fruitful results. Even though there was much "bitterness," as Galloway recorded, Wolf Creek Baptist Church never became two separate churches—a very telling fact about the stability and longevity of many mountain church communities, especially those built around kinship ties.[9] Because of Parker's leadership, a split in the church did not prevent many of those holding weekly Sunday school and occasional preaching services at the community church house from attending worship with the family members and neighbors who chose to remain in the schoolhouse for their monthly services, despite the fact that "[a]t times the members who refused to go to the community church would suggest excluding the members who did." The key word here was "suggest." Expulsion was not carried out, despite the "bitterness." Wolf Creek Church, according to Galloway, still continued as one church community, albeit in two separate locations (p. 3).

"In 1940, there was a flood that washed the schoolhouse away. The element that disapproved of the community church had no place to meet, so they met in various homes until 1943, when the new brick church building was completed." Now the dissenting members of Wolf Creek Baptist Church had their own church house, still holding services once a month, but because of the split the majority members continued to meet three out of four Sundays at the community or "rock church," as it was called because of the material out of which it was constructed. Various members made efforts over the years to heal the split, but to little avail. "At this time, Brother Burnett made arrangements for young preachers from Bob Jones University to meet with the group at the rock church." Bob Jones University in Greenville, South Carolina, was a radically fundamentalist and extremely politically conservative institution that was highly antagonistic toward organizations and individuals or "unbelievers" not reflecting its standards. The "Bob Jones boys," as they were called in the Wolf Creek Church community, caused dissension not only within the church community but also in the local community.[10]

In 1949, as a result of the use of preachers from Bob Jones University, the local Methodist bishop had the community church house locked one Sunday, without prior notice. A note was posted on the door informing the Wolf Creek Baptist Church members who had helped to build the church

on the main road. As we set up to photograph the church house that had once been a one-room schoolhouse, we met Sister Annie Roark, then in her early eighties, who had attended Cumbo UMC since 1916. I asked Sister Annie how the revival was going. She replied that "five preachers showed up two nights ago"—two Methodist, one Baptist, one Presbyterian, and one Holiness—not by any formal invitation but on their own initiative. And they all preached that night.

In *Religion in the Highlands,* Hooker wrote that revivals in the mountains were "far more important in the church program than Sunday schools. . . . The 'big meetin'' is the great event of the year" (p. 183). Hooker also frequently called mountain revivals "protracted meetings," a term which she misapplied, for it was once widely employed for the tradition of the type of revival meetings held in towns and cities that had entered into the institutional frameworks of denominationalism through Finney-esque revivalism. Nonetheless, in 1933 Hooker recorded language that was current in the 1850s and decades earlier as still part of the nomenclature of the region—a "big meeting," "praying through," "getting religion." She observed that for the people of rural Appalachia, "The climax of human experience is the conversion" (p. 153), foreshadowing by fifty years Albanese's conclusion, "[T]he episodic conversion experience became the mainstay of Southern Appalachian religion."[11] The climactic experience of conversion at a revival meeting, wrote Hooker, was widely considered to be "the only possible entrance into the Christian life" (p. 184). Indeed, even today the yearly revival meetings of local churches are the principal means of adding new members to a church community in non-Calvinist traditions, not endless verses of "Just as I Am" at the close of an evangelistic worship service.

People attended not only their own church's yearly revival but those of other churches too. Galloway recorded that people who had been attending Wolf Creek Church had been added to its church community through conversion experiences at revivals held by other nearby churches. Galloway wrote of Sunday, September 28, 1986, "As a result of a revival at the Promise Land Baptist Church, several were baptized . . . and taken into our church" (p. 23). Throughout his history, Galloway also records that people baptized into the church were baptized by immersion either in Tannessee Creek or Tuckasegee River, reflecting the nearly universal tradition that continues to thrive of baptism in a natural body of water, "in living waters," as it is still commonly called today.

The absence of musical instruments to accompany singing was a long part of Wolf Creek Baptist Church's history. Galloway recorded the period when this tradition underwent change and why. For 1950, the year Wolf Creek Church reunited, Galloway wrote, "As yet there was not any musical instruments in the church. Because of this, the song service was suffering. Most of the old singers who were used to singing without music were gone and the new generation was not able to carry on without some kind of music to accompany them" (p. 7). In *Religion in the Highlands,* Hooker wrote that the absence of musical instruments in churches was perceived as a virtue: "This view not only prevails for the whole of certain primitive denominations, but is also common among many churches of other denominations" (p. 150). She attributed it to the privation of mountain people's "pioneer ancestors" turned into "tradition."

Hooker's (and other's) theory of privation regarding musical instruments—meaning pianos and especially organs—to accompany singing in worship did not apply to church traditions such as the Old Regular Baptists, with their extraordinary style of hymn lining that had nothing to do with the lack of either instruments or songbooks; nor did it apply to people who became independent Holiness beginning in the late nineteenth century, as we shall learn in a few lines from a Presbyterian missionary to the mountains at the same time Hooker did her field research. In the early years of the century, settlement workers in the mountains, almost all of them women, would cart their portable organs from site to site on Sunday for gatherings with mountain people otherwise "deprived" of regular Sunday worship, and these organs literally and symbolically set the tone for the type of worship these earnest women sought to promote. In 1959, Galloway records, Wolf Creek Baptist Church acquired a piano. "This was a special year as the church voted with a big majority to purchase a piano. . . . This was the first time any kind of musical instrument had been allowed in Wolf Creek Church" (p. 8). Today, Sunday worship at Wolf Creek Church also includes a guitarist, and has for some years. Guitars are pervasive in mountain churches of a variety of traditions, and I have often heard banjos and mandolins at services.

Capwell Wyckoff, a missionary for the "Department of Sunday School Missions of the Board of National Missions of the Presbyterian Church in the U.S.A.," worked in the Ozarks and the Appalachian mountains at the time Hooker was doing her research. In 1931, Wyckoff published *The Challenge of the Hills,* a wonderful account of mountain religious life of his era, on a par with Pierson's *In the Brush* (1883) about the Appalachian wilderness of the 1850s. Like Pierson, Wyckoff wrote in detail about a wide range of worship life in which he took part in homes and churches of these two closely related mountain populations. Wyckoff apparently spent a great deal of time among Holiness churches, whose distinctive music had a pronounced, vigorous "swing" to it. In his chapter "Worship in Song," Wyckoff wrote about this style of music and the commonness of banjos in worship:

The people of the mountains enjoy singing. Singing was one of the ac-
complishments of the pioneers who pushed their way into the new
lands of the West and Southwest in covered wagons [i.e., the New West
and New Southwest beyond the Mississippi River], and in many of the
homes [of mountain people] a banjo or a guitar, suspended from the
wall or dusty on a shelf, testifies to this fact. Many of the roving religious sects of the mountains hold their services out of doors and the
hymns are vigorously played on the banjo, imparting to the sacred
music a swing not in keeping with the general tenor of holy things. . . .
My experience was to go into a service, hurt my throat by singing the
hymns picked out by the local song leader, and then wonder who had
ever written such high-pitched, galloping melodies. . . . Though I am
no judge of music myself, I can distinguish the music of the splendid
old hymns of the Church from the rollicking swing of the hill-country
hymns.[12]

Even though he did not name them, most likely, if not most certainly, Wyckoff was working among independent Holiness people, "the roving religious
sects of the mountains," as did J. Alva Stafford, a Presbyterian and missionary for the American Sunday School Union in eastern Kentucky and east
Tennessee from the late 1920s until the 1940s. Stafford was Warren Brunner's next-door neighbor for nearly twenty-five years until his death. One of
Stafford's daughters who, as a child, accompanied her father during his extensive work among Holiness people in Knox County, Kentucky, said to me
in an oral history interview, "Holiness is the religion of the mountains. Anyone knows that."

Today there is no piano or organ at Cranks Holiness Church in eastern
Kentucky and Red Hill Holiness Church in southwest Virginia, as is true for
innumerable (but certainly not all) independent Holiness churches; only
tambourines belong to these churches. The people bring their own musical
instruments, which they carry with them from church to church (like Wyckoff's "roving religious sects of the mountains")—guitars, banjos, mandolins, even harmonicas. Wyckoff's use of the word "sects" reflects the overriding prevalence of the church-sect typology model of his era and today for
understanding independent nondenominational churches in the mountains,
especially Holiness. We observed this pattern in chapter 1, "Brother Callaway of Avery County," where outsiders see each independent nondenominational church as a random, discrete "sect," unconnected and peculiar unto
itself, instead of realizing that all of these unaffiliated churches make up part
of a large, intelligible, mountain church tradition.

Although independent Holiness churches such as Cranks Holiness
Church are clearly distinct from Wolf Creek Church, an independent Missionary Baptist church, they nonetheless share the same fundamental simi-

larities or "common characteristics" Hooker enumerated decades ago, making them part of the interconnected patterns unique to Appalachian mountain religion. During the tenure of Brother Owen as pastor from 1961 to 1964, Galloway notes that Wolf Creek Baptist Church "had our first full-time pastor" (p. 8). By "full time" Galloway did not mean that Wolf Creek Church now provided for the full financial support of a preacher who earned his way in the world by being a preacher. Galloway simply meant that the pastor now preached all four Sundays, rather than once a month when "other preachers would drop in on the 'off preaching' days and preach" (p. 7). His statement reflects the tradition of mountain preachers traveling from church to church on their own initiative, "dropping in" on a regular worship service or a Sunday school meeting with no scheduled preaching service that week ("'off preaching' days") and being invited to preach, although prearrangements also were frequently made.

The pastor of Wolf Creek Church, now preaching every Sunday, did receive more pay than before, the amount of one weekly collection a month which, at the conclusion of Galloway's history in 1987, averaged one hundred dollars. The first Sunday's collection went to the missionary supported by the church, the second Sunday to the pastor, the third Sunday to the church and Sunday school, the fourth Sunday to the building fund, and the fifth Sunday (approximately every three months) to whatever the church saw fit for its use. Not only did Wolf Creek's preachers receive little or no pay, in the manner of the mountain preachers Hooker observed, but their preaching also reinforced her findings. The style for most of Wolf Creek's preachers and pastors according to my host, Pat Parker Brunner, was that of the "Great Gaspers," as she and her brothers used to call practitioners of "the holy tone," the chanting preaching style where preachers punctuate each phrase with an "ah!" Indeed, Brother Vess ("Bud") Galloway, who was the guest preacher when I attended services, preached in this "old time" style.

In *Religion in the Highlands,* Hooker listed several forms of "church gatherings" that were normative for mountain churches and that characterized Wolf Creek Baptist Church. Hooker wrote of "circuit meetings" (for Methodists), "foot-washings," "'union' meetings," "home-coming day," "protracted meetings" or "revivals," "funerals," and "decoration days." Over the years Wolf Creek Baptist Church has held footwashings only sporadically. Brother Galloway does not participate in footwashings for theological reasons, but has prepared the basins, towels, and communion utensils for the church in his capacity as deacon. Today footwashings are no longer practiced by Wolf Creek Church. Homecoming is always held by this church on the first Sunday in June. On Sunday, May 4, 1978, a special collection was taken up "for cement to build tables . . . on the church grounds" (p. 13). Dinner on the ground is universally held on homecoming Sunday, and a very large num-

historical identity in the mountains—was reflected in the degree to which such a church felt it needed organized programs of "community service" to justify its presence. Mountain people's understanding of what is community and how a local church serves its community's needs was very different from that of the home missionaries and those who set their policies and priorities. This basic difference put them at odds with each other throughout this era of home missions, as it does still today. It also accounted for the failure of a significant number of home mission churches (as Hooker noted, "Indeed, a not inconsiderable number of missionary churches have been abandoned" [p. 226]), even though these home mission churches were replete with programs covering "service to the community in every department of life" that were nothing less than religious social work, the leading priority that the denominations of this era of American Protestantism were determined to establish in mountain communities. This priority would continue into the late twentieth century, transformed by new theological language and broader ideological agendas grouped under the catch phrase "social justice."

Hooker also identified the several "difficulties of particular denominations" engaging in home mission work in the mountains. For the Southern Baptist Convention, it was the influence of the anti-missionary movement throughout the Appalachian mountains with regard to missions, educated preachers, church expenditures, and auxiliary societies. For the Methodist denomination North and South, their connectional system clashed badly with the congregational polity and autonomy of individual church communities, as did their tradition of christening infants and their stated rejection of baptism by immersion (although many Methodist ministers in Appalachia have always accommodated baptism by immersion if asked). In addition, "Methodist churches are peculiarly liable to be weakened by the Holiness services in the vicinity" (p. 213), for reasons we explored in chapter 11, "Methodism in Appalachia—A Clash of Religious Values." The Presbyterians, U.S.A. and U.S., both shared the liability of highly centralized polity, for which Presbyterianism was famous, and baptism by means other than immersion. The Presbyterian emphasis on intellectualization, its demand for a learned ministry, and its lack of emotional appeal were deadly to mountain people, the exceptions being individual Presbyterian churches long planted in the region that had been influenced to some extent by the region's distinctive religious ethos.

As of 1933 the nine denominations which Hooker determined had "the most extensive missions in the region" were (in modified alphabetical order) the Northern Baptist Convention; Southern Baptist Convention; Congregational Churches; Protestant Episcopal Church; Methodist Episcopal Church; Methodist Episcopal Church, South; Presbyterian Church, U.S.; Presbyterian Church, U.S.A.; and Reformed Church in America (p. 215). Their most common home mission program other than schools and community centers was supplementing ministers' salaries through home mission grants. Hooker stated that denominations making such grants had "two highly contrastive attitudes." The denominations that had been present in the region "from the early days" whom Hooker designated "long-established denominations"—notably the Methodist Episcopal Church, the Methodist Episcopal Church, South, and the Southern Baptist Convention—tended to "regard the Highlands as just another group of conferences or associations in which they apply a standardized policy of supplementing by small grants the salaries of ministers assigned to the weaker charges." In contrast, the denominations regarded as "foreign" by mountain people "because they have few or no indigenous churches in typically Highland territory," notably the Presbyterian Church, U.S. and U.S.A., the Congregationalists, the Reformed Church in America, and the Episcopalians, "all regard the region as a mission field" (pp. 216–17). The long-established denominations usually had native ministers in their mountain churches, and the foreign denominations imported ministers from outside of the region, as was the case when Schermerhorn and Mills made their tour of the Old Southwest of the Appalachian frontier in 1812–13.

Hooker identified the long-established denominations with some form of home mission interests in the Appalachian region as Methodist Episcopal; Methodist Episcopal, South; Southern Baptist Convention; Church of the Brethren; Disciples of Christ; Cumberland Presbyterian Church; Associated Reformed Presbyterian Church; United Brethren; and United Brethren, Old Constitution. Of these groups, two had their origins on the very fringes of the present boundaries of the Appalachian region—Cumberland Presbyterians and Disciples of Christ. Some were pietist bodies established in the Appalachian region since the early eighteenth century by German settlers who were the region's first founding population—United Brethren; United Brethren, Old Constitution; and Church of the Brethren. The Associated Reformed Presbyterian Church represented the early Scottish Seceder Church known for its plain-style worship practices and its codifying as the heart of true Scottish reformed tradition the Holy Spirit-centered emotional piety and spontaneity associated with the sacramental revivalism of Scots-Irish people who were Appalachia's largest founding population in the eighteenth century. The Methodist church exploded in numbers for the first time in the United States through its work on the Appalachian frontier of the Great Revival period, as did what became the Southern Baptist Convention.

In contrast to these long-established denominations' deeply rooted histories in Appalachia, which reached into its mountain regions, the denominations "operating from outside the Highlands" that Hooker identified as "foreign" or "outside" denominations with active home mission interests were the Presbyterians, U.S. and U.S.A.; Protestant Episcopal; Congregational; Reformed Church in America; Seventh Day Adventist; and Society of Friends (Quakers) (p. 217). She allowed that the Presbyterians and Episcopalians had been long settled in the valley regions of Appalachia, but "they have never been well-established in the hills"; hence their foreignness, which they themselves confirmed by adjudging the mountain regions to be home mission territory ("all [foreign denominations] regard the region as a mission field"). As a result, these foreign denominations have always seen their churches in the mountains as the church not at home but in home mission territory. This was especially true for the Presbyterians and Congregationalists who considered themselves to be "the exponents of the purest form of Protestantism" (Goodykoontz) at the beginning of the national home missions movement and who sponsored Schermerhorn and Mills on their missionary tour in 1812–13 in order to investigate the "religion and morals" of the Old Southwest.

Hooker concluded by summarizing the barriers to home missions in the mountains of Appalachia, which she grounded in the conflict of two very different understandings of what is religion:

> An almost insurmountable barrier between missionaries of *all* denominations and the people they have come to assist, lies in differences regarding basic conceptions as to the nature of religion. . . . Holding such divergent views, both the Highlanders and the missionaries find it almost impossible to recognize the validity of the religious experiences of the other party. The missionary tends to *minimize the religious values* possessed by the Highlander, characterizing them, in the words of one such minister, as "intense and strange spiritual vagaries." The Highlander, for his part, tends to believe that the "brought-on religion" with its coldness and its heretical doctrines is not religion at all. (p. 214, emphasis added)

Hooker lodged the fundamental divide between "the Highlanders and the missionaries" in a radical conflict of "religious values." She described that conflict in terms of "differences" in "basic conceptions as to the nature of religion" that were "[a]n almost insurmountable barrier between" them, making it "almost impossible [for them] to recognize the religious experiences of the other party." As we have seen throughout this study, for mountain churches in particular, these differences in religious values were summarized not only in a difference in theological predisposition determining much of their orientation to the world around them but in an understanding of the nature of religious experience itself—their "intense and strange spiritual vagaries" as it was seen by outsiders—which determined how they understood who God is and who people are in relation to God and to each other.

Capwell Wyckoff, the Presbyterian Sunday school missionary to the Ozarks and the Appalachian mountains, provides a more lyrical understanding of that "almost insurmountable barrier" Hooker identified dividing the religious lives of mountain people from the denominations of American Protestantism. Wyckoff illustrated that "barrier" by creating a sensitive canvas of words about the mountain church house, the premier icon in the material culture of Appalachian mountain religion. On that word canvas Wyckoff captured the fundamental differences in religious values separating the world of this uniquely American, Protestant, regional religious tradition from what was still the nation's dominant religious culture of American Protestantism when he worked among mountain people as a representative of that culture.

> These mountain churches are humble because they serve humble people, a people who take readily to Christ because he was such as they. . . . In these unpretentious temples of the mountains there is no stained glass, no lofty arches, no choir loft or stately pulpit. The feet of the worshiper sink in no soft carpet, and no sounding board is required to carry the voice of the preacher to the rearmost seat. There is no physical glory, no splendid architecture to delight the artistic and no blendings of color and light to captivate the lover of beauty, but only a spiritual glory and the beauty of unseen things in the lives and souls of men and women who have given themselves to God, requiring no cathedral and content with the limitless personality of Him who has redeemed them.[15]

Sixty years later Brother Coy Miser also said, "These are humble people." Emma Bell Miles wrote in 1905 about mountain people's "real passion for simplicity" and how they valued "humility."

This passion for simplicity is embodied in their church houses. The Primitive Baptists have a saying about the historical development of their religion that interprets this passion for simplicity within a theological context. The basic meaning of that saying within mountain religion, apart from the Primitive Baptists' own highly developed interpretation of it, is as inviolate throughout mountain religious culture as any rubric in canon law: "It is one of neither adding nor taking away."[16] Many will pounce on this saying as proof positive of mountain religion's willful, self-conscious stagnation and as a perverse self-justification of its regressive, insular traditionalism. Some will see that the saying encapsulates an entirely different perspective representing mountain people's own understanding of their religion as exemplified by the carefully maintained, only rarely changed church house itself. The mountain church house embodies the historical integrity of mountain people's religious lives by tightly interweaving past and present through the generations of people sharing like belief and practice who have worshiped in it. This value of personally interconnected continuity—made brilliantly, passionately alive by the homecomings and memorial meetings and decoration days embedded in mountain religious culture—stands apart from the vagaries and instabilities of ceaseless winds of change and the world's eager embrace of the "new," change that mountain people through their religion believe undermines the stability of Christ's established church on earth which was made whole and complete at the time of its institution as a spiritual institution by spiritual design.

Mountain people have always taken the spiritual very seriously. Their religious identity is atemporal, aligned with the spiritual realm, as Schermerhorn observed in 1812–13 about Baptist elders' "effort to spiritualize every passage of Scripture" and Hooker's conclusion that "[t]he missionary tends to minimize the religious values possessed by the Highlanders, characterizing them, in the words of one such minister, as 'intense and strange spiritual vagaries.'" Mountain people through their spiritually derived values of simplicity and humility, as expressed by their church houses and worship lives, seek to uphold Christ's church here on earth as a spiritual reality. They embody that reality in their profoundly heart-centered worship services, the heart being the home of the Holy Spirit whom Christ sent to help and to sustain his church until he comes again. They translate that spiritual reality into their social relationships and everyday social action beyond the church house door, emboldened by the manifestation of that reality in the transformative power of their fleeting yet sustaining and dearly treasured experiences of heaven on earth in their worship services. They lean heavily on their highly developed intuitive sensibilities, or listening to their hearts, that their spiritual orientation compels in order to keep close to the path directed by the foremost command Christ gave when he still walked the earth to "love one another, as I have loved you" (John 13:34).

All the many religious "improvements" in beliefs and practices and social action American Protestantism has sought to bring to (impose on) mountain people since Schermerhorn first met with Elder John Taylor, in order to absorb mountain people into itself as the nation's dominant religious culture and thus make them "normal," were "improvements" that deflected from this spiritual reality which needs no improvement, a reality that their religious culture has personified and nurtured since Appalachia's earliest days of settlement. Consistently, stubbornly, mountain people leave these "improvements" for others to embrace. As for themselves, their religious lives which teach them how to love God, live in the world, and treat one another are guided by the value of "neither adding nor taking away," which leaves in its wake, as Wyckoff wrote, "not a physical glory, . . . but only a spiritual glory and the beauty of unseen things in the lives and souls of men and women who have given themselves to God, requiring no cathedral and content with the limitless personality of Him who has redeemed them."

Appalachia's "Victims"
and Their "Liberators" Today

The Social Gospel provided much of the ideological impetus and interpretive framework for home mission work in the mountains of the Appalachian region through the 1930s and beyond. The home mission priorities of education and especially religious social work have changed little over the years, although their ideological language, mode of programming, and scope of vision have certainly undergone revision. The two most important factors influencing this revision were the War on Poverty of the 1960s and the concomitant shift in theological discourse culminating in the emergence of liberation theology in Latin American countries during the 1960s and 1970s. Liberation theology's imperative of identification with and social justice for the radically oppressed was quickly appropriated by Protestant denominations as the latest development in the history of American Protestantism's liberal traditions, now framing in new ideological terms its vision for realizing God's kingdom here on earth. For Appalachia, the effect was like new wine poured into the old wineskins that had held American Protestantism's other tightly interconnected ideologies—from American Benevolence to a Christian America to the Social Gospel.

Home mission work in Appalachia today is better described as church-based interest in remedying dysfunctional socioeconomic conditions and environmental tragedies in the region caused solely by systemic, institutionalized greed. Ostensibly, Douglass's cooperative pair of "the millionaire and the missionary" (1909) had finally parted company. Home mission work today thus involves taking a stand on wide-sweeping, multifaceted "social justice" issues to help Appalachia's "victims," its "poor" and its "hopeless" and "oppressed," confront and remedy their plight of being used and abused by outside interests otherwise unaccountable for their incremental destruction of a land and its people. Redemptive "help" comes to Appalachia's oppressed (however they are defined) through the giant supporting arm of the denominations of American Protestantism, as a statement of "solidarity" and identification with their plight. The denominations of American Protestantism, through their home missions presence in the region (now technically an anachronism), commit themselves to stand with Appalachia's "exploited" populace, who are trapped in a position of "powerlessness," through radical critique of socioeconomic hegemonic structures and by challenging the power relationships of Appalachia's controlling interests. Their commitment involves direct action at local, subregional, regional, national, and international levels. Their goal is to bring social justice to Appalachia and its people, which they equate with the effort to bring God's kingdom on earth to fruition.

The pastoral letter *God's Face Is Turned toward the Mountains: A Pastoral Letter of Hope from the Bishops of Appalachia of the United Methodist Church, December 1992,* gives a solid jolt of reality to the preceding summary. It was addressed to the people of the United Methodist Church throughout Appalachia, enjoining them to respond to the social justice emergency in Appalachia as a powerful Christian people whose help the people of Appalachia need. Indeed the bishops stated bluntly near the close of the letter, "At our recent meeting, members of the Council of Bishops entered covenant with each other *to develop personal relationships with the poor.* Many of us will develop those relationships within Appalachia. *We pledge ourselves to become the friends of the poor* and to be advocates, servants and leaders in Appalachia,"[1] having already outlined just how the bishops expected to be "advocates, servants and leaders in Appalachia."

The pastoral letter as it was excerpted in *Sojourners* (June 1993), a publication that could not have been more sympathetic and supportive, gave a useful edited version under the revealing title, "God's Word to the Mountains," capturing much of the pastoral letter's essence, beginning with the words,

> To our sisters and brothers in the mountains, grace to you all and peace in the name of our Lord Jesus Christ.
> There is a long low cry of pain that moves through the mountains like the wind. And our God, the God of Exodus and Easter, hears that cry, and turns God's face toward the mountains, and speaks God's Word to the people, and it is a Word of justice and hope. . . .
> Our region reveals all the characteristics of American economic life at its worst, and connects our people by chains of suffering to sisters and brothers in other exploited places like South America and Africa. So Appalachia has been properly defined as a part of the Third World within the United States.
> [Poverty, unemployment, illiteracy] . . . All of this translates into two words—suffering and hopelessness.
> So, while the mountains carry mineral deposits in their breasts, and wear garlands of timber on their brow, the lament of the people moves through the valleys like the wind.[2]

The United Methodist bishops of Appalachia summed up their response to the problems of the region and its people first under "The Stewardship of

Creation. . . . If the wealth is being carried away; if tax structures are so regressive that those who own the land pay the lowest rate of taxation; if politics are so corrupt that government does not represent the people; . . . if the hopelessness of the people causes them to litter the streams and the roads; then the Church must remember and must remind that 'the Earth is the Lord's and the fullness thereof, the world and those who dwell therein' [Ps. 24:1]" (pp. 5, 6). In these words, the bishops made clear that they had caught the drift of what had been driving Appalachian activists since the 1960s, although they assumed that the people "litter the streams and the roads" because they felt "hopeless" (a distinctly Methodist interpretation), failing to recognize the wide absence of landfills for trash and limited, if any, garbage pickup in many rural areas. What would the bishops do with *their* trash if they lived under the same conditions?

The Church Incarnate must be "for" and "against," the Appalachian bishops of the United Methodist Church declared as their "second theological principle" of response to Appalachia's social justice crisis. Their pastoral letter made clear that the bishops saw that their task was not just to help Appalachia's "victims" through local social action projects, as was true of earlier home mission policies. Today the leadership of the United Methodist Church in Appalachia called upon the church "to be involved in the struggle. . . . to take sides on behalf of the victims. Jesus of Nazareth was 'for' and 'against' and so has the Church been at its best. Martin Luther was not neutral; Dietrich Bonhoeffer was not neutral; Martin Luther King Jr. was not neutral. Archbishop Desmond Tutu is not neutral. We cannot be neutral in Appalachia." The UMC Appalachian bishops were especially forthcoming about how they understood just who were "the victims" to whom the Church Incarnate must respond: "The Church that extends the Incarnation always asks: 'Who is the sick? Why are they sick? Who is the hungry? Why are they hungry? Who is the homeless? Why are they homeless? Who are the victims? Why are they victims?' We will be for *them*. We will speak for *them*. We will be on *their* side—on the side of the victims" (pp. 6–7, emphasis in the original). The tradition the bishops claimed as their responsibility and their prerogative, "We will speak for *them*," was long-standing, defining the presence of American Protestantism in Appalachia throughout its history of involvement with the region, a tradition we shall address further on.

The bishops proclaimed "costly grace" as their "third theological principle," meaning what their courageous stand "for" Appalachia's "victims" could cost the church. For the UMC Appalachian bishops, "'to take up the cross and follow Jesus' . . . means to stand at the side of the victim." The bishops declared, "Ministry in Appalachia will not only give a food basket and a cup of cold water, but it will also 'wrestle against principalities and powers, against spiritual wickedness in high places' [Eph. 6:12]" (p. 7), not-so-subtle code language for the "principalities and powers" of multinational conglomerates and corporate interests and local, state, and national governments where corruption in "high places" only "exploits" Appalachia and its people. The bishops saw the dramatic, adrenalin-pumping big picture, one that could cost them dearly by committing them to spend some of their church's worldly capital of influence and prestige. Once the principal church of the South's slaveholders, and then the principal church of the industrialists in Appalachia, how did the bishops imagine their church would be different today? Yet, what could be more redemptive of that past than to risk taking a stand between Appalachia's "victims" and their oppressors, jousting in the name of social justice with the national and international power brokers held responsible for their suffering?

"Liberation and Resurrection" constitute the fourth premise summing up the bishops' "theological foundation of our church's mission in Appalachia" (pp. 8, 5). Although compelled to address the material and social foundations of injustice, nonetheless "[t]he Church is more than an agent of political and economic reform." The church was also "a community of hope" that helped to impart to mountain people "'a vision' of new life." "Exodus and Easter," said the Methodist bishops, were "*our* words" to "our beautiful agonized Appalachia" (p. 8, emphasis in the original). To the United Methodist people throughout Appalachia, their bishops "plead with" them to support "our church's mission in Appalachia":

> —To serve the mission of the one who said that "The Spirit of the Lord is upon me because he has anointed me to preach good news to the poor" [Luke 4:18];
> —To rejoice in the Creation, springtime green and autumn gold, so beautiful in our mountains;
> —To cherish the children, all the children who live up the hollows and on the farms and in the cities of Appalachia;
> —To be a church that has as many colors as an Appalachian quilt; . . .
> —To be optimists in a pessimistic culture; . . .
> —To be the Church, the community of the covenant, which enables discouraged people to see in your faces the reflection of God's smile.
> (p. 12)

The bishops urged their people to be "a church that has as many colors as an Appalachian quilt" that will "enable" Appalachia's "discouraged" populace with their "pessimistic culture," especially "up the hollows" in the rural mountains, to see in the "faces" of United Methodist folk "God's smile."

The Appalachian bishops of the United Methodist Church defined and delimited the people of the mountains as an "exploited," "hopeless" people with a "pessimistic culture" for whom God had enjoined the United Methodist Church "to be involved in the struggle" and "stand with the victims."

As for Methodist people themselves, their bishops "rejoice[d] in the gifts and commitments of pastors and church and community workers, of deaconesses and district superintendents, of mission project directors, of conference staff persons," but especially "the laos [laity], the people of God who in the congregations of Appalachia live the Gospel in such a way as to offer an *alternative vision*" (p. 9, emphasis added) to the people of Appalachia, taking no account of the "alternative vision" the congregations of mountain churches offered the United Methodist Church—indeed, all of American Protestantism—in how they lived the Gospel.

On this same page of the pastoral letter the bishops exulted, "We find joy in every evidence of the inclusiveness of the church in Appalachia." Yet how inclusive? Two pages later, as an illustration of the progress "of our church's mission in Appalachia," the bishops made special mention of the World Methodist Evangelism Institute, which had conducted "[t]he Appalachian Regional Seminar," noting with pride that it was "the only seminar to date to be held within the United States." It "was an important and helpful event, and we are grateful for it" (p. 11). The bishops failed to recognize that the Appalachian Regional Seminar, following historical precedent, only excluded from this "inclusive" church the Appalachian region and the regional religious tradition unique to it: Appalachia was singled out for its "otherness" in the United States through this unprecedented special attention by the World Methodist *Evangelism* Institute, which had not accorded any other region or population group in the United States this same distinction.

The seminar was about how to evangelize Appalachia, with special attention to its "indigenous" factors affecting how evangelization should be tailored in a way "appropriate to the area." Indeed, the bishops stated, "We pledge ourselves to develop forms of evangelization that are indigenous and appropriate to the area" (pp. 10–11), in no way suggesting a return to the Methodist church of the pre-1840s, which still had much in common with "indigenous," mountain religious culture. Instead, the bishops made their pledge according to the now requisite heightened sensitivity to "indigenous" folk and their traditions associated with liberation theology, but in order to absorb these "indigenous" folk into the "inclusive" church, ostensibly without violating their "indigenous" integrity. Historical echoes for institutionalizing Appalachia's regional and religious "otherness" in order to justify evangelization of its people fairly quaked in the walls holding up the bishops' "pledge" of an "evangelization . . . appropriate to the area." Its meaning was in no way cloaked by a mode of evangelistic accommodation meant to enhance the church's stated value of "inclusiveness," where "we are called to place before an oppressed people a vision of a beloved community that is male and female, 'red and yellow, black and white.' . . . It will not be so unless

all the colors of the mountains are seen in the faces of the church's people"
(pp. 9–10).

The bishops' particular focus on Appalachia's mountain regions and "the
people in the mountains" (p. 1), Appalachia's most "indigenous" areas and
populations, was driven home by the pastoral letter's closure with a passage
from Isaiah:

> No more shall the sound of weeping be heard in the land, or the cry of
> distress.
>   —No more shall there be in it an infant who lives but a few days or
> an old person who does not live out a lifetime;
>   —They shall build houses and inhabit them;
>   —They shall plant vineyards and eat their fruit.
>   —They shall not build and another inhabit;
>   —They shall not plant and another eat;
>   For like the days of a tree shall the days of my people be, and my
> chosen shall long enjoy the work of their hands.
>   They shall not labor in vain or bear children in calamity; for they
> shall be offspring blessed by the Lord—and their descendants as well.
>   Before they call, I will answer, while they are yet speaking, I will hear!
> They shall not hurt or destroy on all my holy mountain, says the Lord.
>   —Isaiah 65:19–20, 21–24, 25 (pp. 12–13)

"O God," concluded the pastoral letter, "make us the stewards and servants
of that dream. And let it come true! Amen."

The UMC Appalachian bishops' pastoral letter demonstrated once again
a religious paternalism toward the "victims" of Appalachia in need of "liberation" and "'a vision' of new life" with which the powerful denominations
of American Protestantism such as the Methodists could endow them. The
bishops asked God to let them be "the stewards and servants of" God's
"dream" for Appalachia, a dream that the bishops had discerned and articulated in their letter. Again, the bishops took no notice of the wealth of religious life already long flourishing in the mountains, which had nourished
and sustained a large host of Appalachia's mountain populations since the
early nineteenth century when mountain religion differentiated itself from
the quickly evolving Protestant mainstream. The bishops took no notice
either because they were oblivious to it or, more likely, because they assumed
it was bankrupt, as demonstrated by its "failure" to meet these much larger,
systemic needs that only the denominations of American Protestantism, as
well as American Catholicism, had the moral authority and religious institutional power to address.

Co-opting the language of liberation theology while freezing out the
involvement of mountain people's own authentic, honest-to-God, religious
"base communities" (in the argot of liberation theology) compromised the

seriousness and genuineness of intent of the UMC Appalachian bishops' statement, which proclaimed itself to be *A Pastoral Letter of Hope* articulating to the people of Appalachia the prophetic reality that *God's Face Is Turned toward the Mountains*. Much of that prophetic reality had to do with the denominations of American Protestantism turning their faces "toward the mountains." Indeed, the pastoral letter declared, "The Church is called to be the reflection of God's face, so that when the people see the Church, they should know that God's face is turned toward them" (p. 5). The UMC Appalachian bishops failed to recognize and acknowledge that the prophetic reality they proclaimed for Appalachia had been made real and immanent for generations in the already long-established, profoundly influential presence of "God's Face" *in* the mountains through the church traditions and religious culture shaping the life-sustaining values and worldview of the people the pastoral letter addressed as Appalachia's "victims."

As always, American Protestantism was *bringing to* the mountains as though it were filling a void, with the intention of absorbing what it found into itself. Once it brought Christian civilization; today it was bringing liberation and social justice. Once it sought to absorb mountain people into itself by "normalizing" or "nationalizing" them as part of the nation's dominant religious culture; today it was seeking to absorb them by promoting an "inclusiveness" that affirmed and celebrated their diverse, "indigenous" qualities. The question arises, how much of a real difference is there between the two agendas? I suggest that little has changed since the Christian America movement defined home missions to mountain people as service to a needy people who must be saved from the appalling conditions of their lives, and ultimately from themselves and their religion. Only the language justifying home missions has changed.

Once again, neither the United Methodist Church nor its Appalachian bishops stood alone among the denominations of American Protestantism in their posture toward Appalachia and its people. The UMC Appalachian bishops provided in their pastoral letter what was actually a plain vanilla, typical illustration of how mainstream Protestant denominations of nearly all stripes now applied the language of liberation theology to Appalachia, expressing the most recent ideological shift in home missions to Appalachia and the latest discourse mobilized for articulating denominations' national policies toward the region (although the Appalachian bishops' pastoral letter was not an official statement of the UMC Council of Bishops). Since liberation theology originated out of the Latin American Roman Catholic church, the Roman Catholic bishops of Appalachia had a jump on their Protestant brethren by some years, issuing their own liberation-theology-based pastoral letter on Appalachia in the mid-1970s, *This Land Is Home to*

Me: A Pastoral Letter on Powerlessness in Appalachia by the Catholic Bishops of the Region (1975).

Despite the foment over liberation theology and Appalachia, mountain religion, providing the premier "base communities" among mountain people, continued to be shunted aside as irrelevant to the larger demands of "social justice" the denominations felt God had commanded them to help Appalachian people realize. Given that liberation theology rose up from the religious lives and the indigenized Roman Catholic religious culture of rural Latin American people, the outright refusal of American Protestantism to look at all, let alone first, to the religious lives and the indigenized Protestant religious culture of rural mountain people in Appalachia invalidated completely its appropriation of liberation theology: American Protestantism had violated liberation theology's methodological core by dispensing with the essential source of its life and integrity. This refusal to look to mountain people and their religious culture, while claiming for them the social justice goals of liberation theology, was an obvious clue to what lay beneath American Protestantism's new ideological stance in the region, adding to the clues that had already laid a clear, two-hundred-year track of evidence.

Unlike the Appalachian bishops of the United Methodist Church, who spoke to their denomination's evangelistic interests in the mountains, the major "home mission" groups that today have taken over both cooperative efforts and the representation of their denominations' commitments to the Appalachian region have little or no interest in evangelization, apart from proclaiming justice for the downtrodden. Among these groups yet again, after nearly two centuries of ongoing conflict between Appalachian mountain religion and the nation's dominant religious culture, there is little in the way of acknowledging or understanding or affirming—let alone having any direct interaction with—the religious life and church traditions historically consistent with Appalachia's mountain regions. The new home mission organizations with their new portfolios of commission thus maintain what has always been the historical constant in denominational activity in Appalachia, whether as established churches or part of home mission efforts in the field.

The home mission landscape today has been transformed by a sea of acronyms representing various denominational and interdenominational groups now engaged in some type of activity in the Appalachian region. I shall only go so far as to name a few of the more prominent ones now operating. I shall give special attention to the AMERC consortium that, as of the mid-1980s, was the most recent Appalachian-based organization of American Protestantism, and certainly one of the most ambitious and extensive during its history in the region. AMERC provides perhaps the best illustration in microcosm of the difference between what American Protestantism says and what it means when defining its "helping" posture in Appalachia today.

The interdenominational and interagency Commission on Religion in Appalachia (CORA) was founded in 1965, partly as a response to Brewer's "Religion and the Churches," published in Ford's *The Southern Appalachian Region: A Survey* (1962), which summarized the findings of the 1959 Southern Appalachian Studies (a project which had returned to the seventeen counties Hooker had surveyed in 1931); partly as an outgrowth of the Spiritual Life Commission of the Council of the Southern Mountains (CSM), founded by John C. Campbell in 1913; and partly as a response to the War on Poverty programs of the period. CORA is the largest Appalachian-based interdenominational agency today, with official ties to the National Council of Churches. With headquarters in Knoxville, Tennessee, its efforts have little to do with religion per se in the region, except as an ecumenical umbrella organization and national outreach arm for the Appalachian concerns of church agencies and denominations in the region. Instead, its emphases are primarily on creating task forces and research groups on socioeconomic issues such as land ownership and funding grassroots social action projects. CORA prides itself in being an unromantic, hard-nosed realist about the big picture of Appalachia's plight and its needs as a region and how an organization like CORA can help.

The Coalition for Appalachian Ministry (CAM) represents Presbyterian and Reformed denominations in the Appalachian region. A small organization, CAM publishes materials to alert its members to socioeconomic issues in the Appalachian region, such as land reform, and their theological significance; holds weeklong orientation meetings for new ministers and church workers in the region to acquaint them with Appalachian issues and culture; and forms committees on various subjects related to church work in Appalachia as influenced in part by the larger social justice priorities of liberation theology. The Christian Appalachian Project (CAP), with headquarters in Lancaster, Kentucky, is a Roman Catholic organization that accepts volunteers from all backgrounds to help with social needs. CAP engages in more traditional religious social work activities such as work projects, food and clothing pantries, literacy, and crafts industry for self-support, doing little if anything in the way of evangelization. The Appalachian People's Service Organization (APSO) represents the interests of the Episcopal church in Appalachia, supported by fifteen Episcopal dioceses from New York to Georgia. With headquarters in Blacksburg, Virginia, APSO focuses mostly on funding projects such as research studies and research groups as well as building and literacy campaigns.

Throughout its history, Berea College in Madison County, Kentucky, in the foothills of the Cumberlands, has been characterized by a "missionary spirit" in the region,[3] beginning with its abolitionist and biracial origins in the mid-nineteenth century, and most recently as a sponsor and the host of the Appalachian Ministries Educational Resource Center (AMERC). AMERC is the newest of the major interdenominational organizations in Appalachia, initiated in 1983 by a preliminary, site-by-site survey of sixty seminaries conducted by Mary Lee Daugherty and sponsored by CORA. Soon after it opened its doors in December 1985, AMERC quickly achieved the distinction of being the largest consortium of graduate schools in the nation, made up of seminaries and theological and divinity schools, and was featured in the *Chronicle of Higher Education* during its first summer semester in 1986.[4] Although AMERC focuses on feeder schools into the region, with member institutions ranging from Asbury Theological Seminary in Wilmore, Kentucky, to the Interdenominational Theological Center in Atlanta, Georgia, AMERC's consortium members also include such tony eastern institutions as Yale Divinity School, Princeton Theological Seminary, and Union Theological Seminary (New York City).

AMERC's stated mission is educational, training clergy and church workers—with the overwhelming majority of its participants coming from mainstream Protestantism—in the skills and sensitivities needed for ministry especially in rural and small-town Appalachia, with particular emphasis in its curriculum on the larger issues of Appalachia's pressing socioeconomic and environmental needs. AMERC originally offered a two-month summer program and a January intercession travel seminar for graduate credit accepted by all of its member institutions, with the intention of placing interns throughout the Appalachian region for three to twelve months, a goal that foundered. As the first years came and went, the type of students AMERC sought were not forthcoming, and AMERC's core faculty and administration soon laid the blame on the two-month block of time consumed by the summer term. Beginning with its "Seventh 1992 Appalachian Summer Term NEW AND REVISED," as its promotional literature declared, revamped enrollment options included a three-week term, a six-week term, or the six-week term plus a six-week internship placement, along with the January travel seminar.

Through all of its jump-and-shift scrappiness to make itself marketable, and therefore viable, from its first year AMERC has emerged as the largest and most ambitious program yet for training the representatives of American Protestantism and American Catholicism for religiously based service in Appalachia, coming from a long line of less far-reaching and less academically grounded efforts. AMERC is the progeny of the most recent of the shifting theological front lines of liberal Protestantism. Its ecumenical character is reinforced by strong Roman Catholic representation among its students, faculty, and consortium-member institutions.

AMERC's original purpose in the minds of its creators was to introduce students to the best in current Appalachian studies and scholarship, and to focus in depth on the religious life long distinctive to Appalachia's mountain regions in order to break, for the first time, what Hooker in 1933 referred to as a pattern of "discounting the value of the existing [mountain] churches."[5] Unfortunately, what AMERC turned itself into within three short years of opening its doors was entirely predictable. As a product of do-or-die political realism, AMERC accommodated all of the requirements of its support network by acquiescing to ingrained attitudes toward denominational church work in Appalachia, stiff prejudices against mountain religious life, and an academic and partisan elitism that excluded several recognized authorities in Appalachian studies from playing central roles in the formation of AMERC's curriculum as well as from being "core faculty."

AMERC thus chose as its guiding priorities the familiar goals of training clergy for serving in their denominations' established churches in the region, alternative areas of service (religious social work) or what AMERC's curriculum called "direct service ministries," and dealing with the region's "important" larger issues of the day. Mountain religion was quietly dropped from the picture, even though it was originally meant to have a prominent, central role in AMERC's curriculum, where the perspective was to have been, for the first time, from the inside out. The denominations of American Protestantism were placed at the forefront for understanding "The Appalachian Religious Context," part of AMERC's core curriculum about religious life and history in the Appalachian region, with only a requisite nod toward "Appalachian religion" in terms of "traditional and contemporary life" dominated by the perspective of American Protestantism.

The reasons why mountain religion was reduced to an "Oh, by the way" in AMERC's curriculum betray what is by now a very familiar, fixed pattern throughout the history of the presence of American Protestantism in Appalachia. AMERC's consortium member schools and agencies, and the foundations that paid its bills, had entrenched positions about what is religion and what is the church and what is church life, positions they brought with them to the "AMERC experience" that molded it to their requirements. More than half a century before, Hooker called this entrenchment the "insurmountable barrier" between mountain people and the home missionaries of American Protestantism, made up of "differences regarding basic conceptions as to the nature of religion,"[6] a barrier into which AMERC was completely absorbed in its struggles to solidify itself. Nonetheless, AMERC appropriated the symbol of the quilt so ubiquitous today in American Protestantism's description of its role in Appalachia. Indeed, its 1988 promotional film, *A Pattern of Love: The AMERC Story,* whose controlling image was quilt patterns and the process of quilt making, declared AMERC "rich in religious diversity" like a "cultural quilt," failing to admit that AMERC's "quilt" of "religious diversity" had a very large hole right in the center of it.

AMERC thus confirmed and reinforced the unbroken continuum defining American Protestantism's historical presence in the region, rather than breaking with the old by establishing new patterns, as it had originally meant to do. The pressure on AMERC to capitulate was enormous from the start. The foundations largely underwriting AMERC responded only to certain themes. By 1993, AMERC's forty-one "sponsoring" consortium member institutions, along with its thirty additional "participating theological institutions" ranging from the Seventh Day Adventist Theological Seminary in Michigan to the divinity schools of the University of Chicago and Harvard University, represented a substantial part of the bulwark of American Christianity's educational system for its ongoing religious leadership, from the local church to national headquarters. AMERC successfully met its primary challenge of establishing an overall unified support base by dashing its original vision, discerning quickly what overriding expectations its support base required that it meet—and what its support base would not tolerate. AMERC responded by developing early on a strong home missions bias and a standard Social Gospel orientation, topping them off with the ideological discourse of liberation theology that certified AMERC's mission and strategy as "new."

AMERC's reformulated "goals," which appeared for the first time in the promotional literature for its 1993 summer term, clearly marked the extent, indeed, the complete 180-degree turn, to which AMERC had distanced itself from its original vision:

> Goals of AMERC:
> (1) *to preach the gospel message* to the people of Appalachia; and
> (2) *to strengthen* church leadership and *the role of religion* in this deeply-troubled region.[7]

AMERC's evolution to this point of full-blown home missions hubris duly reinforced the stereotypes and met the expectations of the nation's Protestant—and Catholic—leadership. This was especially true regarding stereotypes and expectations about preaching the gospel and strengthening the role of religion (as though that role needed strengthening in Appalachia) in the lives of the people "in this deeply-troubled region," the same people about whom Catherine Albanese wrote a radically different appraisal: "By the twentieth century, . . . this intensely religious people would have the least need for official church structures of perhaps any people in the United States" (1981).[8] Albanese's appraisal echoed and reinforced Elizabeth Hooker's who wrote of mountain people and mountain religion, "[T]heir religion . . . is part of their very selves to a degree rare in this age" (1933),[9] an iconoclastic statement of powerful force exposing the stereotypes and expectations of American Protestantism in Appalachia now personified, at the conclusion of the twentieth century, by AMERC.

Indeed, the Appalachian bishops of the United Methodist Church certified in their pastoral letter of December 1992 that AMERC had now fully integrated itself into the historical, ongoing mission of the Protestant mainstream in Appalachia, writing, "We commit ourselves to work with the Appalachian Ministries Educational Resource Center (AMERC) and with our theological seminaries to better train our clergy, both conference members and local pastors, for ministry in the mountains" (p. 10). Despite its original intentions, which AMERC found impossible to uphold and which were lost from sight in less than a decade, AMERC showed yet again that old attitudes toward Appalachia and its people died hard, if they died at all.

One anecdote from the 1987 AMERC summer session will suffice as illustration of old attitudes that have yet to die. A Roman Catholic brother had spent several years as a carpenter building low income housing mostly in rural areas. He was going to be sent by his religious order to one of their home mission churches in central Appalachia, established in the 1940s, to see what he could do to build up a church membership that had known almost negligible increase since its founding. For this reason he was enrolled in the AMERC summer program to get retooled before taking up his new duties. In a theological reflection group he used the language of liberation theology to describe his planned strategies. He was going to build up "base communities" by creating local prayer groups. The reflection leader, a prominent black feminist theologian, asked him why he chose not to work with some of the many, many church communities indigenous to the area that already existed. But he maintained that his purpose was to increase membership in the home mission church, and so he insisted upon the strategy of building up new "base communities" in order to eventually draw its participants into the waning Roman Catholic outpost.

When the leader of the theological reflection group asked him if he had any goal beyond simply increasing membership in a Roman Catholic mission church in the mountains, he replied, "Why, *I want to raise them to my level and give them my values.*" The stunned leader of the group wrote his statement on the board to make sure she had heard him correctly and to see if he had any problems with his statement if he actually read it. To her dismay, and to the dismay of some of the participants in the group, she did understand him correctly and the student found no problems with how he had formulated a goal that was indistinguishable from what home missionaries a century before had identified as the goal of "the mountain work." Later the leader of the theological reflection group repeated the student's statement to West Virginia native Mary Lee Daugherty, founder and executive director of AMERC as of this writing. Daugherty shook her head and said, "If I tore my hair out over every student who didn't 'get it' I'd be snatched bald!"

This student's goal for his home mission efforts among mountain people illustrated that even in 1987 centuries-old attitudes of paternalism and superiority died hard when it came to the presence of American Christianity, Protestant and Catholic, in the Appalachian region. Basic attitudes toward Appalachia and its people simply had not changed, even though the emphasis today may be on issues of land ownership and environmental struggles, social and economic justice, social services to meet immediate local needs, and radical critique of Appalachia's plight from the standpoint of liberation theology. Indeed, seminary students are almost always enthralled by the comparison of Appalachia as an economic colony of the United States with the Third World countries of Latin America, Africa, and Asia.

This Roman Catholic brother embodied in the microcosm of his own personal vision the prevailing institutional attitudes about mountain religion and the ongoing institutional strategy of establishing a religious counterpresence in the mountains. Mountain religion was not part of today's religious discourse about "justice" for Appalachia. As for earlier ideological movements propelling American Protestantism into the mountains, mountain religion was still seen as inferior to Catholicism's and the Protestant mainstream's redeeming and ennobling social justice commitments to Appalachia. At the close of the twentieth century, mountain religion continued to be ignored by them. When considered at all, it was still seen as a major barrier to actions that would "help the people." For this one Roman Catholic brother, it made little difference that he had invested many years of his life in concrete social justice efforts by building low-cost housing. When it came to religion, his attitudes were regressive. He saw no reason to engage himself in any way with the pervasive religious culture already long established in the Appalachian mountains; it offered him nothing except to reinforce the extent to which he needed "to raise them to my level and give them my values," a goal stunning in its clarity and directness, with loudly reverberating historical echoes throughout the history of home missions in Appalachia. A couple of years after the Roman Catholic brother departed to his home mission post in central Appalachia, another AMERC student, this time a Protestant seminarian, received vocal support from within the AMERC program for his bold initiative to create an "Appalachian Liberation Theology."

Linda Johnson summarized extremely well the emerging tensions between the "new" social-justice-propelled American Protestant presence in Appalachia and the values of native mountain churches. In her 1976 article in *Christian Century*, "The Foot-Washin' Church and the Prayer-Book Church: Resisting Cultural Imperialism in Southern Appalachia," Johnson especially took to task the Commission on Religion in Appalachia (CORA), which had just completed its first decade since it was launched at the height of the War on Poverty. Johnson's article generated quite a few letters from readers, published several months later as "Readers' Response: Pluses and Minuses of Mountain Religion." The "Readers' Response" included a lengthy reply from Paul J. Albers, then chairman of CORA, defending it against Johnson's critique; letters from Presbyterian and Methodist ministers who were certainly not in agreement with Johnson; and letters from some folk attached to universities also not in agreement.

Only the published letter by Michael E. Maloney of the Urban Appalachian Council in Cincinnati was genuinely supportive and affirming of what Johnson had to say. His one caveat was, "In many communities the only voice raised against this oppressive system is that of a local or regional organization *supported by the political shelter and economic power of the mainstream churches.* . . . [W]e do need allies. . . . Until the foot-washin' churches begin to help their people deal with Caesar in a more realistic way, they are not going to have much impact on the Appalachian struggle for justice."[10] Maloney had apparently forgotten Jesus' words, "'Render to Caesar the things that are Caesar's, and to God the things that are God's.' And [the religious leaders] marvelled at him" (Mark 12:17). In this saying, which has stirred up so much debate over the millennia, Jesus gave voice to a radically different way of undertaking the "struggle for justice" for a community also trapped in an "oppressive system" that was looking for an activist leadership that would compel confrontation. This perplexing way of justice, when identified with mountain churches, is invariably labeled "passive" and "fatalistic." Mountain churches do not lose sight of "the Appalachian struggle for justice," but they define the conduct of that struggle through the terms of their religious lives and values and their religious worldview, all of which distinguish many of their priorities from the priorities of Appalachian activists such as Maloney and the denominations of American Protestantism.

Maloney had also apparently forgotten that mountain churches played one of the central roles in organizing coal miners during the region's labor struggles throughout the twentieth century. Many of these labor leaders were mountain preachers and many church houses provided meeting places for organizing. As but one example, in 1987 in Welch, West Virginia, in McDowell County, Warren Brunner and I photographed a church house that had a sign beside its doorway declaring that it was also the meeting hall for the area's local of the United Mine Workers of America.

Maloney's qualified support of Johnson's affirming premises about mountain religion and her criticism of organized religion in Appalachia was based on an activist political realism which defined the stance of many Appalachian activists and tempered their own affirmations of mountain religion. This same stance of activist political realism and its embedded critique of mountain religious culture was assumed by the denominations and agencies of American Protestantism (as Appalachia's Methodist bishops made note, the church serves as "an agent of political and economic reform"). But the reasons for their stance were very different, grounded in American Protestantism's religious identity and religious action in the Appalachian region for nearly two centuries, much of it hegemonic, which mountain religion had challenged and contradicted and resisted throughout. Since no respectful, mutual interaction has ever taken place on a significant, sustained level between American Protestantism and Appalachian mountain religion, the questions remain, "On whose terms are mountain churches supposed to engage in the 'struggle for justice'? Whose definition of justice and whose determination of its priorities should prevail?"

Thus far, only the voice of the nation's dominant religious culture has been heard. American Protestantism and American Catholicism have prevailed as the recognized religious arbiters of Appalachia's social justice priorities and as the recognized religious critics of Appalachia's oppressors. However, those who know best what it really means to "struggle for justice" in Appalachia in terms of both their religious values and their lived experiences are found in the most elemental "base communities" that Appalachia's mountain religious culture represents. But these "base communities" are told to step aside by mainstream clergy and academics and regional agency directors and Appalachian bishops who nonetheless celebrate the possibility of "a church that has as many colors as an Appalachian quilt" and mourn the "long low cry of pain that moves through the mountains like the wind." Who knows better that "long low cry of pain"—the ones from whom it comes, or those who hear it from afar while making earnest pledges "to develop personal relationships with the poor"? And whose remedy is better, those who busy themselves with "principalities and powers," or those whose values of simplicity and humility intimately connect them with God and with each other, values and connections that translate into a strong social identity which they struggle mightily to make real outside the doors of the mountain church house in their everyday social action?

I cannot propose at this time what genuinely mutual, equitable, respectful, and sensitive interaction would create between the church traditions of Appalachian mountain religion and the denominations of American Protestantism (which need first to take a lesson in humility and simplicity as their mountain "brothers and sisters" understand it). Nor do I have much reason to think that such interaction is either likely or desirable—or even possible—at this time. The Congregationalist John C. Campbell in *The Southern Highlander & His Homeland* (1921) had warned the American Protestantism of his day that mountain preachers, mountain religion's principal leadership, have "a combination of endowments which makes them leaders *not* to be ignored in any effort for betterment."[11] American Protestantism has never heeded Campbell's advice, any more than it heeded that of Elizabeth R. Hooker, commissioned to study the home mission situation in Appalachia as of 1931.

Today's social justice priorities are no more than Campbell's "effort for betterment," and his warning not to ignore mountain preachers and mountain religion in order to help accomplish some real good in the region remains in effect today. Mountain religion has played a large and indispensable role in nourishing and sustaining the integrity of the sociocultural life of the Appalachian region, a triumph accomplished at ground zero, where the ravages and injustices heaped upon its land and its people have had greatest impact, an impact that the leadership of American Protestantism has rarely, if ever, experienced. These are the same issues of social justice that denominational involvement in Appalachia has rightly identified through American Protestantism's normative "moral reform and social benevolence" ideology that has energized it throughout its history in the region and is currently promoted in the guise of liberation theology. But, although the ideology rightly names Appalachia's social justice issues, there is a flaw that still proves fatal.

We explored to some extent in the introduction the underlying rationale that American Protestantism has maintained throughout its home missions presence in Appalachia and that today it cloaks in the ennobling goals of liberation and social justice. That underlying rationale has predetermined and governed the involvement of all of the denominations of American Protestantism with Appalachia and its people, regardless of whatever ideological discourse was at the forefront at the time. That underlying rationale is identified with American Protestantism's long, uninterrupted history of trying to overcome mountain people and mountain religion by either absorbing them into the mainstream of American life and into itself as the nation's dominant religious culture or, failing that (as it did), by focusing on mountain people while either ignoring or debasing mountain religion.

A large part of the energy American Protestantism has expended to ignore or debase mountain religion comes from the fundamental clash of religious values mountain religion creates as a radical sign of contradiction to the nation's dominant religious culture. American Protestantism long ago developed a set of strategies to defeat the challenge to its values and worldview that mountain religion compels at the foundational level of American Protestantism's basic identity. One prominent thematic motif in this pattern of behavior toward mountain religion is the implicit and explicit negative critique of "do-nothing" mountain churches that Maloney had alluded to in gentler terms, a critique first voiced by the Baptist historian David Benedict in 1860 about anti-missionary Baptists "found in the southern and western regions" dominated by Appalachia as "the do-nothing class at home."[12] Home missionaries who invaded Appalachia beginning in the late nineteenth century were quick to generalize Benedict's critique, applying it universally to mountain people's "native churches," their dismissive attitude motivated by the busy "works-righteousness" priorities of "moral reform and social benevolence" that were the antithesis of mountain churches' communal role.

In the ideological device of liberation theology, this pattern of historical abuse of mountain religion persists in revivified form. Today American Protestantism dismisses Appalachia's mountain churches as "do-nothing" because they take no active part in the categorical imperative of achieving social justice in Appalachia as American Protestantism has construed it. American Protestantism does not voice this critique often, because it continues to ignore mountain religion almost entirely. But whenever it is acknowledged at all within the framework of liberation theology, mountain religion is condescended to as "the religion of the poor," and therefore "powerless" in the "struggle for justice" apart from the salvific forces brought to bear by American Protestantism. Indeed, American Protestantism's unilateral conduct of the "struggle for justice" confirms the historical contempt behind its hollow identification of mountain religion as "the religion of the poor," conveniently placing mountain religion in the ranks of Appalachia's voiceless "victims" who need not be heeded because they cannot speak for themselves (as the UMC Appalachian bishops declared, "We will speak for *them*"). At the same time, American Protestantism does not hesitate to exploit the highly manipulatable image that mountain religion as "the religion of the poor" conveys to create copy that sells everything from grant proposals and direct-mail funding appeals, to articles appearing in a variety of publications and speaking engagements about the religion of the United States' own "Third World," all the while providing theologians and seminary students with a new "hot topic" about which to engage in earnest but ill-informed discourse.

How American Protestantism employs liberation theology in Appalachia as but the latest justification of its historical contempt for mountain religious culture shows that this ideological construct is no clean break with the past. Liberation theology does not redeem the long history of American Protestantism's extremely paternalistic and ideologically driven—and largely self-serving—interaction with Appalachia, beginning in the early nineteenth century with the American Benevolence movement. How American Protestantism applies liberation theology simply reinforces its long-standing pattern of ignoring the value of the religious identity of a very large portion of Appalachia's people when not dismissing or demeaning or trivializing their distinctive religious culture. By doing so, American Protestantism refuses to recognize and acknowledge the significant place of mountain people's religious culture on the landscape of American religions, as one of the largest regional religious traditions in the United States and one of the very few "native" religious traditions to which American Christianity can lay claim.

This pattern of bigotry and intolerance and not a little loathing toward mountain religious culture must be broken if American Protestantism is not to defeat the good it would do by trampling under its own feet the biblical prophecy quoted by the UMC Appalachian bishops, "They shall not hurt or destroy on all my holy mountain, says the Lord." This pattern *cannot* be broken until American Protestantism confronts and defeats its centuries-old assumptions of religious superiority—whether as "the exponents of the purest form of Protestantism" that backed the first home mission tour of the Appalachian frontier by Schermerhorn and Mills at the beginning of the nineteenth century, or as late twentieth-century "liberators" bringing the good news of "social justice" to Appalachia's "victims," its "poor" and "exploited" and "hopeless" and "oppressed." These labels for those whom American Protestantism discerns its divine commission "to stand at the side of" in order "to be involved in the struggle" are in fact labels of domination and control that only disempower and disable and diminish the very people it would "liberate." (Whatever happened to the imperative of "collegiality" that sounded like a trumpet in mainstream church life, Protestant and Catholic, in the 1960s and 1970s?) These labels loudly, unambiguously reinforce traditional assumptions of mountain people's neediness and the salvific remedies that American Protestantism is best qualified to bring to them, whether it be the Christian civilization of an earlier era or an all-encompassing "social justice" today. These labels also reinforce how American Protestantism's long-term relationship with Appalachia over a period of nearly two centuries was determined in large part by its unquestioned assumptions of mountain religion's radical inequality and inherent inferiority.

Quoting Isaiah's "They shall not hurt or destroy on all my holy mountain, says the Lord," the UMC Appalachian bishops meant "they" in the context of "principalities and powers" (Eph. 6:12), the oppressors of the "victims" at whose side the churches of national institutional power and national moral influence must stand. But from the perspective of many mountain people, the denominations of American Protestantism are the "principalities and powers" of organized religion which, not so long ago, they saw as twin to the looting industrialists, Douglass's "the millionaire and the missionary." American Protestantism has much it needs to repent of in its long history in the mountains in order to redeem its presence there today by fulfilling its long-standing debt of religious justice to the people of the mountains and their distinctive religious culture, a debt American Protestantism has yet to acknowledge, let alone begin to make good on. Perhaps the first step is to recognize just who all "They" include from the perspective of the "victims" whom American Protestantism and American Catholicism would liberate from the fetters of worldly oppression so that God's kingdom may come.

Perhaps the second step is to see that, for many mountain people through the transformative power of their worship lives, God's kingdom has already come. They have partaken of it in the here and now. They have the certainty of religious experience. They know God's grace in their lives and they know what it means in terms of their religious values. Mountain religion empowers them to deal with the physical reality and psychic stress of the world in which they live with courage and grace and humor and, for many, with a genuine love for their brothers and sisters in Christ, and for their families and friends, their neighbors and associates and acquaintances, freeing them to express goodwill and humanity and the love of God toward those who cross their daily paths and whose paths they cross in kind.

Mountain religion does not numb them to the "long low cry of pain" the United Methodist bishops of Appalachia heard coming from the mountains "like the wind." That cry does not exist apart from the people who give life to mountain religious culture, and they are very aware of why they cry out. John Gaventa wrote about his own surprising discovery, which American Protestantism should find instructive. Gaventa found among the people of a small Appalachian valley, and specifically among its coal miners, that they had a clear understanding, without despair, of "the long-standing inequities" of their "past experiences" and how "the local injustices" of their "present situation" had emerged out of them:

> Near the Cumberland Gap, stretching between the Pine and Cumberland Mountains across parts of Tennessee and Kentucky, lies [Clear Fork] Valley about which this book is written. Of the many experiences remembered from that summer [1971] when I first entered the Valley, one perhaps marks my introduction to the questions here pursued. With a community organizer in the area, I had climbed a narrow path to a mountain cabin to talk to a retired miner about joining with others in a law suit challenging the low taxation of the corporate coal property which surrounded his home. The miner listened attentively to the account of the local injustices which several other students and I had "discovered." He showed no surprise, though his response might have been anticipated. The land of his father had been taken by the coal lords. He knew of the inequities of the Valley since.
>
> In this opportunity to move against one of the long-standing inequities, though, the miner showed no particular interest. His response did not seem one of apathy or ignorance. It seemed to grow from past experiences in the Valley, as well as from his situation in the present. The miner understood something of powerlessness, of power, and of

how the two could serve to maintain inaction upon injustice, even in a "democracy." Of that knowledge, my rather traditional schooling at the nearby university [Vanderbilt] had taught me very little.[13]

While recognizing the importance of "religion" in "power relationships,"[14] in fact Gaventa was able to speak only a very few words about religion in his book.

Many of the people whom Gaventa observed in Clear Fork Valley, and the people whom the UMC Appalachian bishops sought to address in their "pastoral letter of hope," and the people to whom AMERC expects the "church leadership" it trains "to preach the gospel message" and "to strengthen the role of religion in this deeply-troubled region," share an understanding without despair along with Brother Coy Miser, who "*learned* something from" his "troubles" and "these heart aches and these hard times" that was redemptive in his life. Appalachia's "victims," its "poor" and its "hopeless" and "exploited" and "oppressed" with their "pessimistic culture," resist the heart-deadening role of the victim which American Protestantism insists that they must play, and they resist it largely through their religion. The dynamics of the "struggle for justice" in Appalachia need to be renegotiated if justice is to be done.

Brother Coy Miser died late in 1992 of complications from black lung contracted from his years as a coal miner in the 1940s and 1950s. He died after a lifetime of proclaiming with great power and authority and, above all, with a transforming joy God's love for all people, as Brother Coy's wide-ranging ecumenism made real in his own life. God's love and God's Word became flesh through Brother Coy's life, which he lived with grace and humility and a full commitment to serve God in any way God called him wherever he lived or worked, which was mostly in the heart of the mountains of central Appalachia, but also reached into the region's border areas. Brother Coy said of his life as a Christian,

> [I]t's a wonderful life. It's just something that you can't explain, you can't tell it when the blessing that God gives you, why it's just untold. You can't tell it all. But I've really enjoyed my life. . . . I've had a lot of heart aches and a lot of bad things through my life and I've had a lot of troubles but I thank God for my life because I learned, through these heart aches and these hard times, I learned something from it and through my mistakes I learned a lot. It helps us because if we don't make mistakes, or if we don't do something for the Devil to get after us, then we're not doing much, you know. I've had hard times and I've had good times, and through them all I thank God for *all* my life because I've enjoyed it.

"I've really enjoyed my life," said Brother Coy, despite his many, many "hard times" whose accumulation would crush or corrupt a lesser soul. Like the retired miner Gaventa talked with, Brother Coy knew exactly what larger wrongs had happened to him and why. When he spoke about "that disease" which was eating away his life, it was the only time I saw just the faintest touch of bitterness. Brother Coy knew in his bones what the UMC Appalachian bishops could only render in *faux* biblical language tinged with the condescension of those who mean well from afar but don't really know what they're talking about.

The religious lives of these "powerless" people, these "victims" so "hopeless" and "oppressed" and "exploited," exercise the *nevertheless* of their powerful faith birthed and nurtured by their distinctive religious culture to "enable discouraged people to see in [*their*] faces the reflection of God's smile." Before American Protestantism embarks once again to fix these people's lives under the impetus of the latest ideological fashion justifying the current state of its long, ongoing mission in Appalachia (as the Appalachian bishops of the United Methodist Church claimed up front "our church's mission in Appalachia"), it should "humble itself down" and take a lesson from mountain people's even longer-lived religious culture, which has so much to teach. American Protestantism should also take a lesson from the meanings undergirding its own set patterns of attitudes and behaviors, like stone pillars set into a rock foundation, that have determined how it has treated Appalachia and mountain religion throughout nearly two centuries of less than noble interaction with the region and its people. Brother Coy's nondefensive, straightforward stance of owning and learning from his "mistakes"—by which he meant the wrongs he had done—as both his responsibility as a Christian and a gift from God should be a model of encouragement to American Protestantism if it ever seeks to redeem the "mistakes" it has committed against Appalachia and its people throughout most of the life of the republic. After all, says Brother Coy, "[T]hrough my mistakes I learned a lot. It helps us because if we don't make mistakes, or if we don't do something for the Devil to get after us, then we're not doing much."

American Protestantism must finally take a hard look at itself and ask God for the courage of a broken, humble, and contrite heart in the manner of the people it seeks to liberate. Only then will American Protestantism stop assuming its historical role as the prophetic arbiter identifying and addressing Appalachia's woes in whatever ideological discourse reigns for a season to justify "our church's mission in Appalachia" while actually pursuing its own interests. Pastoral letters proclaiming that *God's Face Is Turned toward the Mountains* must give way to seeking God's face and hearing God's voice *in* the mountains. Indeed, hearing God's voice in the mountains compels a very specific response: "Today, after so long a time, as it is said, Today if ye will hear [God's] voice, harden not your hearts" (Heb. 4:7). American Protestantism will be able to learn how to redeem its past in the mountains "after so long a time," if it will hear God's voice in the mountains *and* "harden not your hearts." Only then will it be possible for American Protestantism to learn how to be present in Appalachia and doing God's will, so that "They shall not hurt or destroy on all my holy mountain, says the Lord."

Afterword

As the Pieces Begin to Fall into Place

The "invisibility" of Appalachian mountain religion has created a large, gaping hole in the writing of American religious history. That it is an oral religious tradition known primarily through its oral literature and material culture is one reason for this invisibility. Perhaps the more potent reason is the history of American Protestantism's "attack and run" relationship to mountain religion, obscuring the religious culture of mountain people with the stereotypes and prejudices of its own projections over its nearly two centuries of interaction with the Appalachian region. Scholars have scurried around many of the major themes and components integral to American religious history, unable to quite fit all the pieces together and formulating hypotheses to accommodate the missing links, or simply misconstruing—usually unintentionally, for lack of additional perspectives—what the data mean in their efforts to create a narrative framework that makes sense and rings true. Such benign misconstruing fades when confronted with the type of scholarship that attempts to control and dominate (and even demolish) a subject the scholar finds personally threatening, as is the case for many who have addressed the subject of mountain religion in some form or another.

Mountain religion is, in a number of these integral themes and components, the "missing link"—or certainly one of the most significant links yet to be explored—that has been in front of scholars all along. Situated at the geographic core of the United States east of the Mississippi and covering a very large area, mountain religion is a long-recognized, but little-known, regionally specific Protestant tradition whose formative history extends back to the early eighteenth century and is clearly distinct from the larger Protestant culture that has dominated, until recent years, the writing and interpretation of the nation's religious history. Mountain religion is in many ways an axis around which certain defining traditions and religious movements of American Christianity have revolved, not only in their actual operations but also in terms of how they may be understood in relation to each other.

We cannot understand the history of revivalism in the United States—especially in terms of intellectual history—without understanding Appalachian mountain religion. Nor can we move beyond the response of a deer frozen in the headlights, which it then turns on and charges, when faced with the reality of the central place of a continuous, centuries' old heritage of religious experience—manifested as expressive and ecstatic worship practices that promote profoundly emotional, physical, and psychic vulnerability—without understanding the uninterrupted tradition history of such emotional piety through Appalachian mountain religion, and nowhere else in the white, Euro-Protestant religious culture of the United States. Throughout the history of American Protestantism, comparable emotional piety would periodically flare up (usually a demarcation of one of American Protestantism's defining eras), only to die down and, more often than not, nearly die out altogether, until the firm establishment of the Holiness-Pentecostal movements on the American landscape by the late nineteenth and early twentieth centuries. Although it is perhaps the most compelling drama in American religious history, and the most universal, we also cannot hope to understand very well at all the ongoing divide between the traditions of piety and reason—the heart and the head—and how issues specific to American religious history have framed that debate, especially with regard to the central role of religious experience as galvanized by strong emotional piety, without understanding very deeply Appalachian mountain religion.

Without recognizing the crucial role played by Appalachian mountain religion, from independent Holiness to Old Regular Baptists (although, without question, this would amaze most Old Regular Baptists), our understanding of the rise and development of the Holiness-Pentecostal movements is woefully incomplete. Mountain religion provides one of the most helpful, reliable, and broad routes of transmission in the United States for the earlier, and especially the earliest, stages in the tradition histories and symbol systems of these movements' worship practices and beliefs—from ancient practices such as anointing with oil that did not die out altogether in America because of the influences of pietism and early Baptist revival culture in a number of church traditions regionally specific to Appalachia; to spontaneous, emotional expressions originating in a very specific heritage of revival religiosity permeating mountain people's worship services and private lives; to the centrality of the Holy Spirit in which these expressions were consciously grounded in mountain church communities' doctrinal traditions and popular beliefs.

The central role of emotional piety in mountain religion's normative tradition of a conservative system of beliefs, profoundly influenced by a Calvinist theological heritage pivoting on grace and the Holy Spirit, should put into a very different light the role and heritage of emotional piety in the Holiness-Pentecostal and Charismatic movements. Moreover, Baptist contributions to the development of the Holiness-Pentecostal movements, a topic in Holiness-Pentecostal scholarship just beginning to peek over the edges of the coverlet, should no longer be such a question mark. Understanding how mountain religion provides one of the most important and historically far-reaching "missing links" for the Holiness-Pentecostal movements will enable scholars to fit together and even reconfigure all the widely scattered pieces in a way that will allow them to begin to see more clearly the commonalities and variations on commonalites that are the primary clues to these pieces' histories on the American landscape. How mountain religion's groundwaters fed the Holiness-Pentecostal movements, especially the earliest formative years of their distinctive religiosity, is a story waiting to unfold.

Mountain religion as a *regional* religious tradition is more generally equated with other subtraditions and religious movements, especially evangelical fundamentalism, of which it is, in fact, no more a direct part—although evangelical fundamentalists are certainly found throughout Appalachia—than it is of more liberal Protestant traditions (and liberal Protestants are also found throughout Appalachia), even though all of these traditions and movements are interrelated. Mainstream American Protestants in Appalachia will, for example, airily label West Virginia—while looking bemused and knowing and sorrowful all at the same time—as "the buckle of the Bible belt." This "sounds like, looks like, smells like" (even though it really isn't) form of typecasting mountain religion for a role that, in reality, does not fit it has to do especially with the high level of mutual ignorance not just among the general populace but within academic circles. We can no longer presume that we understand as well as we should the many larger religious movements and subtraditions of American Protestantism, especially the largest blocks such as evangelicalism—which, let us not forget, by the mid-nineteenth century encompassed all the nonliturgical denominations of American Protestantism—unless we understand not only how they are like mountain religion but how they are different from it (namely, that mountain religion in a generalized form is not simply a quirky variant of evangelicalism or, more specifically, evangelical fundamentalism infused with "mountain culture").

It is highly probable that further studies of mountain religious history will clarify to an extent not before possible the historical dynamics of the interrelationships of earlier and later religious movements and their subtraditions—notably the revival traditions of evangelicalism and its subtraditions such as the Holiness-Pentecostal movements—that did not simply bypass Appalachia and its people, like the national roads after 1850, but coursed through it and were, quite probably, influenced directly or indirectly by its distinctive religious culture. (For example, considering the unrecognized mountain religion "factor" in the background of William Branham will not only enlighten our understanding of his contributions to the healing revival that clearly emerged with him and Oral Roberts in the late 1940s but also of the religious "peculiarities" that overtook him in the last years of his life.) Factoring mountain religious history and culture into the historical, sociocultural, and theological equations of these subtraditions and religious movements may well change significantly how we understand them within the broader framework of American religious history by enabling our ears, now tuned differently to their historical echoes, to understand better what we hear. Through Appalachian mountain religion, as a major and long-lived regional religious tradition clearly distinct from any other Protestant tradition in the United States, we should be able to hear these historical echoes "differently" than before by including for the first time a far-reaching and highly relevant perspective heretofore lacking. This complementary perspective should allow our perceptions and presentations to become sharper and cleaner, more precise and more true to who these subtraditions and religious movements are today in the religious culture of the United States. Not only will this increase our understanding of their histories but perhaps our tolerance for and even a genuine appreciation of their differences.

As the study of Appalachian mountain religion instructs us, the gleaning fields of written documentation, so sparse in some areas, so misleading in others, must be replenished by the equally fruitful and often even richer fields of oral literature and material culture that are an integral part of the religious movements and subtraditions of American Christianity—as well as of non-Christian American religions—not merely to supplement but to complement the portrait we attempt to paint of them in our descriptive narratives and analyses. The people who give life to the predominantly oral culture of mountain religion bear in themselves its clearest living chronicles and are, therefore, our most important "primary source documents." We need to begin to see that the same applies to many of the subtraditions, religious movements, and the variety of religions on the American landscape that are known as much, if not more, through their oral literature and material culture as they are through whatever written sources—be they many or few, by or about them—they may have. As with mountain people and mountain religion, we shall know we are getting closer to creating more authentic portraits of these variegated expressions of American religions, which challenge us to see and to listen in new ways, once those who give life to them yet today and continue to shape what they become begin to recognize and affirm those portraits as akin to their own self-understanding.

Essay on Sources

Bibliographies on Mountain Religion

No bibliographies specifically about Appalachian mountain religion exist as of this writing, other than the one I have created and am preparing for publication. A lengthy section on religion may be found in Charlotte T. Ross, ed., *Bibliography of Southern Appalachia* (1976), representing the holdings of the member institutions of the Appalachian Consortium.

The bibliographic preparation for this book represents two years of on-site research in the Weatherford-Hammond Mountain Collection of Berea College in Berea, Kentucky; the Appalachian Collection at Appalachian State University, Boone, North Carolina; and the Pentecostal Research Center at Lee College in Cleveland, Tennessee. Although I did not go to the Appalachian Collection at West Virginia University in Morgantown, I used the collection's *Appalachian Bibliography* (1980), which compiled the annotated quarterly *Appalachian Outlook* since October 1964 on holdings in the Appalachian Collection, and I have consulted all issues of the *Outlook* published since 1980. The result of my efforts was a single-spaced eighty-page bibliography on Appalachian mountain religion. I divided the bibliography as follows:

> *Secondary Sources:* History, Religious Studies; Sociology, Anthropology, Psychology; Regional Denominational Histories.
> *Primary Sources:* Appalachian Preachers/Pastors/Ministers; Home Missionaries; Archives and Oral History Collections; General.
> Fiction Treating of Religion in Appalachia.
> Reference Materials Pertaining to Religion in Appalachia.
> *American Missionary Magazine* (1858–1933); *Mountain Life & Work* (1925–80).

I also sent out a survey to over eighty archives and resource collections in the Appalachian region that had indicated some holdings in "religion/church history." There were thirty-five respondents to the survey. I plan to process the results into publishable information.

Of the material listed in the above bibliographic outline, most were chapters in books, short articles, and as little as one or two pages of text—even a single paragraph. The material on mountain religion per se is very skimpy indeed, especially historical material. The recent monographs by Dorgan and Titon represent the first book-length studies of mountain religion as religion. My own bibliography represents the first bibliographic study of Appalachian mountain religion as a regional religious tradition. A copy of the bibliography has been deposited in Special Collections of Hutchins Library at Berea College and is available for public use until it is published.

Materials on Primitive and Old Regular Baptists

Two resource collections exist on Primitive Baptists: Primitive Baptist Library, Rt. 2, Elon College, North Carolina 27244, "owned and sponsored by Old School Primitive Baptists," publisher of the *Old Faith Contender* and the *Primitive Baptist Library Quarterly*, repository for all materials (from annual minutes of associations to spiritual diaries) dealing with Primitive Baptists; William P. Lewis Collection on Primitive Baptists, Library of the American Baptist Historical Society, Rochester, New York, at the Colgate Rochester Divinity School. The key "insider" book-length history is by Cushing Biggs Hassell and Sylvester Hassell, *History of the Church of God, from the Creation to A.D. 1885; Including Especially the History of the Kehukee Primitive Baptist Association* (1886).

Most writings on Primitive Baptists in secondary sources are limited to brief mention in Baptist denominational histories and chapters or subsections on the anti-mission controversy of ca. 1800–1840. A small number of doctoral dissertations and master's theses are available, one of the better ones being Lawrence Edwards's "History of the Baptists of Tennessee with Particular Attention to the Primitive Baptists of East Tennessee" (1941). The best available succinct historical outline is by Arthur Carl Piepkorn, "The Primitive Baptists of North America" (1971). On white Primitive Baptists in Appalachia the most significant work has been done by Melanie Sovine. In addition to the three essays by Sovine included in "Works Cited," her master's thesis is of particular interest, "A Sweet Hope in My Breast: Belief and Ritual in the Primitive Baptist Church" (1978). Brett Sutton has produced the only extensive studies to date on African-American Primitive Baptists in Appalachia. He is the author of several essays, and his dissertation, "Spirit and Polity in a Black Primitive Baptist Church" (1983), makes a significant contribution. The first book to incorporate a religious studies perspective on Primitive Baptists in Appalachia is the ethnographic investigation by James L. Peacock and Ruel W. Tyson, Jr., *Pilgrims of Paradox: Calvinism and Experience among the Primitive Baptists of the Blue Ridge* (1989), representing the emerging of religious studies interpretations of Appalachian mountain religion that have appeared in monograph form only since the late 1980s.

Primary source material on Old Regular Baptists is much less organized. There is no repository for associational minutes or other material. The one published collection is by Dexter Dixon and Walter Akers, comps., *Minutes of the Burning Spring Association of Baptist, 1813–1824, and Minutes of the New Salem Association of Old Regular Baptist, 1825–1983,* 2 vols. (1983). The one published history is by Rufus Perrigan, *History of Regular Baptist and Their Ancestors and Accessors* (1961), mostly about the Union Association of Old Regular Baptists, which was armed off of the New Salem Association.

Howard Dorgan of Appalachian State University is the first scholar to study Old Regular Baptists in depth. In addition to his *Giving Glory to God* (1987), in which he examines the worship practices of Primitive, Old Regular, Regular, Union, Free Will, and independent Missionary Baptists, his *Old Regular Baptists of Central Appalachia: Brothers and Sisters in Hope* (1989) goes a long way toward laying the historical groundwork for a contextual interpretation of Old Regular Baptists. Dorgan has collected and borrowed as many Old Regular Baptist associational minutes as he can, and the Appalachian Center at Appalachian State University has been microfilming the material. Two other articles of real significance to understanding Old Regular Baptists are by Loyal Jones, "A Preliminary Look at the Welsh Component of Celtic Influence in Appalachia" (1983)—in which both Primitive and Old Regular Baptist history are treated together—and John Wallhausser, "I Can Almost See Heaven from Here" (1983).

Only a very small smattering of articles by insiders are available, notably Verna Mae Slone's chapter on "Religion," a glossary of Old Regular Baptist vocabulary, in her book, *How We Talked* (1982), and two articles by the former moderator of Old Regular Baptist Thornton Union Association, Ray Collins, "True or False?" (in which Brother Collins takes strong exception to the ways mountain preachers have been portrayed in writings on mountain religious life) and "Amen, Brother Ray," a transcript of one of Brother Collin's sermons (both published in 1974). The Appalachian Center of Berea College has a small collection of tapes of Old Regular Baptist services in eastern Kentucky from the late 1970s and early 1980s, approximately twenty nonprofessionally recorded cassette tapes. The William H. Tallmadge Baptist Hymnody Collection includes tapes of Old Regular and Primitive Baptist worship services as well as a collection of associational minutes and is housed in Special Collections of Hutchins Library at Berea College.

The one available professional recording of Old Regular Baptist preaching and hymn lining is by Alan Lomax, *The Gospel Ship: Baptist Hymns & White Spirituals from the Southern Mountains* (1977), Side One. The one article that treats of Old Regular Baptist hymn lining, a practice for which they are especially known, is by William H. Tallmadge, "Baptist Monophonic and Heterophonic Hymnody in Southern Appalachia" (1975). A comparative sound recording of hymn lining is *Gaelic Psalms from Lewis* (1975), this island off the west coast of Scotland being the only known location for hymn lining today outside of the region between the Cumberlands and the Blue

Ridge mountains in the United States. Few recordings exist of hymn lining in Appalachia: Walter Evans, *Old Hymns Lined and Led by Elder Walter Evans*, 2 vols. (n.d.), recorded in a Sparta, North Carolina, Primitive Baptist church; Charles K. Wolfe, ed., *Children of the Heav'nly King: Religious Expression in the Central Blue Ridge* (1981), two-record set with booklet, with only a few selections of hymn lining; Brett Sutton, *Primitive Baptist Hymns of the Blue Ridge* (1982), single record with booklet. Sutton's recording has the distinction of being equally distributed between white and African-American Primitive Baptist hymn singing. Again, only a few of the selections are lined hymns.

I know of one other small collection of primary source material, two file drawers in the Appalachian Collection at Appalachian State University of photocopies of associational minutes dating from the mid-nineteenth to the mid-twentieth century for Primitive Baptists, Regular, Old Regular, Regular Predestinarian, Regular Primitive, United Baptists, Separate Baptists in Christ, and Free Will Baptists.

Monographs on Mountain Religion

In chapter 7, "Mountain Religion and Denominationalism," we looked at the contributions to the study of Appalachian mountain religion as a regional religious tradition by John C. Campbell (1921), Elizabeth R. Hooker (1933), and Catherine L. Albanese (1981). We also noted the habitual blindness of denominational traditions to religious life and history distinctive to the mountains of the Appalachian region as demonstrated by W. D. Weatherford's ironically titled *Religion in the Appalachian Mountains: A Symposium* (1955). This section of the Essay on Sources notes briefly the monographs that have been published on Appalachian mountain religion, mostly by a single author, and the stages through which the study of mountain religion has gone as it has achieved recent recognition for an autonomy that makes it distinct from the "Southern religion" label under which it has traditionally been subsumed.

The most complete efforts to trace the development of denominational traditions in the Appalachian region, including the Mississippi Valley, up to the end of the Great Revival are by Walter Brownlow Posey: *The Baptist Church in the Lower Mississippi Valley, 1776–1845* (1957); *The Development of Methodism in the Old Southwest, 1783–1824* (1933); *Frontier Mission: A History of Religion West of the Southern Appalachians to 1861* (1966); *The Presbyterian Church in the Old Southwest, 1778–1838* (1952); *Religious Strife on the Southern Frontier* (1965). The first formal acknowledgment in Southern religious studies that Appalachian mountain religion—usually identified as religion in the "upland South"—is not one and the same as religion in the deep South came in Samuel S. Hill's *Encyclopedia of Religion in the South* (1984), which has an article by Loyal Jones on "Appalachian Religion."

A breakthrough book yet to be matched is *Revival!* (1974), by Eleanor Dickinson and Barbara Benziger. Ranging from the Great Smoky Mountains of Tennessee to southern West Virginia to eastern Kentucky, *Revival!* is a powerful, vivid work that integrates oral literature, the artifacts of material culture, music traditions, and oral history, replete with dozens of photographs, facsimile pages from songbooks, oral history transcriptions, explanatory passages, and Dickinson's own riveting line drawings of participants at these worship gatherings. *Revival!* was the first book about the breadth of religious life distinctive to the mountains of Appalachia—from tent revivals to serpent handling to footwashing to baptism "in living waters"—since Weatherford's very narrow attempt in *Religion in the Appalachian Mountains* (1955), which focused almost exclusively on mainstream denominations.

In 1978 appeared a collection of essays of varying quality edited by John D. Photiadis, *Religion in Appalachia: Theological, Social, and Psychological Dimensions and Correlates.* Many of the essays had been published previously, and the predominant methodological biases were structural functionalism, statistical studies, and a subculture-of-poverty model. Still, some regional scholars with particular interest in mountain religion welcomed the collection because it recognized mountain religion as a distinctive category for serious research,[1] while others with equally strong interest in Appalachian mountain religion castigated it.[2]

Since 1978 only nine additional book-length works have been published that attempt to look at some aspect of Appalachian mountain religion from a descriptive and, to a much more limited extent, historical perspective, accompanied by varying levels of theoretical analysis. The first two came out in 1982. *Foxfire 7: Ministers, Church Members, Revivals, Baptisms, Shaped-note and Gospel Singing, Faith Healing, Camp Meetings, Footwashings, Snake Handling, and Other Traditions of Mountain Religious Heritage,* edited by Paul F. Gillespie, is a collection of oral history interviews and photographs, most of which had appeared in issues of *Foxfire* magazine. Troy D. Abell's *Better Felt Than Said: The Holiness-Pentecostal Experience in Southern Appalachia* (1982) is a social science study about how people living on the "economic periphery" of American society make sense out of their world and their hardships through their religion. Four works came out in the late 1980s and represented the emergence for the first time of a humanities approach (other than *Revival!* [1974]), especially in religious studies: Howard Dorgan, *Giving Glory to God in Appalachia: Worship Practices of Six Baptist Subdenominations* (1987); Dorgan, *The Old Regular Baptists of Central Appalachia: Brothers and Sisters in Hope* (1989); Jeff Todd Titon, *Powerhouse for God: Speech, Chant, and Song in an Appalachian Baptist Church* (1988); and James L. Peacock and Ruel W. Tyson, Jr., *Pilgrims of Paradox: Calvinism and Experience among the Primitive Baptists of the Blue Ridge* (1989).[3] In 1993 appeared Thomas Burton's *Serpent-*

Handling Believers and Howard Dorgan's *Airwaves of Zion: Radio and Religion in Appalachia.*

The first monograph in the emerging specialization of mountain religious studies to investigate a single motif—death and its religious focus within a secular framework—was published in 1994, *Death and Dying in Central Appalachia: Changing Attitudes and Practices,* by James K. Crissman. Crissman explores material culture, from grave houses to embalming practices, emphasizing the insights he has gleaned from mountain music and religious songs that address death.

The nine books by Dickinson and Benziger, Abell, Dorgan, Titon, Peacock and Tyson, Burton, and Crissman are the only works so far that reflect, in whole or at least in part, a religious studies perspective guided by the conscious awareness of religious life and culture distinctive to the mountains of the Appalachian region. Except for Dickinson and Benziger (1974) and Abell (1982) as the transitional bridge, signaling a radical change in emphasis, all were published since 1987, demonstrating the nascent stage of the study of Appalachian mountain religion informed by a religious studies perspective not predetermined by models of church-sect typology or of dysfunction. Moreover, these nine monographs are among only twelve scholarly book-length works published thus far by a single or joint author on some aspect of religion distinctive to Appalachia, except for Hooker's 1933 study, which was the first.

The remaining three works, social science studies, were published prior to the Photiadis essay collection (1978), which also concentrated on the social sciences. Two were studies in psychology, focusing on sensationalistic and supposedly aberrant or dysfunctional religious phenomena, such as serpent handling and the ecstatic worship traditions of Holiness-Pentecostal people, with no appreciable awareness on the part of the authors that they were dealing with religious traditions found only in the Appalachian region (except through out-migration) that at some level should have informed their findings. The third sought to expand on data gathered for the 1959 Southern Appalachian Studies project.

The best known of the three is by Weston La Barre, *They Shall Take Up Serpents: Psychology of the Southern Snake-Handling Cult* (1962). For La Barre, Freudian phallic fixation theory explained much of the "function" of serpents in the religious rituals. Research for a study in an unidentified part of Appalachia produced William W. Wood's *Culture and Personality Aspects of the Pentecostal Holiness Religion* (1965). Rorschach tests showing that the subjects tended to see animals more often than people in the ink blots indicated to the author that his subjects did not integrate with people very well (never mind the fact that his subjects were rural people rather than townspeople). An expansion of the findings summarized in Brewer's "Religion and the Churches" in Ford's 1962 *Southern Appalachian Region: A Survey* appears in W. D. Weatherford and Earl D. C. Brewer, *Life and Religion in Southern Appalachia: An Interpretation of Selected Data from the Southern Appalachian Studies* (1962). One prominent Appalachian studies scholar has remarked on more than one occasion that the Brewer summary seemed intent on proving how little Appalachian people knew about religion.

Numerous articles, book chapters, doctoral dissertations, and master's theses are available on mountain religion from a social science perspective (sociology, anthropology, psychology), with a much smaller number representing the humanities. There are a growing number of social science works informed by an Appalachian studies perspective, such as F. Carlene Bryant, *We're All Kin* (1982), whose treatment of mountain religion in her chapter "Churches" is especially useful. Melanie Sovine's own training is in anthropology and she demonstrates repeatedly in her essays the possibilities opened up by careful study of historical theology and religious history when the anthropologist makes religion her primary subject of investigation.

Other than Dickinson and Benziger (1974), Dorgan (1987) and Titon (1988) provided the first two monographs to study Appalachian mountain religion *as* religion. They sought to explore what religious language and traditions meant in the lives of their practitioners, rather than how religion "functioned" in their lives from the standpoint of the outside looking in (a mode of "explaining" that concentrates on adaptations to environment). Taken together, Dorgan's three books (1987, 1989, 1993), often characterized in reviews as ethnography, provide the first in-depth descriptions of worship practices and beliefs, complemented by initial efforts at historical study of previously uncharted religious groups that most represent the religious life distinctive to the mountain regions of Appalachia. Dorgan does not attempt to do what he calls "academic theorization," but concentrates entirely on vibrant yet seasoned descriptive discourse about what he has observed, which he unpacks with interpretations guided primarily by his painstaking efforts to represent the perspective of his subjects. Given the oral character of Appalachian mountain religion, Dorgan's approach provides what is most needed at this stage of investigation—a solid foundation in field study that puts at the forefront worshipers' own self-understanding. At the time of this writing, Dorgan's descriptive work is the cornerstone of the new Appalachian religious studies. His books will be considered "primary sources" of an otherwise unrecorded religious culture in the decades to come.

Titon, an ethnomusicologist, is the first to engage in a comprehensive investigation of language in religious practice (speech, chant, and song), focusing on a single church community. His *Powerhouse for God* ranges from in-depth discussions of phenomenological issues to detailed social history. Both Dorgan and Titon have undertaken extensive fieldwork and participant-observation over many years in Appalachia (although Titon's has been limited primarily to Brother John Sherfey's Fellowship Independent Baptist Church in Page County, Virginia),[4] as well as analysis of the literary forms of both oral and written documentation.

Melanie Sovine threw down the gauntlet in 1979 in the first essay to challenge the methodological assumptions prevailing in social science studies that had dominated the limited number of investigations of mountain religious life up to that time. As the first to name the need for—and state the absence of—a religious studies perspective, Sovine Reid wrote,

> From Photiadis to Lewis, these are the present alternatives for understanding Appalachian religion: either religion functions to maintain social order, or it is a retardant to modernization, or it is exploitative, or it functions to resist "cultural imperialism." Perhaps the greatest weakness of both the subculture of poverty model and the internal colonialism model is the fact that both are more suited to an analysis of—and were actually intended to deal with—the lack of economic development in Appalachia. Stretching the models to interpret other phenomena—religion, for example—ends in making religion just another product of prevailing economic conditions. . . .
>
> . . . Religion is not just another name for economics or government or—for that matter—the unconscious. *The challenge is to study religion as religion.* Religion is distinctive in that it claims contact with the supernatural—God—as its goal. The challenge of modern Appalachian religious commentary recalls us to attempt a more complete understanding of religious beliefs themselves and to understand systems of beliefs in general.[5]

No one would pick up Sovine's challenge in the following decade except Loyal Jones (whose writings prior to 1979 reflected the same outlook as Sovine's and basically stood alone), John Wallhausser in his one essay, "I Can Almost See Heaven from Here" (1983), and Sovine herself in several essays. Despite their contributions, neither Dorgan nor Titon have fully incorporated into their writings the Appalachian studies and religious studies concerns expressed by Jones, Sovine, and Wallhasser. However, even though Dorgan and Titon are not principally religion scholars or Appalachian studies scholars (their primary disciplines are in other fields that largely determine their approaches to investigating mountain religion), their contributions mark the earliest stages of the study of mountain religion as an emerging discipline within religious and Appalachian studies, quickly followed by the contributions of Peacock and Tyson in *Pilgrims of Paradox.*

In his attempt to create a religious history context for the church community that was the focus of his investigations, Titon found that by far most of the material available on mountain religion was by home missionaries and social scientists. He wrote of the need for what he called a "long view" of the history of Appalachian mountain religion: "The importance of tradition suggests that the literature on Appalachian religion needs a historical framework and a long view, something notably absent from the writings of the missionaries and social scientists."[6] Given the paucity of available material on mountain religious life, especially from a religious history perspective, this book has been an attempt to create the beginnings of "a historical framework and a long view" for the study of Appalachian mountain religion. The complexity of the task, primarily due to the oral character of mountain religion and the general absence of written primary source material, imposes its own limitations on these first efforts in the investigation of what is tantamount to an emerging discipline in American religious studies.

As an emerging discipline, the study of Appalachian mountain religion challenges traditional categories of historical research that have been dependent on a plethora of written documentation. Now other forms of documentation—the preaching, singing, and praying, the visions, dreams, and trances, the testimonies and conversion narratives, oral history interviews, photographs, and material culture—provide the basis for research and are the primary source documents of mountain religious life, along with the obscure published material and church records yet to be identified, and the letters, diaries, and private memoirs of mountain people still to be found, which may speak about their religious lives.

Notes

Introduction

1. The second edition (1986) is titled *Protestantism in the United States: Righteous Empire,* inverting the title and subtitle to distinguish it from the first edition (1970).

2. See Loyal Jones, "Mountain Religion: The Outsider's View" (1976); and Albanese, *America: Religions and Religion* (1981), on "mountain religion" in the "Southern Appalachians," pp. 226–29, 233–34, 237, 241–42.

3. The invisibility of mountain religion is discussed in detail in chapter 11, "Methodism in Appalachia: A Clash of Religious Values."

4. Quoted in Ergood, "Toward a Definition of Appalachia," p. 39.

5. Raitz and Ulack, "Regional Definitions," p. 18. That "distinctive 'upland' culture subregion . . . in the southeastern portion of the United States" is referred to in Southern studies as the "upland South," where plain-folk camp-meeting religion developed and thrived during the first half of the nineteenth century.

6. John C. Campbell, *Southern Highlander,* p. 18.

7. Schermerhorn wrote of his tour in Kentucky about the country between the Kentucky and Green rivers, a region heavily dominated by traditional Baptist groups, "Some Presbyterian societies could also be formed, particularly in the county towns, for wherever you find men well informed there is a decided preference to that denomination, and rather than hear the Baptists and Methodists." Of what became identified as the Appalachian region, Schermerhorn wrote, "The Presbyterian ministers are mostly settled in the villages, of which there is generally at least one in each county. The whole space of country around them is therefore the field for other sects" (Schermerhorn and Mills, *A Correct View of That Part of the United States Which Lies West of the Allegany Mountains, With Regard to Religion and Morals* [1814], pp. 21, 37). We shall explore in depth the observations and conclusions of this report, which focused primarily on western Pennsylvania, "New Virginia" (West Virginia), Kentucky, and Tennessee.

8. All Bible quotations are from the King James Version (KJV). All Bible references are also to the KJV, the English translation mountain people overwhelmingly prefer.

9. Best, "Stripping Appalachian Soul," p. 14.

10. When I asked Brother Coy Miser, "Is there a way of helping the Holy Ghost come into a worship service?" he replied, "Hope, having hope that he will be there and ask the Lord, Lord you let the Holy Ghost take over. You let the Holy Ghost rule and you let the Holy Ghost bless somebody. If you can't bless me Lord, you bless somebody else and that's the way I pray. I pray that if there's not a blessing for me, because I see somebody else get a blessing, I'm going to

get one too. It's a blessing to me to see somebody else get a blessing. That makes me feel good inside. In other words, if God was to move on you right now, and start you a shouting or start you a running or start you dancing, that would make me feel good. See what I mean?"

11. Wadhwani, "Appalachian Religion and American Capitalism: Iron Cages and Transformative Power," pp. 7–10.

12. A *Time* magazine cover story in December 1991 on the separation of church and state summarized the diversity of religion in the United States with this sentence: "Millions of Americans attend worship services each week, but the locales range from Hindu temples in California to churches of snake-handling Pentecostalists in Appalachia" ("America's Holy War," p. 63). The *New York Times* also makes regular human interest pilgrimages to Appalachia for the edification of its readers, usually focusing on poverty, the odd, the quaint, the heroic, and—in its coverage of religion in Appalachia—the spectacular. On September 11, 1992, an article about serpent handlers, titled "When the Faithful Tempt the Serpent," took up nearly half a page and was placed on the first page of the "National Report" section, accompanied by a three-column photograph of a serpent-handling worship service in Jolo, West Virginia (the locale for serpent handling known best by reporters looking for a story and researchers looking for subjects), and further complemented by a detailed map of its location ("When the Faithful Tempt the Serpent," p. A14).

13. Melanie Sovine's essays explicitly challenge the historical manipulation of such a portrayal of mountain religion's Calvinist, anti-missionary Baptist church traditions. Lewis, Kobak, and Johnson's "Family, Religion, and Colonialism in Central Appalachia" also addresses it, but less specifically and not in depth.

14. Jack Weller's writings, crowned by "The Mountaineer and the Church" in his *Yesterday's People: Life in Contemporary Appalachia* ([1965], pp. 121–33), epitomize this type of source. Weller was a United Presbyterian minister called into the Appalachian region to take up work in a church in the coalfields of West Virginia. In his book he castigated mountain religion as individualistic, uncooperative, fatalistic, and incapable of the social service activity needed to redeem the region. Weller's interpretations of religion and other aspects of the mountain culture of Appalachia have had wide influence. For example, in "Impact of Great Revival Religion on the Personal Characteristics of the Southern Appalachian People," Barbara J. Redman used Weller's "six major personality traits of mountaineers" as her theoretical foundation.

15. Sovine, "Traditionalism, Antimissionism, and the Primitive Baptist Religion," p. 38.

16. Ahlstrom, *A Religious History of the American People,* pp. 420, 422.

17. Spencer, *A History of Kentucky Baptists from 1769 to 1885,* vol. 2, p. 671 (emphasis in the original).

18. Livingston, "Coal Miners and Religion" (1951), p. 224.

19. Even the third edition of Robert G. Torbet's *A History of the Baptists* (1963), still in print in the 1980s, continued this uninterrupted trend in denominational histories with sections on "Hyper-Calvinism" (p. 275) and "Hyper-Calvinistic Baptist bodies" (pp. 261–63), among whom he included "[t]he Primitive, Old School, or Anti-mission Baptists" (p. 262).

20. Piepkorn, "The Primitive Baptists of North America," p. 301.
21. McLoughlin, *Modern Revivalism*, pp. 65–66 (emphasis added).
22. Cratis D. Williams, "The Southern Mountaineer in Fact and Fiction," pp. 622–23. See also George Brosi, "Mountain Novels before 1890: 28. The Prophet of the Great Smoky Mountains, by Charles Egbert Craddock (Mary Murfree)," p. 21.
23. Ray Collins, "True or False?" p. 7.
24. Beginning in 1985, publication of *Appalachian Heritage* was taken over by Berea College, with the poet-author Sidney Saylor Farr as editor. Albert Stewart was the founding editor of *Appalachian Heritage* while it was at Alice Lloyd College.
25. Cratis Williams, who died in 1985, is considered the founding dean of Appalachian studies.
26. Hartman, "Origins of the Mountain Preacher," p. 55.
27. Cratis D. Williams, "The Southern Mountaineer in Fact and Fiction (Part III)" (1976), pp. 212–13. Fox (1862–1919) published in the 1890s and during the first two decades of the twentieth century. Two of his best-known novels on Appalachia are *The Little Shepherd of Kingdom Come* (1903) and *The Trail of the Lonesome Pine* (1908).
28. Hartman, "Origins of the Mountain Preacher," p. 61.
29. Fristoe, *The History of the Ketocton Baptist Association, 1766–1808*, p. 32.
30. Hartman, "Origins of the Mountain Preacher," p. 66.
31. Sovine, "Traditionalism," p. 40.
32. Hartman, "Origins of the Mountain Preacher," p. 56.
33. "'If I Were Beginning Again': A Reflective Symposium by Seven Rural Ministers of the Mountains." Whisnant in *Modernizing the Mountaineer* devoted "Part 1: The Missionary Background" to a single chapter entitled "Workers in God's Grand Division: The Council of the Southern Mountains" (pp. 3–39).
34. Titon, *Powerhouse for God: Speech, Chant, and Song in an Appalachian Baptist Church* (1988), focuses for more than five hundred pages on Brother John Sherfey and his church. See also Titon's two-record set and booklet, *Powerhouse for God* (1982).
35. Wolfe, *Children of the Heav'nly King: Religious Expression in the Central Blue Ridge*. This two-record set with an extensive booklet features a broad range of religious expression (gospel singing, hymn lining, conversion narratives, prayer and preaching, baptisms, revival meetings, black and white churches). See pp. 20–25 of the booklet for Elder Millard Pruitt and the Laurel Glenn Regular Baptist Church.
36. National Geographic Society, *American Mountain People*, features Preacher Dan Gibson on pp. 86–87.
37. Daugherty's "Saga of the Serpent-Handlers" is a large unpublished manuscript about Brother Joe Turner, his family, and his church community.
38. The largest Pentecostal denomination in the South today is the Assemblies of God, with headquarters in Springfield, Missouri, in the northern foothills of the Ozarks. The third largest is the Pentecostal Holiness Church out of Franklin Springs, Georgia, in the southern foothills of the Appalachians. As the second largest, the Church of God (Cleveland, Tennessee) is not to be confused

with the Church of God (Anderson, Indiana), the oldest Holiness denomination in America (1881). Nor is it to be confused with the myriad of small, independent Holiness-Pentecostal churches throughout the mountains of Appalachia that have named themselves "Church of God," but have no connection with the national denomination of the same name based in Cleveland, Tennessee. "Church of God" is one of the most common and popular names for the region's independent Holiness churches, going back at least to the 1880s.

Part 1: Mountain Religious Life, Mountain Religious History

1. Brother Coy Miser, a commanding presence in this book, was called by "Death's Angel" (in his words) while I was in the final stages of revising the book manuscript. I have maintained his voice and active involvement throughout as originally written, in the present tense.

Chapter 1: Brother Callaway of Avery County

1. Hooker, *Religion in the Highlands,* p. v. Fannie W. Dunn, a contributor to this study, was a professor at Teachers College, Columbia University.

2. Ibid., p. viii.

3. Only Melanie L. Sovine in her "Traditionalism, Antimissionism, and the Primitive Baptist Religion" (1986) has developed discussion about how mountain religion has been portrayed in terms of a passive traditionalism corresponding to the mythical image of Appalachia. Sovine is also the one scholar who has redirected discussion about mountain religion toward social and historical context; see "Studying Religious Belief Systems in Their Social Historical Context" (1983). This essay includes an examination of the political questions affecting theological decisions by religious traditions most characteristic of the mountains of Appalachia.

4. William Goodell Frost was president of Berea College in Berea, Kentucky, when he published "Our Contemporary Ancestors in the Southern Mountains" in the March 1899 issue of *Atlantic Monthly.* Originally founded in the late 1850s by the American Missionary Association home missionary John G. Fee as an abolitionist school for biracial education, Berea College was transformed by Frost to focus upon the educational needs of Appalachian young people. Frost is often credited with "discovering" Appalachia as a bastion of Anglo-Saxon heritage, and this well-known article only served to reinforce that description in the national consciousness. The phrase "yesterday's people" was current for half a century and culminated in popular usage as the title of Jack Weller's *Yesterday's People* (1965). This book is credited with being instrumental in solidifying Appalachia's central place in the mid-1960s War on Poverty programs, following almost immediately on the heels of Harry Caudill's *Night Comes to the Cumberlands* (1962) and strongly reinforcing *Night's* extraordinary national impact. *Night's* impact as a dynamic symbol came along at an appropriate time, building on the growing focus on Appalachia that began with many press pieces from the late 1950s. *Night* articulated Appalachia's distinction of being "the first frontier in the war on

poverty" (as the 1963 paperback edition proclaimed on its cover, complete with a photograph of a decrepit, whitewashed mountain log cabin); it did not, however, have the distinction sometimes accorded it of "starting" the War on Poverty in Appalachia. The seed planted for the War on Poverty is attributed to the shock John F. Kennedy felt at the poverty he saw when he campaigned in West Virginia. That seed was, however, a seed of politics. The Democratic party wanted to see if Kennedy could win a primary in a predominantly southern Protestant state, and West Virginia was chosen as the test. Kennedy won West Virginia and from there went on to win the nomination from Hubert Humphrey. (My thanks to Ron D Eller for his clarification of my questions about Caudill's *Night Comes to the Cumberlands* and also the role of West Virginia in the presidential elections of 1960.)

5. Loyal Jones, "Appalachian Values," p. 508 (emphasis added).

6. Sovine Reid was the first to lay down the methodological challenge to other researchers and scholars to study mountain religion as religion, not as a subcategory of another field. See Reid, "On the Study of Religion in Appalachia" (1979). I quote the particular passage referred to here in the Essay on Sources.

7. Loyal Jones, "Appalachian Values," p. 508.

8. Albanese, *America: Religions and Religion*, pp. 8–9.

9. Ibid., p. 222.

10. Bruce, *And They All Sang Hallelujah: Plain-Folk Camp-Meeting Religion, 1800–1845*, p. 24.

11. Gerrard, "Churches of the Stationary Poor in Appalachia," is the premier example of this genre of social science writing on mountain religion. Gerrard uses a subculture of poverty model for understanding the independent, nondenominational Holiness church in Appalachia, and his language of description is extremely condescending (for example, he refers to Holiness mountain people as "contemporary primitives"). However, Gerrard does recognize the preponderance of such churches in rural areas (pp. 103–4) and that mountain people more often than not identify themselves as "Holiness," even though outsiders would call them Pentecostal (see esp. p. 112, n. 5). See Loyal Jones's critique of Gerrard's essay in "Mountain Religion: The Outsider's View," p. 44.

12. See Parker, "Folk Religion in Southern Appalachia," the bulk of which traces the development of church-sect typology in academic research, from Ernst Troeltsch to H. Richard Niebuhr to Earl D. C. Brewer. Parker argues against using church-sect typology for describing and analyzing Appalachian mountain religion. Brewer, an ordained Methodist minister, was the sociologist who directed the religion survey of the 1959 Southern Appalachian Studies and summarized its findings in "Religion and the Churches," in Ford, *The Southern Appalachian Region: A Survey* (1962). Brewer's summary and research data set the direction for most of the social science doctoral and postdoctoral research on Appalachian mountain religion for the next fifteen years and is still called upon today. Berea College and the Council of the Southern Mountains sponsored the Southern Appalachian Studies, funded by a Ford Foundation grant, which resulted in the 1962 *Survey*, the first survey of the Appalachian region since the 1935 USDA study.

13. Albanese, *America: Religions and Religion,* p. 234.

14. 1935 Religious Survey, Box 5, Series VII, 11–5: Avery County, North Carolina, Survey of Ministers. The survey is dated 1935 rather than 1931 in the Berea College Archives because that is the year the USDA study was published.

15. Remarks about these and other individuals, unless otherwise indicated, are from my personal meetings and interviews with them, along with my attendance at their worship services.

16. Warren Brunner is a photographer of mountain life and culture with a studio in Berea, Kentucky.

17. The Church of Christ, Christian Church, and Disciples of Christ are preceded in the United States only by the Rogerenes, the Separate Congregationalists, and the Separate Baptists in Connecticut.

18. Bush, *Dorie, Woman of the Mountains,* pp. 137–39. An expanded version was published in 1992 under the same title by the University of Tennessee Press. *Dorie, Woman of the Mountains* is that rarest of documents for which religion historians of the Appalachian region search: a detailed, comprehensive account by the very people who lived the events and transitions of a period that forever changed the face of traditional mountain life and culture. Florence Cope Bush understands very well indeed the transition from nonindustrial to industrial society that her mother and father, grandmother and grandfather, lived through and what it meant not only for them but for the region in which they lived. Vignettes about religious life in the Great Smokies are laced throughout the book. Bush's parents were Baptists initially (what "flavor" is never indicated). Her father, Rev. Fredrick Arnold Cope, after spending decades working as a laborer in timber camps and then building power lines in the surrounding counties, moved to Knoxville in the early 1940s. "After completing the required educational background, he became a Methodist minister," serving in various churches in the Knoxville area until his death in 1961 (p. 183).

19. A representative article is by R. H. Randolph, "Religion: Highland Churches" (1950), about "several common problems" found in mountain churches. These "common problems" are listed under various titles, "Denominational Overlapping," "Lack of Cooperation," "Under Churching," "Non-Church People," "Inadequate Church Program," and "Obsolete Church Buildings." *Mountain Life & Work* (*ML&W*), in which this article appeared, was the publication of the Council of the Southern Mountains or CSM, originally named the Conference of Southern Mountain Workers. The conference was organized by John C. Campbell, an American Missionary Association home missionary assigned full-time to Appalachia beginning in 1896. Campbell founded the conference in 1913 as the umbrella organization to help coordinate the endeavors of secular and church workers alike in the Appalachian region and provide outreach to national agencies. *ML&W* began publication in April 1925. Over the years *ML&W* upheld mainline churches—especially Presbyterian, Congregational, Lutheran, and Episcopalian—nestled in mountainous rural areas as the ideal to be striven for. Indigenous mountain preachers were a bane. Mountain religion itself was seen as a retardant, hence the need for a "true" Christianity in Appalachia to lead the way to progressiveness and humane social problem solving.

In 1925 the conference also opened an office in Berea, Kentucky. This move began a tight association with Berea College for nearly half a century.

Chapter 2: Emma Bell Miles and "The Old-time Religion"

1. See Gaston, *Emma Bell Miles* (1985), the first book-length biography.
2. Miles, *The Spirit of the Mountains,* pp. 119–20. Further references to this work will be cited by page number within the body of the text.
3. Wicks, "Life and Meaning: Singing, Praying, and the Word among Old Regular Baptists of Eastern Kentucky"; Dorgan, *Giving Glory to God in Appalachia: Worship Practices of Six Baptist Subdenominations;* Titon, *Powerhouse for God.*

Chapter 3: The New Salem Association of Old Regular Baptists, org. 1825

1. Lewis, Kobak, and Johnson, "Family, Religion, and Colonialism in Central Appalachia." Helen Lewis is the scholar most credited with development of the colonialism model in its application to Appalachia. Linda Johnson, "The Foot-Washin' Church and the Prayer-Book Church: Resisting Cultural Imperialism in Southern Appalachia," especially took to task the Commission on Religion in Appalachia (CORA), an interdenominational agency founded in 1965 in part as a result of the findings of the 1962 Ford *Survey* and in part as a response to the War on Poverty. CORA is now the largest umbrella organization for denominational work in the Appalachian region. True to the spirit of the times and the Protestant denominations that make up the bulwark of its representation, CORA offers significant support for projects such as economic critique and grassroots development.
2. Reid, "'Neither Adding nor Taking Away': The Care and Keeping of Primitive Baptist Church Houses," p. 170.
3. I provide a summary of primary and secondary sources on Primitive and Old Regular Baptists in the Essay on Sources.
4. Whisnant, Introduction to the new edition of *Spirit of the Mountains,* p. xxv.
5. "Armed off" is an expression stemming from early Baptist revival culture during the Great Awakening in the South. It means that a church or association, called a "mother" church or association, constitutes or "arms off" "daughter" churches or associations. The expression is very common in the Appalachian region.
6. Spencer, *Kentucky Baptists,* vol. 2, p. 394.
7. Dorgan, *The Old Regular Baptists of Central Appalachia,* p. 1.
8. Ahlstrom, *Religious History of the American People,* p. 442. Ahlstrom includes the full text of the 1801 confession, pp. 441–42.
9. Wallhausser, "I Can Almost See Heaven from Here," p. 4.
10. Ibid.
11. See *The Articles of the Synod of Dort,* trans. Scott (1841).
12. Torbet, *History of the Baptists,* p. 25.

13. Ibid., pp. 29–30.

14. Ibid., p. 65.

15. Some of the "combination of factors" Torbet lists for the solidifying "ecclesiology" of the Southern Baptist Convention were "(1) an early union of Baptist forces to protect themselves against persecution; (2) a General Baptist background with its more centralized polity; (3) a developing centralization of state conventions quite early in the nineteenth century" (ibid., p. 442).

16. Dorgan, *Old Regular Baptists,* pp. 204–5.

17. Pittman, comp., *In Defense of the Truth: Or, Danville Church Division Investigated . . . May, 1926.* The Danville Church was a Primitive Baptist church in southern Virginia caught up in an internal dispute over absolute predestination. Pittman, beginning on p. 87, attacks "association Baptists," because the Danville Church had referred the issue "to the association!" (p. 6) rather than settling with the messengers sent in the dispute.

18. Only James E. Cushman, a Presbyterian minister who served in the Presbytery of Greenbrier in West Virginia for several years, has recognized and analyzed these characteristics of Appalachian mountain churches and how they are reflected in the rural mountain churches of mainstream denominations such as Presbyterian, Methodist, and Southern Baptist. See Cushman, *Beyond Survival (Revitalizing the Small Church),* "Historical Foundations of the Small Church Today," pp. 11–75.

19. Dixon and Akers, comps., *Minutes of the Burning Spring Association of Baptist, 1813–1824, and Minutes of the New Salem Association of Old Regular Baptist, 1825–1983,* vol. 1, p. 146.

20. Ibid., vol. 1, p. 225.

21. Dorgan, *Old Regular Baptists,* p. 37.

22. Dixon and Akers, *Minutes,* vol. 1, p. 276.

Chapter 4: "We Believed in the Family and the Old Regular Baptist Church"

1. See the Essay on Sources for insider pieces written by or about Old Regular Baptists.

2. Dorgan, *Old Regular Baptists,* p. 8.

3. Short, "We Believed in the Family and the Old Regular Baptist Church," p. 62.

4. Benedict, *Fifty Years among the Baptists* (1860), pp. 160, 162–63.

5. Ibid., pp. 160, 165–68.

6. Short, "We Believed," p. 62.

7. Spencer, *Kentucky Baptists,* vol. 2, p. 394.

8. Sovine has explored this tradition of conversion experience in greatest depth, "A Sweet Hope in My Breast: Belief and Ritual in the Primitive Baptist Church."

9. Short, "We Believed," p. 62.

10. See Selement and Woolley, eds., *Thomas Shepard's Confessions.*

11. See Mullen, "Ritual and Sacred Narrative in the Blue Ridge Mountains," a paper originally written for the American Folklife Center, Library of Congress.

12. Short, "We Believed," p. 63.

13. See Reid, "'Neither Adding nor Taking Away': The Care and Keeping of Primitive Baptist Church Houses."

14. See the Essay on Sources for material on hymn lining.

15. C. C. Collins, "Church Work in North Carolina" (1891).

16. Pinkston, "Lined Hymns, Spirituals, and the Associated Lifestyle of Rural Black People in the United States."

17. Short, "We Believed," p. 64.

18. Dorgan, "'Ol' Time Way' Exhortation: Preaching in the Old Regular Baptist Church," p. 28.

19. Bruce, *And They All Sang Hallelujah,* p. 86 (emphasis added).

20. For many years Brother Sam Johnson (1892–1975) was moderator of Ivory Point Regular Baptist Church, an Old Regular Baptist Church in eastern Kentucky. (To add to the outside observer's confusion, many churches that are Old Regular Baptist call themselves simply "Regular Baptist"—just as many Regular Baptist churches are not Old Regular Baptist.) Brother Johnson said in an oral history interview, "It's a great big job, moderator of the church. He does the church work and preaches. He asks them all whuther they're in 'love and fellowship' with one another and if anything is wrong. They generally answer, 'Love and fellowship' all the time [whether] they is or not" (Shackelford and Weinberg, *Our Appalachia: An Oral History,* pp. 287–88).

21. Short, "We Believed," p. 65.

22. Sovine, "Sweet Hope in My Breast," pp. 48–49, quoting her interview with Mrs. Carolyn P. Alston (emphasis added).

23. Short, "We Believed," p. 65.

24. Ibid., p. 62.

25. Ibid., p. 65 (emphasis added).

26. R. Chesla Sharp in a review of Dorgan's *Giving Glory to God* concluded that "in some cases, the study is probably the record of dying sects." Sharp also described the book's eight photographs of Appalachian church houses: "One is a beautiful country gothic church, two are non-descript clapboard structures, and the rest are hideous buildings." Sharp's "beautiful country gothic church" was the one that looked most like the church building of a mainline denomination. The "non-descript clapboard structures" and "hideous buildings" were the architecture most representative of church houses in rural Appalachia. Sharp's comment demonstrates that beauty is very much in the eye of the beholder. This review appeared in *Now and Then* (Summer 1988), published by the Center for Appalachian Studies and Services/Institute for Appalachian Affairs, East Tennessee State University.

27. See Beaver, *Rural Community in the Appalachian South,* which explores especially kinship as a cultural idea or idiom through which community homogeneity and cooperation are derived. See also F. Carlene Bryant, *We're All Kin: A Cultural Study of a Mountain Neighborhood,* especially the chapter "Churches," pp. 89–120. Bryant in particular recognized that while kinship is a key factor in mountain churches, it is transcended by the kinship of a religious community as brothers and sisters in Christ not determined or de-

limited by blood kinship ties. See also Sweet, "The Churches as Moral Courts of the Frontier," for the impact of a disciplined church within the broader framework of social community.

Chapter 5: Baptists, Methodists, and the Radical Decline of Religious Experience, 1825–27

1. See Handy, *A Christian America.* See also Marty, *Protestantism in the United States: Righteous Empire.*
2. Sovine, "Traditionalism," p. 36.
3. The word "mountain" and the phrase "Hill Country of Holston" are repeated motifs in Martin, *Methodism in Holston* (1945).
4. Frank Richardson, *From Sunrise to Sunset* (1910), p. 35.
5. Ibid., pp. 37, 38. Emphasis added.
6. Bruce, *And They All Sang Hallelujah,* p. 56.
7. Charles A. Johnson, *The Frontier Camp Meeting,* p. 249.
8. Frank Richardson, *From Sunrise to Sunset,* p. 37.
9. Mickel, "The Change in the Perspective on Camp Meetings in *The Methodist Magazine* between 1818 and 1826," p. 4. I am indebted to Rev. Mickel for sharing with me his research paper.
10. Ibid., pp. 15–17. These three pages contain mostly notes documenting Mickel's conclusions.
11. Sovine, "Traditionalism," p. 38.
12. Taylor, *Thoughts on Missions* (1819), p. 12.
13. Alexander Campbell, *The Christian Baptist* (1835), vol. 1, p. 16, col. 2.
14. Hassell and Hassell, *History of the Church of God, . . . Including Especially the History of the Kehukee Primitive Baptist Association* (1886), pp. 736–38.
15. Short, "We Believed," p. 62.
16. See Spencer, *Kentucky Baptists,* vol. 2, p. 671.
17. Benedict, *Fifty Years among the Baptists,* pp. 126–27 (emphasis added).
18. For a statistical chart of distribution in 1846 taken from the *Baptist Reporter* (1847), pp. 341, 344, see Sweet, *Religion on the American Frontier: The Baptists,* p. 66, n. 22.

Chapter 6: Old Father Nash and Charles Grandison Finney

1. McLoughlin, *Revivals, Awakenings, and Reform,* pp. 131, 106, 122.
2. See Mead, *Nathaniel William Taylor, 1786–1858.*
3. McLoughlin, *Modern Revivalism: Charles Grandison Finney to Billy Graham,* p. 132.
4. Finney, *Lectures on Revivals of Religion* (1835), p. 12.
5. See Dolan, *Catholic Revivalism: The American Experience, 1830–1900.*
6. Cross, *The Burned-Over District: The Social and Intellectual History of Enthusiastic Religion in Western New York, 1800–1850,* p. 9.
7. Olafson, *1860 Census Book of Boone County, West Virginia,* pp. 10, 23, 32,

34, 59, 68, 73, 88, 99, 122, 125; cited in Daugherty, "Saga of the Serpent-Handlers," p. 26.

8. Cross, *Burned-Over District*, p. 15.

9. Torbet, *History of the Baptists*, p. 256.

10. Cross, *Burned-Over District*, p. 278.

11. Ibid., p. 160.

12. Finney, *Charles G. Finney: An Autobiography*, p. 52.

13. Perkins, *A "Bunker Hill" Contest, A.D. 1826, etc.* (1826), p. 65.

14. Lillard G. Rouse was born in 1887 and lived throughout the central Appalachian region, ministering in small churches with little means of support as far north as Chillicothe in southeastern Ohio and as far south as Anniston, Alabama, with many years in eastern Kentucky and east Tennessee. In his later years his healing ministry was centered in the Knoxville area. See his autobiography, *Modern Miracles: Life of L. G. Rouse.*

15. Mahan, *Autobiography* (1882), p. 226.

16. Myrick to Finney, Verona, N.Y., Jan. 30, 1832, Charles G. Finney papers, Oberlin College Library, Oberlin, Ohio (hereafter, "Finney papers").

17. Nash to Finney, Albia, N.Y., Oct. 27, 1828, Finney papers.

18. Nash to Finney, Wynants Kill, N.Y., Nov. 12, 1828, Finney papers.

19. Mahan, *Autobiography*, p. 227.

20. Finney, *Charles G. Finney*, pp. 70–71.

21. Weaver, "The Praying Rock."

22. Brockway, *A Delineation of the Characteristic Features of a Revival of Religion in Troy, in 1826 and 1827* (1827), p. 54 (emphasis in the original). This pamphlet was an attack on the "new system" of the "prayer of faith" or "particularity in prayer," especially as practiced and defended by the Presbyterian minister Nathaniel Beman, who hosted a revival in Troy, New York, by Finney and Nash. Brockway seemed unaware that the "new system" of prayer originated from Nash in the Finney revivals.

23. Finney, *Charles G. Finney*, p. 134.

24. Nash to Finney, Wynants Kill, N.Y., Nov. 12, 1828, Finney papers.

25. Nash to Finney, Verona, N.Y., Nov. 26, 27, 1831, Finney papers.

26. Nash to Brother James, Palmyra, N.Y., Apr. 12, 1831, Finney papers.

27. Fowler, *Historical Sketch of Presbyterianism within the Bounds of the Synod of Central New York* (1877), p. 216.

28. Nash to Finney, Palmyra, N.Y., Feb. 2, 1831, Finney papers.

29. Fowler, *Historical Sketch of Presbyterianism*, p. 217 (emphasis added).

30. Cross, *Burned-Over District*, p. 161.

31. Ibid., p. 163. Cross provides no citation for the original source of this resolution.

32. Barnes, *The Antislavery Impulse, 1830–1844*, p. 12.

33. Quoted in Cross, *Burned-Over District*, p. 162. Gale's unpublished autobiography is in the collection at Oberlin College Library.

34. Ibid., p. 161.

35. Nash to Brother [Leonard?], Utica, N.Y., Oct. 22, 1827, Finney papers.

36. *A Narrative of the Revival of Religion, in the County of Oneida* (1826), pp. 12–13 (emphasis added).

37. Frank Richardson, *From Sunrise to Sunset,* p. 35 (emphasis added).

38. Nash to Finney, Wynants Kill, N.Y., Nov. 12, 1828, Finney papers.

39. Nash to Finney, Verona, N.Y., Nov. 26, 27, 1831, Finney papers.

40. McLoughlin, *Modern Revivalism,* pp. 65–66.

Part 2: Roots of Mountain Religiosity

1. Mead, *The Lively Experiment: The Shaping of Christianity in America,* p. 38.

2. Ibid., p. 36.

Chapter 7: Mountain Religion and Denominationalism

1. Vance, Foreword to *Southern Highlander,* p. ix.

2. Shapiro, Introduction to *Southern Highlander,* p. xxii.

3. Weatherford, editor of *Religion in the Appalachian Mountains,* was at the time president of Berea College. He would be instrumental in securing funding for the 1959 Southern Appalachian Studies that would take John C. Campbell's *The Southern Highlander & His Homeland* and Hooker's *Religion in the Highlands* as its base for devising a strategy for a social survey of the Appalachian region.

4. Campbell, *Southern Highlander,* p. 176. Further references to this work will be cited by page number within the body of the text.

5. Hooker, *Religion in the Highlands,* p. 209.

6. Despite the strong admonitions of its founder, John C. Campbell, this last advice—not to ignore the leadership of mountain preachers "in any effort for betterment"—would later be discountenanced in particular by *Mountain Life & Work,* the periodical of the Conference of Southern Mountain Workers first published in 1925. Some early articles of note are: Doran, "Some Church Problems in the Southern Mountains" (1926); Tadlock, "Church Problems in the Mountains" (1930); and Warren H. Wilson, "The Educated Minister in the Mountains" (1930). Wilson lamented the long-sufference of "the educated minister" among "the mountain people" and applauded "the educated minister" for his courage. A Berea College alumnus and Columbia University Ph.D., he had been Superintendent of Church and Country Life Work of the Presbyterian Church, U.S.A. (northern Presbyterians), since 1908 and was a regular contributor to *ML&W.* One article, however, stands out in particular: Kelly, "The Mountain Preacher and the Mountain Problem" (1933). Kelly was the founder of Clear Creek Mountain Preachers' School in Pineville, Kentucky, now called the Clear Creek Baptist Bible College and associated with the Southern Baptist Convention. See Carvin Bryant, *Voice in the Mountains: The Incredible Story of Lloyd C. Kelly* (1987).

7. In fact, in his forty-two pages on religion, Campbell mentions Holiness-Pentecostal churches in only two sentences, identifying them with the "Holiness Methodist Church."

8. Lowther, *Laughter and Tears in the Mountains,* pp. 41–43.

9. Cushman elaborated on Campbell's insights in *Beyond Survival,* "The Small Church Pastor," pp. 84–107. He says that in small denominational churches in Appalachia, "[T]he pastor has often been part of the problem." As part of the problem, Cushman listed three types of pastors mainline denominations send to Appalachia: "First are the ones who possess a retirement mentality. . . . The second type of pastor . . . is the young pastor motivated by the stepping stone mentality. . . . The third type of pastor . . . is the pastor with the missionary mentality" (pp. 84–86). Cushman writes, "One underlying problem with all three types of small church pastors is that they are often cultural foreigners. This is especially true in small, rural churches. The pastor is an urban, upper middle class, seminary educated pastor, who possesses a certain cultural superiority over the laity of the small church. Therefore, the pastor feels that he/she knows what is best for that congregation. Any program development becomes the pastor's thing. In any case, the pastor is usually gone in less than five years. And in each case it is not the church laity that is the problem. It is the pastor who is the main problem" (p. 86).

10. Albanese, *America: Religions and Religion,* p. 231; Loyal Jones, "A Preliminary Look at the Welsh Component of Celtic Influence in Appalachia."

11. Albanese, *America: Religions and Religion,* pp. 221–43.

12. Ibid., p. 229.

Chapter 8: Pietism, Pietists, and Holiness People

1. See George H. Williams, *The Radical Reformation.*

2. Torbet, *History of the Baptists,* p. 29.

3. Anabaptist traditions in the United States range from the Old Order Amish to the Evangelical United Brethren, who later merged with the Methodist church. See Piepkorn, *Profiles in Belief,* vol. 2, *Protestant Denominations,* part 4, "Churches with Origins in the Radical Reformation," subsection entitled "Churches That Perpetuate Continental Free Church Tradition," pp. 478–530. Piepkorn also included in part 4 the Puritans, "Churches Perpetuating the Congregationalist Tradition," "Churches of the Mennonite Tradition," and "Baptist Churches."

4. See Stein, *Philip Jakob Spener.*

5. See Sattler, *God's Glory; Neighbor's Good: A Brief Introduction into the Life and Writings of August Hermann Francke.*

6. Stoeffler, *The Rise of Evangelical Pietism,* p. 8 (emphasis added). See also Stoeffler, ed., *Continental Pietism and Early American Christianity.*

7. Ibid., p. 13.

8. Ibid., p. 21.

9. Ibid., p. 5.

10. Ahlstrom, *Religious History of the American People,* p. 236.

11. Westerkamp, *Triumph of the Laity: Scots-Irish Piety and the Great Awakening, 1625–1760,* p. 207.

12. Caruso, *The Appalachian Frontier,* pp. 30–31.

13. Ahlstrom, *Religious History of the American People,* p. 324.

14. "They [Sandy Creek Association] formerly held nine Christian rites, viz. *baptism, the Lord's supper, love-feasts, laying-on-of-hands, washing feet, anointing the sick, right hand of fellowship, kiss of charity, and devoting children*" (Benedict, *A General History of the Baptist Denomination in America* [1813], vol. 2, p. 107 [emphasis in the original]). All of these practices or "rites" were also carried out by pietist groups in Appalachia, especially the Mennonites and German Baptist Brethren.

15. Brunk, *History of the Mennonites in Virginia, 1727–1900*, vol. 1, p. 23. Vol. 2 covers 1900 to 1960.

16. Handy, *A History of the Churches in the United States and Canada*, pp. 98–99.

17. Albanese, *America: Religions and Religion*, p. 231.

18. Mary Lee Daugherty has noted this in her "Saga of the Serpent-Handlers" about serpent-handling Appalachian Christians in southern West Virginia. The holy kiss, footwashing, and refusal to take oaths are especially prevalent among the serpent handlers Daugherty has studied.

19. Wust, *Saint-Adventurers of the Virginia Frontier*, covers the Virginia frontier in the late 1740s from the vantage point of separatists from the Ephrata community. Corliss Fitz Randolph, *A History of Seventh Day Baptists in West Virginia* (1905).

20. Ahlstrom, *Religious History of the American People*, p. 233.

Chapter 9: Scots-Irish Religiosity and Revivalism

1. Albanese, *America: Religions and Religion*, p. 231. Serpent handling is also among the celebrations creating "a new sacramentalism which spoke to their condition." See Daugherty, "Serpent-Handling as Sacrament."

2. Dorgan, *Giving Glory to God*, p. 128.

3. Albanese, *America: Religions and Religion*, p. 230.

4. Tallmadge, "Anglo-Saxon vs. Scotch-Irish"; Caudill, "Anglo-Saxon vs. Scotch-Irish, Round 2"; Drake, "Anglo-Saxon vs. Scotch-Irish, Round 3."

5. Drake, "Round Three," p. 18.

6. Leyburn, *The Scotch-Irish*, p. 185.

7. Campbell still provides the best succinct outline of settlement in the Appalachian region in his *Southern Highlander*, "Pioneer Routes of Travel and Early Settlement," pp. 22–49. Drake writes, "In this matter of a judicious seeking for the ancestors to Southern Appalachians, we have not progressed much further than the able account of this left by John C. Campbell" ("Round Three," p. 19).

8. Blair, "Memoir of the Rev. Samuel Blair," p. 158.

9. Ibid., pp. 159–60.

10. Trinterud, *The Forming of an American Tradition*, p. 77.

11. Bailie, *The Six Mile Water Revival of 1625*.

12. Schmidt's dissertation, "Scottish Communions and American Revivals" (1987), on which *Holy Fairs* is based, will also be cited.

13. Schmidt comes very close to the term "sacramental revivalism" at several points in his text. Once he uses the term "sacramental revivals" (Schmidt,

Holy Fairs, p. 49) for sacramental meetings, which he also calls sacramental occasions, communion seasons, and communion festivals, to name the most frequent variations. Repeatedly he emphasizes that sacramental meetings were "intertwined from the first with revival" (ibid., p. 11). Indeed, Schmidt borrowed the concept of "sacramental evangelicalism" (Schmidt, "Scottish Communions and American Revivals," p. 7) from Dolan's *Catholic Revivalism* on revivalism among Roman Catholics in America in the nineteenth century. Dolan's helpful concept conveys a combination of conversionist preaching with eucharistic practice and, hence, a recognition of the compatibility of "sacramentalism and revivalism" which, as Schmidt stated, "it will become clear, could happily intertwine" (ibid., p. 8). Dolan wrote that the term "evangelicalism" is generic, descriptive of a perspective that "represents a mood or style of religion which is not peculiar to any one denomination and thus best describes the central thrust of the revival tradition in American religion" (Dolan, *Catholic Revivalism,* p. 91). Dolan went on to say that, unlike Protestant revivalism, "Catholic revivalism blended the gospel of evangelicalism with the ritual of sacraments; the end result was a sacramental evangelicalism" (ibid., p. 112). Through his study of Scots-Irish sacramental meetings, Schmidt saw the "continuity between" Catholic revivalism and "Protestant evangelism," thus extending Dolan's insight of "sacramental evangelicalism" to the "revivalism of American Protestants" (Schmidt, "Scottish Communions and American Revivals," pp. 7–8). We have already heard Catherine Albanese argue that mountain people "wove their Protestantism with a new sacramentalism which spoke to their condition" (Albanese, *America: Religions and Religion,* p. 231). I further argue that the base of mountain religion is a revival religiosity infused with a sacramental consciousness permeating all of mountain religious culture and its church traditions, from the most doctrinally conservative to the most free-flowing. Fortified by the insights of Albanese, Dolan, and Schmidt, as well as my own, I have consolidated their tightly interconnected terminology by extending it to embrace the substance of mountain religiosity which I identify as "sacramental revivalism." Given that the Scots-Irish provided Appalachia's largest population base during its earliest years of settlement, I also apply the term "sacramental revivalism" to Scots-Irish religiosity throughout this chapter, which the combined insights of Westerkamp and Schmidt on the religious culture of the Scots-Irish laity reinforce.

14. Westerkamp, *Triumph of the Laity,* p. 14.

15. Ibid., p. 9.

16. Schmidt, "Scottish Communions and American Revivals," p. 13.

17. Schmidt, *Holy Fairs,* p. 24.

18. Ibid., p. 11.

19. See Morgan, *Visible Saints: The History of a Puritan Idea.*

20. See Schmidt, *Holy Fairs,* p. 237, n. 105, where he faults Dickson D. Bruce for not recognizing that plain-folk camp-meeting religion did not simply spring up in the frontier of the upland South, making a decisive break with previous revival traditions; instead, Schmidt identifies the emergence of plain-folk camp-meeting religion with the heritage of Scots-Irish sacramental revivalism, especially as it expressed itself on the Appalachian frontier. While recog-

nizing the eventual localization of Scots-Irish religiosity in the Appalachian region, Schmidt seems unaware to what extent the Scots-Irish heritage of sacramental revivalism pervaded all of mountain religious culture, especially in Calvinist-based mountain church traditions.

21. Westerkamp, *Triumph of the Laity*, p. 34.

22. Schmidt, *Holy Fairs*, p. 20.

23. Westerkamp, *Triumph of the Laity*, p. 31.

24. Schmidt, *Holy Fairs*, p. 58.

25. Ibid., p. 59.

26. Ibid., p. 53.

27. Westerkamp, *Triumph of the Laity*, p. 40.

28. Both Westerkamp and Schmidt consider popular versus official religion and popular versus elite culture. See especially Schmidt, *Holy Fairs*, chap. 4, "The Autumn of the Sacramental Season," pp. 169–212.

29. Schmidt, *Holy Fairs*, pp. 145–46.

30. Westerkamp, *Triumph of the Laity*, p. 86. See chapter 8, "Pietism, Pietists, and Holiness People," for Stoeffler's reference to the Scottish Kirk.

31. Westerkamp, *Triumph of the Laity*, p. 108.

32. Ibid., p. 135.

33. Lingle and Kuykendall, *Presbyterians: Their History and Beliefs*, pp. 92–93. See also Alexander, "The Covenanters Come to East Tennessee."

34. Westerkamp, *Triumph of the Laity*, pp. 204–5. Westerkamp made her determination by identifying the origins and ethnic backgrounds of the Presbyterian ministers involved in the Great Awakening at the time of schism in 1741 and of reunion in 1758.

35. Ibid., p. 166.

36. Ibid., pp. 195–96 (emphasis added).

37. Albanese, *America: Religions and Religion*, p. 229.

38. Westerkamp, *Triumph of the Laity*, p. 212 (emphasis added).

39. Lawless, *God's Peculiar People: Women's Voices & Folk Tradition in a Pentecostal Church*, pp. x, 4. This work focuses on a single church community in southern Indiana near the Kentucky border, an independent Jesus Only or Oneness Pentecostal church. The people who make up this church community support themselves by working in limestone quarries. The church itself, especially its worship practices, is particularly characteristic of independent Jesus Only churches in coal mining communities, as well as other independent Holiness churches, in central Appalachia.

40. Ibid., p. 5.

41. On James McGready, see McGready, *The Posthumous Works of the Reverend and Pious James McGready, Late Minister of the Gospel in Ky. [Kentucky]*; Posey, *The Presbyterian Church in the Old Southwest, 1778–1838*; Sweet, *Religion on the American Frontier: The Presbyterians, 1783–1840*; Boles, *The Great Revival, 1787–1805*; Schmidt, *Holy Fairs*; and Conkin, *Cane Ridge: America's Pentecost*.

42. Schmidt, *Holy Fairs*, p. 63.

43. McGready, "A Short Narrative of the Revival of Religion in Logan Coun-

ty," *Western Missionary Magazine*, 1 (1803), pp. 173, 177, quoted in Schmidt, *Holy Fairs*, p. 11.

44. Conkin, *Cane Ridge*, p. 55.

45. Schmidt, "Scottish Communions and American Revivals," p. 113. Schmidt's marked conservatism in revising his dissertation into *Holy Fairs* is demonstrated by his very constricted reformulation of this statement: "Throughout much of the West and South—including western Pennsylvania, the valley of Virginia, backcountry North Carolina, Kentucky, and Tennessee—the old forms of renewal, based upon the sacramental practices of Scotland and Ulster, were often preserved for another generation or more [into the 1820s and 1830s]" (Schmidt, *Holy Fairs*, pp. 65–66). In his much more narrowly focused revision of his original statement, Schmidt lost sight of—or simply rejected the prospect of—the far-reaching influences and power of the traditional religiosity of Scots-Irish people he had originally discerned in the areas he named that made up most of the core of the Appalachian region and, like Marilyn Westerkamp (see Westerkamp, *Triumph of the Laity*, p. 14), he was initially not hesitant to proclaim. Indeed Westerkamp, unlike Schmidt, recognized the influential prevalence of what she termed "Scots-Irish religiosity" (ibid.), which Schmidt, though he does not use her term, restricted solely to the Scots-Irish's "Holy Fairs," without recognizing the wide-sweeping influence of the revivalistic behavior of the Scots-Irish that originated in their tradition of sacramental meetings but reached far beyond this limited context. Apparently for Schmidt, and contra Westerkamp, once the specific practice of the "Holy Fairs" or communion "festivals" died away altogether on the American landscape (notwithstanding the clear variations on Scots-Irish sacramental meetings I argue are present throughout mountain religion still today), so did the religiosity unique to the Scots-Irish (which I also argue was one of the foundational movements in the creation of Appalachian mountain religion).

46. As I noted in part 1, talking about the Old Regular Baptists, common usage of the term "sacrament" among mountain people when referring to the communion service usually precludes a definite article with it; that is, mountain people rarely say "*the* sacrament." Instead, they say simply "sacrament."

47. Schmidt noted that evangelical Scots-Irish Presbyterians in the celebration of their sacramental meetings "covered the eucharistic elements and the place of celebration with fine cloth to suggest the solemnity of the event" (*Holy Fairs*, p. 19). This "fine cloth" did not just cover the burse and the chalice used in the Catholic and Anglican Mass; it was a large cloth dramatically draped over all of the cups and plates, reaching well past the edge of the tabletop, which was also separately covered. In *Giving Glory to God*, Dorgan refers to "[a] communion table, covered by a linen cloth" at Bethany Old Regular Baptist Church in Kingsport, Tennessee (p. 126). A few pages later, Dorgan provides a full-page photograph of a communion-footwashing service at Mount Paran Baptist Church, an independent Missionary Baptist Church at Deep Gap in Watauga County in western North Carolina (p. 131). In this photograph the communion utensils and elements are all draped by a large white cloth reaching nearly halfway down the

length of the table legs. The basins and towels for footwashing are casually placed on the floor around the table legs.

48. See Schmidt, *Holy Fairs,* pp. 49–50.

Chapter 10: The Baptist Revival and the Power of Self-Definition

1. Campbell, *Southern Highlander,* p. 174.

2. Fristoe, *Ketocton Baptist Association* (1808), p. 15. The Ketocton was the first association of Regular Baptists in Virginia, organized in 1766.

3. See Pilcher, *Samuel Davies.*

4. Leland, "The Virginia Chronicle," in *The Writings of the Late Elder John Leland* (1845), p. 104.

5. See Lumpkin, *Baptist Foundations in the South: Tracing through the Separates the Influence of the Great Awakening, 1754–1787.*

6. Morgan Edwards, "Virginia," in *Materials Towards a History of the Baptists,* vol. 2, pp. 44–45. Edwards made his first public appeal in the late 1760s for materials that would allow him to write the first comprehensive history of the Baptists in America. He collected and wrote on Pennsylvania, New Jersey, Rhode Island, Delaware, Maryland, Virginia, North Carolina, South Carolina, and Georgia, but published only the pieces on Pennsylvania and New Jersey. Until the 1984 publication of this two-volume set, the other histories, except that on Delaware, existed only on microfilm and in manuscript form (though the material on North Carolina was published in 1930 by G. W. Paschal with annotations in the *North Carolina Historical Review*). Edwards died in January 1795. See McKibbens and Smith, *The Life and Works of Morgan Edwards.*

7. Morgan Edwards, "Virginia," *Materials,* vol. 2, p. 43.

8. Semple, *History of the Baptists in Virginia* (1810), p. 101, quoting the minutes of the General Committee for Friday, Aug. 10, 1787 (emphasis in the original).

9. Berry, comp., *The Kehukee Declaration and Black Rock Address,* pp. 23–43.

10. Dickerson, "The Baptist of the Cumberland Mountains," pp. 64–65 (emphasis added).

11. See Loyal Jones, "Old-Time Baptists and Mainline Christianity."

12. "The cant word was that they are an ignorant, illiterate set and are of the poor and contemptible class of people" (Fristoe, *Ketocton Baptist Association,* p. 32).

13. See for example Titon, *Powerhouse for God,* "Land and Life," pp. 58–140, for the social origins and conditions of some of the members of Fellowship Independent Baptist Church in Stanley, Virginia (Page County).

14. Kroll-Smith, "In Search of Status Power: The Baptist Revival in Colonial Virginia, 1760–1776," p. 25. Further references to this work will be cited by page number within the body of the text.

15. Rhys Isaac, *The Transformation of Virginia, 1740–1790,* has explored in greatest depth the power of the gentry class to assign social identity in Virginia society and the Baptist revival challenge to this presumption of social power.

16. "It was not uncommon at their great meetings for many hundreds of

men to camp on the ground, in order to be present the next day. The night meetings, through the great work of God, continued very late. The minister would scarcely have an opportunity to sleep. Sometimes the floor would be covered with persons struck down under conviction of sin. . . . There were instances of persons traveling more than one hundred miles to one of these meetings; to go forty or fifty was not uncommon" (Semple, *Baptists in Virginia,* pp. 23–24).

17. Morgan Edwards, "Virginia," *Materials,* vol. 2, pp. 38–39, transcribing Daniel Fristoe's journal.

18. John Williams, "Journal (1771)," quoted by Kroll-Smith, "Status Power," p. 203.

19. Kroll-Smith, "Status Power," p. 192.

20. Loyal Jones, "Preliminary Look," pp. 31–32. See also Dorgan, *Giving Glory to God,* chap. 2, "Hanging Their Toes in the Heavens," pp. 55–85, for a communications analysis of traditionally intoned or chanted preaching styles among mountain preachers that very closely parallel the following description of the practice of *hwyl* in late nineteenth-century America by Welsh Baptist preachers.

21. Erasmus W. Jones, "The Welsh in America" (1876), pp. 309, 310 (emphasis added). I am indebted to Loyal Jones for bringing this article to my attention.

22. Pierson, *In the Brush* (1883), pp. 73–74. See chapter 16, "In the Brush."

23. Semple, *Baptists in Virginia,* p. 15.

24. Wadhwani, "Appalachian Religion and American Capitalism," p. 9, quoting Bachelard, *The Poetics of Space* (1964), p. xii, and Dorgan, *Giving Glory to God,* p. 59 (emphasis added).

25. Ibid., p. 8 (emphasis added).

26. Leland, "Virginia Chronicle," *Writings,* pp. 114–15.

27. Benedict, *General History,* vol. 2, p. 107 (emphasis in the original).

28. Ibid., vol. 2, pp. 107–8 (emphasis added).

29. Morgan Edwards illustrated churches' autonomy and selective prerogative in their worship traditions in his record of Fall Creek Church (Separate Baptist), one of many whose individual worship traditions Edwards enumerated: "In this church are admitted Evangelists, Ruling elders, deaconesses, laying on of hands, love feasts, anointing the sick, kiss of charity, washing feet, right hand of fellowship, and devoting children. No estate. No salary, except presents" ("Virginia," *Materials,* vol. 2, p. 46). Samuel Harris was pastor of this church, a renowned revival Baptist preacher to whom Semple attributed much of the earliest important work done in establishing the Baptist revival in Virginia.

30. See Sovine, "Sweet Hope in My Breast."

31. Torbet, *History of the Baptists,* p. 256.

32. Piepkorn, *Profiles in Belief,* vol. 2, *Protestant Denominations,* p. 433.

33. Ibid., vol. 2, pp. 480–81.

34. See Harney, "A Strange Land and Peculiar People" (1873).

35. Benedict, *General History,* vol. 2, p. 407.

36. Ibid., vol. 2, p. 108.

37. "The thing referred to is this: when a woman is safely delivered in child-bearing, and raised to health enough to go to meeting, she brings her child to the minister, who either takes it in his arms, or puts his hands upon it, and thanks God for his mercy, and invokes a blessing on the child; at which time the child is named" (Leland, "Virginia Chronicle," *Writings*, p. 120).

38. Benedict, *General History*, vol. 2, p. 5.

39. Ibid., vol. 2, p. 6.

40. Morgan Edwards, "Virginia," *Materials*, vol. 2, p. 61.

41. Benedict, *Fifty Years*, pp. 162–63 (emphasis in the original).

42. See Dorgan, *Giving Glory to God*, chap. 4, "Do As I Have Done," pp. 113–46.

43. Benedict, *Fifty Years*, p. 130.

44. Benedict, *General History*, vol. 2, p. 107.

45. Campbell, *Southern Highlander*, p. 181.

46. Fristoe, *Ketocton Baptist Association*, p. 15.

47. Semple, *Baptists in Virginia*, pp. 20–21.

48. Ibid., p. 249.

49. Ibid., p. 242.

50. Morgan Edwards, "North Carolina," *Materials*, vol. 2, p. 82.

51. Burkitt and Read, *A Concise History of the Kehukee Baptist Association from Its Original Rise down to 1803*, pp. 175, 178–79 (emphasis in the original).

52. Ibid., p. 179 (emphasis in the original). See Sweet, "The Churches as Moral Courts of the Frontier."

53. In agreement with Lawless and Westerkamp, Kroll-Smith wrote, "[A] particular type of authority . . . is dependent in part on the communicative context within which it is enacted. . . . [T]raditional authority, it may be argued, [is] best served by a non-literate or oral culture" ("Status Power," p. 112).

54. Campbell, *Southern Highlander*, p. 181.

Chapter 11: Methodism in Appalachia

1. Dickerson, "Baptist of the Cumberland Mountains," pp. 64–65.

2. Livingston, "Coal Miners and Religion," p. 179. Further references to this work will be cited by page number within the body of the text.

3. Partridge, "Our Highland Institutional Church at Bon Air" (1902), pp. 436–37 (emphasis in the original).

4. Albanese, *America: Religions and Religion*, p. 234.

5. A popular novel by John Fort, *God in the Straw Pen* (1931), imagined what a Methodist revival in the tradition of plain-folk camp-meeting religion in "the up-country of Georgia in 1830" must have been like for his great-grand-father: "Hearty of laughter and with gay song he who was my great-grandfa-ther rode to camp-meeting to hear and see a mighty evangelist. He sat unmoved at the thunderous words, at the delirium of the multitude for he was doubtful of his own sin and doubtful of the vengeance of God. That night as he rode alone through the darkness the 'Power' followed him. He fell from his horse and saw into Heaven and into Hell. So was he convinced of the vengeance of

God, so did the gay song die. I, understanding a little of myself, know what that visitation in the night-time meant. In spite of struggle, I share his conviction of sin. . . . There is no complete escape from the ancestral mould" ("Foreword"). Fort's first chapter, "An High Mountain," introduced in its first sentence this highly wrought-up historical novel's protagonists: "Men of God, Methodist evangelists, Isham Lowe and John Semple traveled through the mountains of Tennessee towards the uplands of Georgia where they were going to save souls from Hell" (p. 1). Fort's imaginings contradicted the experiences of legions of people in the mountains of Appalachia like Sister Mae June Hensley, who are part of the Holiness tradition that best preserves today the camp-meeting religion of his great-grandfather. Sister Mae June said of the night meetings of one dour, sanctimonious Holiness preacher who had long since placed greater emphasis on right belief than on a tender heart, "Not very happy, are they?"

6. Hooker, *Religion in the Highlands*, p. 213.

7. "Coming to Appalachia," *Church Herald* (Sept. 1992), pp. 3, 27.

8. Ibid., p. 28. A caption for one of the article's accompanying photographs (p. 28) from the "new RCA slide program" reads, "The Commission on Religion in Appalachia (CORA), of which the RCA is a part, has helped sponsor an innovative project that helps farmers raise sorghum rather than tobacco, then uses the juices to make sweeteners and candies. This is one way the church is bringing financial and social stability to small communities and individual families." The churches of American Protestantism brought what Appalachia lacked— "financial and social stability." One of the jars of sorghum in the photograph to which this caption is attached was labeled "Sorghum Praline Topping with Kentucky Bourbon." Apparently Kentucky bourbon as an additive was a better source of "social stability" than tobacco.

9. *God's Face Is Turned toward the Mountains*, p. 12.

10. In the RCA article "Coming to Appalachia," a photograph caption reads, "In Jackson County, three Reformed churches provide a pastoral calling program that *blankets the area with spiritual nurture*. Many of the thousands of people the pastors . . . visit will never attend services at a Reformed church, but they still have the opportunity to hear the gospel of Jesus Christ" (p. 27, emphasis added). This caption represents a perspective established universally among American Protestant home mission efforts in Appalachia: the people will not come to our churches, but at least they will "still have the opportunity to hear the gospel of Jesus Christ"—the immediate implication being that without the home missions' presence, rural mountain people did not "have the opportunity to hear the gospel." Most simply, they were unchurched, meaning that they had no churches of their own, or no "real" or "adequate" churches among themselves other than what the home missionaries provided. It is deeply discouraging, yet highly revealing, that the home mission attitudes of the 1880s persisted without interruption or any substantial change into the 1990s. Like the Methodists, the Reformed Church in America did not stand alone, but was highly representative of the overall perception American Protestantism has had of its "place" in Appalachia.

Part 3: The Independent Holiness Church

1. Dorgan to author, 1991.

Chapter 12: Mountain Religion and the Holiness-Pentecostal Movements

1. Ahlstrom, *Religious History of the American People,* pp. 420, 422.
2. Hunter, "Spirit-Baptism and the 1896 Revival in Cherokee County, North Carolina," p. 8.
3. Henry, *Shouting* (1859), p. 292. Further references to this work will be cited by page number within the body of the text.
4. See Loyal Jones, "The Welsh Component of Celtic Influence in Appalachia."
5. See Ffirth, *The Experience and Gospel Labours, of the Rev. Benjamin Abbott* (1813).
6. Wallis, Introduction to *Autobiography of Peter Cartwright,* p. 5.
7. McLoughlin, *Modern Revivalism,* pp. 65–66.
8. See Westerkamp, *Triumph of the Laity,* and Schmidt, *Holy Fairs.*
9. Schmidt, "Scottish Communions and American Revivals," p. 113.
10. Charles Edwin Jones, *A Guide to the Study of the Holiness Movement,* p. xxi.
11. Ibid., p. 235.
12. See Price, *Without Scrip or Purse; Or, "The Mountain Evangelist," George O. Barnes* (1883).
13. See McConnell, *Hitherto and Henceforth in the Kentucky Mountains* (1949) and *The Pauline Ministry in the Kentucky Mountains* [1942].

Chapter 13: How an Independent Holiness Church Became a Major Denomination

1. Traditional Church of God history puts Richard Spurling's dates as 1812–86. I shall discuss this important discrepancy later in the chapter.
2. "W. F. Bryant said his personal ordination came at the hands of Spurling and Porter" (Bryant interview by Chesser, p. 18; quoted in Hunter, "Beniah, TN: A Case of the Vanishing Flame" [1993], p. 33); "Lemons said that Porter introduced the Camp Creek group to him around 1900. Lemons did not join until 1903 and would eventually find himself out of the mainstream" (Lemons interview by Chesser, p. 19; quoted in ibid., p. 33, n. 72).
3. Abbott, *The Forgotten Church* (1962), p. [38]. Abbott frequently used a semicolon to end a sentence; in these cases I have substituted a period.
4. Ibid., pp. [28–30].
5. Both of these accounts are self-published, Abbott's *Forgotten Church* (1962) and *The Flight of the Dove: Roots of Pentecost in Eastern Ky.* [1982], by Alfred Carrier, a 253-page work of brief and many historical sketches, mostly by county, replete with numerous photographs of church houses, preachers, and other individuals. Brother Carrier sold me his last copy.

6. W. F. Bryant, quoted in Charles W. Conn, *Like a Mighty Army: A History of the Church of God, 1886–1976*, p. 79; originally quoted in the *Minutes of the Seventh Annual Assembly* (1912), p. 8.

7. W. F. Bryant, Chesser interview with W. F. Bryant [1949].

8. Almost all of the material that follows about the Spurling family, and later about Richard Green Spurling and the Church of God, Wade Phillips shared with me in several telephone interviews in May and June 1993, making the venue of this book its first appearance in print. All direct quotations from Phillips without attribution are from these several interviews. Given the extraordinary historical importance of this material for the Church of God (Cleveland, Tennessee) and the Church of God of Prophecy, I asked him why he would allow me to publish the information and much of the analysis he had pieced together, rather than keeping that privilege for himself, as most scholars would. Phillips said that he was "anxious to get the correct focus of the history of the Church in print in the proper context." As well as publishing his own works and presenting numerous papers, Phillips has handed over large chunks of his original research in related topics to other scholars who have published it and of whom he requested only that credit be given his research and opinions.

9. Contra June Glover Marshall, *A Biographical Sketch of Richard G. Spurling, Jr.* (1974), there is no evidence that the Spurlings settled in Whitley County, Kentucky. Nor was Richard G. born in Germany.

10. Phillips has copies of the deeds for the Spurling land in the Holly Springs area of Monroe County, Tennessee.

11. Phillips, "Richard Spurling and the Baptist Roots of the Church of God," p. 15, n. 35.

12. Ibid., p. 22. Phillips writes, "Eventually Landmarkers withdrew from the Southern Baptist Convention, forming in 1905 the Baptist General Association (American Baptist Association since 1924). This Association continues to represent and perpetuate the Landmark tradition today" (p. 25). Phillips gives a thorough treatment of Landmarkism and its influence on the Spurlings in this paper and in his "Richard Spurling and Our Baptist Heritage" (1993).

13. Phillips, "Our Baptist Heritage," p. 2. Phillips's conclusion is drawn from Clear Creek Church records and minutes.

14. Ibid., p. 1.

15. Ibid., p. 3.

16. Ibid.

17. Phillips, "Baptist Roots," p. 19.

18. Ibid., p. 28.

19. "Brief History Of the Church That is Now Recognized as The Church of God," in *Book of Minutes* (1922), p. 8. This volume was compiled and edited by L. Howard Juillerat and Minnie Hayes up through the 1917 Thirteenth Annual Assembly. Juillerat died in the flu epidemic of 1918. The unattributed "Brief History" was taken verbatim from A. J. Tomlinson's *The Last Great Conflict* (1913), pp. 205–15.

20. A photocopy of Richard G. Spurling's ordination certificate is in the James Marshall Church of God Collection.

21. Interview with James Marshall and June Glover Marshall, Cleveland, Tenn., Nov. 1987.

22. Richard G. Spurling, *The Lost Link* (1920), p. 45. Further references to this work will be cited by page number within the body of the text.

23. Phillips, "Our Baptist Heritage," p. 2.

24. Abbott, *Forgotten Church*, pp. [2–20].

25. G. P. Spurling, untitled early history of Richard G. Spurling's religious work (n.p., n.d.). The document is just four typed pages, single-spaced. A photocopy is available in the James Marshall Church of God Collection.

26. Hunter, "Spirit-Baptism and the 1896 Revival in Cherokee County, North Carolina," p. 8. Hunter, now a member of the Church of God, was at the time he published this essay a minister in the Church of God of Prophecy. He has taught on the Church of God School of Theology faculty, holds a Ph.D. in systematic theology from Fuller Theological Seminary, and is past president of the Society for Pentecostal Studies. It is significant that an "insider" has challenged the official or traditional Church of God interpretation supported by scholars such as Charles W. Conn in his history of the denomination.

27. Phillips, "Baptist Roots," p. 38.

28. Nettie Bryant interview, n.d.

29. *Samson's Foxes* (1901), p. 2.

30. Simmons, *History of the Church of God*, p. 15.

31. Phillips, "Baptist Roots," pp. 39–40.

32. Conn, *Like a Mighty Army*, p. 140. Conn, a former general overseer and longtime member of the Council of Twelve, wrote in the denomination's official history (which he authored), "This attitude of trust [by the people of the Church of God] has continued with the Council through the years, for its work has been sincere and its members worthy of people's confidence."

33. Stone, *The Church of God of Prophecy: History & Polity* (1977), pp. 66–67 (see also pp. 62–67). Contra Conn, *Like a Mighty Army* (1977), p. 188n.

34. W. F. Bryant, "Work in the Mountains of Tennessee," p. 8.

35. W. F. Bryant, "Work in Tellico Mountains of Tennessee," p. 7.

36. Bower, "Work in the Mountains of Tennessee Near Tellico Plains," p. 3.

37. W. F. Bryant, "The Mountain Work," p. 4.

38. Edney, "Roan Mountain, Tenn.," p. 3.

39. W. F. Bryant, "To the Readers of The Evangel," p. 8.

40. Conn, *Like a Mighty Army*, p. 152.

41. For the strong presence of cultural and socioeconomic divisions that now exist within the Church of God, as demonstrated by various churches' music selections for their worship services, see Philip Wesley Conn, "The Relationship between Congregational Hymn Preference and Socioeconomic Status: A Study of Congregational Variation in Religious Orientation." Conn's study is based on three Church of God congregations, urban and rural. Conn grew up in the Church of God, the son of Charles W. Conn, official church historian and the denomination's general overseer in the mid-1960s. For the definitive history of North Cleveland Church of God, "The exciting story of a congregation from its

beginning as a mission in 1905 to its present position of leadership in the Pentecostal world," see Charles W. Conn, *Cradle of Pentecost.*

42. See Richard G. Spurling, *Lost Link*, pp. 25–26.

43. Wallhausser, "I Can Almost See Heaven from Here," p. 4.

Chapter 14: Brother Coy Miser

1. Nash to Brother James, Palmyra, N.Y., Apr. 12, 1831, Finney papers.

2. Richard G. Spurling, *Lost Link*, p. 12.

3. Miles, *Spirit of the Mountains*, p. 138.

4. Blair, "Memoir of the Rev. Samuel Blair," pp. 159–60.

Part 4: The Home Mission to "Mountain Whites"

1. Loyal Jones, "Old-Time Baptists," p. 120.

2. The full title tells the tale. See Baird, *Religion in America; Or, an Account of the Origin, Progress, Relation to the State, and Present Condition of the Evangelical Churches in the United States. With Notices of the Unevangelical Denominations* (1844), pp. xii, 219–20.

3. Ahlstrom, *Religious History of the American People*, p. 8 (emphasis in the original).

4. Handy, *Christian America*, p. 155.

Chapter 15: "Mr. Schermerhorn's Statement"

1. Goodykoontz, *Home Missions on the American Frontier: With Particular Reference to the American Home Missionary Society*, p. 15.

2. Ibid., p. 16.

3. In 1869 Will Wallace Harney, a physician, traveled to the Cumberland Mountains. As Shapiro observed, there was little in Harney's 1873 article for *Lippincott's Magazine* to justify its title, "A Strange Land and Peculiar People." It was among the first to highlight the focus on "otherness" in the local-color movement of the period. Shapiro identified Harney and the editors of *Lippincott's* as being the first to "discover" Appalachia by being the first to assert its "otherness," a matter more of perception than of objective reality (Shapiro, *Appalachia on Our Mind: The Southern Mountains and Mountaineers in the American Consciousness, 1870–1920*, pp. 3–4).

4. Dwight, *Travels; in New-England and New-York* (1821–22), vol. 2, p. 459 (emphasis in the original).

5. Ibid., vol. 2, p. 462.

6. Goodykoontz, *Home Missions*, pp. 31–34.

7. Here I deliberately lowercase "spirit." Writers on mountain religion usually ignore the prevailing emphasis on the Holy Spirit in mountain worship life, lowercasing the word "spirit" in their own writings to explain the "spirit-possession" that takes place in worship services. Lawless, an anthropologist and ethnologist, did this in her work, *God's Peculiar People* (1988), about a church

in southern Indiana very similar to churches in the coalfields of central Appalachia. Even Howard Dorgan, whose studies of Old Time Baptists in Appalachia, especially Old Regular Baptists, have laid a foundation of descriptive discourses, failed to recognize the principal role of the Holy Spirit in their traditions, as demonstrated by his consistent lowercasing of "spirit" in his writings, especially in his *Giving Glory to God*. To date, only Jeff Todd Titon has given clear recognition to the centrality of the Holy Spirit in the worship life of the Appalachian church community he studied in *Powerhouse for God*.

8. Goodykoontz, *Home Missions*, p. 139.

9. Torbet, *History of the Baptists*, pp. 249–50.

10. Schermerhorn and Mills, *A Correct View of That Part of the United States Which Lies West of the Allegany Mountains, With Regard to Religion and Morals* (1814), p. 38 (emphasis in the original). Further references to this work will be cited by page number within the body of the text.

11. Elder I. D. Back is featured in song and testimony on side 1 of Alan Lomax's *The Gospel Ship: Baptist Hymns & White Spirituals from the Southern Mountains*. In the jacket notes Elder Back is misidentified as Beck.

12. Otto, *The Idea of the Holy: An Inquiry into the Non-rational Factor in the Idea of the Divine and Its Relation to the Rational*, p. 30 (emphasis in the original).

13. Short, "We Believed in the Family," p. 62.

14. Miles, *Spirit of the Mountains*, p. 121.

15. For one of the very few articles written on the life of Taylor, despite his widely recognized significance, see Thompson, "John Taylor of the Ten Churches." Thompson was Taylor's great-great-granddaughter by way of his youngest daughter, Sally.

16. Taylor, *History of Ten Baptist Churches* (1827), pp. 55–57, 65. Further references to this work will be cited by page number within the body of the text.

17. Taylor, *Thoughts on Missions* (1819), pp. 5–6.

Chapter 16: "In the Brush"

1. Maltby, "Connexion between Domestic Missions and the Political Prospects of Our Country" (1825), quoted in Goodykoontz, *Home Missions*, pp. 170–71.

2. "The South West" (1851), pp. 48–49. Emphasis in the original. All following quotations from this article are from p. 49.

3. Goodykoontz, *Home Missions*, p. 172.

4. Davidson, *History of the Presbyterian Church in the State of Kentucky* (1847), pp. 131–41, 142–69, 170–89.

5. Pierson, *In the Brush; Or, Old-Time Social, Political, and Religious Life in the Southwest* (1883), p. 316. Further references to this work will be cited by page number within the body of the text.

6. The text of the tribute appears on p. 317.

7. Ellen Myers, "Mountain White Work in Kentucky" (1884), p. 14.

8. Albanese, *America: Religions and Religion*, p. 231.

9. Campbell, *Southern Highlander*, p. 177.

10. On the persistence of the "holy tone" in mountain preaching, see Dorgan, *Giving Glory to God,* chap. 2, "Hanging Their Toes in the Heavens," pp. 55–85.

11. See chapter 4, "We Believed in the Family," on "singing down" the preacher.

12. Bush, *Dorie, Woman of the Mountains,* p. 137.

13. Miles, *Spirit of the Mountains,* pp. 132–33.

14. *Five Years in the Alleghanies,* p. 206 (capitalization in the original).

Chapter 17: A Christian America and the Appalachian "Problem"

1. McMillan, *"Unfinished Tasks" of the Southern Presbyterian Church* (1922), pp. 94–95.

2. Morris, *At Our Own Door* (1904), p. 95.

3. Dwight, *Travels; in New-England and New-York* (1821–22), vol. 2, p. 459.

4. Morris, *At Our Own Door,* pp. 94–95 (emphasis added).

5. Masters, *The Home Mission Task* (1912), p. 218.

6. "Coming to Appalachia," p. 28.

7. Douglass, *Christian Reconstruction in the South* (1909), pp. 303–34, 335–66.

8. Ibid., p. 335.

9. For a book-length exegesis of the peripheralization theme, see Cunningham, *Apples on the Flood: The Southern Mountain Experience.*

10. Eller, "Industrialization and Social Change in Appalachia, 1880–1930," pp. 38–39.

11. Ibid., p. 40.

12. Sweet, *The Story of Religion in America,* p. 345.

13. Douglass, *Christian Reconstruction,* p. 366.

14. Ibid., pp. 350, 361.

15. See Shapiro, *Appalachia on Our Mind,* pp. 40ff.

16. The masthead of *American Missionary Magazine,* 61, no. 6 (June 1907), reads, "The American Missionary Magazine: Devoted to Christian Education and Evangelization among Eight Races in America, White, Negro, Indian, Alaskan, Porto Rican, Chinese, Japanese, Hawaiian." The only "white race" served by the AMA were the mountain people of Appalachia.

17. Roy, "Americans of the Midland Mountains" (1892), p. 85. Further references to this work will be cited by page number within the body of the text.

18. J. C. Richardson, "Williamsburg, Whitley Co., September 16, '59," p. 19 (emphasis in the original).

19. Handy, *Christian America,* p. 65.

20. Drake, "The Mission School Era in Southern Appalachia: 1880–1940," p. 4.

21. Mrs. A. A. [Ellen] Myers, "Mountain White Work in Kentucky," p. 14 (emphasis in the original). Further references to this work will be cited by page number within the body of the text.

22. See for example "The History of Wolf Creek Baptist Church," by Terry

Galloway. Until the early 1960s, its worship services were held once a month over Saturday and Sunday.

23. Wilson's *The Southern Mountaineers* went through five editions between 1906 and 1915.

24. Stephenson, "The Mountain Whites," p. 7, quoted in Marcia Clark Myers, "Presbyterian Home Missions in Appalachia—A Feminine Enterprise," p. 74.

25. Marcia Clark Myers, "Presbyterian Home Missions," p. 74.

26. Wilson, *Southern Mountaineers*, pp. 100–101.

27. Morris, *At Our Own Door*, p. 103.

28. Morris, *The Romance of Home Missions* (1924), p. 59 (emphasis added).

29. See Edward O. Guerrant, *The Soul Winner* (1896) and *The Galax Gatherers: The Gospel among the Highlanders* (1910). See also McAllister and Grace Owings Guerrant, *Edward O. Guerrant: Apostle to the Southern Highlanders* (1950). Grace Owings Guerrant was his daughter.

30. Guerrant, "Fifty Years among the Highlanders," a folder quoted by Hooker, *Religion in the Highlands*, p. 200.

31. Morris, *At Our Own Door*, pp. 108–9.

32. Craig, comp. and ed., *Highways and Byways of Appalachia* (1927), p. 3 (emphasis added).

33. McMillan, *Other Men Labored* (1937), p. 40.

34. Armstrong, "Appalachia" (1923), p. 103.

Chapter 18: Elizabeth Hooker and Brother Terry Galloway

1. Hooker, *Religion in the Highlands*, p. v. Further references to this work will be cited by page number within the body of the text.

2. Handy, *Christian America*, pp. 209–10.

3. Ibid., pp. 210–11.

4. Ibid., pp. 212–13.

5. Hooker divided her study among six geographic areas: Northeastern Cumberland Plateau, Northwestern Cumberland Plateau, Allegheny Plateau, Blue Ridge, the Central Ridges, and the Central Valleys.

6. Galloway, "History of Wolf Creek Baptist Church," p. 1. Further references to this work will be cited by page number within the body of the text.

7. Many of the older one-room church houses still in existence today are indistinguishable in architecture from the one-room schoolhouse. Indeed, many churches simply bought one-room schoolhouses when they were abandoned. The architectural style and minor variations on it prevail in the construction of many new church houses today.

8. Mountain church houses tend to be wood frame or cement block structures painted white. Brick church houses are not very common in rural areas. Possibly Wolf Creek Baptist Church was built in brick to withstand future flooding. See below on how flooding washed away the old schoolhouse.

9. In *We're All Kin*, F. Carlene Bryant provided another account of splits in a family church that resulted in the founding of other churches in the area ("Churches," pp. 89–120).

10. In 1943 Bob Jones University was located in Cleveland, Tennessee. The school moved to Greenville, South Carolina, its present location, in 1946. For additional insight into why the presence of young preachers from Bob Jones University would cause such dissension, see Queen, "Bob Jones, Sr., Jr., and III."

11. Albanese, *America: Religions and Religion,* p. 230.

12. Wyckoff, *The Challenge of the Hills* (1931), pp. 17, 19, 20.

13. Masters, *The Call of the South* (1918), p. 83.

14. Masters, *Home Mission Task* (1912), "The Southern Highlands," p. 230 (emphasis added).

15. Wyckoff, *Challenge of the Hills,* pp. 14, 15–16.

16. See Reid, "'Neither Adding nor Taking Away'" (1982).

Chapter 19: Appalachia's "Victims" and Their "Liberators" Today

1. *God's Face Is Turned toward the Mountains,* p. 11. (emphasis added). Further references to this work will be cited by page number within the body of the text.

2. "God's Word to the Mountains" (1993), p. 16. See *God's Face Is Turned,* pp. 1, 2, 4, 5.

3. Whisnant, *Modernizing the Mountaineer,* p. 7.

4. See Ingalls, "An Appalachian Summer: Student Interns and Seminarians Encounter Rural Poverty."

5. Hooker, *Religion in the Highlands,* pp. 200–201.

6. Ibid., p. 214.

7. *Appalachian Ministries Educational Resource Center (AMERC) Presents the Eighth Appalachian Summer Term—June 1 through July 14, 1993.* Promotional literature (emphasis added).

8. Albanese, *America: Religions and Religion,* p. 229.

9. Hooker, *Religion in the Highlands,* p. 209.

10. "Readers' Response: Pluses and Minuses of Mountain Religion" (1977), letter from Michael E. Maloney, p. 333 (emphasis added).

11. Campbell, *Southern Highlander,* p. 182 (emphasis added).

12. Benedict, *Fifty Years among the Baptists,* pp. 126, 127.

13. Gaventa, *Power and Powerlessness: Quiescence and Rebellion in an Appalachian Valley* (1980), p. [v].

14. Ibid., p. x.

Essay on Sources

1. Loyal Jones, "A Major Contribution: A Review of *Religion in Appalachia.*"

2. Reid, "On the Study of Religion in Appalachia."

3. For an in-depth review essay on *Giving Glory to God* and *Powerhouse for God,* see McCauley, "The Study of Appalachian Mountain Religion." For a solid examination of *Pilgrims of Paradox,* see Ostwalt's review in *Appalachian Journal.*

4. With access provided by Loyal Jones and John Wallhausser of Berea College, for the past few years Titon has begun fieldwork in the Indian Bottom

Association of Old Regular Baptists in eastern Kentucky. He hopes to produce a film or at least a professional recording of their music during worship.

5. Reid, "On the Study of Religion in Appalachia," pp. 242–43 (emphasis added).

6. Titon, *Powerhouse for God,* p. 162.

Works Cited

Abbott, Joe. *The Forgotten Church*. N.p., 1962.

Abell, Troy D. *Better Felt Than Said: The Holiness-Pentecostal Experience in Southern Appalachia*. Waco, Tex.: Markham Press, 1982.

Ahlstrom, Sydney E. *A Religious History of the American People*. New Haven: Yale University Press, 1972.

Albanese, Catherine L. *America: Religions and Religion*. Belmont, Calif.: Wadsworth Publishing Co., 1981.

Alexander, Theron. "The Covenanters Come to East Tennessee." Master's thesis, University of Tennessee, 1939.

"America's Holy War." *Time*, 138, no. 23 (Dec. 9, 1991), 60–68.

Appalachian Center. Berea College, Berea, Ky. Oral history collection of Old Regular Baptist services and interviews.

Appalachian Collection. Appalachian State University, Boone, N.C. Photocopies of associational minutes dating from the mid-nineteenth to the mid-twentieth century for Primitive Baptists, Regular, Old Regular, Regular Predestinarian, Regular Primitive, United Baptists, Separate Baptists in Christ, and Free Will Baptists.

Appalachian Ministries Educational Resource Center. *A Pattern of Love: The Story of the Appalachian Ministries Educational Resource Center*. [Berea, Ky.]: AMERC, [1988]. Video.

Armstrong, Mrs. Gale. "Appalachia." In *Pioneer Women of the Presbyterian Church, United States*, edited by Mary D. Irvine and Alice L. Eastwood, 103–17. Richmond, Va.: Presbyterian Committee of Publication, 1923.

The Articles of the Synod of Dort. Translated by Thomas Scott, introduction by Samuel Miller. Philadelphia: Presbyterian Board of Publication, 1841.

Bachelard, Gaston. *The Poetics of Space*. Boston: Beacon Press, 1964.

Bailie, W. D. *The Six Mile Water Revival of 1625*. New Castle, Ire.: Mourne Observer Press, 1976.

Baird, Robert. *Religion in America; Or, an Account of the Origin, Progress, Relation to the State, and Present Condition of the Evangelical Churches in the United States. With Notices of the Unevangelical Denominations*. New York: Harper and Brothers, 1844. 1st Amer. ed.

Balling, Kevin M., and Howard Dorgan. *While the Ages Roll On . . . A Memorial*. White Light Video, 1990. Video.

Barnes, Gilbert H. *The Antislavery Impulse, 1830–1844*. New York: D. Appleton-Century, 1933.

Beaver, Patricia Duane. *Rural Community in the Appalachian South*. Lexington: University Press of Kentucky, 1986.

Benedict, David. *Fifty Years among the Baptists*. New York: Sheldon and Co., 1860. Reprint. Little Rock, Ark.: Seminary Publications, 1977.

———. *A General History of the Baptist Denomination in America, and Other Parts of the World.* 2 vols. Boston: Lincoln and Edmands, 1813. Reprint. Gallatin, Tenn.: Church History Research and Archives, 1985.

Berry, W. J., comp. *The Kehukee Declaration and Black Rock Address, with Other Writings Relative to The Baptist Separation between 1825–1840; Gilbert Beebe, A Biographical Sketch.* Elon College, N.C.: Primitive Publications, n.d.

Best, Bill. "Stripping Appalachian Soul: The New Left's Ace in the Hole," *Mountain Review,* 4, no. 3 (Jan. 1979), 14–16.

Blair, Samuel. "Memoir of the Rev. Samuel Blair." In *The Log College: Biographical Sketches of William Tennent and His Students, Together with an Account of the Revivals under Their Ministries,* edited by Archibald Alexander, 147–77. 1851. Reprint. London: Banner of Truth Trust, 1968.

Boles, John B. *The Great Revival, 1787–1805: The Origins of the Southern Evangelical Mind.* Lexington: University Press of Kentucky, 1972.

Bower, Flora E. "Work in the Mountains of Tennessee near Tellico Plains." *Evening Light and Church of God Evangel,* 1, no. 8 (June 15, 1910), 2–4.

Brewer, Earl D. C. "Religion and the Churches." In *The Southern Appalachian Region: A Survey,* edited by Thomas R. Ford, 201–18. Lexington: University of Kentucky Press, 1962.

Brockway, J. *A Delineation of the Characteristic Features of a Revival of Religion in Troy, in 1826 and 1827.* Troy, N.Y.: Francis Adancourt, 1827.

Brosi, George. "Mountain Novels before 1890." *Appalachian Mountain Books: News, Reviews, Catalog,* 2, no. 5 (1986), 18–23.

Bruce, Dickson D., Jr. *And They All Sang Hallelujah: Plain-Folk Camp-Meeting Religion, 1800–1845.* Knoxville: University of Tennessee Press, 1974.

Brunk, Harry Anthony. *History of the Mennonites in Virginia, 1727–1900.* Staunton, Va.: McClure Printing Co., 1959.

Bryant, Carvin. *Voice in the Mountains: The Incredible Story of Lloyd C. Kelly.* Pineville, Ky.: Clear Creek Baptist Bible College, 1987.

Bryant, F. Carlene. *We're All Kin: A Cultural Study of a Mountain Neighborhood.* Knoxville: University of Tennessee Press, 1981.

Bryant, Nettie. Interview. N.d. Document 8-A. Church of God Collection, Pentecostal Research Center, Lee College, Cleveland, Tenn.

Bryant, W. F. H. L. Chesser Interview with W. F. Bryant. [1949.] Document 27-A. Church of God Collection, Pentecostal Research Center, Lee College, Cleveland, Tenn.

———. "The Mountain Work." *Evening Light and Church of God Evangel,* 1, no. 9 (July 1, 1910), 4.

———. "To the Readers of The Evangel and All whom it May Concern." *Church of God Evangel,* 5, no. 2 (Jan. 10, 1914), 8.

———. "Work in Tellico Mountains of Tennessee—And in the Mountains North of the Blue Ridge, near North Carolina and Georgia Line." *Evening Light and Church of God Evangel,* 1, no. 7 (June 1, 1910), 7–8.

———. "Work in the Mountains of Tennessee." *Evening Light and Church of God Evangel,* 1, no. 1 (Mar. 1, 1910), 8.

Burkitt, Lemuel, and Jesse Read. *A Concise History of the Kehukee Baptist Association from its Original Rise down to 1803.* 1803. Rev. ed., ed. Henry L. Burkitt. Philadelphia: Lippincott, Grambo and Co., 1850. Reprint. New York: Arno Press, 1980.

Burton, Thomas. *Serpent-Handling Believers.* Knoxville: University of Tennessee Press, 1993.

Bush, Florence Cope. *Dorie, Woman of the Mountains.* Sevierville, Tenn.: Nandel Publishing Co., 1988.

Campbell, Alexander, ed. *The Christian Baptist.* 2d ed., ed. D. S. Burnet. Cincinnati: D. S. Burnet, 1835. Reprint. Joplin, Mo.: College Press Publishing, 1983.

Campbell, John C. *The Southern Highlander & His Homeland.* New York: Russell Sage Foundation, 1921. Reprint. Lexington: University Press of Kentucky, 1969.

Carrier, Alfred. *The Flight of the Dove: Roots of Pentecost in Eastern Ky.* N.p.: Privately printed, [1982].

Cartwright, Peter. *Autobiography of Peter Cartwright.* 1856. Reprint. Nashville: Abingdon Press, 1984.

Caruso, John Anthony. *The Appalachian Frontier: America's First Surge Westward.* Indianapolis: Bobbs-Merrill Co., 1959.

Caudill, Harry. "Anglo-Saxon vs. Scotch-Irish, Round 2." *Mountain Life & Work,* 45, no. 3 (Mar. 1969), 18–19.

————. *Night Comes to the Cumberlands: A Biography of a Depressed Area.* Boston: Little, Brown and Co., 1962.

Collins, C. C. "Church Work in North Carolina." *American Missionary Magazine,* 45, no. 5 (May 1891), 202–3.

Collins, Ray. "Amen, Brother Ray." *Mountain Review,* 1, no. 1 (Sept. 1974), 8, 29, 36.

————. "True or False?" *Mountain Review,* 1, no. 1 (Sept. 1974), 7.

"Coming to Appalachia." *Church Herald,* 49, no. 8 (Sept. 1992), 26–29.

Conkin, Paul K. *Cane Ridge: America's Pentecost.* Madison: University of Wisconsin Press, 1990.

Conn, Charles W. *Cradle of Pentecost: North Cleveland Church of God.* Cleveland, Tenn.: Pathway Press, 1981.

————. *Like a Mighty Army: A History of the Church of God, 1886–1977.* Rev. ed. Cleveland, Tenn.: Pathway Press, 1977.

Conn, Philip Wesley. "The Relationship between Congregational Hymn Preference and Socioeconomic Status: A Study of Congregational Variation in Religious Orientation." Master's thesis, University of Tennessee, 1972.

Craddock, Charles Egbert. Pseud. See Mary Noailles Murfree.

Craig, Edward Marshal, comp. and ed. *Highways and Byways of Appalachia: A Study of the Work of the Synod of Appalachia of the Presbyterian Church in the United States.* Kingsport, Tenn.: Kingsport Press, 1927.

Crissman, James K. *Death and Dying in Central Appalachia: Changing Attitudes and Practices.* Urbana: University of Illinois Press, 1994.

Cross, Whitney R. *The Burned-Over District: The Social and Intellectual History of Enthusiastic Religion in Western New York, 1800–1850.* Ithaca, N.Y.: Cornell University Press, 1950.

Cunningham, Rodger. *Apples on the Flood: The Southern Mountain Experience.* Knoxville: University of Tennessee Press, 1987.

Gaston, Kay Barker. *Emma Bell Miles.* Signal Mountain, Tenn.: Walden's Ridge Historical Association, 1985.

Gaventa, John. *Power and Powerlessness: Quiescence and Rebellion in an Appalachian Valley.* Urbana: University of Illinois Press, 1980.

Gerrard, Nathan L. "Churches of the Stationary Poor in Appalachia." In *Change in Rural Appalachia: Implications for Action Programs,* edited by John D. Photiadis and Harry K. Schwarzweller, 99–114. Philadelphia: University of Pennsylvania Press, 1971.

Gillespie, Paul F., ed. *Foxfire 7: Ministers, Church Members, Revivals, Baptisms, Shaped-note and Gospel Singing, Faith Healing, Camp Meetings, Footwashings, Snake Handling, and Other Traditions of Mountain Religious Heritage.* Garden City, N.Y.: Anchor Books, 1982.

God's Face Is Turned toward the Mountains: A Pastoral Letter of Hope from the Bishops of Appalachia of the United Methodist Church, December 1992. Hagerstown, Md.: Appalachian Development Committee of the United Methodist Church, 1992.

"God's Word to the Mountains: Excerpts of a Pastoral Letter from the United Methodist Bishops of Appalachia." *Sojourners,* 22, no. 5 (June 1993), 16–17, 49.

Goodykoontz, Colin Brummitt. *Home Missions on the American Frontier: With Particular Reference to the American Home Missionary Society.* Caldwell, Idaho: Caxton Printers, 1939.

Guerrant, Edward O. *The Galax Gatherers: The Gospel among the Highlanders.* Richmond, Va.: Onward Press, 1910.

———. *The Soul Winner.* Lexington: John B. Morton and Co., 1896.

Handy, Robert T. *A Christian America: Protestant Hopes and Historical Realities.* New York: Oxford University Press, 1971.

———. *A History of the Churches in the United States and Canada.* New York: Oxford University Press, 1976.

Harney, Will Wallace. "A Strange Land and Peculiar People." *Lippincott's Magazine,* 12 (Oct. 1873), 429–38.

Hartman, Robert H. "Origins of the Mountain Preacher." *Appalachian Heritage,* 9, no. 4 (Fall 1981), 55–69.

Hassell, Cushing Biggs, and Sylvester Hassell. *History of the Church of God, from the Creation to A.D. 1885; Including Especially the History of the Kehukee Primitive Baptist Association.* Middletown, N.Y.: Gilbert Beebe's Sons, 1886. Reprint. Ellenwood, Ga.: Old School Hymnal Co., 1983.

Henry, G. W. *Shouting: Genuine and Spurious, In All Ages of the Church, from the birth of Creation, when the Sons of God shouted for joy, until the shout of the Arch-Angel: with numerous extracts from the works of Wesley, Evans, Edwards, Abbott, Cartwright and Finley. Giving a history of the outward demonstrations of the Spirit, such as Laughing, Screaming, Shouting, Leaping, Jerking, and Falling under the Power, &c.* Oneida, N.Y.: Privately printed, 1859.

Hooker, Elizabeth R. "The Church Situation." In *Economic and Social Problems and Conditions of the Southern Appalachians.* U.S. Department of Agriculture, Miscellaneous Publication no. 205, Jan. 1935, 168–84.

—————. *Religion in the Highlands: Native Churches and Missionary Enterprises in the Southern Appalachian Area; With a Section on Missionary and Philanthropic Schools by Fannie W. Dunn.* New York: Home Missions Council, 1933.

Hunter, Harold D. "Beniah, TN: A Case of the Vanishing Flame." [1993.] Typescript.

—————. "Spirit-Baptism and the 1896 Revival in Cherokee County, North Carolina." *Pneuma,* 5, no. 2 (Fall 1983), 1–17.

"'If I Were Beginning Again': A Reflective Symposium by Seven Rural Ministers of the Mountains." *Mountain Life & Work,* 23, no. 1 (Spring 1947), 6–10, 30.

Ingalls, Zoë. "An Appalachian Summer: Student Interns and Seminarians Encounter Rural Poverty." *Chronicle of Higher Education,* 32, no. 24 (Aug. 13, 1986), 22–23.

Isaac, Rhys. *The Transformation of Virginia, 1740–1790.* Chapel Hill: University of North Carolina Press, 1982.

James Marshall Church of God Collection. 514 Cedar Drive, SE, Cleveland, Tenn. 37323.

Johnson, Charles A. *The Frontier Camp Meeting: Religion's Harvest Time.* Dallas: Southern Methodist University Press, 1955.

Johnson, Linda. "The Foot-Washin' Church and the Prayer-Book Church: Resisting Cultural Imperialism in Southern Appalachia." *Christian Century,* 93, no. 35 (Nov. 3, 1976), 952–55.

Jones, Charles Edwin. *A Guide to the Study of the Holiness Movement.* Metuchen, N.J.: Scarecrow Press, 1974.

Jones, Erasmus W. "The Welsh in America." *Atlantic Monthly,* 37, no. 221 (Mar. 1876), 305–13.

Jones, Loyal. "Appalachian Religion." In *Encyclopedia of Religion in the South,* edited by Samuel S. Hill, 38–42. Macon, Ga.: Mercer University Press, 1984.

—————. "Appalachian Values." In *Voices from the Hills: Selected Readings of Southern Appalachia,* edited by Robert J. Higgs and Ambrose N. Manning, 507–17. New York: Frederick Ungar Publishing Co., 1975.

—————. "A Major Contribution: A Review of *Religion in Appalachia: Theological, Social, and Psychological Dimensions and Correlates,* ed. by John D. Photiadis." *Mountain Review,* 4, no. 4 (Apr. 1979), 31–32.

—————. "Mountain Religion: The Outsider's View." *Mountain Review,* 2, no. 3 (May 1976), 43–46.

—————. "Old-Time Baptists and Mainline Christianity." In *An Appalachian Symposium: Essays in Honor of Cratis D. Williams,* edited by J. W. Williamson, 120–30. Boone, N.C.: Appalachian State University Press, 1977.

—————. "A Preliminary Look at the Welsh Component of Celtic Influence in Appalachia." In *The Appalachian Experience: Proceedings of the Sixth Annual Appalachian Studies Conference,* edited by Barry M. Buxton et al., 26–33. Boone, N.C.: Appalachian Consortium Press, 1983.

Juillerat, L. Howard, and Minnie Hayes, comps. and eds. *Book of Minutes: A Compiled History of the Work of the General Assemblies of the Church of God.* Cleveland, Tenn.: Church of God Publishing House, 1922.

Kelly, L. C. "The Mountain Preacher and the Mountain Problem." *Mountain Life & Work*, 9, no. 1 (Apr. 1933), 12–16.

Kroll-Smith, J. Stephen. "In Search of Status Power: The Baptist Revival in Colonial Virginia, 1760–1776." Ph.D. diss., University of Pennsylvania, 1982.

La Barre, Weston. *They Shall Take Up Serpents: Psychology of the Southern Snake-Handling Cult*. Minneapolis: University of Minnesota Press, 1962.

Lawless, Elaine J. *God's Peculiar People: Women's Voices & Folk Tradition in a Pentecostal Church*. Lexington: University Press of Kentucky, 1988.

Leland, John. *The Writings of the Late Elder John Leland, Including Some Events of his Life, Written by Himself, with Additional Sketches, &c. by Miss L. F. Greene*. New York: G. W. Wood, 1845. Reprint. Gallatin, Tenn.: Church History Research and Archives, 1986.

Lewis, Helen Matthews, Sue Easterling Kobak, and Linda Johnson. "Family, Religion, and Colonialism in Central Appalachia: Or, Bury My Rifle at Big Stone Gap." In *Colonialism in Modern America: The Appalachian Case*, edited by Helen Matthews Lewis, Linda Johnson, and Donald Askins, 113–39. Boone, N.C.: Appalachian Consortium Press, 1978.

Leyburn, James G. *The Scotch-Irish: A Social History*. Chapel Hill: University of North Carolina Press, 1962.

Lingle, Walter L., and John W. Kuykendall. *Presbyterians: Their History and Beliefs*. Atlanta: John Knox Press, 1978.

Livingston, William John Bryant. "Coal Miners and Religion: A Study of Logan County." Th.D. diss., Union Theological Seminary (Richmond, Va.), 1951.

Lomax, Alan. *The Gospel Ship: Baptist Hymns & White Spirituals from the Southern Mountains*. New World Records 294. New York: Recorded Anthology of American Music, 1977.

Lowther, Russell D. *Laughter and Tears in the Mountains*. Huntington, W.Va.: Cook Printing Co., 1968.

Lumpkin, William L. *Baptist Foundations in the South: Tracing through the Separates the Influence of the Great Awakening, 1754–1787*. Nashville: Broadman Press, 1961.

McAllister, J. Gray, and Grace Owings Guerrant. *Edward O. Guerrant: Apostle to the Southern Highlanders*. Richmond, Va.: Richmond Press, 1950.

McCauley, Deborah Vansau. "The Study of Appalachian Mountain Religion." *Appalachian Journal*, 16, no. 2 (Winter 1989), 138–52.

McConnell, Lela G. *Hitherto and Henceforth in the Kentucky Mountains: A Quarter of a Century of Adventures in Faith—The Year of Jubilee*. N.p.: Privately printed, 1949.

———. *The Pauline Ministry in the Kentucky Mountains: Or a Brief Account of the Kentucky Mountain Holiness Association*. Louisville, Ky.: Pentecostal Publishing Co., [1942].

McGready, James. *The Posthumous Works of the Reverend and Pious James McGready, Late Minister of the Gospel in Ky. [Kentucky]*. Edited by James Smith. Nashville: J. Smith's Steam Press, 1837.

———. "A Short Narrative of the Revival of Religion in Logan County." *Western Missionary Magazine*, 1 (1803), 27–28, 45–54, 99–103, 172–73.

McKibbens, Thomas R., Jr., and Kenneth L. Smith. *The Life and Works of Morgan Edwards*. New York: Arno Press, 1980.

McLoughlin, William G. *Modern Revivalism: Charles Grandison Finney to Billy Graham*. New York: Ronald Press Co., 1959.

———. *Revivals, Awakenings, and Reform: An Essay on Religion and Social Change in America, 1607–1977*. Chicago: University of Chicago Press, 1978.

McMillan, Homer. *Other Men Labored*. Richmond, Va.: Presbyterian Committee of Publication, 1937.

———. *"Unfinished Tasks" of the Southern Presbyterian Church*. Richmond, Va.: Presbyterian Committee of Publication, 1922.

Mahan, Asa. *Autobiography: Intellectual, Moral and Spiritual*. London: T. Wolmer, 1882.

Maltby, John. "Connexion between Domestic Missions and the Political Prospects of Our Country." Address before the Society of Inquiry respecting Missions, Andover Theological Seminary, 1825. [Congregational Home Missionary Society Archives, Amistad Research Center, New Orleans?]

Marshall, June Glover. *A Biographical Sketch of Richard G. Spurling, Jr.* Cleveland, Tenn.: Pathway Press, 1974.

Martin, Isaac Patton. *Methodism in Holston*. Knoxville: Methodist Historical Society, Holston Conference, 1945.

Marty, Martin E. *Protestantism in the United States: Righteous Empire*. 2d ed. New York: Charles Scribner's Sons, 1986.

Masters, Victor Irvine. *The Call of the South: A Presentation of the Home Principles in Missions, Especially as It Applies to the South*. Atlanta: Publicity Department of the Home Mission Board of the Southern Baptist Convention, 1918.

———. *The Home Mission Task: Its Fundamental Character, Magnitude and Present Urgency*. Atlanta: Home Mission Board of the Southern Baptist Convention, 1912.

Mead, Sidney E. *The Lively Experiment: The Shaping of Christianity in America*. New York: Harper and Row, 1976.

———. *Nathaniel William Taylor, 1786–1858: A Connecticut Liberal*. Chicago: University of Chicago Press, 1942.

Mickel, Christopher A. "The Change in the Perspective on Camp Meetings in *The Methodist Magazine* between 1818 and 1826." [1984.] Typescript.

Miles, Emma Bell. *The Spirit of the Mountains*. New York: J. Pott, 1905. Reprint. Knoxville: University of Tennessee Press, 1975.

Morgan, Edmund S. *Visible Saints: The History of a Puritan Idea*. Ithaca, N.Y.: Cornell University Press, 1963.

Morris, S. L. *At Our Own Door: A Study of Home Missions with Special Reference to the South and West*. Richmond, Va.: Presbyterian Committee of Publication, 1904.

———. *The Romance of Home Missions*. Richmond, Va.: Presbyterian Committee of Publication, 1924.

Mullen, Patrick B. "Ritual and Sacred Narrative in the Blue Ridge Mountains." *Papers in Comparative Studies* (Ohio State University), 2 (1983), 17–38.

Murfree, Mary Noailles. *The Prophet of the Great Smoky Mountains*. Boston: Houghton, Mifflin and Co., 1885.

Myers, Mrs. A. A. [Ellen]. "Mountain White Work in Kentucky." *American Missionary Magazine*, 38, no. 1 (Jan. 1884), 12–16.

Myers, Marcia Clark. "Presbyterian Home Missions in Appalachia—A Feminine Enterprise." M.Div. thesis, Princeton Theological Seminary, 1979.

A Narrative of the Revival of Religion, in the County of Oneida, Particularly in the Bounds of the Presbytery of Oneida, in the Year 1826. Utica, N.Y.: Hastings and Tracy, 1826.

Nash, Daniel, Sr. Correspondence. Charles G. Finney papers, Oberlin College Library, Oberlin, Ohio.

National Geographic Society. *American Mountain People.* Washington, D.C.: Special Publications Division, National Geographic Society, 1973.

1935 Religious Survey. Southern Appalachian Archives, Special Collections, Hutchins Library, Berea College, Berea, Ky.

Olafson, S. *1860 Census Book of Boone County, West Virginia.* Madison, W.Va.: Privately printed, 1979.

Ostwalt, Conrad E., Jr. Review of *Pilgrims of Paradox: Calvinism and Experience among the Primitive Baptists of the Blue Ridge,* by James L. Peacock and Ruel W. Tyson, Jr. *Appalachian Journal*, 17, no. 4 (Summer 1990), 420–25.

Otto, Rudolf. *The Idea of the Holy: An Inquiry into the Non-rational Factor in the Idea of the Divine and Its Relation to the Rational.* 2d ed. Translated by John W. Harvey. 1923. Oxford: Oxford University Press, 1979.

Parker, Gerald Keith. "Folk Religion in Southern Appalachia." Th.D. diss., Southern Baptist Theological Seminary, Louisville, 1970.

Partridge, H. E. "Our Highland Institutional Church at Bon Air." *American Missionary Magazine*, 56, no. 10 (Oct. 1902), 436–37.

Peacock, James L., and Ruel W. Tyson, Jr. *Pilgrims of Paradox: Calvinism and Experience among the Primitive Baptists of the Blue Ridge.* Smithsonian Series in Ethnographic Inquiry, no. 17. Washington, D.C.: Smithsonian Institution Press, 1989.

Perkins, Ephraim. *A "Bunker Hill" Contest, A.D. 1826, etc.* Utica, N.Y.: Hastings and Tracy, 1826.

Perrigan, Rufus. *History of Regular Baptist and Their Ancestors and Accessors.* Haysi, Va.: Privately printed, 1961.

Phillips, Wade. "Richard Spurling and Our Baptist Heritage." *Reflections*, 3, no. 2 (Spring 1993), 1–3.

———. "Richard Spurling and the Baptist Roots of the Church of God." Paper presented at the annual meeting of the Society for Pentecostal Studies, Guadalajara, Mexico, Nov. 11–13, 1993.

Photiadis, John D., ed. *Religion in Appalachia: Theological, Social, and Psychological Dimensions and Correlates.* Morgantown: Center for Extension and Continuing Education, Division of Social and Economic Development, Office of Research and Development, West Virginia University, 1978.

Piepkorn, Arthur Carl. "The Primitive Baptists of North America." *Concordia Theological Monthly*, 42, no. 5 (May 1971), 297–314.

———. *Profiles in Belief: The Religious Bodies of the United States and Canada.* Vol. 2. *Protestant Denominations.* San Francisco: Harper and Row, 1978.

Pierson, Hamilton W. *In the Brush; Or, Old-Time Social, Political, and Religious Life in the Southwest.* New York: D. Appleton and Co., 1883.

Pilcher, George William. *Samuel Davies: Apostle of Dissent in Colonial Virginia.* Knoxville: University of Tennessee Press, 1971.

Pinkston, Alfred Adolphus. "Lined Hymns, Spirituals, and Associated Lifestyle of Rural Black People in the United States." Ph.D. diss., University of Miami, 1975.

Pittman, R. H., comp. *In Defense of the Truth: Or, Danville Church Division Investigated . . . May, 1926. . . .* Front Royal, Va.: Buck Press, [1926].

Posey, Walter Brownlow. *The Baptist Church in the Lower Mississippi Valley, 1776–1845.* Lexington: University of Kentucky Press, 1957.

————. *The Development of Methodism in the Old Southwest, 1783–1824.* Tuscaloosa, Ala.: Weatherford Printing Co., 1933.

————. *Frontier Mission: A History of Religion West of the Southern Appalachians to 1861.* Lexington: University of Kentucky Press, 1966.

————. *The Presbyterian Church in the Old Southwest, 1778–1838.* Richmond, Va.: John Knox Press, 1952.

————. *Religious Strife on the Southern Frontier.* N.p.: Louisiana State University Press, 1965.

Price, W. T. *Without Scrip or Purse; Or, "The Mountain Evangelist." George O. Barnes.* Louisville, Ky.: Privately printed, 1883.

Primitive Baptist Library. Rte. 2, Elon College, N.C. 27244.

Queen, Edward L., II. "Bob Jones, Sr., Jr., and III." In *Twentieth Century Shapers of American Popular Religion,* edited by Charles H. Lippy, 196–202. Westport, Conn.: Greenwood Press, 1989.

Raitz, Karl B., and Richard Ulack. "Regional Definitions." In *Appalachia: Social Context Past and Present,* 3d ed., edited by Bruce Ergood and Bruce E. Kuhre, 10–26. Dubuque: Kendall/Hunt Publishing Co., 1991.

Randolph, Corliss Fitz. *A History of Seventh Day Baptists in West Virginia; Including the Woodbridge and Salemville Churches in Pennsylvania and the Shrewsbury Church in New Jersey.* Plainfield, N.J.: American Sabbath Tract Society (Seventh Day Baptist), 1905.

Randolph, R. H. "Religion: Highland Churches." *Mountain Life & Work,* 26, no. 3 (Fall 1950), 1–7.

"Readers' Response: Pluses and Minuses of Mountain Religion." *Christian Century,* 94, no. 17 (Apr. 6, 1977), 332–35.

Redman, Barbara J. "Impact of Great Revival Religion on the Personal Characteristics of the Southern Appalachian People." *Southern Studies,* 20 (Fall 1981), 303–10.

Reid, Melanie Sovine (see also Sovine, Melanie L.). "'Neither Adding nor Taking Away': The Care and Keeping of Primitive Baptist Church Houses." In *Perspectives in Vernacular Architecture,* edited by Camille Wells, 169–76. Annapolis, Md.: Vernacular Architecture Forum, 1982.

————. "On the Study of Religion in Appalachia: A Review/Essay." *Appalachian Journal,* 6, no. 3 (Spring 1979), 239–44.

Richardson, Frank. *From Sunrise to Sunset: Reminiscence.* Bristol, Tenn.: King Printing Co., 1910.

Richardson, J. C. "Williamsburg, Whitley Co., September 16, '59." *American Missionary Magazine,* 4, no. 1 (Jan. 1860), 18–19.

Ritchie, Jean. *Sweet Rivers.* JA 037. Whitesburg, Ky.: June Appal, 1981.

Roosevelt, Theodore. *The Winning of the West.* 6 vols. New York: G. Putnam's Sons, 1900.

Ross, Charlotte T., ed. *Bibliography of Southern Appalachia.* Boone, N.C.: Appalachian Consortium Press, 1976.

Rouse, L. G. *Modern Miracles: Life of L. G. Rouse.* N.p., n.d.

Roy, District Secretary. "Americans of the Midland Mountains." *American Missionary Magazine,* 46, no. 3 (Mar. 1892), 85–90.

Samson's Foxes, 1, no. 1 (Jan. 1901).

Sattler, Gary. *God's Glory; Neighbor's Good: A Brief Introduction into the Life and Writings of August Hermann Francke.* Chicago: Covenant Press, 1982.

Schermerhorn, John F., and Samuel J. Mills. *A Correct View of That Part of the United States Which Lies West of the Allegany Mountains, With Regard to Religion and Morals.* Hartford: Peter B. Gleason and Co., 1814. Facs. rpt. in *To Win the West: Missionary Viewpoints, 1814–1815,* edited by Edwin S. Gaustad. New York: Arno Press, 1972.

Schmidt, Leigh Eric. *Holy Fairs: Scottish Communions and American Revivals in the Early Modern Period.* Princeton: Princeton University Press, 1989.

———. "Scottish Communions and American Revivals: Evangelical Ritual, Sacramental Piety, and Popular Festivity from the Reformation through the Mid-Nineteenth Century." Ph.D. diss., Princeton University, 1987.

Selement, George, and Bruce C. Woolley, eds. *Thomas Shepard's Confessions.* Boston: Colonial Society of Massachusetts, 1981.

Semple, Robert Baylor. *History of the Baptists in Virginia.* 1810. Revised by G. W. Beale. 1894. Reprint. Lafayette, Tenn.: Church History Research and Archives, 1976.

Shackelford, Laurel, and Bill Weinberg. *Our Appalachia: An Oral History.* New York: Hill and Wang, 1977.

Shapiro, Henry D. *Appalachia on Our Mind: The Southern Mountains and Mountaineers in the American Consciousness, 1870–1920.* Chapel Hill: University of North Carolina Press, 1978.

———. Introduction to *The Southern Highlander & His Homeland,* by John C. Campbell. Lexington: University Press of Kentucky, 1969.

Sharp, R. Chesla. "Dorgan's *Giving Glory to God in Appalachia,*" *Now and Then,* 5, no. 2 (Summer 1988), 31–32.

Short, Ron. "We Believed in the Family and the Old Regular Baptist Church." *Southern Exposure,* 4, no. 3 (1976), 60–65.

Simmons, E. L. *History of the Church of God.* Cleveland, Tenn.: Church of God Publishing House, 1938.

Slone, Verna Mae. *How We Talked.* Pippa Passes, Ky.: Pippa Valley Printing, 1982.

"The South West. Prejudices—Distracted Meetings." *Home Missionary,* 24, no. 2 (June 1851), 48–49.

Sovine, Melanie L. (see also Reid, Melanie Sovine). "Studying Religious Belief Systems in Their Social Historical Context." In *Appalachia and America:*

Autonomy and Regional Dependence, edited by Allen Batteau, 48–67. Lexington: University Press of Kentucky, 1983.

———. "A Sweet Hope in My Breast: Belief and Ritual in the Primitive Baptist Church." Master's thesis, University of Georgia, 1978.

———. "Traditionalism, Antimissionism, and the Primitive Baptist Religion." In *Reshaping the Image of Appalachia,* edited by Loyal Jones, 32–44. Berea, Ky.: Berea College Appalachian Center, 1986.

Spencer, J. H. *A History of Kentucky Baptists from 1769 to 1885; Including More Than 800 Biographical Sketches.* Revised and corrected by Mrs. Burrilla B. Spencer. 2 vols. Cincinnati: J. R. Baumes, 1885. Reprint. Gallatin, Tenn.: Church History Research and Archives, 1984.

Spurling, G. P. [Untitled early history of the religious work of Richard G. Spurling]. Manuscript, 4 pp. James Marshall Church of God Collection.

Spurling, R. G. *The Lost Link.* Turtletown, Tenn.: Privately printed, 1920.

Stein, K. James. *Philip Jacob Spener: Pietist Patriarch.* Chicago: Covenant Press, 1986.

Stephenson, Florence. "The Mountain Whites." Pamphlet, 1890. Presbyterian Historical Society, Philadelphia.

Stoeffler, F. Ernest, ed. *Continental Pietism and Early American Christianity.* Grand Rapids: Wm. B. Eerdmans Publishing Co., 1976.

———. *The Rise of Evangelical Pietism.* Leiden: E. J. Brill, 1971.

Stone, James. *The Church of God of Prophecy: History & Polity.* Cleveland, Tenn.: White Wing Publishing House and Press, 1977.

Sutton, Brett. "Spirit and Polity in a Black Primitive Baptist Church." Ph.D. diss., University of North Carolina, 1983.

———. *Primitive Baptist Hymns of the Blue Ridge.* American Folklore Recordings. Chapel Hill: University of North Carolina Press, 1982.

Sweet, William Warren. "The Churches as Moral Courts of the Frontier." *Church History,* 2 (Mar. 1933), 3–21.

———. *Religion on the American Frontier: The Baptists, 1783–1830.* New York: Henry Holt and Co., 1931.

———. *Religion on the American Frontier: The Presbyterians, 1783–1840; A Collection of Source Documents.* New York: Harper and Brothers, 1936.

———. *The Story of Religion in America.* New York: Harper and Brothers, 1950.

Tadlock, E. V. "Church Problems in the Mountains." *Mountain Life & Work,* 6, no. 1 (Apr. 1930), 6–8.

Tallmadge, William H. "Anglo-Saxon vs. Scotch-Irish." *Mountain Life & Work,* 45, no. 2 (Feb. 1969), 10–12.

———. "Baptist Monophonic and Heterophonic Hymnody in Southern Appalachia." *Yearbook for Inter-American Musical Research,* 11 (1975), 106–36.

Taylor, John. *A History of Ten Baptist Churches, of which The Author Has Been Alternately a Member: In Which Will Be Seen Something of a Journal of the Author's Life for More Than Fifty Years; Also a Comment on Some Parts of Scripture, in which the Author Takes the Liberty to Differ from Other Expositors.* 1823. 2d ed. Bloomfield, Ky.: Will. H. Holmes, 1827.

———. *Thoughts on Missions.* N.p., 1819.

This Land Is Home to Me: A Pastoral Letter on Powerlessness in Appalachia by the Catholic Bishops of the Region. Prestonsburg, Ky.: Catholic Committee of Appalachia, Commission on Religion in Appalachia, 1976.

Thompson, Dorothy B. "John Taylor of the Ten Churches." *Register of the Kentucky Historical Society,* 46, no. 156 (July 1948), 541–72.

Titon, Jeff Todd. *Powerhouse for God: Sacred Speech, Chant, and Song in an Appalachian Baptist Church.* American Folklore Recordings. Chapel Hill: University of North Carolina Press, 1982.

———. *Powerhouse for God: Speech, Chant, and Song in an Appalachian Baptist Church.* Austin: University of Texas Press, 1988.

Tomlinson, A. J. *The Last Great Conflict.* Cleveland, Tenn.: Walter E. Rodgers, 1913. Reprint. Cleveland, Tenn.: White Wing Publishing House, 1984.

Torbet, Robert G. *A History of the Baptists.* 3d ed. Valley Forge, Pa.: Judson Press, 1963.

Trinterud, Leonard J. *The Forming of an American Tradition: A Re-examination of Colonial Presbyterianism.* Philadelphia: Westminster Press, 1949.

Tucker, George. *The Valley of Shenandoah; Or, Memoirs of the Graysons.* 2 vols. New York: Charles Riley, 1824.

Vance, Rupert B. Foreword to *The Southern Highlander & His Homeland,* by John C. Campbell. Lexington: University Press of Kentucky, 1969.

Wadhwani, Anita. "Appalachian Religion and American Capitalism: Iron Cages and Transformative Power." 1992. Typescript.

Wallhausser, John. "I Can Almost See Heaven from Here." *Katallagete,* 8, no. 2 (Spring 1983), 2–10.

Wallis, Charles L. Introduction, Bibliography, and Index to *Autobiography of Peter Cartwright,* by Peter Cartwright. Nashville: Abingdon Press, 1984.

Weatherford, W. D., ed. *Religion in the Appalachian Mountains: A Symposium.* Berea, Ky.: Berea College, 1955.

Weatherford, W. D., and Earl D. C. Brewer. *Life and Religion in Southern Appalachia: An Interpretation of Selected Data from the Southern Appalachian Studies.* New York: Friendship Press, 1962.

Weaver, Curtis. "The Praying Rock." In *Foxfire 9,* edited by Eliot Wigginton and Margie Bennett, 321–28. Garden City, N.Y.: Anchor Books, 1986.

Weller, Jack E. *Yesterday's People: Life in Contemporary Appalachia.* Lexington: University of Kentucky Press, 1965.

Westerkamp, Marilyn J. *Triumph of the Laity: Scots-Irish Piety and the Great Awakening, 1625–1760.* New York: Oxford University Press, 1988.

"When the Faithful Tempt the Serpent." *New York Times,* Sept. 11, 1992, A14.

Whisnant, David E. Introduction to the new edition of *The Spirit of the Mountains,* by Emma Bell Miles. Knoxville: University of Tennessee Press, 1975.

———. *Modernizing the Mountaineer: People, Power, and Planning in Appalachia.* Boone, N.C.: Appalachian Consortium Press, 1980.

Wicks, Sammie Ann. "Life and Meaning: Singing, Praying, and the Word among Old Regular Baptists of Eastern Kentucky." Ph.D. diss., University of Texas, 1983.

William H. Tallmadge Baptist Hymnody Collection. Southern Appalachian Archives, Special Collections, Hutchins Library, Berea College, Berea, Ky.

William P. Lewis Collection on Primitive Baptists. Library of the American Baptist Historical Society, Colgate Rochester Divinity School, Rochester, N.Y.

Williams, Cratis D. "The Southern Mountaineer in Fact and Fiction." Ph.D. diss., New York University, 1961.

———. "The Southern Mountaineer in Fact and Fiction (Part III)." *Appalachian Journal,* 3, no. 3 (Spring 1976), 186–261.

Williams, George H. *The Radical Reformation.* Philadelphia: Westminster Press, 1962.

Williams, John. "Journal (1771)." Virginia Baptist Historical Society, Richmond, Virginia.

Wilson, Samuel Tyndale. *The Southern Mountaineers.* New York: Literature Department, Presbyterian Home Missions, 1906.

Wilson, Warren H. "The Educated Minister in the Mountains." *Mountain Life & Work,* 6, no. 1 (Apr. 1930), 20–24.

Wolfe, Charles K., ed. *Children of the Heav'nly King: Religious Expression in the Central Blue Ridge.* AFC L69–L70. Washington, D.C.: Library of Congress, 1981.

Wood, William W. *Culture and Personality Aspects of the Pentecostal Holiness Religion.* The Hague: Mouton and Co., 1965.

Wust, Klaus G. *Saint-Adventurers of the Virginia Frontier: Southern Outposts of Ephrata.* Edinburg, Va.: Shenandoah History Publishers, 1977.

Wyckoff, Capwell. *The Challenge of the Hills.* Philadelphia: Department of Sunday School Missions of the Board of National Missions of the Presbyterian Church in the U.S.A. by the Presbyterian Board of Christian Education, 1931.

Index

Abbott, Benjamin (eighteenth-century Methodist preacher), 269

Abbott, Joe: Free Holiness Church and Spurlings, 279–80

Ahlstrom, Sydney: New Haven Theology and revivalism, 21, 261–62; 1801 confession, 92; pietism, 158; Robert Baird, 341–42

Albanese, Catherine L.: mountain religion, 1, 49, 79, 154, 155, 241, 493; John C. Campbell, 36, 155; nondenominational churches, 38, 241; religious history, focus, 45, 155; regional religion, 49, 53–54, 90; Elizabeth R. Hooker, 155; institutional/organized religion, 155, 189; mountain people, 155, 189, 453; religious studies versus church history perspective, 155; German Dunkards in Appalachia, 160; sacramental quality in mountain worship, 169, 380, 493; conversion experience, 170, 178, 222, 225–26, 326, 428; mountain religion's "new sacramentalism," 493

Albers, Paul J.: Commission on Religion in Appalachia (CORA), 456

Alexander, Carl: Edna Alexander's son, Holiness and Mennonite, 167

Alexander, Edna: independent Holiness, 34, 67–68, 164; religious leader, 34, 164–65; pietism, 37, 145, 161; attachment to "place," 61; education and literacy, 61–62; "Holiness" versus "Pentecostal," 67–68; private vocal prayer, 130, 166; dream/vision, 162–63; clothes, 164; father, independent Holiness preacher, 164; "prophetess," 164; mother, midwife, 165, 167; lifestyle, 165–66; Mennonites, 166–67; husband, death of, 167; life changes, 167; mentioned, 59

Alston, Carolyn P.: Primitive Baptist interview, 487

Ambiguity: accepted in mountain religion, 77, 78–79, 333, 357

American Benevolence: and a Christian

America, 12; John F. Schermerhorn, 12; revivalism, 21; objectives, 22; national social movement, 113, 144, 371; transformation of revivalistic conversion, 113–14; 1800–1840, 114; nativism, 114; minority resistance, 114; doctrinal shift, 120; implications for Calvinist groups, 120; earliest institutional expressions, 351

American Bible Society, 377

American Board of Commissioners for Foreign Missions, 349, 400

American Home Missionary Society, 349, 371, 372, 400, 401

American Missionary Association: "mountain white work," 399–400, 401

American Missionary Magazine, 404, 505

American Protestantism: definition, 1; and liberal traditions, 8, 99, 467; fear of mountain religion, 12–13, 27; revivalism, 14; perceptions of mountain religion, 26, 40, 47, 53, 208, 247, 248–49, 250, 253; conflict with Appalachian Calvinism, 29; mountain people, 53; ordination, 63; establishing new churches, 73; hierarchical structures, failure, 95; social justice, 99, 449, 457; literacy, 195; status, 208, 210; national versus regional identity, 245; affirms Appalachia, rejects mountain religion, 247; in Appalachia versus mountain religion, 250; stereotyping mountain religion, purpose, 250; "romance" of Appalachia, 253; "spiritual recession," 1920s–1930s, 417; "second disestablishment," 417–18; end of Christian America movement, 417–18; violation of liberation theology, 449; American Catholicism, 457; triumphalism in Appalachia, 457, 460; bigotry toward mountain religion, 460; labels of domination over mountain religion, 460; debt of religious justice, 460; need to redeem its history in Appalachia, 463; and mountain churches, 484

perience, 314–15; love of God and neighbor, 315–16; heart religion, 317; joy, 317; and Richard G. Spurling, 317; "mistakes" and suffering, 317–18; rejection of fatalism, 317–18; on the Devil, 319; on individual responsibility, 319; Bible and oral memory, 320–21; ecumenism, 322–23, 329–30; death of, 337; legacy, 337–38; footwashing, 388; understanding without despair, 462–63; hope and the Holy Spirit, 479; voice continued in present tense, 482; mentioned, 59
—as a mountain preacher: representative, 11, 39–40; self-supporting, 60; legally ordains others, 67; model of Baptist revival itinerant, 234–35; how he became a mountain preacher, 320
—preaching: tolerance of differences, 75; Holy Spirit and, 78, 319–20, 333–34; and contradiction, 356–57; style, 383
Miser, Dewey: Coy Miser's son, Holiness preacher, 312
Miser, George Edward: Coy Miser's son, 312
Miser, Hassie: Coy Miser's spouse, *Last Supper* gift, 168–69; sacrament meeting, 198
Missions: basis for denominational centralization, 121. *See also* Home missions
Moderator, Old Time Baptist tradition: description, 102–3
Moody, Dwight L.: and Finney, 14
Moravians: description, 157; early Appalachian settlers, 157; background in U.S., 159; missionaries to Cherokee and Creek Native Americans, 159; and John Wesley, 159–60; first to document Mennonites in Blue Ridge, 160; love feast, 222
Morris, S. L.: valley people versus "the typical mountaineer," 393; racial and patriotic motives for missions to mountain people, 394; equated Scots-Irish with Anglo-Saxon, 394; educate mountain people in order to convert them, 411; linked "illiteracy" with "religious destitution," 411–12; same motives for home missions as Southern Baptists, 434–35
Mountain Baptists: and Presbyterians, Scots-Irish heritage, 124–25. *See also* Old Time Baptists
Mountain churches: as the majority of

churches in the mountains, 34; small numbers of worshipers, 68; annual occasions, scheduling, 69; meeting schedules, 69; cooperative character, 70; collections infrequent in, 71, 81; size not relevant, 72; general absence of membership rolls, 73; reject aggressive evangelization, 73; fellowshiping, 81; home church, 81; log churches, examples, 81; power of self-definition, 145; emphasis on purity of life, 159; art about Jesus in a social setting, 168; reject Arminianized evangelization of revivalism, 188; autonomy, description, 190, 427; oral tradition, 190; one-room schoolhouses, 421; Sunday school usually held weekly, even if preaching was once a month, 422–23; common characteristics, partial list, 426; gatherings, types of, 431; "off-preaching days," 431; role in local communities, 435, 436; coal mining labor struggles, 456; different definition of the "struggle for justice," 456, 457; characterized as passive, fatalistic in the "struggle for justice," 456; premier, yet ignored, "base communities" in Appalachia, 457; characterized as "do-nothing," 458–59; disciplined church and social community, 488; splits in family churches, 506. *See also* Anti–mission board Baptists
Mountain church traditions: autonomy and free church polity, 65; doctrinally diverse, shared features, 88, 89; share Old Regular Baptist atonement doctrine, 99
Mountaineers: term, 392–93; "two classes of," 392
Mountain Life & Work: on mountain religion and mountain preachers, 490
Mountain people: definition, 3, 6; as "the oppressed," 8, 446; "purest Anglo-Saxon stock," 26, 211, 393–94; as preservers of colonial era, 50, 401; power of religious self-definition, 53, 206–13 passim; distinction between "religion" and "faith," 58; attachment to "place," 61; commonly attend more than one church (fellowshiping), 68; reasons why missions offend, 121; Scots-Irish versus Anglo-Saxon, 171; attitudes toward centralization, 306; seen as an "exceptional population,"

New Lebanon Convention: and Finney's career, 134; background, 135; demise of evangelical Calvinism, 135–36; response of Old Father Nash, 136–37; revivalism and human initiative, 137

"New Lights." See Christian Church; Stone, Barton W.

New Lights, Great Awakening, Middle Colonies: emphasized conversion, 187; and mountain religion, 410. See also Old Lights and New Lights

"New measures": and Finney, 134–35; popularized New Haven Theology, 135; similar to Great Awakening and Appalachian frontier, 135; definition, 272

New Salem Association: significance, 46; description, 91; as United Baptists, 91; name change, significance, 96–97; antimission controversy, 97; 1905 articles of faith, 98, 99; Old Regular Baptists, 101

New School Baptists: description, 46–47, 123

Niebuhr, H. Richard: church-sect typology, 483

Night meetings/services: Holiness churches, 69; independent Baptist churches, 69; tradition history, 69–70; children imitating, 380–81; in Southwest, 1850s, 380–81

Night watch service: description, 195

Nondenominational: indifference to a preacher's affiliation, 385; worship lives of private households, 385–86. See also Appalachian mountain religion; Church of God; Cope, Dora Woodruff; Independent nondenominational churches

Northern Baptist Convention: West Virginia, 365

Old Lights, Great Awakening, Middle Colonies: emphasized holy life, 187, 410

Old Lights and New Lights: differences characterize mountain religion and Presbyterian church, 187; differ on beliefs, 187–88; differ on institutional structure of church, 187–88; differ on clerical authority, 188; 1758 reunion, 188

Old Regular Baptists: atonement doctrine, 14, 98–99; and religious experience, 14; perceived as epitome of mountain religion, 17–19; modified Calvinism, 46; or-

dination in local church, 62–63; church meeting schedules, 69; size of churches, 72; polity and theology, 89; geographic range, 91; strongly traditional, 91; expressive and ecstatic worship practices, 92; "grace covenant," 92; grace, Holy Spirit, and religious experience, 92; Calvinist doctrinal heritage, 96; and Arminianism, 97; first occurrence of name, 97, 98; mediating doctrinal position, 97; "election by grace," 98; grace as center of mediating position, 98; church membership, 101–2; church seating arrangements, 102; as perceived by outsiders, 111; revival culture and institutionalism, 233; primary and secondary sources, 470–71, 485; moderators, 487. See also Short, Ron

Old School Baptists: and American Benevolence, 22; and nineteenth-century American Protestantism, 24; and Appalachian mountain religion, 25; claim apostolic rather than Calvinist origins, 25; description, 46–47. See also Old Regular Baptists; Primitive Baptists

Old Southwest: description, 40. See also Baptists, Old Southwest; Home missions; Holy Spirit; Schermerhorn, John F.

Old Time Baptists: majority of Baptists in mountains, 145; preaching traditions, 352

Oral religious culture: oral literature and material culture, 6, 37, 468; listening skills and religion, 382; and religious music, 382; and "traditional authority," 498

Oral tradition: hymns, religious music, 82; traditional religion, definition, 189–90; transmitted mountain religion's revival religiosity, 235–36

Ordination: and the local church community, 352. See also American Protestantism; Bryant, W. F.; Holiness churches; Mountain preachers; Old Regular Baptists

Original Freewill Baptists: Virginia and North Carolina, description, 129

Otto, Rudolf: the nonrational in religious experience, 354–55

Parker, Gerald Keith: church-sect typology, critique, 483

DEBORAH VANSAU MCCAULEY was born in Texas and grew up in southeastern Ohio. She holds an undergraduate degree from Ohio University, a master's degree from Harvard University Divinity School, and the Ph.D. in American religious history from Columbia University. Her religious upbringing in one of the church traditions originally indigenous to the Appalachian region was of great help in the preparation of this book. Not until her late teens did she discover that shape-note hymnals were all but nonexistent in the denominations of American Protestantism.